Driftin' on a Memory

American Made
Music Series

ADVISORY BOARD

David Evans, General Editor
Barry Jean Ancelet
Edward A. Berlin
Joyce J. Bolden
Rob Bowman
Curtis Ellison
William Ferris
John Edward Hasse
Kip Lornell
Bill Malone
Eddie S. Meadows
Manuel H. Peña
Wayne D. Shirley
Robert Walser

Driftin' on a Memory

Celebrating 70 Years of The Isley Brothers

TRENTON BAILEY

University Press of Mississippi / Jackson

The University Press of Mississippi is the scholarly publishing agency of the Mississippi Institutions of Higher Learning: Alcorn State University, Delta State University, Jackson State University, Mississippi State University, Mississippi University for Women, Mississippi Valley State University, University of Mississippi, and University of Southern Mississippi.

www.upress.state.ms.us

The University Press of Mississippi is a member of the Association of University Presses.

Copyright © 2025 by Trenton Bailey
All rights reserved
Manufactured in the United States of America
∞

Publisher: University Press of Mississippi, Jackson, USA
Authorised GPSR Safety Representative: Easy Access System Europe - Mustamäe tee 50, 10621 Tallinn, Estonia, *gpsr.requests@easproject.com*

Library of Congress Cataloging-in-Publication Data

Names: Bailey, Trenton author
Title: Driftin' on a memory : celebrating seventy years of the Isley Brothers / Trenton Bailey.
Other titles: American made music series
Description: Jackson : University Press of Mississippi, 2025. |
Series: American made music series | Includes bibliographical references and index.
Identifiers: LCCN 2025035794 (print) | LCCN 2025035795 (ebook) | ISBN 9781496859747 hardback | ISBN 9781496859754 trade paperback | ISBN 9781496859761 epub | ISBN 9781496859778 epub | ISBN 9781496859785 pdf | ISBN 9781496859792 pdf
Subjects: LCSH: Isley Brothers | Rock musicians—United States—Biography | Soul musicians—United States—Biography | Rhythm and blues musicians—United States—Biography | African American musicians—Biography | LCGFT: Biographies
Classification: LCC ML421.I84 B35 2025 (print) | LCC ML421.I84 (ebook) | DDC 782.42166092/2 [B]—dc23/eng/20250905
LC record available at https://lccn.loc.gov/2025035794
LC ebook record available at https://lccn.loc.gov/202503579

British Library Cataloging-in-Publication Data available

This book is dedicated to the memory of all The Isley Brothers who have transitioned: Vernon, O'Kelly, Jr., Marvin, Rudolph, and Chris (Jasper).

This narrative is also a tribute to Ronald and Ernie Isley who continue to build upon the legacy of The Isley Brothers. This group has produced timeless music for several generations and is part of the soundtrack of my life.

Contents

Acknowledgments vii

Introduction 3

1. Brother, Brother, Brother 7
2. Soul on the Rocks 22
3. Freedom 35
4. 3 + 3 56
5. Keep On Doin' 80
6. Fire and Rain 98
7. The Next Phase 117
8. Brother, Brother 135
9. Winner Takes All 149
10. The Heat Is On 170
11. Forever Gold 186
12. Eternal 203

Afterword 223

Notes 227

Bibliography 263

Index 285

Acknowledgments

First and foremost, I must give glory and honor to The Most High Creator for giving me the zeal and tenacity to complete this project. I thank the staff at the Auburn Avenue Research Library for helping me get started on this task. I most certainly salute the late, great Mr. Chris Jasper for providing information on this subject.

I acknowledge my mentor and Morehouse brother Dr. Marcellus C. Barksdale, who guided me as a historian. I express gratitude to my Morehouse brother Dr. Byron K. Edmond, who has supported my career from the beginning. And I commend my Morehouse and Alpha Phi Alpha fraternity brother Dr. Anthony Sean Neal, who is always motivating me to stay on the right path.

I appreciate Dr. Nina J. Staples for her advice and encouragement and Dr. Tamara R. White who is always willing to listen and give advice. I show appreciation to my fraternity brother Mr. Michael A. Philips, for his input and interest in this project. I thank my colleagues Dr. Samuel T. Livingston and my Morehouse brother Dr. Ovell Hamilton for supporting my work.

I am filled with gratitude for the blessings of Mr. Frank L. Sims and Mrs. Robyn F. Sims. I am beholden to Mr. Craig Damon Sanders and Mrs. Sherry Ann Sanders for all their love and kindness. I give a special thanks to Ms. Jean C. Ray who attended all my graduation ceremonies.

I recognize those who have shown a keen interest in and support for my work: Ms. Audra Y. Johnson, Mr. Wronald T. Webster, and Mr. Arthur Peters II. I must also recognize those who have made great impacts on my life: Mr. Romel Andrews, Pastor Fred Bailey, Sr., and Mr. Marvin L. Grant. Lastly, I am thankful for all my family, friends, acquaintances, and colleagues who appreciate and support my work.

Driftin' on a Memory

Introduction

The Isley Brothers, also known as The Isleys, are one of the most successful acts in pop music history. Since their inception over seventy years ago, they have recorded thirty-three studio albums, and countless compilation albums have been issued. Ten of the albums have been certified platinum and five have been certified gold. In the 1970s, The Isleys released six consecutive platinum albums.[1] The first of those reached number two on the *Billboard* pop chart. The other five made it to number one.[2] The group has been inducted into the Rock & Roll Hall of Fame and the Vocal Group Hall of Fame. The Isley Brothers received the Grammy Lifetime Achievement Award in 2014, and they have received additional lifetime achievement awards and prestigious honors throughout their career.

The Isley Brothers acquired their first hit song with "Shout" in 1959. They have reached the *Billboard* Hot 100 songs chart with new music in six different decades, from the 1950s to the 2000s. The Isleys have covered various genres of music, including gospel, doo-wop, rock 'n' roll, the Motown sound, funk, disco, quiet storm, and neo-soul. Music historian and musicologist Bob Gulla declared, "With the possible exception of the Beatles, no band in the history of popular music, and certainly no African American act, has left a more substantial legacy on popular music than the Isley Brothers." Because of this, The Isleys are considered the most important group of all time.[3]

The Isley Brothers formed in 1954 as a gospel quartet in suburban Cincinnati, Ohio. The Isleys included O'Kelly, Rudolph, Ronald, and Vernon. Later that year, the youngest member of the quartet, Vernon, was killed in a traffic accident. After this, the other brothers took a hiatus but decided to continue as a trio. They also decided to sing more secular music, including doo-wop and rock 'n' roll. In 1956, The Isleys decided to move to New York

City to pursue a career in popular music. While in NYC, they hit the chitlin circuit and recorded a few singles. The Isley Brothers recorded their first album, *Shout*, on RCA Records in 1959, which included the title track, their first hit record.

"Shout" is dipped heavily in rock 'n' roll, one of many genres The Isley Brothers covered during their career. By the time "Shout" became a hit, The Isleys had developed an energetic stage show. Godfather of Soul James Brown stated, "They hardly had to sing at all. They'd already killed 'em [with their performance]."[4] Follow-up recordings on RCA failed to chart, and the brothers left the label in 1961, later signing with Scepter Records. The Isleys scored another rock 'n' roll hit in 1962 with "Twist and Shout." But the brothers still struggled with recordings and started T-Neck Records in 1964. During that year, famed guitarist Jimi Hendrix worked with the group for a few months. After the singles featuring Hendrix failed to chart, The Isleys signed with Motown Records.

In 1966, The Isley Brothers captured the Motown sound with their top-forty hit "This Old Heart of Mine."[5] But their time at Motown Records was not ideal. The Isleys failed to score another top-forty hit with the label. They left Motown in 1968 and resurrected T-Neck Records. The brothers also decided to change their image. They traded in the suits for a more casual, yet sophisticated style. This change would serve them well as they incorporated funk music into their next album.[6] According to Teresa Reed, "Funk is a style of music in which elements of jazz, pop, rock, gospel, and the Blues are fused to create a rhythmic, soulful sound."[7] The origin of funk music is attributed to James Brown.

In 1969, The Isley Brothers released *It's Our Thing*, which includes the funk hit "It's Your Thing," for which they earned their first Grammy. The song also solicited a lawsuit from Berry Gordy, who claimed the brothers recorded the song while they were at Motown. The suit dragged on for nearly a decade. In the early 1970s, The Isleys continued their use of funk music, but they also began to cover rock songs, adding their own brand of soul. Those rock songs include "Lay Lady Lay," "Love the One You're With," and "It's Too Late." But it was in 1973 when the brothers took their career to another plateau.

In 1973, younger brothers Ernie (lead guitarist) and Marvin (bass guitarist) along with Chris Jasper (keyboardist), Rudolph's brother-in-law, joined the group. The Isley Brothers had gone from a vocal trio to a self-contained band. With the younger brothers on board, they released *3 + 3*. This album contains the hit "That Lady," which features a fierce guitar solo by Ernie. One can't help but notice the Jimi Hendrix influence in Ernie's work. "That Lady" started The Isleys' golden age, which lasted until 1983, when they were most popular and most successful.

During the golden age, The Isley Brothers released seven studio albums that have been certified platinum and three studio albums that have been certified gold.[8] From 1973 to 1983, The Isleys were radio regulars with several hit singles. Those included funk tracks, such as "Live It Up," "Fight the Power," and "The Pride." The group became synonymous with sultry ballads, such as "For the Love of You," "Don't Say Goodnight," and "Between the Sheets." The Isleys also released songs that have been considered "Black rock" because of Ernie's distinctive guitar sound. Those include "That Lady," "Summer Breeze," and "Voyage to Atlantis." The brothers even dabbled in disco with "Winner Takes All," "It's a Disco Night," and "Hurry Up and Wait." They had proven they could cover various genres of music.

In the latter years of the golden age, tension had been building between the three older brothers and the three younger brothers. In 1984, the younger brothers formed a splinter group titled Isley-Jasper-Isley. The group had a few hit singles, including "Look the Other Way," "Insatiable Woman," and the brotherhood anthem "Caravan of Love." Isley-Jasper-Isley split in 1987, and Chris Jasper started a record label and became a solo artist.[9]

In the mid-1980s, the older brothers decided to continue as a trio, but eldest brother O'Kelly died suddenly in 1986. Rudolph and Ronald carried on the Isley name. They teamed up with multitalented Angela Winbush for *Smooth Sailin'* (1987) and *Spend the Night* (1989). Before the latter was released, Rudolph left the group for Christian ministry. Ronald was practically a solo artist. Ernie and Marvin rejoined Ronald in 1991 to make the group a trio again. This set of brothers recorded two albums, but Marvin left the group in 1996 due to health complications. Ronald and Ernie continued to record and perform as a duo.

By the mid-1990s, The Isley Brothers became popular among the hip-hop generation. Their music was sampled for hit songs by Ice Cube, the Notorious B.I.G., Bone Thugs-N-Harmony, and others. In 1995, The Isleys began working with R&B singer and producer R. Kelly, and Ronald's alter ego, Mr. Biggs, was created. This also helped the brothers connect with younger listeners. In addition to Kelly, The Isleys worked with other prominent producers in the 2000s, including Babyface, Raphael Saadiq, and Jimmy "Jam" Harris and

Terry Lewis. *Eternal* (2001) was certified platinum and *Body Kiss* (2003) was certified gold.[10] Ronald released his first solo album, *Here I Am: Isley Meets Bacharach*, in 2003, and The Isleys' first Christmas album, *I'll Be Home for Christmas*, was released in 2007.

In August 2007, Ronald was forced to take a hiatus from the music business, but he returned to performing with Ernie in 2010. In the same year, youngest brother Marvin died after a long illness. Ronald also released his second solo album, *Mr. I*, in 2010 and his third, *This Song Is for You*, in 2013. The Isley Brothers teamed up with Santana in 2017 to release their first studio album in nearly ten years, titled *Power of Peace*. Their follow-up album, *Make Me Say It Again, Girl*, was released in 2022. Despite the changes, challenges, and time, The Isley Brothers are still popular in today's ever-changing music landscape.

This narrative examines the career of The Isley Brothers from 1954 to 2024. The first chapter is about the brothers' formative years, their move to New York City, and early recordings. Chapter 2 deals with the formation of T-Neck Records, the employment of Jimi Hendrix, and The Isleys' time at Motown Records. The third chapter details how the brothers changed their image, the incorporation of funk music, and their niche for covering songs by other artists. Chapter 4 assesses the beginning of the group's golden age (1973–1983) with the addition of the three younger brothers and a new, distinctive sound. The fifth chapter covers the continued success of The Isleys during the late seventies and the beginning of the eighties, including the incorporation of disco. Chapter 6 deals with the last three years of the group's golden age, the breakup that led to a splinter group, and the older brothers' return to being a trio. The seventh chapter is about the group's music in the late eighties and early to mid-nineties, personnel changes, and Ronald's relationship with Angela Winbush. Chapter 8 discusses the group's musical partnership with R. Kelly in the late nineties and Ronald's alter ego, Mr. Biggs. The ninth chapter describes the group's success in the new millennium, Ronald's finances, and his first solo album. Chapter 10 details three studio albums, including Ronald's second solo album, and the brothers' return to performing. The eleventh chapter is about Ronald's third solo album, The Isleys' project with Santana, awards, and touring. The final chapter is about The Isley Brothers' sixtieth anniversary tour, navigating through the pandemic, their thirty-third studio album, seventieth anniversary, and legacy.

Chapter 1

Brother, Brother, Brother

The Isley Brothers phenomenon began around Cincinnati, Ohio. The Isley family started when O'Kelly Isley, a US Navy veteran from Greensboro, North Carolina, married Sallye Bernice Bell from Georgia.[1] O'Kelly Isley was in a vaudeville group called the Brown Skin Models, and they traveled the South with The Red Caps, The Ink Spots, Cab Calloway, and Ethel Waters. Sallye Isley sang and played the piano and organ and gave lessons.[2]

The couple settled in Lincoln Heights, Ohio, an independent Black city just outside Cincinnati. From its early beginnings after World War I, Lincoln Heights was a haven for Black families seeking refuge from racism in the South and those seeking economic opportunity through home and land ownership. Strong and interdependent families are the result of the early settlers to the land. Early Black residents thrived given the proximity to the Wright Aeronautical plant, the first major factory for the Wright Brothers to build their plane engines; the settlement of its surrounding land; and the uphill climb to incorporate as a municipality in 1938. The first public housing project, the Valley Homes, came courtesy of a Department of Defense contract during World War II that led to decades of gainful employment at the plant nearby.[3]

O'Kelly and Sallye moved into Valley Homes. According to Ronald Isley, his father told his mother that he wanted a musical group like the Mills Brothers, the African American jazz quartet that became popular during the 1930s.[4] Within six years, the couple had four sons. O'Kelly Jr. was born December 25, 1937. Rudolph was born April 1, 1939. Ronald was born May

21, 1941. Vernon was born June 18, 1943.[5] Two other sons were born a decade later: Ernest (1952) and Marvin (1953).

Mr. O'Kelly Sr. had confidence that his sons would someday be famous. Ronald Isley, also known as Ron Isley, remembers when he was two years old, his mother bought them suits and ties, and he stood on a box singing for war bonds with his brothers. Ronald claims that he came of age when he was around four or five years old. By that time, the brothers could imitate several vocalists, including Frank Sinatra, Sammy Davis Jr., and Clara Ward and the Ward Singers.[6] In addition to singing, the Isley boys were active in normal youth behavior, such as going down to the creek to throw rocks, swim, or other things that could make their parents nervous.[7] Marvin Isley declared, "I used to love to play as kids. We had cap guns, and at night, you could see the sparks flash in the dark. Ronald wore this gold handkerchief, and he refused to die, no matter how many times we'd shoot him."[8] The brothers had a good Christian upbringing. The Isley family were members of First Baptist Church in downtown Cincinnati. Their mother played the organ and piano, and she taught the choir. It was the type of church in which parishioners actively expressed their love for God. Marvin Isley recalled, "Every Sunday, me and Ernie sat in the first row. People got excited, shouting, falling over each other, screaming 'Hallelujah, Sweet Jesus!' Then, they'd get the smelling salts! We were young so that really scared us! All those arms and hands flying! Sometimes we really got knocked around." This type of energy would be rendered in The Isley Brothers' music.[9]

O'Kelly Sr. wanted to make sure the brothers were nurtured properly and protected. He always reminded his sons to stay close to one another because they were blessed to have each other as both brothers and friends. Mr. Isley felt strongly about his sons defending one another, and the boys were encouraged to never choose an outsider over their own flesh and blood. He was a serious disciplinarian, who instilled in his sons core values, such as honesty and taking pride in all things they did.[10] Mrs. Isley was determined to move her boys out of Valley Homes because she knew if she could get them out, their talents would have a chance to grow. The family eventually moved to the nearby town Blue Ash.[11]

Rudolph recalled those early days: "Our parents were college-educated and our father taught us that we could do anything that anyone else could do. We went to a mixed school. We sang at socials and school functions." He added, "I can remember coming home from berry picking with my brothers—we'd bring a bucket and our mother would make the most delicious pies—and getting a lift home from our white friends. People are people and we just got along with everyone."[12] Being a close group of brothers and having a strong Christian background, the Isley boys formed a gospel quartet in 1954.

Throughout their young lives, The Isley Brothers had been listening to the most popular gospel music artists. Ronald declared, "At first, we patterned ourselves after Billy Ward and the Dominoes. Then, listening to the Dixie Hummingbirds and Mahalia Jackson, Jackie Wilson, and Sam Cooke, we developed our own style." Clyde McPhatter was a huge influence on the brothers, personally and professionally. Ronald added, "We spent a lot of time talking with him about singing styles and techniques."[13] Also, in 1954, a major campaign for civil rights started in America.

The civil rights movement began with the Supreme Court case of *Brown v. Board of Education of Topeka*. On May 17, 1954, the Supreme Court ruled unanimously that racial segregation in public schools violated the Fourteenth Amendment to the Constitution. The decision declared that separate educational facilities for White and Black students were inherently unequal. The court ordered segregated school districts to integrate with "with all deliberate speed." After this case, more action was taken by African Americans to challenge injustice and inequality. The problems of America would be the subject for several songs recorded by the group.

When the brothers first started singing as a group, they were entered in local church talent shows, which gave them local notoriety and exposure to the dynamics of show business. Soon, people recognized the young brothers had serious talent. Other singers and musicians recognized them as serious competition.[14] The Isley Brothers appeared on television with Dinah Washington, Nat King Cole, and Erskine Hawkins. Ronald declared several people asked, "Where did you find them kids?" One of their most exciting gigs was singing on Ted Mack's *The Original Amateur Hour*. This is the same show on which Gladys Knight appeared when she was seven years old.

According to Rudolph, Ted Mack wanted The Isley Brothers to sing a gospel song. The brothers begged him to sing what they wanted, and he relented. They sang "You Belong to Me" by Sonny Til and The Orioles, and their mother accompanied them. The next week, the family watched the television show at home. Mack announced that The Isley Brothers received the most write-in votes ever. The brothers won a watch with diamonds and red rubies, and they took turns wearing it. The brothers were very close and loved to have fun and make each other laugh.

Rudolph detailed how funny Vernon Isley was. Vernon was the lead singer. Rudolph stated, "He used to crack us up. He had a famous routine going for this song we'd do about a love bug. We'd call it 'The Itch,' and during the chorus, Vernon would scratch himself like crazy! Man, people ate that up!"[15] The family moved from Lincoln Heights to Blue Ash on the first of September, and the good times soon came to a halt.

On September 24, while riding his bike, Vernon was hit and killed by an automobile. On his was to school, Vernon was pedaling on a gravel path beside the road when his bike hit an obstruction and went out of control. Thrown from his bicycle, he landed headfirst against the steel bed of a truck and suffered a broken neck. Exonerated by witnesses, the driver, Elmer Vance, told police he was driving about twenty miles per hour when the accident occurred. Vernon was eleven years old.[16] The surviving brothers were so devastated that they quit singing for a while. Less than a year after Vernon's death, the tragic fate of another African American boy would shine a light on racism in America.

On August 28, 1955, Emmett Till of Chicago, Illinois, was lynched while visiting his family in Money, Mississippi. He was kidnapped from his uncle's home, tortured, and shot for allegedly disrespecting a White woman inside her family's grocery store. His mutilated body was found in the Tallahatchie River. The two White men responsible for his murder were acquitted by an all-White jury. Mamie Till, Emmett's mother, insisted on having an open casket for his funeral. She wanted the world to see how barbaric lynching is in America. The images of Till's body in newspapers and magazines rallied Black support and White sympathy across the country.

Three months after Till's murder, on December 1, 1955, Rosa Parks was arrested in Montgomery, Alabama, for refusing to surrender her seat to a White person. This arrest led to the Montgomery bus boycott, which lasted more than twelve months. The boycott was a protest strategy against the racial segregation on the public transit system of Montgomery. The Supreme Court would eventually declare bus segregation laws unconstitutional. Social issues of this kind had a long-lasting effect on African American musicians, including The Isley Brothers. Their music has never forgotten the Black mass, the forgotten, the oppressed. Over the years, their music would capture the essence, the frustration, and the anger of African Americans.[17]

While American citizens, Black and White, were fighting racism, The Isleys were fighting the pain of losing their brother and trying to figure out how to move forward. They felt no one could sing lead like Vernon. They got over that obstacle and made a pact to continue their love for singing in honor of their brother.[18] They were encouraged by their parents, who convinced them that going forward would fulfill a higher purpose. The Isleys re-formed as a trio, and Ronald volunteered to sing lead. The brothers were conflicted about singing gospel music again. They talked with their parents about singing more secular music. The sound of doo-wop was popular, and the brothers admired The Diablos, The Spaniels, and The Crests.[19]

Doo-wop music is a genre of rhythm and blues music that originated in the 1940s among African American youth in large cities, such as New York, Los Angeles, Chicago, Detroit, and Philadelphia. It features vocal group harmony that carries an engaging melodic line to a simple beat with little or no instrumentation. At that time, segregation was at its highest point. Young African American musicians were often too poor to afford musical instruments. Because of that, they had to be creative. They would meet together, mostly as groups of four, and start producing sounds by using only a wide range of vocal parts. They would sing a cappella and simultaneously generate meaningless words that imitate or suggest the sound it describes, for example, "doo doo-wop" or "do wop de wadda."[20] Doo-wop became the style of choice for The Isleys. The parents gave in to the idea and gave their blessings.[21] Life began to move fast.

Rudolph married his childhood sweetheart, Elaine Elizabeth Jasper, on January 13, 1956. They were sixteen years old. And because of The Isley Brothers' growing reputation, O'Kelly Sr. told his sons to go to New York City to pursue their dreams. But shortly thereafter, tragedy struck the family again. O'Kelly Sr. died of a heart attack in his sleep. As the shock of this loss eased slowly, the brothers held themselves together and asked God for guidance. With their deep spiritual conviction and with the promise to their deceased relatives Vernon and O'Kelly Sr., the brothers were now on a mission. They knew they had to fulfill their father's prophecy about the imminent fame ahead. They understood what their father envisioned was not just wishful thinking. It was predestined. So, according to Rudolph's daughter, Elizabeth Isley Barkley, with their mother's love, strength, and constant guidance, on April, 17, 1956, The Isleys traveled to New York City to pursue their music career.[22]

The Isley Brothers took a Greyhound bus from Cincinnati to New York City. A friend of The Isleys was on the bus, and she promised to make some introductions. They stayed in a hotel near Times Square, and on the second day, someone had stolen Rudolph's wallet with all their food money. But he was street smart enough to pay two weeks of rent in advance.[23] Things were shaky for The Isleys soon after they arrived in New York City.

Rudolph told a story to his daughter Elizabeth about the brothers' hardship of being in the big city. One day, the brothers were walking down a street in New York City. They didn't have much money between them, but they were very hungry. As they walked, they began to smell the wonderful aromas from a bakery nearby. Their mouths began to water, and they stood so close to the bakery that their noses pressed against the window. A woman who worked there saw the brothers and felt sorry for them. She assumed they were nice young men who were just hungry and harmless. The woman came out of the store with a bag full of assorted donuts. The brothers thanked her and walked down the street stuffing themselves with pastry. After they ate all the donuts, they became ill and had stomachaches from eating so much.[24] But their luck in the Big Apple would get better.

The brothers eventually called Richard Barrett, a talent scout who had supervised sessions for Frankie Lymon and The Teenagers' "Why Do Fools Fall in Love" in 1955. He literally found the brothers on the street and was struck by their enthusiasm and natural talent. Barrett thought Ronald sounded like a combination of Jackie Wilson and Clyde McPhatter. He fed them and helped them find the right contacts in NYC's recording industry.[25] While in NYC, The Isley Brothers performed at several venues, including the famous Apollo Theater.

The Apollo Theater was the place at which all new musical talent wanted to perform. The Apollo had a reputation for audiences to be very honest in their responses to new artists. If the audience thought a performance was bad, they could hurt the performer's feelings. On the other hand, if the audience liked a performance, it could have a positive impact on the performer's career. It was public knowledge that powerful agents and record company executives often sat in the audience, scouting for potential recording artists. This was one of the benefits of being invited to perform at the Apollo. When The Isley Brothers performed there, they were well-received by the audience.[26] They soon began to record songs.

One of the contacts from Richard Barrett was George Goldner, the producer of The Teenagers' sessions. George Goldner took The Isleys into the studio and recorded their first doo-wop sides, including "Angels Cried" and

"The Cow Jumped Over the Moon," for various independent labels in New York City, such as Teenage, Mark X, and Cindy. Those records were released between 1957 and 1959. They never sold outside of Cincinnati. However, the songs did gain the attention of RCA Records.[27] With these records, The Isley Brothers toured the East Coast circuit of Black theaters, often called the chitlin circuit, from the Howard Theatre in Washington, DC, to the Uptown in Philadelphia.

The Isley Brothers developed a reputation for a rousing stage show. One particular show was described by singer James Brown in his autobiography. Brown stated, "We saw The Isley Brothers coming from the back of the theater, swinging on ropes, like Tarzan, onto the stage. They hardly had to sing at all. They'd already killed 'em."[28] And in 1959, The Isley Brothers acquired their first hit record.

The year 1959 has been dubbed "the year that changed everything." Journalist Fred Kaplan declared, "There was this growing sense that things were changing. The new is good. The new is something worth embracing." From science and technology came the birth of the microchip. This year also brought the first steps toward birth control, which allowed the sexual revolution and women to get jobs and advance professionally. In music, Miles Davis and Ornette Coleman were breaking the chord structure of older jazz.[29] And 1959 is the year The Isley Brothers recorded their first album.

At that time, The Isley Brothers were perfecting their neo-gospel doo-wop, a soulful blend of secular and spiritual music. Jackie Wilson's "Lonely Teardrops" is one of the songs they performed onstage. During a particular gig in Washington, DC, Ronald Isley ad-libbed, "WELLLLLLLLLL... you know you make me want to SHOUT!" O'Kelly and Rudolph joined the improvisation. The crowd went into a frenzy. RCA executive Howard Bloom signed them based on that performance and suggested they release it as their first RCA single.[30] The song is simply titled "Shout" and would be featured on the forthcoming album.

Shout!

"Shout (Part I)" was released in August 1959. The B-side of the single is "Shout (Part II)," which is a wilder version of the song. "Shout" evolved from the call-and-response style The Isley Brothers sang in church.

You know you make me wanna (shout)
Kick my heels up and (shout)
Throw my hands up and (shout)
Throw my hands back and (shout)[31]

The organist from their church, Professor Herman Stephens, played on the record. The brothers did not consider this a song at first. It's just something they did onstage that made the crowd go wild. They knew they were on to something when Jackie Wilson, for whom they were opening, started using the stop-and-go style in his performance.[32] "Shout" peaked at number forty-seven on the *Billboard* Hot 100 songs chart on October 26.[33]

Although "Shout" was not a chart success on its initial release, it sold over a million copies and became an R&B classic. The Isley Brothers bought their mother a house in Englewood, New Jersey, with the money they earned from this song. Ernie remembered the night the phone rang. Rudolph called his mother, and he was jiggling something in the background. He asked, "Hear that noise?" Sallye replied, "Yeah, what's that?" Rudolph answered, "That's the keys to your new house in New Jersey." Ernie stated that he couldn't get to sleep that night. Within a few days, Mrs. Isley moved her young sons eastward to join her older sons who were swiftly becoming one of the top musical acts in America. Their hit song "Shout" had turned her world and the rock 'n' roll world upside down.[34]

"Shout" has its own dance. When The Isley Brothers sing "little bit softer now," the dancer goes a little lower, then gradually rises up for the "little bit louder now" part. For the rest of the song, people just jump around and get wild. It's an easy dance, which makes it popular at social events where many awkward people may end up on the dance floor. "Shout" has constantly been used in American pop culture.

"Shout" has been used in movies such as *Animal House* (1978), *Troop Beverly Hills* (1989), *Glory Road* (2006), and more. The song has also been featured on television shows, including *Fame* ("A Different Drummer," 1986), *The Wonder Years* ("Night Out," 1990), and *Ally McBeal* ("I Want Love," 2001). Nike re-created the *Animal House* scene with "Shout" in a 2015 video celebrating University of Oregon athletics. This song is known to several generations and demographics. Other artists have covered "Shout," including Joey Dee and the Starlighters, Lulu, The Chambers Brothers, and more.[35] The album on which the song serves as the title track was released on November 1, 1959, on RCA Victor.

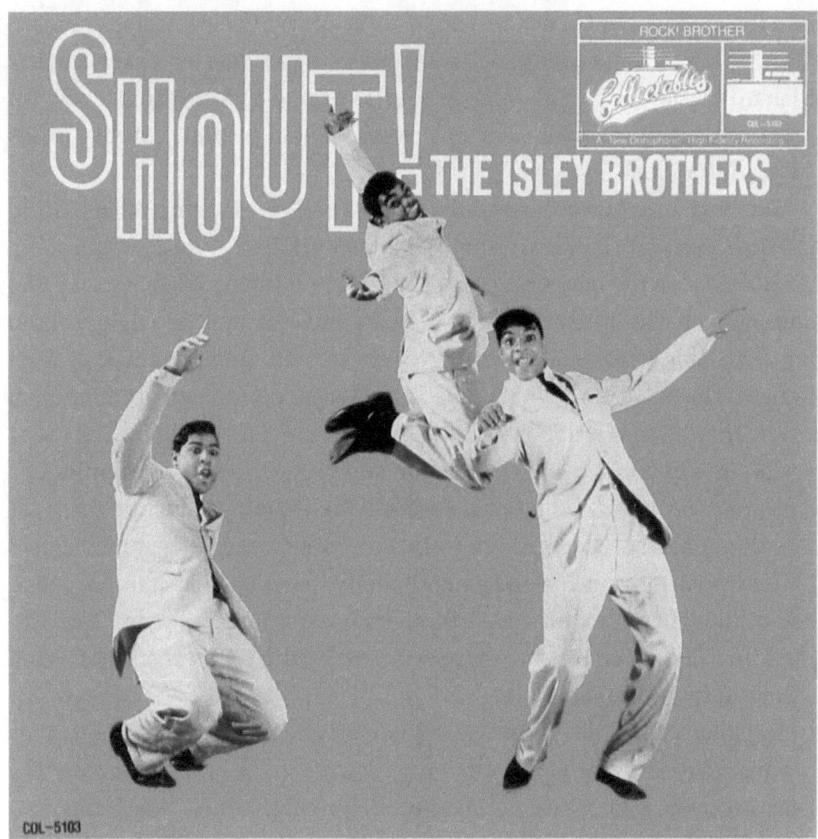

The *Shout* cover displays the brothers dancing in tan suits with conked hairstyles.

Shout! was produced by the songwriting and production team of Hugo Peretti and Luigi Creatore. The album contains twelve tracks: "When the Saints Go Marching In," "St. Louis Blues," "Yes, Indeed," "How Deep Is the Ocean," "Ring-A-Ling-A-Ling (Let the Wedding Bells Ring)," "Rock Around the Clock," "He's Got the Whole World in His Hands," "That Lucky Old Sun," "Respectable," "Without a Song," "Shout (Part I)," and "Shout (Part II)." The album cover is a photo of the brothers wearing tan suits and conked hairstyles. The photo appears to capture them while they are dancing and shouting.[36]

Shout! opens with a jazzy version of the gospel hymn "When the Saints Go Marching In." Ronald's vocals and a strong saxophone highlight W. C. Handy's classic "St. Louis Blues." There is a nice mix of rocking guitar and organ on Sy Oliver's "Yes Indeed," which has a part of "Shout" incorporated into the ending. Next is the up-tempo cover of Irving Berlin's pop standard "How Deep Is the Ocean," which was released as a single but never charted. Richard Jackson's "Ring-A-Ling-A-Ling" is a good rocker with a nice horn break at the halfway point. Side one closes with an accurate cover of "Rock Around the Clock."

Side two opens with the traditional spiritual "He's Got the Whole World in His Hands," which almost sounds like a Chuck Berry–style guitar rocker. Next, they turn the tale of hardship from the pop standard "That Lucky Old Sun" into a lively celebration of life. "Respectable" is another single that did not chart. It is an original guitar-driven rocker with some great vocals from Ronald. The mid-tempo "Without a Song" is a mediocre, overproduced pop cover. They close the album with the two parts of "Shout." While The Isleys' vocals are top notch, the song selection and production are hit or miss.[37]

Shout! was not a commercial success. The Italian production team for this album had been assigned to work with Sam Cooke. They were inclined to use lush arrangements and smooth, fluffy material. This brand of music had nothing to do with The Isley Brothers' background and style.[38] But with their first album and the showstopper "Shout," The Isley Brothers performed across America in 1960.

In January 1960, the Regal Theater in Chicago, Illinois, made good on its promise to present the top acts in music. Starred in the production were The Isley Brothers, Etta James, Bo Diddley, Bobby Blue Bland, Will Gains, and more. Regal management hoped to outdo its phenomenal stage show from the previous year, which included Miles Davis, Della Reese, Ray Charles, Jackie Wilson, and others. Throughout the year, the Regal compounded nationally known artists with famous stars from around the world. Top name-bookers of Las Vegas venues booked several Regal stage shows in America's top show places because of their tremendous success at the Regal.[39] This was a transformative time for Americans, especially African Americans.

By 1960, the civil rights movement was in full swing. In February, the sit-in form of protesting began in Greensboro, North Carolina, when four students from the Agricultural and Technical College of North Carolina orchestrated a sit-in at Woolworth Drug Store, protesting its policy of segregation. In April, the Student Nonviolent Coordinating Committee (SNCC) was formed at Shaw University by over two hundred students from different races to challenge Jim Crow laws.[40] Like many African American musicians, The Isley Brothers had experienced the ugliness of Jim Crow in the South.

Rudolph explained, "When we saw our first 'Colored Only' signs at toilets and drinking fountains in Myrtle Beach, South Carolina, we laughed. Then we got angry. I thought, 'We're the new generation. We don't eat in kitchens.' So, I drank at that fountain for whites." Rudolph spoke of another incident. "I remember being in Selma, Alabama, around the time of Dr. King's Freedom March, and we were asked about canceling our appearance at a white college. Of course not! That was our own march toward equality."[41] Progress was coming along slowly.

On May 6, 1960, President Dwight D. Eisenhower signed the Civil Rights Act of 1960 into law. The act allows for federal inspection of local voter registration rolls and improves on the Civil Rights Act of 1957, which failed to put in place permanent procedures and agencies for investigating voter discrimination and enforcing policies against it. The Civil Rights Act of 1960 made it easier to prove when African American voters were being discriminated against by requiring election officers to maintain proper voting-related documentation.[42] This helped John F. Kennedy defeat Richard Nixon in the 1960 presidential election by a slim margin of 112,000 votes. Many Americans, especially African Americans, perceived this victory to be a step in the right direction. In the following year, America continued to take steps toward equality.

On January 9, 1961, the University of Georgia admitted its first African American students, Charlayne Hunter-Gault and Hamilton E. Holmes. From May to December, a group of Black and White Americans took Freedom Rides on buses across the South to end segregation practices on interstate buses.[43] By this time, The Isley Brothers were yearning for another hit record. They caught wind of "Twist and Shout" and began work on this song and their second album in early 1962.

Twist and Shout

"Twist and Shout" was written by Bert Berns and Phil Medley. It was originally recorded by The Top Notes in 1961. The Top Notes were a promising act already signed to Atlantic Records. The Isley Brothers believed "Twist and Shout" would be a better fit for them. The song was produced by Bert Berns and The Isleys. "Twist and Shout" is the title track for the album that was recorded at Bell Sound Studio in New York City and released on the Wand label.[44]

Twist and Shout was produced by Bert Berns and was released in April 1962. The album contains twelve songs: "Twist and Shout," "I Say Love," "Right Now," "Hold On Baby," "Rubber Leg Twist," "The Snake," "You Better Come Home," "Never Leave Me Baby," "Spanish Twist," "Time After Time," "Let's Twist Again," and "Don't You Feel."[45] This album was reissued in 1966 under the title *Take Some Time Out for The Isley Brothers*.[46] The first single from *Twist and Shout* is the exciting title track.

The song "Twist and Shout" was released in May 1962. It combined the twist dance craze with the energy of the 1959 hit song "Shout" and proved to be a winning combination. The Isleys' version used the same lyrics but with a totally different sound.[47]

> Well, shake it up, baby, now
> Twist and shout
> Come on, come on, come, come on, baby, now
> Come on and work it on out[48]

"Twist and Shout" climbed to number two on the *Billboard* Hot R&B Singles chart on July 28. It also peaked at number seventeen on the *Billboard* Hot 100 Songs chart on August 11.[49] "Twist and Shout" was a success for The Isley Brothers. In November, the song reached gold record status after selling over one million copies.[50] The money came rolling in, and it was evident in The Isley Brothers' appearance. They quickly began dressing more stylishly in sharp suits.[51]

"Twist and Shout" would be an even bigger success for The Beatles, who recorded it in 1963. The fact that The Beatles took the song to a higher social and cultural level underlines what was a hindrance for The Isley Brothers for many years. They were so entrenched in the African American community that they were barely recognized outside of it. Culturally, this was their strength, but a weakness in terms of achieving widespread exposure and corresponding financial success. This would not change until the early 1970s.[52] Hip-hop powerhouse Salt-N-Pepa also released a version of "Twist and Shout" on their 1988 album *A Salt with a Deadly Pepa*. The Isleys released more singles in 1962.

The Isley Brothers followed up "Twist and Shout" with other twist-themed songs, including "Let's Twist Again," "Rubberleg Twist," and "Twistin' with Linda."[53] "Twistin' with Linda" is the only other single to reach the *Billboard* chart. This song was written by the three Isley brothers.⁵⁴ It peaked at number fifty-four on the *Billboard* Hot 100 Songs chart on October 27.⁵⁵ No other singles were released from *Twist and Shout*, and the title track basically carries the album.

According to Richie Unterberger of AllMusic, *Twist and Shout* was a "stone classic." He believes many songs on the album do their best to emulate "Twist and Shout" with Latin rhythms and gospel-styled vocals. Unterberger claims "some of the tracks do little more than rework the basic riff, and even the ones that aren't blatant rewrites don't measure up to 'Twist and Shout.'" For this album he describes the brothers as "never less than energetic and entertaining."⁵⁶

The Isleys released another single titled "Nobody but Me" in December. This song has the typical groove of an early 1960s dance song. It was not featured on *Twist and Shout*, and it failed to chart.⁵⁷ After having two charting records in 1962, The Isley Brothers continued to perform across America.

In January 1963, The Isley Brothers and Dee Clark shared the spotlight in a stage show at the Regal Theater in Chicago, Illinois. The show began on January 18 and lasted for one week. Other artists in the show were Redd Foxx and Gladys Knight, who made her debut as a single artist without her Pips.⁵⁸ About three weeks later, The Isley Brothers traveled to New York City to perform. On Friday, February 8, The Isley Brothers and other artists began performing at the Apollo Theater for one week. The Isley Brothers headlined the bill with Etta James. The exciting rhythm and blues show featured a supporting cast that included Joe Henderson, The Miller Sisters, Curley Mays, ET Pankins, and comedian Baron Harris.⁵⁹ The Isleys soon began work on their next album.

Twisting and Shouting

Twisting and Shouting, the third album by The Isley Brothers, was released in July 1963 on the United Artists label. The album is credited as The Famous Isley Brothers and produced by Bert Berns. It consists of twelve songs: "Surf and Shout," "Please, Please, Please," "She's the One," "Tango," "What'cha Gonna Do," "Stagger Lee," "You'll Never Leave Him," "Let's Go, Let's Go, Let's Go," "She's Gone," "Shake It with Me Baby," "Long Tall Sally," and "Do the Twist." The album cover shows the brothers in tan suits with conked hairstyles.⁶⁰

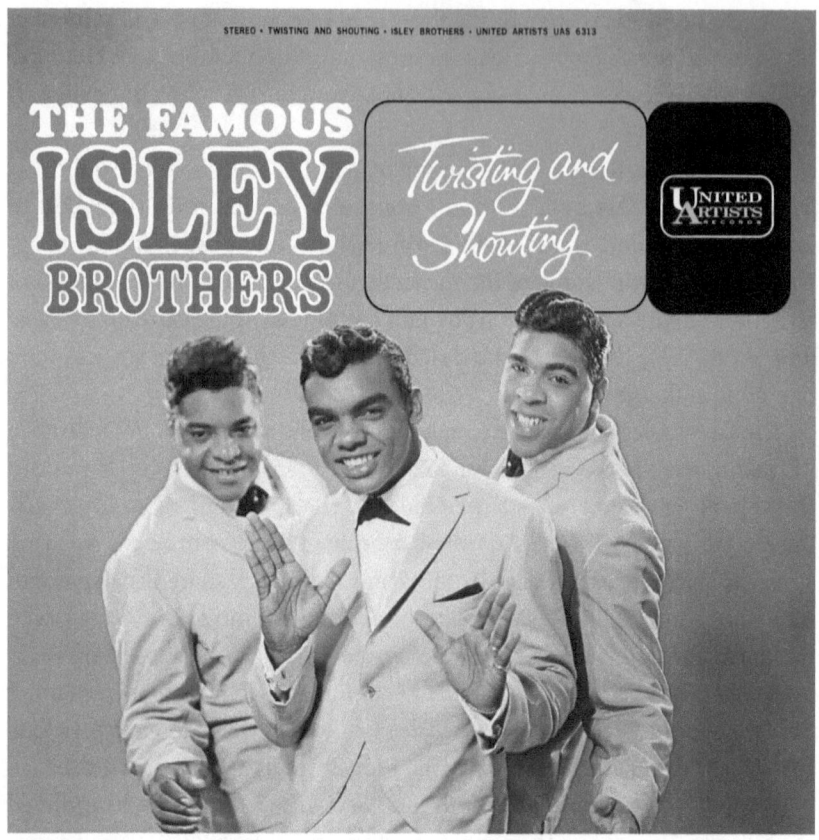

The *Twisting and Shouting* cover is a photo of The Isleys posing in tan suits with conked hairstyles.

The American suit had a cut to broaden the shoulders and a slow drop down to the trousers, slouching over the feet like an exhausted lover. The look screamed celebrity. This suit was the uniform of the chitlin circuit. With hair conks slicker than waves, The Isleys were larger than life or large enough to fool White teenagers into believing they were groomed by Motown.[61] *Twisting and Shouting* has good songs, but it was not what The Isleys needed to make a huge impact. None of the songs made the singles charts.

According to John Alroy and David Bertrand Wilson of Wilson and Alroy's Record Reviews, *Twisitng and Shouting* is "a well-made album with a lot of variety." The songs are considered "tuneful and intriguing, either up-tempo rock and roll or moody ballads." The critics wrote, "They show off flawless imitations of James Brown ('Please, Please, Please'), Little Richard ('Long Tall Sally'), and Chubby Checker ('Do the Twist')—you may think you're listening to a compilation by the original artists."[62] *Twisting and Shouting* should have had a better reception. This was a challenging time for The Isley Brothers and for America in general.

On June 11, Alabama Governor George Wallace and state troopers defied federal district court orders by blocking Black students from entering the University of Alabama. President John F. Kennedy federalized the state's National Guard to force the governor's compliance. On the following day, Medgar Evers, National Association for the Advancement of Colored People (NAACP) field secretary, was assassinated in Jackson, Mississippi, by a White supremacist. On August 28, 250,000 people attended the March on Washington for Jobs and Freedom, just two and a half weeks before Ku Klux Klan members bombed the Sixteenth Street Baptist Church in Birmingham, Alabama, which killed four girls and wounded many others.[63] And on November 22, President Kennedy was assassinated in Dallas, Texas. He had brought much hope to a troubled nation. Also, The Isleys had become tired of hassling with different record labels and maneuvering through the politics and wishes of various music executives.[64] They believed it was time to make a change, and change was on the horizon.

Chapter 2

Soul on the Rocks

The year 1964 was a critical time for America. The Civil Rights Act of 1964 was signed into law by President Lyndon Johnson. The outspoken boxer Cassius Clay, later known as Muhammad Ali, defeated Sonny Liston for the World Heavyweight Championship. President Johnson was reelected for a second term, and Martin Luther King Jr. was awarded the Nobel Peace Prize. In the world of popular music, the British band The Beatles took the world and America by storm by releasing a series of number one hits. The Supremes and Bob Dylan became household names. Sam Cooke was killed under mysterious circumstances, and The Isley Brothers were still navigating their trajectory.

In early 1964, The Isley Brothers released "Who's That Lady" on the United Artists label. This is a gentle groove with a nice melody, but it did not chart. This song would come back in a much bigger way for the brothers almost a decade later. Unfortunately, United Artists was not a good fit for The Isleys, and they left the label after a brief association. The Isley Brothers decided to form their own record label called T-Neck. It was named after the nearby New Jersey town. The Isley Brothers became the first Black group to have their own label and one of the first Black artists to do so, in addition to Sam Cooke, Curtis Mayfield, and Ray Charles. Having their own record company gave the brothers creative and financial control of their own careers. Going against the grain would be a recurring theme throughout their tenure.[1]

In February 1964, a guitarist in The Isley Brothers backup band, the I. B. Specials, quit, despite the fact that a spring tour and recording dates had been booked. Tony Rice, a friend of The Isleys, suggested a young guitarist named

Jimi Hendrix. Ronald recalled Rice's enthusiasm for Hendrix: "Tony said this kid—he was about fifteen or sixteen—was the best and that he played right-handed guitar with his left hand. I said to Tony, 'Aw come on man, man, he can't be that good. Is he better than . . .' and then I started naming all the guitar players we knew we'd like to have in our band, and Tony said, 'He's better than any of them.'"

Ronald and Tony met Jimi at the Palm Café in Harlem. The musicians in the band at the café did not want Jimi to play. They said he played too loud, but Ronald believed it was jealousy. So, he invited Jimi to his house the following weekend to play music. The Isley Brothers were living in a house on Liberty Road in Englewood, New Jersey. They shared the house with their mother and younger brothers, Ernest (also known as Ernie) and Marvin. The Isleys assembled the backup band in their basement, with Al Lucas on bass and Bobby Gregg on drums. Jimi leaped into "Twist and Shout," followed by "Respectable" and "Shout." He played all the songs fluidly. On that afternoon, Jimi was hired as a member of the I. B. Specials.[2] Consequently, he spent much time with the Isley family.

Jimi was given a spare room in the Isley family's home. He quickly adapted to his surroundings and often watched Saturday morning cartoons with Ernie and Marvin. The brothers nicknamed him "Creepy" because he moved so quietly through the house. Ernie was eleven years old at that time. He declared that Jimi was quiet, well-behaved, and minded his own business. Ernie often watched Jimi sit and play his guitar while looking out the front window. He recalled, "Jimi would practice phrases over and over again, turn them inside out, break them in half, break them in quarters, play them slow, play them fast. . . . Jimi would even use the guitar to do his talking for him: 'How are you doing, Jimi?' 'Bading bada dooo' on the guitar. 'Is it cold outside?' 'Wheeooooow.'"[3] Jimi had a great influence on young Ernie, and that influence would be exemplified in The Isley Brothers' music within the next decade. With Jimi Hendrix on board, The Isley Brothers began touring in March.

The tour began in Montreal, Canada, at the Grand National. After that, the group traveled to a baseball stadium in Bermuda, where they headlined. They also traveled to the West Coast, where they played a college circuit. While in Seattle, Jimi ran into his former girlfriend, Betty Jean Morgan, and they reminisced over old times. Jimi wanted to stay over in Seattle and meet the group in the next city. The Isleys assumed he knew where the next gig was, but he didn't. The Isleys performed a concert in Atlanta, Georgia, on May 6 at a street dance in Peters Park set up by the Georgia Institute of Technology (Georgia Tech) to celebrate its Greek Week festival. The group performed without the unique stage persona of Jimi. He had already traveled to New York City, the location for the next gig after Atlanta.

When The Isley Brothers returned to New York City, O'Kelly took Jimi to Manny's Music Shop in Manhattan and bought him a white Fender Duo-Sonic guitar. Jimi customized it with an Epiphone "Temtome" vibrato unit that changed volume and pitch on demand. It was a quantum leap from Jimi's old guitar. Jimi was now ready to perform again with the brothers in NYC.[4] On Friday, June 19, The Isley Brothers and several other recording stars came together at the Rockland Palace in Harlem to throw the largest farewell salute to honor a popular disc jockey named Magnificent Montague. Included in the flock of stars were Ben E. King, Otis Redding, Gladys Knight, Wilson Pickett, Dionne Warwick, and many others.[5] A week later, The Isleys returned to the famed Apollo Theater for an exciting rhythm and blues revue presented by the "Soul Brothers," four disc jockeys at New York City's WWRL radio station. Other artists who performed were Dionne Warwick, The "5" Royales, and the Charades.[6] In the same month, The Isleys published new music.

The Isley Brothers released the single "Testify" on T-Neck. Because the song ran over six minutes during recording, the engineer made it radio friendly by editing it into two parts and splitting them on sides A and B of the single. To testify is to speak about the goodness of God in church. "Testify" is an upbeat song that emulates parishioners expressing the Holy Spirit in the African American church. In the song, each brother individually testifies about R&B acts, such as James Brown, Jackie Wilson, Little Stevie Wonder, paying homage to their unique singing style and stage performance.

> I'm talking about Raymond, I'm talking about Raymond
> Come on, Ray, the genius, come on and testify, son
> Go ahead, son, go ahead[7]

Surprisingly, "Testify" did not chart. That could be attributed to the new soul sounds emerging from Motown Records.[8] Like "Twist and Shout," this tune is another blast of post-gospel rock 'n' roll jubilation that roars with the power of a great gospel group backed by a funk band. "Testify" is a notable track in pop music history because it is the commercial debut of one of the world's greatest guitarists: Jimi Hendrix.[9] The Isleys soon released a second single on their newly formed label titled "Move On Over and Let Me Dance." This song also failed to chart.[10] The Isley Brothers didn't have a current hit record as they toured throughout the summer.

The Isley Brothers' summer tour took them to Georgia, where they performed a show with Carla Thomas, Joe Tex, Esther Phillips, and the Drifters. In most R&B revues, each act was given about thirty minutes of stage time, and Jimi would be lucky if his guitar solo lasted thirty seconds. Occasionally, the tour intersected with a British band, and The Isleys put their great guitarist in the spotlight. Ernie recalled, "In the middle of a show, Kelly might say 'Come on out here Jimi and show them how it's done.'... And he'd do something like play the guitar behind his back, and everyone would go, 'My God, how did he do that?'"[11] Jimi was special and different. Rudolph exclaimed, "Jimi scared our pants off! He was just ... different. He had that hippie look, the rings, the scarves, the bracelets, the jewelry, before we even knew what hippies were! The way his hair fell all the way down his back!" People could be so judgmental. They would ask, "Is that a boy or a girl?" Rudolph added, "We were kind of ashamed of that look. We used to buy the band their clothes, but Jimi didn't want a gold lamé suit like everyone else." The Isleys were in the Bahamas once when he put on a ruffled shirt and wrapped a car chain around his waist for a belt. They couldn't believe it. But Jimi was a nice guy who made beautiful music. Rudolph declared, "Jimi respected that we were clean cut, that we didn't drink or smoke. And we respected him for respecting us."[12] While Jimi was with the group, The Isleys signed a deal with Atlantic Records and hoped to have Jimi play on a session in New York, but shortly after a concert in Macon, Georgia, Jimi was fired.

Jimi Hendrix was a great musician, but apparently, he wasn't a good fit for The Isley Brothers. So, why was Jimi fired? In an interview long after his departure, Jimi confessed that his attitude may have been the dominant factor. He declared. "I got tired of playing in the key of F all the time and turned in my white, mohair silk suit and patent leather shoes."[13] Although Jimi was with the band for only a few months, his impact would last for years. With Jimi gone, The Isley Brothers persevered and continued to perform around the country.

The Isley Brothers concluded 1964 by returning to the Apollo Theater. Tommy Smalls, master disc jockey and genius at predicting stars of the future, brought an exciting holiday revue to the Apollo for the week beginning Christmas Day. His cast included established stars, up-and-coming new singers, and one of the finest big bands in show business. Headline honors were shared by The Isley Brothers and Joe Tex. The supporting cast included King Curtis and his band, Johnny Thunder, Inez and Charlie Foxx, and other newcomers. The holidays were all the merrier for patrons of the Apollo.[14] The beginning of the new year would be challenging for The Isleys.

As the year 1965 came, The Isley Brothers had been without a hit song for nearly three years, since "Twist and Shout" was released in the spring of 1962. Although they had created their own record label, that label didn't produce any hits. The brothers understood they needed a new strategy. The absence of a hit record exasperated The Isleys so much that when the opportunity to record for Motown came around, they put their own T-Neck Records on hiatus. At that time, Motown was the hottest label in America, with some of the hottest recording artists, including The Supremes, The Temptations, Marvin Gaye, Stevie Wonder, and several others. Motown was responsible for the so-called Sound of Young America, a polished pop soul sound that had Black and White audiences pressing for more.[15] The music of Motown has been credited with breaking racial barriers and helping America heal during the challenging times of the 1960s, and that music was much needed in 1965.

On February 21, 1965, world-renowned activist and orator Malcolm X was assassinated in Harlem, New York. On March, 7, about six hundred people crossed the Edmund Pettus Bridge in Selma, Alabama, to begin the Selma to Montgomery march. State troopers violently attacked the peaceful demonstrators, resulting in severe injuries. This event became known as Bloody Sunday. In the same month, America began sending troops to Vietnam to fight in the infamous Vietnam War. In the summer, from August 11 to 16, African Americans rioted in the Watts section of Los Angeles, California. Thirty-four people died and over one thousand were injured. African Americans needed strategic ways to express themselves and challenge oppression.

In June, the Black Arts Movement had begun when Amiri Baraka (LeRoi Jones) established the Black Arts Repertory Theater in Harlem, New York. The Black Arts Movement was a Black nationalism movement that focused on music, literature, drama, and the visual arts, made up of Black artists and intellectuals. This was the cultural section of the Black Power movement that began the following year. Artists shared many of the ideologies of Black self-determination, political beliefs, and culture. Some of those artists include Audre Lorde, Ntozake Shange, James Baldwin, Gil Scott-Heron, and Thelonious Monk. During this movement, Black American artists were encouraged to express themselves through their own institutions. Also, a new style of music was developing among Black musicians.

James Brown released "Papa's Got a Brand New Bag" in June. This is credited with being the first funk song. Funk music, as described by Rickey Vincent in *Funk: The Music, the People, and the Rhythm of the One*, is a deliberate reaction to—and a rejection of—the traditional Western world's preference for formality, pretense, and self-repression.[16] Music educator Howard C. Harris also describes the essence of funk music: "Funk is a style of music in which elements of jazz, pop, rock, gospel, and the Blues are fused to create a rhythmic, soulful sound. Funk thrives on rhythm, and the art of it depends on the level of togetherness between the performers. It is, in essence, togetherness in motion."[17]

James Brown initially played in a style that incorporated ballads, rock 'n' roll, and classic up-tempo R&B, but he soon found that he could do more with less by stripping away the more superfluous elements of his music and arrangements. Multiple chord changes were reduced to pulling on a single chord. Fleshed-out lyrics were tossed in favor of improvised lines. Predetermined sections were dropped as call-and-response between musicians began to take shape. All of those elements soon began to merge into a brand-new sound.[18] With funk music, Black musicians were doing a new thing, their own thing. Within a few years, The Isley Brothers would incorporate this style into their music. But in 1965, there was a more popular style of music in America: the Motown sound. The Isleys felt assured of getting another hit record by signing with Berry Gordy's Motown label.

This Old Heart of Mine

Berry Gordy assigned The Isley Brothers to the renowned hit-songwriting team of Brian Holland, Lamont Dozier, and Eddie Holland (Holland-Dozier-Holland) and set out to make them another successful Motown act.[19] The Isley Brothers' first single on Motown was "This Old Heart of Mine (Is Weak for You)." It was released in January 1966. Holland-Dozier-Holland wrote the song with help from fellow Motown songwriter Sylvia Moy.[20] They had The Supremes in mind to record it, but for once, The Supremes did not get first bite of this fruit. The song has echoes of The Supremes' "Back in My Arms Again."[21] This is one of those upbeat Motown tunes with heart-wrenching lyrics about a man who is devastated over losing his lady friend. The man just can't move on, and like the singer in "Ain't Too Proud to Beg" (The Temptations), he has abandoned his pride.

> If you leave me a hundred times,
> A hundred times I'll take you back
> I'm yours whenever you want me.

Lamont Dozier said the song was inspired by a girl he just couldn't let go. He stated, "The more I tried, the deeper I fell. I made excuses for her and all the wrong she had done to me. She was a necessary evil that I just couldn't overcome." In addition to sensible lyrics, the song has a good sound.[22]

"This Old Heart of Mine" is packed with energy, but it also has an ease. The song has great force but not too fast. It is exactly the right dancing speed with rolling thunder drums, piano, and xylophone. Along the surface are strings, courtesy of the Detroit Symphony Orchestra, supported by brass, including the baritone sax used on so many Motown records, played by Mike Terry. The Isleys add to the energy by moving quickly around the rhythm. Amid a crammed, crowded lyric, they throw in perfectly precise pauses and semi-stutters.[23] This song did extremely well on the music charts

"This Old Heart of Mine" climbed to number six on the *Billboard* Hot R&B Singles chart on April 9, 1966. It also peaked at number twelve on the *Billboard* Hot 100 Songs chart on April 23.[24] "This Old Heart of Mine" would also reach number three in the UK when it was released there in 1968.[25] Motown always made the best of a good song. Later in 1966, The Supremes sped up the song a little; so did Tammi Terrell in 1968.[26] Rod Stewart, a huge fan of both Motown and The Isley Brothers, released his version of the tune in 1975. Stewart's rendition was a big hit in the UK, climbing to number four, but it only went to number eighty-three in America. He did a lot better stateside when he recorded the song as a duet with Ronald Isley in 1989. That version climbed to number ten in America.[27] "This Old Heart of Mine" became the title track for The Isley Brothers' fourth studio album and their first album with Motown.

This Old Heart of Mine was released May 17, 1966. It was produced by Robert Gordy, William "Mickey" Stevenson, and Holland-Dozier-Holland. The album contains twelve tracks: "Nowhere to Run," "Stop! In the Name of Love," "This Old Heart of Mine (Is Weak for You)," "Take Some Time Out for

The cover for *This Old Heart of Mine* displays a White couple on the beach.

Love," "I Guess I'll Always Love You," "Baby Don't You Do It," "Who Could Ever Doubt My Love," "Put Yourself in My Place," "I Hear a Symphony," "Just Ain't Enough Love," "There's No Love Left," and "Seek and You Shall Find." Surprisingly, the cover for this album displays a photo of a White couple on a beach.[28] *This Old Heart of Mine* is a masterpiece for Ronald's wailing vocals, featuring inspired covers of hit songs by The Supremes, Martha and the Vandellas, and Marvin Gaye.[29] After the title track for this album, more singles followed.

"Take Some Time Out for Love" was released in May 1966. It was written by Thomas Kemp and Robert Gordy.[30] It is one of two songs on the album that was not written by Holland-Dozier-Holland. The other one is "Seek and You Shall Find." "Take Some Time Out for Love" has a structure similar to "Twist and Shout." This song peaked at number sixty-six on the *Billboard* Hot 100 Songs chart on June 11.[31] Less than a week later, another social movement began.

On June 16, the first popular use of the term "Black Power" was by Stokely Carmichael (later known as Kwame Toure) and Willie Ricks (later known as Makusa Dada). They were both organizers and spokespeople for the Student Nonviolent Coordinating Committee (SNCC). In a speech in Greenwood, Mississippi, during the March Against Fear, Toure led the marchers in a chant for Black Power that was nationally televised. Many believe this was the beginning of the Black Power movement. This movement would influence several artists, including The Isley Brothers. During the same month, another single was issued.

Hoping to benefit from The Isley Brothers' Motown success, United Artists released "Love Is a Wonderful Thing." This song had been recorded when the group was previously with that label and was written by The Isley Brothers.[32] "Love Is a Wonderful Thing" was not featured on an album. It was only released as a 45 record as a single. Some industry magazines predicted the song would be a hit: *Gavin Report* on August 26, *Cashbox* on August 27, and *Billboard* on September 10. Ironically, "Love Is a Wonderful Thing" stalled at number 110 on a *Billboard* chart titled "Bubbling Under the Hot 100." The song was never listed on any other Top 100 charts.[33] Surprisingly, "Love Is a Wonderful Thing" would be a huge money-maker for The Isley Brothers in the 1990s. That situation is discussed in chapters 7, 8, and 9. In the following month, The Isleys were in NYC again.

On July 1, The Isley Brothers returned to the Apollo Theater after a year and a half. The group headlined there for a week. The Isleys had matured into an exciting act, providing good all-around entertainment, with songs, impressions, and dancing. The supporting cast included Johnny Nash, The Spellbinders, The Diplomats, and others.[34] Also in July, The Isleys released the third single from *This Old Heart of Mine* titled "I Guess I'll Always Love You." This song peaked at number sixty-one on the *Billboard* Hot 100 Songs chart on August 20. It also climbed to number thirty-one on the *Billboard* Hot R&B Singles chart on September 3.[35] Based on this album, signing with Motown seemed to be a good move for The Isleys.

AllMusic gives *This Old Heart of Mine* a four-star rating. According to Andrew Hamilton, the title track has a throbbing beat and memorable melody with irresistible vocals. He declared that Ronald "sings with understated fire in his natural register," as opposed to the falsetto he used mostly in the 1980s and '90s. Hamilton added, "Isley versions of 'Nowhere to Run,' 'Stop in the Name of Love,' 'Baby Don't You Do It,' and 'I Hear a Symphony' are comparable to, if not better than, the originals."[36] *This Old Heart of Mine* peaked at number 140 on the *Billboard* 200 Albums chart on July 2. It also climbed to number 15 on the *Billboard* Hot R&B LPs chart on July 23.[37] With a successful album, The Isleys continued to perform.

On August 14, The Isley Brothers performed at the All-Star Spectacular of 1966 at Village Theatre in New York City. It was presented by the New York Chapter of the National Association of Radio Announcers. The event was split into two shows, the first at 3:00 p.m. and the second at 8:00 p.m. The Isleys performed during the first show. Other artists on the bill included Dionne Warwick, Little Richard, Otis Redding, Sarah Vaughan, and several others.[38] Two months later, the Black Power movement was solidified

On October 15, the Black Panther Party for Self-Defense was founded by Huey P. Newton and Bobby Seale in Oakland, California. The core practice of the party was its open carry armed citizens' patrol to monitor the behavior of the Oakland Police Department. The party had chapters in major cities across America and some foreign countries as well. The Black Panthers encouraged people to arm themselves and "fight the power" by challenging the corruption of the police and other forms of injustice. By this time, The Isleys had begun working on their next studio album.

Soul on the Rocks

Soul on the Rocks is the fifth studio album by The Isley Brothers. It was produced by Norman Whitfield, Ivy Jo Hunter, and Smokey Robinson and released on January 24, 1967. This album contains twelve tracks: "Got to Have You Back," "That's the Way Love Is," "Whispers (Gettin' Louder)," "Tell Me It's Just a Rumor Baby," "One Too Many Heartaches," "It's Out of the Question," "Why When Love Is Gone," "Save Me from This Misery," "Little Miss Sweetness," "Good Things," "Catching Up on Time," and "Behind a Painted Smile." The album cover is a photo of the brothers in a park with dark suits and conked hairstyles.[39] Before the first single was released, The Isleys returned to the Apollo in New York City.

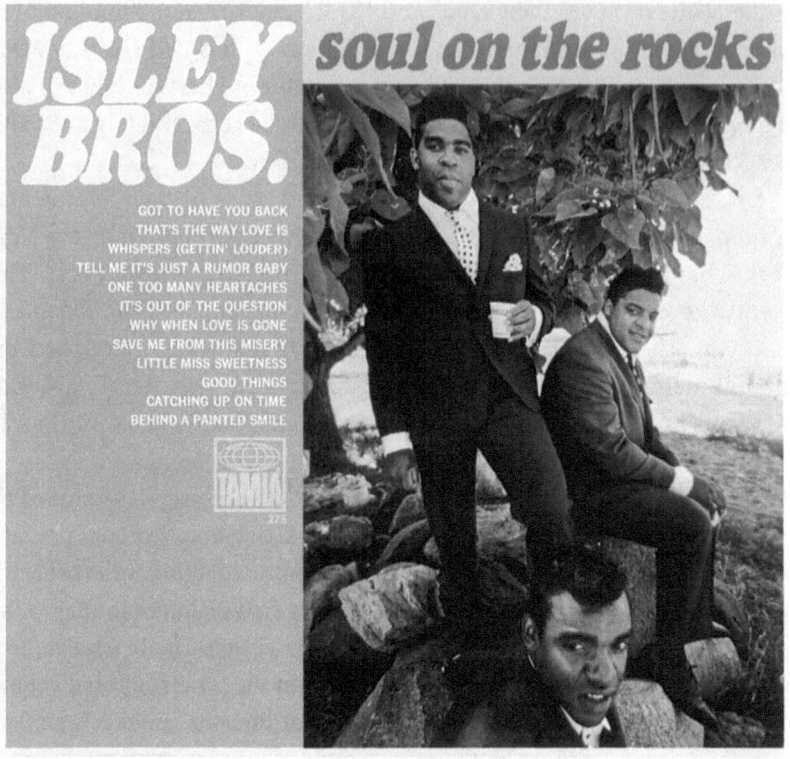

The cover for *Soul on the Rocks* shows the brothers at a park in dark suits with conked hairstyles.

On February 17, The Isley Brothers performed at the Apollo Theater midnight show for "A Salute to Adam Clayton Powell," sponsored by the Women's Alliance for Voter Registration. Adam Clayton Powell Jr. was an outspoken African American pastor and congressman who represented Harlem. The alliance grew out of congressional action against Powell, and plans were finalized to become a permanent organization to provide research and resources without political strings for all African Americans in politics. The Isley Brothers have always exemplified their concerns for the progress of African Americans. Other musicians who performed were Thelonious Monk, Cannonball Adderley, the Booker Ervin Quartet, and Walter Bishop Jr. Muhammad Ali, Dick Gregory, and Georgia state senator

Julian Bond were also invited.⁴⁰ In the spring, The Isleys released "Got to Have You Back."

"Got to Have You Back" was written by Ivy Jo Hunter, Leon Ware, and Stephen Bowden.⁴¹ It has the typical Motown vibe and sounds like it could have been sung by The Four Tops. This song peaked at number ninety-three on the *Billboard* Hot 100 Songs chart on May 6 and climbed to number forty-seven on the *Billboard* Hot R&B Singles chart on May 20.⁴² Another single from this album, "Behind a Painted Smile," would not be released until 1969. It was challenging for The Isley Brothers to have another major hit record with Motown. Things were happening fast at Motown, and for a while, The Isleys were given sufficient attention.

When The Isley Brothers didn't create the excitement Motown expected for them, Berry Gordy pulled his resources back. He had already spread his creative resources too thinly, and so, like any chief executive, Gordy had to make some tough decisions. The Temptations, The Miracles, and The Supremes were still successful and popular, and so were a few other Motown acts. The Isleys had not broken through. So, they received limited assistance.⁴³ This caused tension between the brothers and the record label. During this same time, racial tension was escalating in America.

In the summer of 1967, 158 riots occurred in urban communities across America. Most shared the same triggering event: a dispute between Black citizens and White police officers that escalated to violence. During those violent months, the massive social unrest resulted in 83 deaths and 17,000 arrests. The worst uprising was in Detroit, Michigan; there were 43 deaths, 7,200 arrests, and more than 2,500 buildings looted, damaged, or destroyed in five days of rioting.⁴⁴ Although racial tensions were high, Thurgood Marshall was sworn in as the first African American Supreme Court justice on October 2, 1967. Nevertheless, America's racial anxiety would climax four months later.

On April 4, 1968, Dr. Martin Luther King Jr. was assassinated at the Lorraine Motel in Memphis, Tennessee. He was thirty-nine years old. Violence erupted across America because of his death. The ten days following King's death are known as Holy Week 1968. During that time, nearly two hundred cities experienced looting, arson, or sniper fire. The US experienced its greatest wave of social unrest since the Civil War. Around 3,500 people were injured, 43 were killed, and 27,000 were arrested. The chaos ended on April 14 after local and state governments and President Lyndon B. Johnson deployed a collective total of 58,000 National Guardsmen and Army troops to assist law enforcement officers in quelling the violence.[45] Before the violence ended, President Johnson signed the Civil Rights Act of 1968 into law on April 11. Some consider this to be the end of the civil rights movement. Americans worked to carry on the legacy of Dr. King, and The Isleys continued to work on their career.

Motown released "Take Me in Your Arms (Rock Me a Little While)" in April. This song was written by Holland-Dozier-Holland.[46] It was not featured on a studio album but would later appear on a compilation album. "Take Me in Your Arms" is an upbeat rocker that reached number twenty-two on the *Billboard* Hot R&B Singles chart on April 27.[47] However, it did not break into the Hot 100 in pop and was considered a failure, especially by Motown standards. This did not help the relationship between The Isleys and Motown Records.

Marvin Isley recalled, "The images of the Motown stars on TV were so glamorous. They were living! The clothes, the hair, it looked so great." But his older brothers were coming off the road with a different story. Marvin added, "They'd talk about how the artists were asking for royalty statements and finding out about all the expenses being charged back to them. How they were responsible for all those nice things, like room service and limousines. It made everything about saving money. You know, my brothers always took some of mother's fried chicken." The Isley Brothers became tired of the formula and power games at Motown. "My brothers were so enamored of the Motown writers, they just deferred to super talents like Lamont Dozier and the Holland brothers," Marvin said. The Isleys eventually asked Berry Gordy to let them go, and they left. Ernie stated, "Leaving Motown was considered the kiss of death. Then, after they left, things opened up creatively for a number of artists, especially Stevie Wonder and Marvin Gaye. It just took some time."[48]

After leaving Motown, The Isley Brothers resurrected their T-Neck record label. To help them navigate the risky marketing and distribution, The Isleys contracted the services of Buddah Records in New York City.[49] Now, having their own label again, The Isley Brothers were free to record in a manner that best suited them. They soon began working on their next album, which would take them to another plateau of their career.

Chapter 3
Freedom

The year 1969 was full of milestones. The first communications were sent through the ARPANET (Advanced Research Projects Agency Network), the precursor to the internet. Dr. Denton Cooley implanted the first artificial heart, and the Public Broadcasting Service (PBS) was established. In popular culture, the Woodstock Music and Art Fair attracted more than 350,000 fans, and the Harlem Cultural Festival, nicknamed "Black Woodstock," was also held. A wide range of R&B stars turned up for the Harlem Cultural Festival, which drew more than 300,000 people over six free concerts held in the space now known as Marcus Garvey Park. Some of the performers were Stevie Wonder, Nina Simone, Gladys Knight and the Pips, Mahalia Jackson, The Staples Singers, B. B. King, and The 5th Dimension. The festival is the subject of the 2021 documentary *Summer of Soul*, which reflects significant changes in Black culture and expression at that pivotal time.[1] Changes could definitely be heard and seen among The Isley Brothers.

The Isley Brothers changed their image by trading out their mohair suits to a freer, funkier "West Coast" style. They began wearing a combination of velvets, furs, and smooth eighteenth-century period clothes with radical English and French designs. The look was classy and distinguished and set them apart at a time when, across America, "different" was good. This change would serve them well as they developed a funkier sound for their next album.[2]

Before 1969, The Isley Brothers' style conformed to mainstream America. They wore the standard suits, conked their hair, and produced clean R&B music that could sometimes sound White just as much as it sounded Black.

That type of music is considered easy to cross over. But there would be a distinct change with their new music.

It's Our Thing

In February 1969, The Isley Brothers released "It's Your Thing" from the forthcoming sixth studio album titled *It's Our Thing*. In this song, Ronald is letting a girl know that she is free to spread her love around, as long as he can get some of it too. "It's Your Thing" was a popular saying at the time and wonderfully ambiguous. It could have a sexual connotation or simply be about personal independence.[3]

> It's your thing, do what you wanna do
> I can't tell you, who to sock it to[4]

Aretha Franklin had popularized the "sock it to me" line in her version of "Respect," which could have been for salacious intent. Ronald, who wrote most of the song, liked the double meaning of these lines, which made the song suggestive and radio friendly at the same time. This was the first hit song The Isleys wrote and produced themselves.

In an interview on *The Isley Brothers: Summer Breeze Greatest Hits Live* DVD, Ronald declared that he wrote "It's Your Thing" while dropping his daughter off at school one day. He didn't want to forget the lyrics, so he hummed it in his head and rushed straight to his mother's house to write it out. Ronald sang it for his eldest brother O'Kelly, who thought it would be a hit, so they set up studio time to record it. Ronald, O'Kelly, and Rudolph are the credited writers on the song. "It's Your Thing" was recorded at A&R Studios in New York using musicians who played on the road with Wilson Pickett. Charles Pitts Jr. played the lead guitar—he later played the famous *wah-wah* on "Theme from Shaft" by Isaac Hayes. George Patterson did the arrangement and also played alto sax; Trevor Lawrence played the tenor sax. Ernie Isley, just sixteen years old, played bass.

This was Ernie's first time playing that instrument on a recording. Ernie had played the bass when they were rehearsing the song, but a studio musician was supposed to handle it on the recording. When the hired musician couldn't match what Ernie did at rehearsal, Ronald decided to have his younger brother play it instead. Ernie later said he was in "complete fear" during the recording.[5] The song became a smash hit. Freedom was the key to The Isleys' newfound success.

Rudolph explained, "We've been planning all this for a year and a half now. We pretty much knew what we wanted to accomplish by the time we set up our own record company and started recording." What The Isleys wanted to do was their "own thing," and the hit record proved they were more than capable. "It's Your Thing" was one of the fastest-moving singles in the history of Black music, selling over half a million copies within three weeks of its release. O'Kelly stated, "Anybody can start a record label, but the point is who is the producer, the writer, the arranger? What will the direction be? Where is the material going to come from? If we do everything, we have a full shot at it. It makes sense. So that we wouldn't get bogged down in the details of distribution, we got Buddah to handle it for us. But if we just started a label and hired people to do everything for us, then it wouldn't prove anything. You've got to have full control." Ronald added, "On top of that, you have to have certain ideas and direction. If you produce, write, and have great material and ideas, then you've got a shot." After years of recording for other labels and various producers and writers, The Isleys discovered their own method for success. Ronald declared, "It took us a year and a half to find a formula for a sound. Not a formula for one catchy hit, but a way of doing things that will work for other artists and sounds as well."[6] The formula certainly worked for "It's Your Thing."

"It's Your Thing" was certified gold on April 9, 1969, for having sold more than five hundred thousand units.[7] The song climbed to number one on the *Billboard* Hot R&B Singles Chart on April 19 and stayed in that position for four weeks. It also rose to number two on the *Billboard* Hot 100 Songs chart on May 3.[8] "It's Your Thing" would eventually win the Grammy Award for Best R&B Vocal Performance by a Duo or Group.[9] This tune is still an anthem of personal freedom and has been recorded by more than sixty artists.[10] By this time, both of the younger Isley brothers, Ernie and Marvin, were working as musicians with the three singing brothers. Ernie arranged and played a variety of instruments. Marvin played bass and contributed arrangement ideas.[11] Rudolph's brother-in-law Chris Jasper also began working with the brothers as a keyboardist.

Marvin recalled the care his big brothers gave to the younger brothers. Their daddy died when they were young, so they lived their young lives

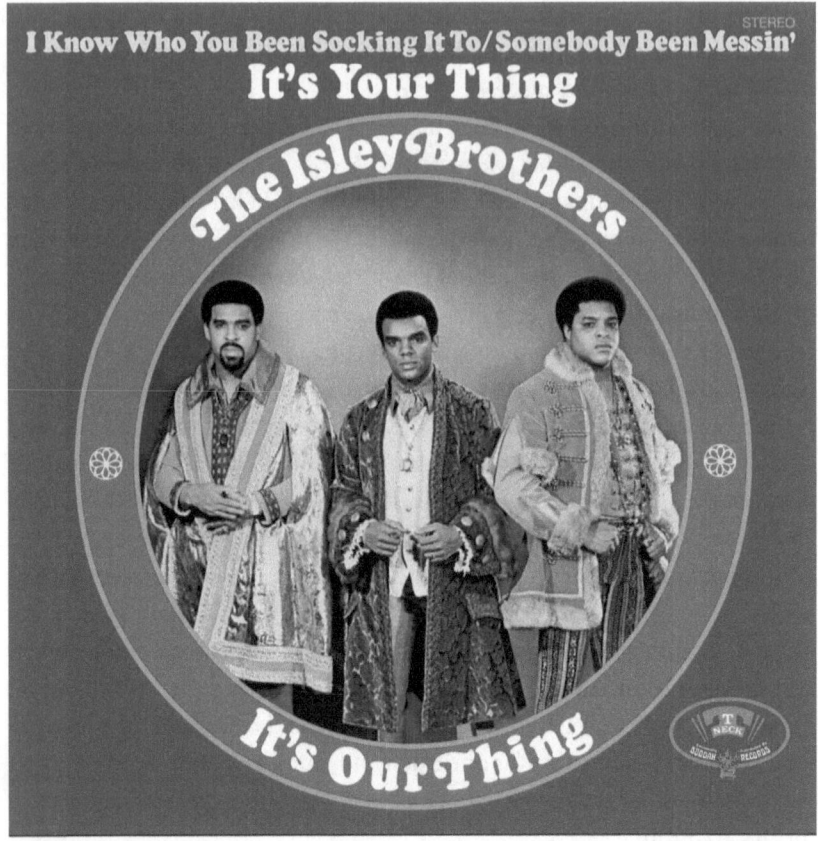

The cover for *It's Our Thing* is a photo of the brothers with afro hairstyles in radically designed clothing.

without a proper father. The three older brothers filled the void. "It was like having three fathers.... They let us enjoy their company, they steered us from trouble. They told us stories about music and helped us with our homework. They explained why it was important to help Mom with the housework. They acted like the difference in our ages wasn't there."[12] At the end of April 1969, The Isley Brothers released their sixth studio album.

It's Our Thing was produced by The Isley Brothers and is the first album recorded on their T-Neck label. The album features ten songs: "I Know Who You Been Socking It To," "Somebody Been Messin'," "Save Me," "I Must Be Losing My Touch," "Feels Like the World," "It's Your Thing," "Give the Women What They Want," "Love Is What You Make It," "Don't Give It Away," and "He's

Got Your Love." The album cover shows the brothers with afro hairstyles in radically designed clothing.[13] This album was The Isleys' first venture into funk music, and the creative freedom made it a commercial triumph, as well as an artistic one.

In addition to "It's Your Thing," Alex Henderson of AllMusic believes other tracks, such as "Give the Women What They Want" and "I Know Who You Been Socking It To" became soul classics. He argues that "He's Got Your Love" and "I Must Be Losing My Touch" give listeners no reason to complain. Henderson declared, "*It's Our Thing* made it clear that Tamla/Motown's loss was Buddah's gain.[14] The album reached number twenty-two on the *Billboard* 200 Albums chart on May 31."[15] Motown was hoping to ride the wave of The Isley Brothers' success.

Doin' Their Thing: Best of The Isley Brothers

In the spring of 1969, Motown released a compilation album for The Isley Brothers titled *Doin' Their Thing: Best of The Isley Brothers*. The album features twelve tracks: "This Old Heart of Mine (Is Weak for You)," "Who Could Ever Doubt My Love," "I Guess I'll Always Love You," "That's the Way Love Is," "One Too Many Heartaches," "Why When Love Is Gone," "Just Ain't Enough Love," "Got to Have You Back," "There's No Love Left," "I Hear a Symphony," "Take Me in Your Arms (Rock Me a Little While)," and "Take Some Time Out for Love."[16] Of course, this album features music that was recorded while The Isleys were with Motown.

Doin' Their Best contains four songs from *This Old Heart of Mine*; four come from *Soul on the Rocks*. "Take Me in Your Arms (Rock Me a Little While)" is the only song not included on a studio album. This is a Holland-Dozier-Holland track that features bongos for percussion as well as a Hammond organ. *Doin' Their Thing* has been described as "a succinct guide through The Isleys' brief stay at Detroit, the essential bridge between their early soul smash hits like "Twist and Shout" and funk bombs like "It's Your Thing" and "That Lady."[17] If you are a fan of The Isley Brothers, this compilation is worth having. Motown also released two more singles by The Isleys that were not featured on *Doin' Their Thing*.

In the spring, Motown issued "Behind a Painted Smile." This song is featured on *Soul on the Rocks*. It did not chart in the United States, but it reached number five in the United Kingdom on April 29. In the summer, Motown issued "Put Yourself in My Place." This track is featured on *This Old Heart of Mine*. Like the aforementioned song, it did not chart in the United States, but it rose to number thirteen in the United Kingdom on August 30.[18] The executives at Motown were so disturbed by The Isley Brothers' recent success that a lawsuit was filed against the group, claiming ownership of "It's Your Thing."

Motown executives claimed "It's Your Thing" had actually been recorded while The Isley Brothers were still under contract with the label.[19] The lengthy lawsuit would not be settled until 1977. The verdict of the case is discussed in chapter 5. The lawsuit certainly did not slow down The Isley Brothers.

The Brothers: Isley

In May 1969, The Isley Brothers released a new single titled "I Turned You On." At the time, the song was not featured on an album, but it would be a part of their next studio album, which was published in the fall of that year. "I Turned You On" was written by The Isley Brothers. It features the popular, provocative catchphrase "sock it to me."[20] The song was almost as big a hit as "It's Your Thing." "I Turned You On" peaked at number twenty-three on the *Billboard* Hot 100 Songs chart on July 12. It also rose to number six on the *Billboard* Hot R&B Singles chart on July 19.[21] The Isley Brothers continued to give their fans a reason to "shout."

On Saturday, June 21, The Isley Brothers presented their first Soul Brothers Summer Music Festival at Yankee Stadium. A substantial percentage of the admission fees was donated to the Minisink Women's Corporation, which sponsored Camp Minisink for underprivileged Blacks, and the Bivins Fund, an educational fund formed by the *New York Amsterdam News* in honor of a citizen of New York's Black community who lost his life while trying to pursue two armed thieves. The festival was coordinated by Betty Sperber of Action Talents, Soul & Style Enterprises, and J & J Productions. The Isley Brothers headlined the event. Additional artists included the Edwin Hawkins Singers, the Chambers Brothers, the Five Stairsteps and Cubie, the Clara Ward Singers, and others.[22] This event was filmed, and the music was recorded for a live album.

This live recording is actually a showcase by The Isley Brothers to conjoin artists who signed to their T-Neck label and Buddah-associated acts. All the guest artists, except the Edwin Hawkins Singers, sang songs written and produced for them by The Isleys. The brothers performed their recent hits "It's Your Thing," "I Turned You On," and the 1959 classic "Shout." As they ended their performance, they invited audience members to join them onstage. This event was independently filmed and funded by The Isleys. A year later, it would be released in theaters as *It's Your Thing* in August 1970.[23] The brothers began working on their next studio album from which they issued their next single.

"Black Berries" was released in late August 1969. It was written by The Isley Brothers. On the album, it is titled "The Blacker the Berrie."[24] This funky track is an ode to the popular phrase "The blacker the berry, the sweeter the juice." "Black Berries" peaked at number seventy-nine on the *Billboard* Hot 100 Songs chart on September 13.[25] It also reached number forty-three on the *Billboard* Best Selling Soul Singles chart on September 20. In the same month, "Was It Good to You?" was published.

"Was It Good to You?" was also written by The Isley Brothers. This song epitomizes the sound of soul music in the late 1960s. The singer asks his ex-lover how she feels after leaving and being with another man.

> How did it feel
> When he held you in his arms?
> I want to know
> How did it feel?[26]

"Was It Good to You?" reached number thirty-three on the *Billboard* Best Selling Soul Singles chart on October 11. It also peaked at eighty-three on the *Billboard* Hot 100 Songs chart on October 18.[27] On the same date of October 18, The Isleys released *The Brothers: Isley*.

The Brothers: Isley is the seventh studio album by The Isley Brothers. This album contains nine songs: "I Turned You On," "Vacuum Cleaner," "I Got to Get Myself Together," "Was It Good to You," "The Blacker the Berrie," "My Little Girl," "Get Down Off of That Train," "Holding On," and "Feels Like the Wind." The album cover shows the brothers dressed in monk-style clothing with a botanical garden–like background.[28] This is one of the lesser-known albums by The Isleys, but it is definitely high-quality.

Alexander Henderson of AllMusic wrote, "The tunes had catchy titles and creative, rhyming lyrics. This recording is loaded with that rocking 'It's Your Thing' style."[29] Three singles are featured on *The Brothers: Isley*. "I Turned You

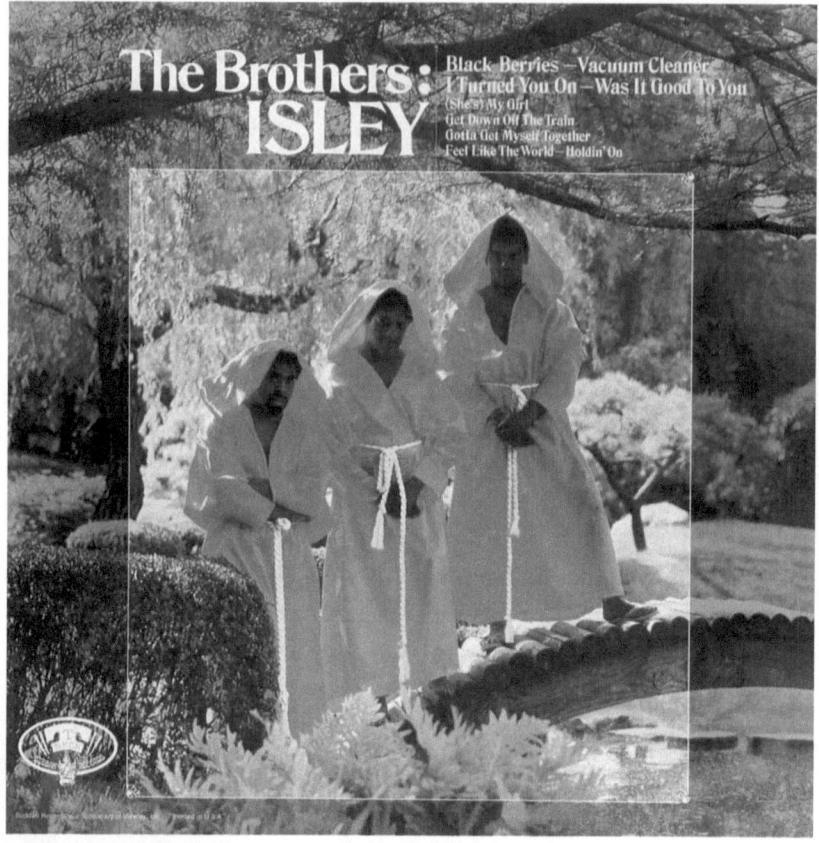

The cover for *The Brothers: Isley* displays the brothers dressed in monk-style clothing with a botanical garden–like background.

On," "Was It Good to You," and "Black Berries (AKA The Blacker the Berrie)" were issued before the album was published. These singles helped *The Brothers: Isley* have a fair run on the music charts. The album peaked at number 180 on the *Billboard* 200 Albums chart on November 1. It rose to number 20 on the *Billboard* Top Soul Albums chart on December 6.[30] The Isleys published their live album on the same date *The Brothers: Isley* was published.

Live at Yankee Stadium

As stated previously, the Soul Brothers Summer Music Festival was recorded for a live album. *Live at Yankee Stadium* was produced by The Isley Brothers

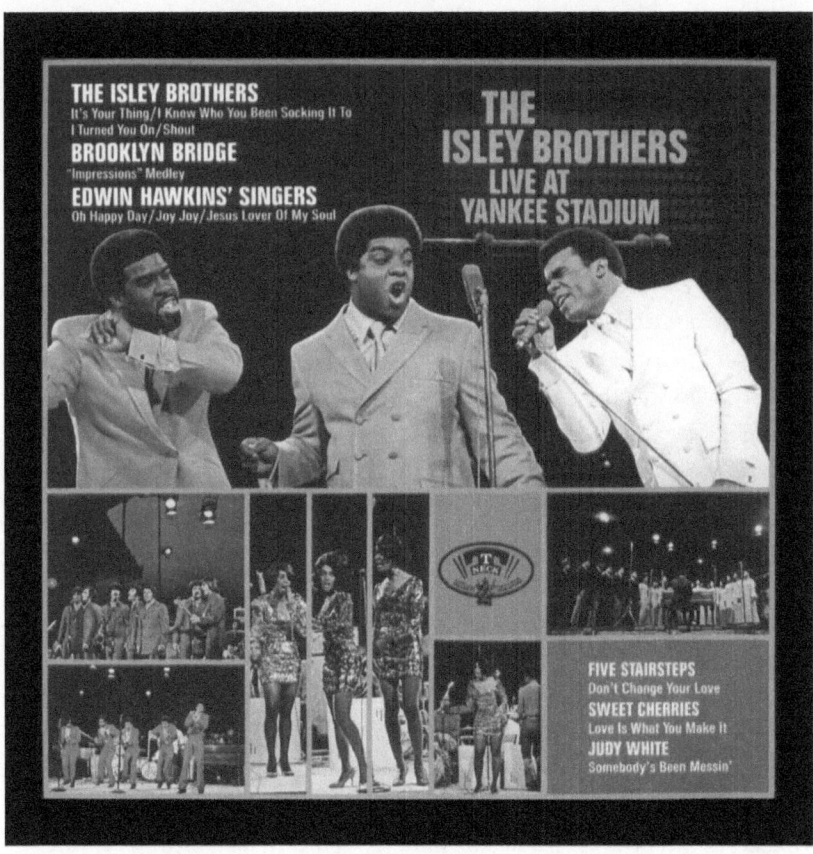

The *Live at Yankee Stadium* cover shows photos of the artists onstage.

and contains thirteen tracks by various artists. The Isley Brothers perform four of their hits: "I know Who You Been Socking It To," "I Turned You On," "It's Your Thing," and "Shout." The Hawkins Singers perform three gospel standards: "Jesus Lover of My Soul," "Joy, Joy," and "Oh, Happy Day." Blue-eyed soul group The Brooklyn Bridge perform a medley of three Curtis Mayfield songs: "People Get Ready," "Talkin' About My Baby," and "It's All Right." The family soul band The Five Stairsteps perform "Don't Change Your Love." Judy White belts out a sassy rendition of The Isleys' "Somebody's Been Messin'," and the girl group Sweet Cherries perform "Love Is What You Make It." The album cover shows photos of the artists onstage.[31] *Live at Yankee Stadium* is an example of the complexity of soul music in 1969. By this time, The Isleys were enjoying the fruits of their labor.

The Isley Brothers performed two concerts at Madison Square Garden on November 15.[32] They also began working on their next studio album. The Isleys issued a new single in December from their upcoming album, titled "Bless Your Heart."[33] This song has the same melody as "It's Your Thing." It climbed to number twenty-nine on the *Billboard* Best Selling Soul Singles chart on December 13. The brothers had a busy and successful year in 1969, and they attributed their success to their faith.

The Isley Brothers' music had evolved from the uninhibited excitement to a more controlled energy that did not overwhelm as much as it inspired. However, their aggression and underlying gospel style remained the same. O'Kelly, who was the spokesman for the group, declared, "Our background was religious and the feeling is still with us. It is still part of everything we do, as is the upbringing our mother and father gave us."[34] With their faith at heart, The Isleys were ready for a new decade.

In this new decade, Black pop culture would become mainstream. Black sitcoms were created, Blaxploitation films were popular, and Black musical artists reached new levels of success. In the 1970s, The Isley Brothers became mainstays on the music charts, producing a plethora of hit records. The Isleys began 1970 by becoming a part of Soul '70. This was a 1970 concert series with a list of talent appearing on the bill that read like the "Who's Who" of soul music. In addition to The Isleys, the artists on the bill included The Dells, Isaac Hayes, Booker T and the MG's, and others. Soul '70 presented its first concert at the Cow Palace in Sacramento, California, on Friday, February 6, 1970.[35] In the same month, The Isley Brothers released "Keep On Doin'" from their upcoming album.

Get Into Something

"Keep On Doin'" was written by The Isley Brothers. In this funky song with a solid bass line and pulsating horns, the singer proclaims he will keep doing whatever he wants to do and encourages the listener to do the same.[36] The message is similar to "It's Your Thing." "Keep On Doin'" peaked at number seventy-five on the *Billboard* Hot 100 Songs chart on March 7. It also rose to number seventeen on the *Billboard* Best Selling Soul Singles chart on March 21.[37] While this song was on the charts, The Isleys released their eighth studio album, *Get Into Something*.

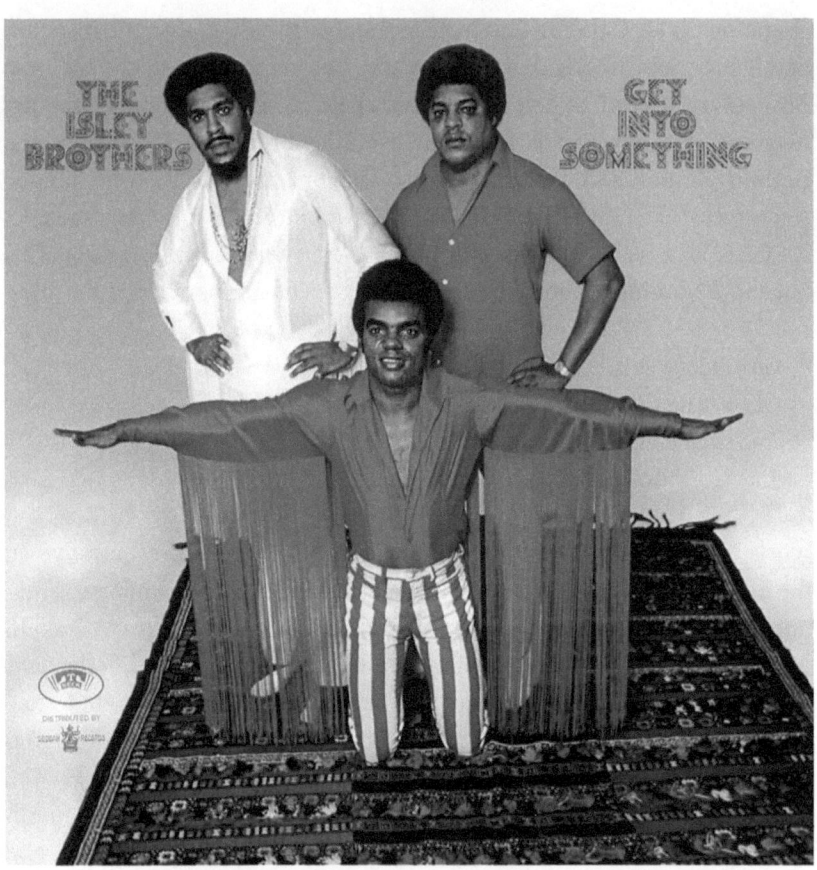

The *Get Into Something* cover is a photo of the brothers in casual attire with afros.

Get Into Something contains ten songs: "Get Into Something," "Freedom," "Take Inventory," "Keep On Doin'," "Girls Will Be Girls, Boys Will Be Boys," "I Need You So," "If He Can, You Can," "I Got to Find Me One," "Beautiful," and "Bless Your Heart."[38] The album cover shows the brothers in casual attire. Although the album did not chart, it includes six songs that appeared in the top-thirty *Billboard* R&B chart between late 1969 and early 1971. Most of these singles appeared on the lower end of the *Billboard* pop chart as well. The third single from *Get Into Something* is "If He Can, You Can."

"If He Can, You Can" was released in April 1970. This song was written by The Isley Brothers with Johnny Brantly. This song proclaims, "Two can play that game" and erases the double standard.[39] It is an indication of women's liberation. "If He Can, You Can" rose to number twenty-one on the *Billboard* Best Selling Soul Singles chart on May 30.[40] During that month, the National Academy of Recording Arts and Sciences held the Twelfth Annual Grammy Awards Ceremony. At this ceremony, The Isley Brothers were awarded the Grammy for Best R&B Performance by a Duo or Group for "It's Your Thing."[41] A few weeks later, the fourth single from *Get Into Something* was issued.

"Girls Will Be Girls, Boys Will Be Boys" was released in July 1969. This is a laid-back groove about the complex nature of a romantic relationship.

> Girls will be girls, boys will be boys
> One day they're lovers
> And you know the next day
> They're fighting one another[42]

"Girls Will Be Girls, Boys Will Be Boys" peaked at number seventy-five on the *Billboard* Hot 100 Songs chart on August 1 and reached number twenty-one on the *Billboard* Best Selling Soul Singles chart on August 15.[43] Also in August, on the twenty-first, the film *It's Your Thing* was released in theaters. In addition to the concert performances at Yankee Stadium, a segment featuring Ike and Tina Turner was added to the film. Performers in the film who are not featured on the live album are Patti Austin, Jackie "Moms" Mabley, Clara Ward Singers, The Young Gents, and The Winstons. Almost a month after the release of *It's Your Thing*, a tragedy saddened The Isley Brothers and many others in the music world.

On September 18, 1970, Jimi Hendrix was found dead in the West London hotel room of his girlfriend Monika Dannemann. Forensic evidence suggested the nine German Vesparax sedatives and an excessive amount of red wine had not been ingested willingly. The attending physician, John Bannister, found red wine soaking in Jimi's hair and oozing out of his lungs. No stories mentioned that many of Jimi's friends knew he feared his manager, Michael Jeffery, a former member of British Intelligence, and wanted to end his contract as soon as possible. In his book *Rock Roadie*, James "Tappy" Wright, who worked for Jimi, claimed Jeffery admitted to him, "I was in London the night of Jimi's death and together with some old friends. . . . We went around to Monika's room, got a handful of pills and stuffed them into his mouth . . . then poured a few bottles of red wine into his windpipe." Wright also insisted Jeffery told him he had taken out a life insurance policy on Jimi worth 1.2

million British pounds, with himself as the beneficiary.[44] No matter the circumstances around Jimi's death, it was devastating to lose a gifted artist at such a young age. The brothers shared good thoughts of Jimi.

Marvin declared, "We'd walk home, Jimi drinking his soda, telling me stories about the road. I was about 10, and they sounded so fantastic! Ernie stated, "I think of Jimi and smile. I'm sure he would have shown up at our gigs had he lived." Rudolph said, "Maybe he was a little strange on the bandstand, but Jimi was always professional. Jimi had a vision. And everything he told us about that vision came true."[45] The Isleys issued two more singles in 1970.

In October, "Get Into Something" was released." In this upbeat song, Ronald tells listeners to follow him if they want to get into something.[46] Maybe it's an invitation to go party or simply have a good time. "Get Into Something" climbed to number twenty-five on the *Billboard* Hot R&B Singles chart on October 24. It also peaked at number eighty-nine on the *Billboard* Hot 100 Songs chart on October 31.[47] In December, The Isleys released their sixth and final single from *Get Into Something*, titled "Freedom."

"Freedom" is a funk song that summarizes *Get Into Something*'s theme of independence as they discuss the meaning of freedom. Ronald explained to Rock Genius, "I wanted to say you can do what you wanna do, say what you wanna say, live how you wanna live, go where you wanna go, that's free. That's what it's about. Then you're free, when you can do all those things—what you should be able to do."[48] "Freedom" rose to number sixteen on the *Billboard* Best Selling Soul Singles chart on February 20, 1971, and it peaked at number seventy-two on the *Billboard* Hot 100 Songs chart on the same date.[49] All the singles and other tracks make *Get Into Something* an admirable album.

Rolling Stone wrote that *Get Into Something* "balances fidgety, syncopated riffs (somebody should sample that title cut) with true-believer gospel harmonies."[50] *Newsday* called the album "a raw raveup with a punchy horn section." Richard Torres wrote, "The Isleys venture into James Brown territory with the stripped-down funk of 'Keep On Doin.'"[51] Andy Kellman of AllMusic declared, "The first side serves up horn-infected party jams." Kellman described *Get Into Something* as an "excellent and vibrant funk/soul album."[52] The music by The Isleys and other artists not only sounded good, but the lyrics gave African Americans hope in the face of oppression.

In early 1971, Black Panthers Bobby Seale, Angela Davis, George W. Sams Jr., Ericka Huggins, and others were in jail. Comedian and activist Dick

Gregory stated, "Just because they put you in jail, don't make you no criminal." African Americans have been an oppressed people who should always strive for liberation. This is especially true in the realm of African American art. And since music is the most prevalent form of art, one of the things that had to happen in 1971 was the closer merging of the people with the arts. Artists were no longer content with only making a hit record, but with how the song relates to the people, which means more and more emphasis on what is being said through the lyrics than with the beat. The beat was good, but the words were also important, especially if the words are saying something like the song "Freedom." The Isleys were singing for the people, not just for profit. Because they loved and wanted to relate to the people, it is in the spirit of the people that they performed.[53] The Isley Brothers released a compilation album during this time.

In the Beginning . . .

In the Beginning . . . by The Isley Brothers and Jimi Hendrix may have been designed as a tribute to Jimi Hendrix after his death. The album consists of twenty-six minutes of old recordings from The Isleys and Hendrix. It features eight tracks: "Move Over Let Me Dance (Part 1)," "Have You Ever Been Disappointed (Parts 1 & 2)," "Testify (Parts 1 & 2)," "Move Over Let Me Dance (Part 2)," "Wild Little Tiger," "The Last Girl," "Simon Says," and "Looking for Love."[54] These sessions were remixed to push Hendrix's guitar up with the voices. Music critic Robert Christgau declared that the music is historic and you can dance to it.[55] Another critic known as Wieden wrote, "If The Isley Brothers had recorded a proper album with Jimi Hendrix, it would have gone down as a turning point for American music. No doubt!"[56] In April of that year, The Isleys released a new single titled "Warpath."

"Warpath" is not featured on an album. This is a funky rock jam about a man who has been betrayed by his woman and his best friend.

> O-ow. I'm on the warpath
> I'm fighting mad (warpath)
> You're all I had
> My best friend has run away with you[57]

"Warpath" climbed to number seventeen on the *Billboard* Best Selling Soul Singles chart on May 1. After this, The Isleys began working on their next studio album.

In June, The Isley Brothers released the first single from their upcoming album, titled "Love the One You're With." This song simply tells the listener, "If you can't be with the one you love, love the one you're with."[58] It is a gospel-driven cover of Stephen Stills's original. "Love the One You're With" rose to number three on the *Billboard* Best Selling Soul Singles chart on July 24. It also climbed to number eighteen on the *Billboard* Hot 100 Songs chart on August 14.[59] While this song was on the charts, The Isleys traveled to New York City to perform.

In the first week of July, The Isley Brothers returned to the Apollo Theater for multiple shows after a five-year absence as one of America's leading attractions. By then, The Isleys had risen to international popularity through connecting events: the massive hit record "It's Your Thing" and an appearance at Yankee Stadium that drew forty thousand people from which came the widely acclaimed film *It's Your Thing*. The show at the Apollo also featured Jean Knight, The Magic Touch, and The Continental Four.[60] Over two months after their stint at the Apollo, The Isleys traveled across the globe to perform.

In September, The Isley Brothers, along with Brook Benton, Aretha Franklin, James Brown, Muhammad Ali, and others, performed in South Africa. Brook Benton started the deal on September 17, and the others followed for two- and three-week stands. Of course, Muhammad Ali was not a musician. He received $300,000 to give ten lectures.[61] At the end of the month, The Isleys published their ninth studio album, *Givin' It Back*.

Givin' It Back

Givin' It Back is a collection of seven tracks. These are songs previously recorded by other artists that The Isley Brothers covered. The first track is a medley of Neil Young's "Ohio" and Jimi Hendrix's "Machine Gun." "Ohio" is a reaction to the Kent State shootings of May 4, 1970. "Machine Gun" is loosely defined as a protest of the Vietnam war. Other tracks include James Taylor's "Fire and Rain," Bob Dylan's "Lay Lady Lay," War's "Spill the Wine," Stephen Stills's "Nothing to Do But Today," and Bill Withers's "Cold Bologna." The last track is Stephen Stills's "Love the One You're With," which was the first single from this album.[62] The album cover may have seemed unusual for some longtime fans.

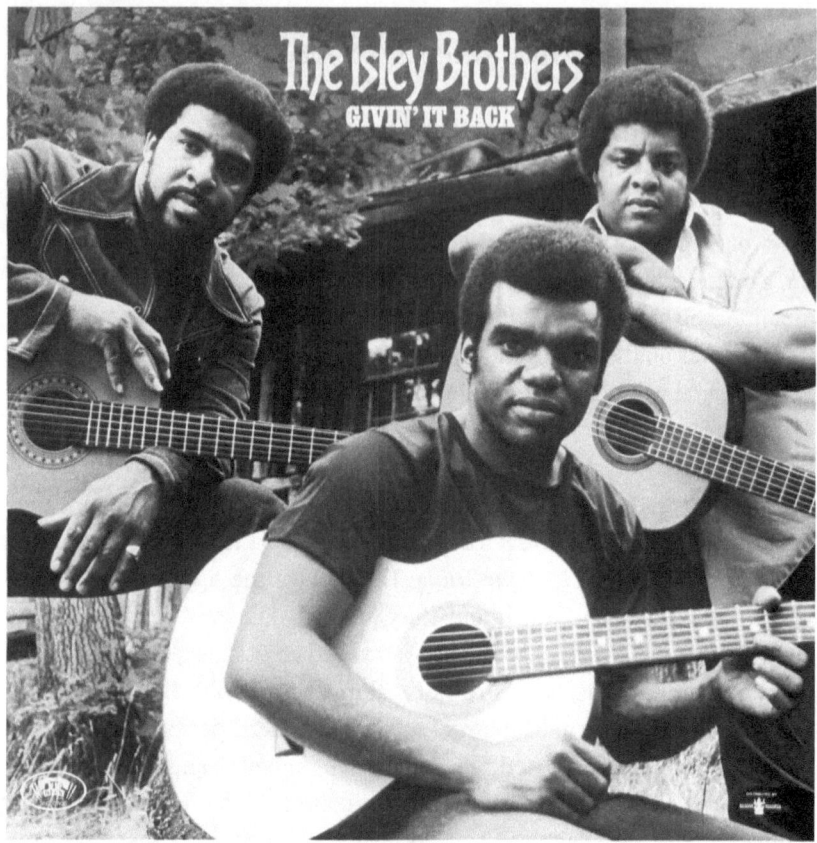

The *Givin' It Back* cover shows the brothers holding guitars and sporting afros.

The cover shows The Isley Brothers immortalized in a sepia-toned portrait. Their afros are strong. Their guitars are poised for new energies. And their facial expressions are comfortable and relaxed. Their appearance was unmistakenly Black and entirely beautiful, much like the music itself.[63] The second single from *Givin' It Back* is "Spill the Wine."

"Spill the Wine" was released in early October. The Isley Brothers do justice to this song. The structure of their version is similar to the original.[64] "Spill the Wine" peaked at number forty-nine on the *Billboard* Hot 100 Songs chart on October 30. It also rose to number fourteen on the *Billboard* Best Selling Soul Singles chart on November 6.[65] During that same week, The Isleys returned to New York City for a special event.

The Southern Christian Leadership Conference (SCLC) Operation Breadbasket held the First International Black Cultural and Business Expo at the Hilton Hotel for three consecutive days: November 4, 5, and 6. The exposition provided a platform from which Black people in America, from Africa, and from the Caribbean could showcase achievements in culture and business. In addition to The Isley Brothers, famed movie and entertainment stars who participated included Nikki Giovanni, Herbie Hancock, Gil Scott-Heron, Stevie Wonder, Hugh Masekela, and several others.[66] Two weeks later, The Isleys were nominated for Male Vocal Group of the Year at the Fifth Annual NAACP Image Awards ceremony on November 21.[67] The award was won by The Jackson 5. Around that time, the single "Lay Lady Lay" was issued.

"Lay Lady Lay" is a sultry bedroom cover of the Bob Dylan standard, and it lasts more than ten minutes.[68] This song reached number twenty-nine on the *Billboard* Best Selling Soul Singles chart on December 11. It also stalled at number seventy-one on the *Billboard* Hot 100 Songs chart on January 1, 1972.[69] This was the last single released from *Givin' It Back*.

Givin' It Back could be considered the most creative album by The Isley Brothers at that time. The brothers departed from the "It's Your Thing" groove and implemented a wedding of rock and soul. Several of the tracks have as much (or more) depth and substance than the versions from the original artists. With these songs, The Isleys took the works of gifted writers and gave back to them a gift of equal merit.[70] On this album, The Isleys do well with latching on to songs that were current in White pop music. But one has to wonder if this is considered "giving it back" or "taking it back." It is most likely the latter.[71] *Givin' It Back* peaked at number seventy-one on the *Billboard* 200 Albums chart on December 4, 1971. It also climbed to number thirteen on the *Billboard* Top Soul Albums chart on December 11.[72] This album is considered a success.

Steven E. Flemming Jr. declares, "The seven self-produced cuts that comprised the original LP were stripped down without coming off as hollow, with the Isleys always-impeccable blends wrapped around a small instrumental nucleus." Flemming adds, "*Givin' It Back* remains a great example of radio-friendly black pop, and a measuring stick for R&B singers who seek to bend and shape categories and move into new territory."[73] Bruce Elder of AllMusic wrote, "The group is so successful at remaking all of the songs here their own in style and approach and sending careful messages in their selection as well as their content, that it really represents a lot of what The Isley Brothers and soul music was about in 1971, and it's still great listening."[74]

Givin' It Back was published when there was much hatred and disunity over the Vietnam War, civil rights, school desegregation, the environment, and other pressing issues between racial and ethnic groups all over America. Bruce Elder argues that "Ohio/Machine Gun," is a slap-in-your-face reminder of just how angry the times and people were. The medley evokes memories of the campus violence of 1970, including the incidents at Kent State and at Jackson State University, where Black students were victimized by a blast of deputy bullets. In music, there was also division.

Black artists usually didn't resonate to the top artists in the White world and were oblivious to, and often resentful of, the adoration accorded Jimi Hendrix by the White community. So, when The Isley Brothers, who were so beloved by the Black community, used Neil Young's "Ohio" and Hendrix's "Machine Gun," they were speaking to anger and bloodshed in the streets, but they were also performing an act of outreach that was as radical as any they could have committed on record in 1971.[75] After the success of *Givin' It Back*, The Isleys were prepared to publish new music.

Brother, Brother, Brother

In March 1972, The Isley Brothers released "Lay Away," the first single from their tenth studio album, *Brother, Brother, Brother*. This is a funk-rock song in which the singer describes his woman's love as so special he needs to have some for keeps. "Lay Away" uses the riff of "Want Ads" by Honey Cone. This song rose to number six on the *Billboard* Best Selling Soul Singles chart on April 22, 1972. It also peaked at number fifty-four on the *Billboard* Hot 100 Songs chart on May 6.[76] On May 2, The Isleys published *Brother, Brother, Brother*.

Brother, Brother, Brother contains nine songs: "Brother, Brother," "Put a Little Love in Your Heart," "Sweet Seasons," "Keep on Walkin'," "Work to Do," "Pop That Thang," "Lay Away," "It's Too Late," and "Love Put Me on the Corner." The album cover art is a drawing of the faces of the three brothers.[77] This was The Isleys' second venture into rock music, but they didn't betray their soul and funk music roots. *Brother, Brother, Brother* is the last Isleys album with Buddah Records as a distributor before moving to Epic

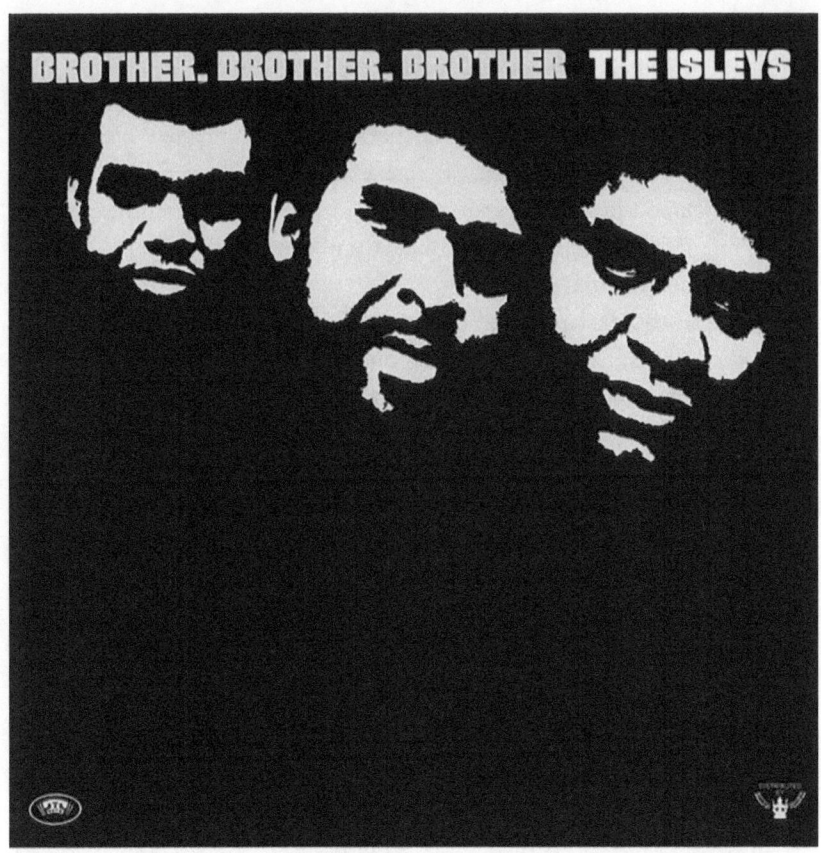

The cover art for *Brother, Brother, Brother* is a drawing of the faces of the three brothers.

Records the next year. The second single from the album, "Pop That Thang," was released in early July.

"Pop That Thang" is a funk song that uses the same formula as "It's Your Thing." It consists of piano notes that sound like gospel music. This song speaks to those involved in intimate activities.

> Hitch up to my wagon
> And get ready to roll
> But don't get on board
> If you can't carry the load[78]

"Pop That Thang" climbed all the way to number three on the *Billboard* Best Selling Soul Singles chart on August 19. It also reached number twenty-four on the *Billboard* Hot 100 Songs chart on September 16.[79] While the song climbed the charts, The Isley Brothers performed with Stevie Wonder, John Lennon, and Yoko Ono on August 30 in a concert at Madison Square Garden, which benefited the plan to establish small community residential facilities for the mentally challenged.[80] Less than two weeks later, The Isleys appeared on national television.

The Isley Brothers headlined the first show of the second season of *Soul Train*. *Soul Train*, the first Black cosponsored weekly national television show, began its second season run Saturday, September 9, 1972, in twenty-six major cities. The Black-oriented dance forum was videotaped in Hollywood. Its executive producer and original host was Don Cornelius, former sports announcer and newscaster for WCIU-TV in Chicago. The variety dance show featured "soul" music performers, and teenage dancing added two attractions for the second season. Each show included a cameo performance by leading personalities in television, motion pictures, and sports, and a "Create-A-Dance" award was presented to the couple who performed the most creative new dance. Also appearing on the episode with The Isleys were Luther Ingram, Melba Moore, and actor Heshimu.[81]

While The Isley Brothers were being interviewed, a member of The Soul Train Gang asked the group how working as brothers impacted their dynamic. O'Kelly told the dancers, "Due to the way we were raised, we find it more convenient being brothers. Basically, the way we made it was the unity that our mother and dad taught us, it really kept us together. That's what we all need, you know? We all gotta be together."[82] The Isley Brothers would make more appearances on *Soul Train* over the next few years, and the hit songs kept coming.

"Work to Do" was released on October 15. This funky track explains a troubled situation between a man and his woman, concerning the lack of quality time spent with each other. The man pleads that as much as he cannot wait to get home and spend time with her, he has a more pressing obligation/commitment to attend to work.[83] "Work to Do" reached number eleven on the *Billboard* Best Selling Soul Singles chart on December 2. It also peaked at number fifty-one on the *Billboard* Hot 100 Songs chart on December 9.[84] This song is considered a classic. It has been covered by several artists, including

The Main Ingredient, Average White Band, Vanessa Williams, and Ian Ross. "Work to Do" was a key factor of *Brother, Brother, Brother*.

Brother, Brother, Brother was well received by the public. The album had risen to number five on the *Billboard* Top Soul Albums chart on August 19. It also reached number twenty-nine on the *Billboard* 200 Albums chart on October 14.[85] By the end of 1972, three hit singles had been issued from this album. Another single from the album would be released in the spring of 1973. *Brother, Brother, Brother* is considered an important album from The Isleys.

Austin Saalman claimed, "*Brother, Brother, Brother* is an important Isley Brother release, its crisp Midwestern soul backbone providing enough support for the group's more ambitious funk and rock aspirations. . . . In retrospect, *Brother, Brother, Brother* feels like a blueprint of explosive greatness to come, the Isleys joining together to function as an unstoppable whole."[86] The album served as a gateway to The Isleys' golden age. This was a good year for the group, and 1973 would be even better.

Chapter 4

3 + 3

The year 1973 was a pivotal time in American history. The United States ended its involvement in the Vietnam War after the signing of the Paris Peace Accords. The Supreme Court ruled on *Roe v. Wade*. About two hundred First Nation people and members of the American Indian Movement (AIM) began their occupation of Wounded Knee in South Dakota, and the price of Organization of the Petroleum Exporting Countries (OPEC) oil increased by 200 percent. During this time, funk music was becoming more prevalent as more artists were incorporating this style. The Isley Brothers published three albums that year.

The Isleys Live

On March 23, *The Isleys Live* was released. This is a double album of live music. It contains eight tracks: "Work to Do," "It's Too Late," "It's Your Thing," "Pop That Thang," "Love the One You're With," "Lay Lady Lay," "Lay Away," and "Ohio/Machine Gun." This album was reissued in 1996 with three bonus tracks: "I Know Who You Been Socking It To," "Turned You On/It's Your Thing," and "Shout."[1] The cover for this album is a collage of the brothers in concert. *The Isleys Live* peaked at number 139 on the *Billboard* 200 Albums chart on May 5. It also climbed to number 14 on the *Billboard* Top Soul Albums chart on May 19.[2] The Isleys also released a single in late May titled "It's Too Late."

"It's Too Late" is featured on *Brother, Brother, Brother*. This is a cover of Carol King's classic. The Isley Brothers' version is a ten-minute psychedelic

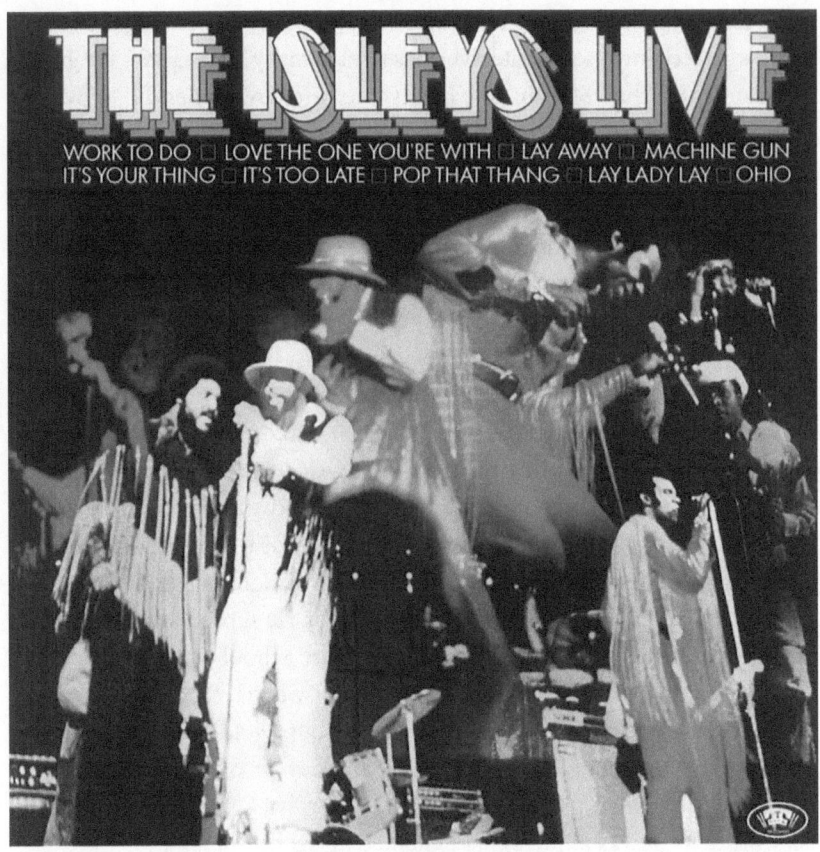

The cover for *The Isleys Live* is a collage of concert photos.

blues song. The piano in the intro reminds the listener of a traditional gospel tune, and Ernie presents his Hendrix-inspired skills on the guitar.[3] The Isleys definitely made this song their own. "It's Too Late" peaked at number thirty-nine on the *Billboard* Hot Soul Singles chart on June 16.[4] At the time, the brothers were working on their next studio album.

Before The Isley Brothers published their next album, younger brothers Ernie and Marvin became official members of the group, as well as Rudolph's brother-in-law Chris Jasper. Ernie was born March 7, 1952, in Cincinnati, Ohio. He was reared there until 1959, when he and his family moved to Englewood, New Jersey. As a teenager, he began to teach himself to become a musician. He was first skilled in drums. Then, he moved on to guitar, bass, and other instruments. Ernie trained himself to be a guitarist after befriending Jimi Hendrix and being influenced by José Feliciano's version of The Doors' "Light My Fire." Ernie is an acclaimed songwriter who has written many hit songs for the group.[5]

Younger brother Marvin was just twenty years old when he joined the group. He was born August 18, 1953. Marvin lived in Cincinnati until he was six years old. He graduated from Dwight Morris High School in Englewood, New Jersey, in 1972. Marvin studied music at C. W. Post College, Long Island, alongside his brother Ernie. Marvin played bass guitar and percussion and cowrote many of the group's hits in the 1970s and '80s.[6] The third instrumentalist to join the group was Chris Jasper.

Chris Jasper became Rudolph Isley's brother-in-law when his sister, Elaine Jasper, married Rudolph. Chris was born December 30, 1951, in Cincinnati, Ohio. His family lived in the same apartment complex as The Isleys in Cincinnati. He began studying classical music at the age of seven. After graduating from high school in Cincinnati, he moved to New York City to study music composition at the Julliard School. Chris received his bachelor of arts degree in music composition from C. W. Post College, where he studied under jazz pianist and composer Dr. Billy Taylor. He subsequently received a juris doctorate degree from Concord University School of Law. Chris was a keyboardist, songwriter, arranger, and producer, who is responsible for many hit records by The Isley Brothers during the group's golden age of 1973–1983. The younger brothers had previously formed their own band called The Jazzmen Trio, which played locally in New Jersey.[7] When they joined The Isley brothers, it was a move that benefited all six brothers.

3 + 3

With the new lineup, The Isley Brothers released the first single from their next album, titled "That Lady," in early July. It is a remake of the 1964 recording "Who's That Lady." This is the funk song that is more widely known.[8] The full title for the song is "That Lady (Parts 1 & 2)." Several other Isley songs have two parts because they run over five minutes. Ernie describes the original version as a cha-cha/bossa nova. He initially did not want to record "That Lady" because he felt it had already been done. Ronald convinced him it would be worthwhile because they were going to change the melody, tempo, and lyrics, and that it would showcase Ernie's guitar work. The original version features a horn section.

The new slickly packaged "That Lady" opened up a new era for The Isley Brothers as Ernie's ferocious guitar solo weaved around a high-energy dance track, bringing the Jimi Hendrix heavy metal influence directly to Black radio and making a cover tune from their sixties years barely recognizable from the original.[9] Ernie learned a lot about the guitar from Jimi Hendrix when he was working with the older brothers. Ernie's work on this song is studied and revered by guitar aficionados in much the same way Hendrix is deconstructed. According to Ernie, recording the song was a magical moment. He declared, "When I finished the solo to 'That Lady,' Kelly looked at me for 15 minutes straight without blinking. I felt like I had one foot on the ground, one on Mount Olympus. I went from a black-and-white world to Technicolor." This song became a crossover hit on both R&B and rock radio.[10]

"That Lady" rose to number two on the *Billboard* Hot Soul Singles chart on September 8. It also climbed to number six on the *Billboard* Hot 100 Songs chart on October 6.[11] "That Lady" reached gold status on October 2 for having sold more than half a million units.[12] The younger brothers were in college when this song hit. They became quite popular on campus. "That Lady" started the golden age for The Isley Brothers. This is the period when they were most popular and most successful. They developed a unique style that helped them sell millions of records and become a mainstay on the music charts over the next decade. The song has become a staple of popular music.

"That Lady" was used during the 2004 comedy *Anchorman: The Legend of Ron Burgundy*. It is used as the intro music for Christina Applegate's character Veronica Cornerstone at Channel 4 News. The guitar solo at the beginning of the song was sampled by The Beastie Boys for "A Year and a Day," which is part of the medley titled "B-Boy Bouillabaisse" featured on *Paul's Boutique*. "That Lady" was also sampled by Kendrick Lamar for his 2014 song "I." Lamar showed up at Ronald's house to personally ask for permission to use the song.[13] Soon after "That Lady" was released, The Isley Brothers issued their eleventh studio album on August 7.

The album *3 + 3* consists of nine songs: "That Lady," "Don't Let Me Be Lonely Tonight," "If You Were There," "You Walk Your Way," "Listen to the Music," "What It Comes Down To," "Sunshine (Go Away Today)," "Summer Breeze," and "The Highways of My Life." The album was reissued in 2003 with the bonus track "That Lady (Recorded Live)." The front of the gatefold displays all the brothers in bold 1970s fashion, with vivid color, velvet, leather,

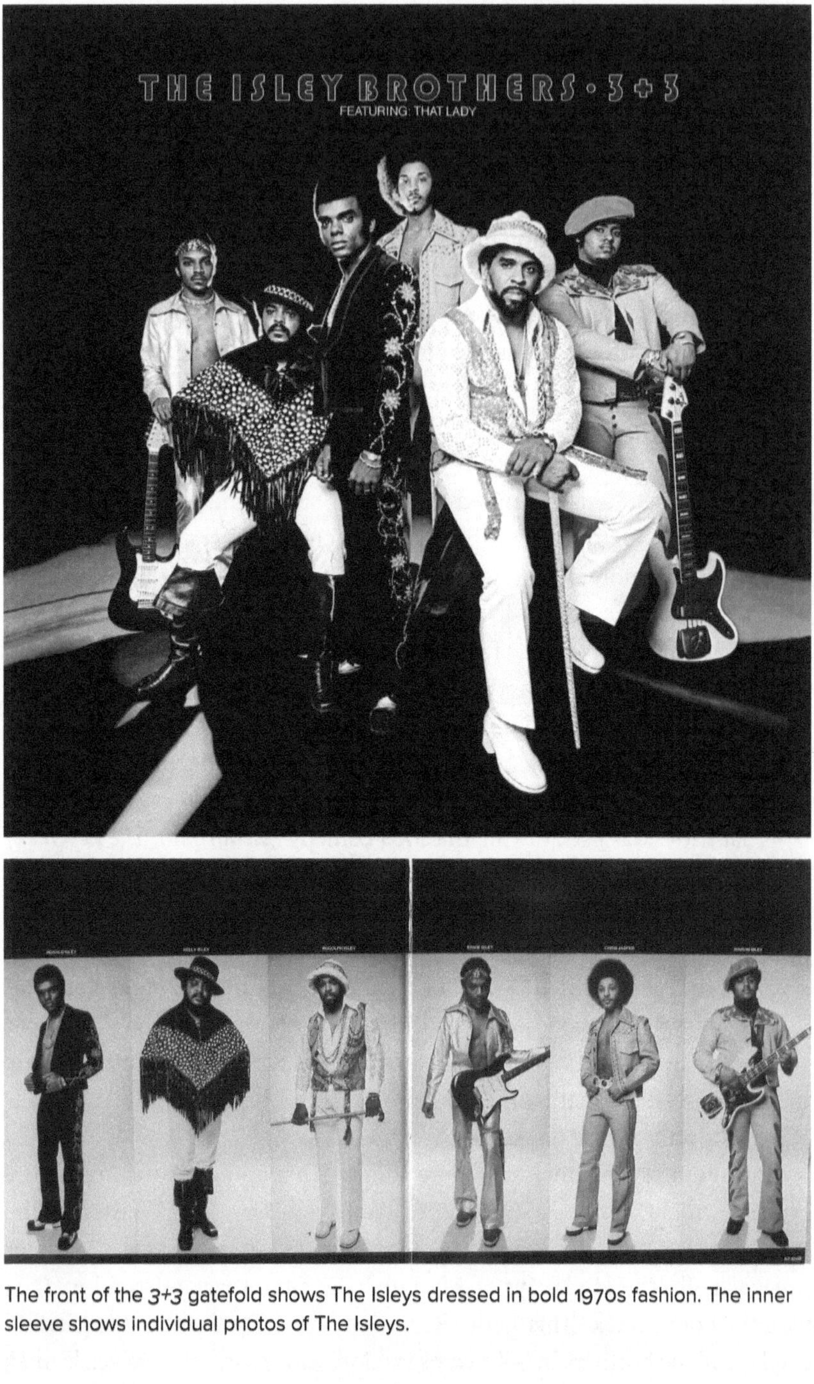

The front of the *3+3* gatefold shows The Isleys dressed in bold 1970s fashion. The inner sleeve shows individual photos of The Isleys.

platform shoes, wide-brimmed hats, and neatly trimmed afros. The inside of the gatefold shows the brothers stylin' and profilin' individually.[14]

The Isley Brothers recorded 3 + 3 in the Record Plant at the same time as Stevie Wonder was recording *Innervisions*. Coincidently, they walked in on him while he was recording "Don't You Worry Bout a Thing." Chris Jasper and Stevie Wonder were users of the ARP synthesizer, and both worked with visionary engineers Robert Margouleff and Malcolm Cecil.[15] Chris Jasper expressed his excitement about working with The Isley Brothers: "You know, all I ever wanted to do with the Isleys was make music that was meaningful. What ideas could we originate? What new avenues could we explore? That was the biggest joy—collaborating with the brothers. Just being in the studio together.... Personalities and business aside—it was always about the music—making positive, hopeful, healing music."[16] Over a month after the album's release, The Isley Brothers appeared at a classic college football game.

On September 22, The Isley Brothers and Patti Austin performed at the third annual Whitney M. Young Jr. Memorial Football Classic between Morgan State College of Maryland and Grambling College of Louisiana. The game was played at Yankee Stadium. The Isleys provided a one-hour pregame show beginning at 2:00 p.m. Austin sang the Black national anthem "Lift Ev'ry Voice and Sing." The football contest was the largest Black event to be held on the East Coast. A capacity crowd of eighty thousand was in attendance. Proceeds from the game were donated to the New York Urban League.[17] On the same date, The Isley Brothers' second appearance on *Soul Train* was televised.[18] In the fifth episode of the third season of *Soul Train*, The Isleys performed "That Lady" and "Don't Let Me Be Lonely Tonight." Other guests were Betty Wright and Jr. Walker & the All-Stars. The Isleys made appearances in other spaces to promote 3 + 3, and it surely helped.

The album 3 + 3 soared to number 2 on the *Billboard* Top Soul Albums chart on October 13. It rose to number 8 on the *Billboard* 200 Albums chart on November 10. This album reached gold status on November 9 and was eventually certified platinum on June 2, 1992.[19] In 2020, 3 + 3 was ranked 464 on *Rolling Stone*'s 500 Greatest Albums of All Time list.[20]

The second single from 3 + 3 is "What It Comes Down To." This song was released in December. It features a synthesizer keyboard solo by Chris and Ernie on guitar and sounds similar to "Family Affair" by Sly and the Family Stone.[21] "What It Comes Down To" reached the number five spot on the

Billboard Hot Soul Singles chart on January 26, 1974. It peaked at number fifty-five on the *Billboard* Hot 100 Songs chart on March 2, 1974.[22] The Isleys also published a compilation album in December 1973.

Isleys' Greatest Hits

Isleys' Greatest Hits contains fourteen songs: "Love the One You're With," "Lay Away," "Freedom," "Get Into Something," "Work to Do," "Keep On Doin'," "It's Your Thing," "Spill the Wine," "Pop That Thang," "Brother, Brother," "I Turned You On," "Vacuum Cleaner," "I Know Who You've Been Socking It To," and "Shout." The cover features the three older brothers dressed in pink.[23] *Isleys' Greatest Hits* stalled at number 195 on the *Billboard* 200 Albums chart on December 29, 1973. However, it reached number 24 on the *Billboard* Top Soul albums chart on January 5, 1974.[24]

By this time, The Isley Brothers had established themselves as a major force in the music world. They had performed on popular television shows like *American Bandstand, Soul Train, The Midnight Special,* and *Don Kirshner's Rock Concert.* They could be seen performing in several venues around the country. On January 11, 1974, The Isley Brothers appeared in concert with the Bar-Kays and New Birth at the Civic Center in Baltimore, Maryland. Frederick I. Douglass of the *Afro-American* described The Isleys' performance:

> The Isley Brothers came onstage and pandemonium broke out. Whistles screeched and trumpets blared. The crowd surged towards the stage, the lemmings making their annual suicide march to the sea. Everybody was dancing. The Isleys went into their bag of tricks and whipped out some treats for the people. They did it all from "Pop That Thang," "It's Too Late," "Love Put Me on the Corner," and "Work to Do," to "That Lady," "SummerRain," "It's Your Thing" and "Love the One You're With." The highlight of their performance was the medley of "Machine Gun" and "Ohio," featuring Ernest Isley on guitar. He really surprised a lot of people in the audience when he got off on a 5-minute solo that had everyone sitting on the edge of their seats. While he is similar to Jimi Hendrix, Ernest has his own thing going. The cat has a lot of potential and may become a wizard in the near future. He and his brothers are definitely worth going to see because they perform from their heart. They give it all up for the people. The Isleys are the best group around.[25]

The cover for *Isleys' Greatest Hits* is a depiction of the three older brothers.

In March 1974, The Isleys issued the third single from 3 + 3, titled "Summer Breeze."

"Summer Breeze" is a cover of the 1972 hit song by soft rock duo Seals and Crofts. The Isleys' version is notable for Ernie's guitar solo, as well as the harmonies of the three vocalists. "Summer Breeze" peaked at number sixty on the *Billboard* Hot 100 Songs chart on April 20. However, it became an R&B hit, rising to number ten on the *Billboard* Hot Soul Singles chart on May 11.[26] "Summer Breeze" is the final single released from 3 + 3, which was a turning point for The Isley Brothers.

With 3 + 3, The Isleys moved their T-Neck label from Buddah to Epic, and it was "epic" that they unveiled their new lineup: Chris on keyboards, Ernie on guitar, and Marvin on bass, adding exciting new elements to The

Isleys' sound. According to Alex Henderson, bassist Marvin Isley was in a class of heavyweights like Larry Graham and Louis Johnson. Ernie is an awesome guitarist who is heavily influenced by Jimi Hendrix but has a style of his own. With the addition of Ernie, The Isleys' sound became more rock influenced. The rock and pop elements didn't alienate R&B audiences, who heavily consumed the album. "That Lady" was a smash hit, and the brothers are equally captivating on Seals and Crofts' "Summer Breeze," James Taylor's "Don't Let Me Be Lonely Tonight," and the Doobie Brothers' "Listen to the Music." With 3 + 3, The Isley Brothers sounded better than ever, and they gained new fans without isolating the old ones.[27] With a new distinct sound, The Isleys continued to show their skills in concert.

On Easter Sunday, April 4, 1974, Universal Concerts presented The Isley Brothers in concert at Oakland Coliseum Arena with special guest Richard Pryor. Kool & the Gang and Bloodstone were also featured. The Isley Brothers had become heavy hitters in entertainment. They were enthusiastic about doing their thing and having their own record label. Ronald called it "our vehicle to do what we think is good" and declared, "We want to surround ourselves with young, creative people, people who have feelings for the new and the now, people who are not afraid to take a stand for something they believe in." O'Kelly explained why the T-Neck setup was geared to more than a simple interest in one aspect of the business: "You see. Motown was like a school to us. All the guys over there are geniuses. They know everything there is to know about the business. During our three years there, we learned everything. We increased our knowledge many times over. With all this knowledge, we feel that now we have our chance."[28] In addition to performing, The Isleys were working on new music.

Live It Up

The Isley Brothers released a new single in July titled "Live It Up (Parts 1 & 2)." This would be the title track for their next album. "Live It Up" is a funk/rock song much like some of The Isleys' "Do What You Wanna Do" records of that time.

> 'Cause everybody's gotta move
> Everybody's gotta groove, yeah

The *Live It Up* cover shows the brothers in colorful 1970s fashion.

Everybody making love, sure 'nough
Everybody's gotta live it up, well

The song's free-love message helped it become an R&B hit. It features a screaming guitar solo from Ernie, and Chris closes it with a clavinet solo.[29] "Live It Up" climbed to number four on the *Billboard* Hot Soul Singles chart on September 7. It peaked at number fifty-two on the *Billboard* Hot 100 Songs chart on September 28.[30] "Live It Up" reached gold status on November 4 for selling over a half million units.[31] On the same date the song peaked on the soul chart, The Isley Brothers released their twelfth studio album.

Live It Up features seven songs: "Live It Up (Parts 1 & 2)," "Brown Eyed Girl," "Need a Little Taste of Love," "Lover's Eve," "Midnight Sky (Parts 1 & 2)," "Hello It's Me," and "Ain't I Been Good to You (Parts 1 & 2)." Like the previous album, *Live It Up* was assisted by the team of Malcolm Cecil and Robert Margouleff. The album also continued their growing trademark of funky dance songs mixed with softer soul ballads. It was reissued in 2004 with one bonus track: "Live It Up (Live on the Dinah Shore Show, 1974)."[32] The album cover shows the brothers in their signature colorful 1970s fashion. *Live It Up* quickly rose to number fourteen on the *Billboard* 200 Albums chart on October 26. It also soared to number one on the *Billboard* Top Soul Albums chart on November 16.[33] This album was certified gold on November 4 after selling half a million copies.[34] A few weeks after *Live It Up* was issued, The Isleys rocked Madison Square Garden.

On October 18, Frankie Crocker presented The Isley Brothers and Graham Central Station in a sold-out performance at Madison Square Garden. The Isleys opened their performance with "That Lady." And they really began to synchronize on the melodious "Don't Let Me Be Lonely Tonight." Ernie was spotlighted on "Ohio," shooting sounds from his electric guitar that at times paralleled those of a machine gun. He played the guitar in the traditional position, behind his head, with the use of his mouth, and on the floor. Hysteria set in when the brothers began "Live It Up," and the crowd really got into the groove.[35] The Isleys made the audience's time worthwhile. Two months later, The Isley Brothers performed on Soul Train for the third year in a row.

On December 14, The Isley Brothers appeared on a special episode of *Soul Train*. Fifteen years after their first hit record, *Shout*, *Soul Train* host Don Cornelius decided to dedicate an entire episode to the brothers. The Isleys were the only act to perform. They performed five songs: "That Lady," "Live It Up," "Summer Breeze," "Midnight Sky," and "Hello It's Me."[36] About a week later, The Isleys released the second single from *Live It Up*, titled "Midnight Sky (Parts 1 & 2)."

"Midnight Sky (Parts 1 & 2)" is another funk/rock song with a guitar solo by Ernie. The lyrics suggest that the nighttime can be romantically enticing.

> I have no sense of direction when loving you
> I lose conception of time
> Ah honey, under the midnight sky, baby, get next to me
> Can you feel it?[37]

"Midnight Sky" stalled at number seventy-three on the *Billboard* Hot 100 Songs chart on January 25, 1975. However, it climbed to number eight on the

Billboard Hot Soul Singles chart on February 15, 1975.³⁸ Although only two singles were released from *Live It Up*, it is considered to be just as good as its predecessor and continues to receive high praise from critics.

According to Wilson and Alroy, *Live It Up* cemented The Isley Brothers for the rest of the 1970s. The title track debuted Ernie's no-nonsense funk drumming and Chris's buzzing synth and clavinet, paving the way for their next smash hit: "Fight the Power." There are ballads featuring Ernie's blazing guitar solos, including "Midnight Sky" and "Ain't I Been Good to You." The White rock cover, Todd Rundgren's "Hello It's Me," sounds like an Isleys original with Ronald's smooth vocals.³⁹ Craig Lytle of AllMusic describes the two singles from *Live It Up* as lengthy vamps that are ideal for parties. As for the romance, "Hello It's Me" is the classic ballad. Ron's melodic intro sets the tone for this beautiful track. "Brown Eyed Girl" is a mid-tempo tune seasoned with a folklike guitar and Ronald's rich vocals. Both songs have become radio regulars despite not being released as singles.⁴⁰ Their following album would also be a memorable production.

In early 1975, The Isley Brothers began recording their thirteenth studio album. This year was a good time for Black pop culture. *The Jeffersons* premiered on CBS, Arthur Ashe became the first person to win the men's singles title at Wimbledon, and disco music became mainstream. Earth, Wind & Fire became the first Black artist to have the number one album and song on *Billboard*'s pop charts simultaneously. They accomplished this feat with *That's the Way of the World* and "Shining Star." The Isley Brothers' next album also topped the *Billboard* pop chart.

The Heat Is On

The first single from the album is "Fight the Power (Parts 1 & 2)." It was released at the end of May 1975. "Fight the Power" is often thought of as a song about the Black experience. It is more of a general statement on rising above the powers that be.

> I tried to play my music, they say my music's too loud
> I tried talking about it, I got the big runaround
> And when I rolled with the punches, I got knocked on the ground
> By all this bullshit going down, hey.⁴¹

In a 1976 interview with *Blues & Soul*, Marvin explained the sentiment behind the song. "'Fight The Power'? Well, we decided not to be passive, to take a stand. And we met hardly any resistance because that power could be anything—we all have our different conceptions of what it is to each of us. And just letting it out—about the bullshit that does go down—is something that everyone wants to do."[42] The sound of this song is just as powerful as the lyrics. It's a loose, percolating jam that accurately encapsulates the political edge and raw funk energy The Isleys observed around them at the time.[43]

The profane word was not originally supposed to be in the song. Ernie stated, "Instead of singing 'bullshit,' I had sung 'nonsense.' But when Ronald started singing it, he used the B.S. word. I thought 'Oh yea, we're going to change that on the album.' I didn't know it was going to be permanent." When it came time to remix the song, Ernie said, "You're going to have grandmothers and kids listening. You're The Isley Brothers, and here you start getting a little street, a little vulgar. Somebody's going to say something." However, the other brothers disagreed and told him that the lyrical direction of the song was such that it merited the use of the word. Therefore, it remained on the final mix of the album.[44]

When "Fight the Power" was sent to Black radio unedited, many stations played the song as delivered. This caused a major controversy as records with profanity were uncommon at the time and definitely not played on the radio.[45] Ernie laughed about performing "Fight the Power" in concert. He declared that when the group got to the bridge of the song, "We had 18,000 people singing 'B.S. going down.'"[46] It makes sense that "Fight the Power" and its disregard for language standards of the time would have such an impact on hip-hop culture in the late 1980s.

In 1989, Public Enemy used the song's title as their inspiration in creating the theme song for Spike Lee's brilliant racially charged *Do the Right Thing*. The idea of fighting the power proved to be a political sentiment that has long informed in different forms, and The Isley Brothers' hit song became a powerful anthem of the Blaxploitation era of the 1970s.[47] The lyrics and groove made it a smash hit.

"Fight the Power" rose to number one on the *Billboard* Hot Soul Singles chart on July 19. It also climbed to number four on the *Billboard* Hot 100 Songs chart on September 27.[48] This song was certified gold on September 11 after selling more than half a million copies.[49] About a week after "Fight the Power" was issued, *The Heat Is On* was released on June 7.

The front of *The Heat Is On* gatefold shows the brothers in peak 1970s fashion.

The inside of the gatefold displays the brothers with their birthdays and zodiac signs.

The Heat Is On features only six tracks: "Fight the Power (Parts 1 & 2)," "The Heat Is On (Parts 1 & 2)," "Hope You Feel Better Love (Parts 1 & 2)," "For the Love of You (Parts 1 & 2)," "Sensuality (Parts 1 & 2)," and "Make Me Say It Again, Girl (Parts 1 & 2)." The first three songs are upbeat funk jams, and the last three are smooth ballads. *The Heat Is On* was reissued in 2001 with the bonus track "Fight the Power (Live)."[50] Marvin declared, "We don't close ourselves away like some entertainers do—we listen to the radio, read the newspapers and generally get into what's happening out there in an attempt to reflect the world as it is. With *The Heat Is On*, we wanted to be as funky as possible musically, and yet for the lyrics to say something unusual."[51] The album gatefold is a reflection of the times.

The front of the gatefold shows The Isley Brothers dressed in peak 1970s fashion—rhinestone studding galore, wide-brimmed hats, and wide collars that reveal a band luxuriating in the glitz and glamour of that time. The inside of the gatefold reveals more and places the band even more firmly in the spirit of 1975. Below each member's picture is his birthdate and zodiac sign. The image captures the era perfectly.[52] A week after the album was released, The Isleys displayed their talents in concert.

The tour of Kool Jazz Festivals around the country began in Oakland, California, on June 13. In addition to The Isley Brothers, several jazz and soul artists performed. Some of the artists were Aretha Franklin, Ramsey Lewis, The Ohio Players, The O'Jays, and Bobbi Humphrey. The tour made stops in other major cities, including Kansas City, Missouri; Atlanta, Georgia; Hampton, Virginia; Cincinnati, Ohio; and Houston, Texas. The tour ended on July 26 in San Diego, California.[53] While The Isleys were touring, *The Heat Is On* was selling rapidly and climbing the charts.

The Heat Is On reached gold status on June 30, 1975. It sold more than five hundred thousand units within its first month of release. It eventually reached platinum status on August 11, 1992, and was certified double platinum on August 17, 1999.[54] *The Heat Is On* soared to number one on the *Billboard* Top Soul Albums chart on July 19, 1975. It stayed in that position for four weeks. The album also rose to number one on the *Billboard* 200 Albums chart on September 13, 1975.[55] While *The Heat Is On* was at the top of the charts, The Isleys established a tour of their own.

On August 22, The Isley Brothers started The Heat Is On Tour in Jackson, Mississippi. For this tour, the brothers performed in seventeen major cities across America, mostly in the South. The tour ended on November 15 in Houston, Texas.[56] While they were traveling and performing, The Isleys published the second single from *The Heat Is On*, titled "For the Love of You (Parts 1 & 2)" in October.

"For the Love of You (Parts 1 & 2)" is a ballad that showcases The Isley Brothers' softer and more mellow sound, coming after the hard-paced funk jam "Fight the Power." The lyrics stimulate the listener to sing along to the song.

> Driftin' on a memory
> Ain't no place I'd rather be
> Than with you, yeah
> Lovin' you, well, well, well[57]

"For the Love of You" became another crossover hit for The Isleys. The song climbed to number ten on the *Billboard* Hot Soul Singles chart on December 6. It also reached number twenty-two on the *Billboard* Hot 100 Songs chart on December 22.[58] "For the Love of You" has become a classic and a fan favorite. It has been covered by several artists, including Whitney Houston, Boyz II Men, and Joss Stone. No other single was released from *The Heat Is On*, but the other four unreleased tracks on the album could have done well on the music charts.

The title track is just as funky as "Fight the Power" and includes a guitar solo by Ernie. According to Patrick Corcoran, Marvin's bass pops like a roll of bubble wrap being jumped on from a great height. "Hope You Feel Better Love" features a solo by Ernie that underlines the sheer genius of his work. The mellow "Sensuality" gives Chris the chance to show the full range of his keyboard skills. The Isley Brothers add layers of warmth to a song that persuades listeners to abandon everything but thoughts of loving. "Make Me Say It Again, Girl" is another bedroom beauty.

"Make Me Say It Again, Girl (Parts 1 & 2)" is a touching ballad in which Ronald showers compliments on his love interest.

> Oh, I believe you are a rainbow
> You are the heaven I need to see
> You're the promise everlasting
> Where you are I hope to be[59]

Ronald continuously sings his sweet lady's praises and ends the song by saying again and again she's all he needs. The Isleys came up with this song near the end of the recording process for *The Heat Is On*. They already had "Fight the Power," "Sensuality," and "For the Love of You," but Ronald felt there was still something else he wanted to say. One day, Ronald and Ernie were kicking around different ideas in their mother's basement. "I picked up my six-string guitar and started playing, then, singing the words, 'Make me say it again,'" Ernie recalled to *Billboard*. "And Ronald's like, 'Oh my God, where did that come from?' Then, I sang, 'I believe you are a rainbow' and Ronald's screaming 'That's it! . . . Here's what I'm trying to say!'"

Though not released as a single, "Make Me Say It Again, Girl" quickly became a concert favorite. "We started playing 'Make Me Say It Again, Girl,'" Ernie recalled of a 1975 Chicago concert. "And Ronald was dressed in this sharp leather outfit. Then, on the last verse and chorus of the song, one of our co-workers came onstage and draped a white mink over Ronald." Ernie figured that every woman at the show probably turned into melted chocolate.

"Make Me Say It Again, Girl" is one of The Isley Brothers' most-sampled songs. The groove of Naughty by Nature's 1993 classic "Hip Hop Hooray" is a sped-up sample. Bone Thugs-N-Harmony based their 1996 hit "The Crossroads" around an interpolation of it, and "Second Nature," the opening track of Destiny's Child's self-titled 1997 debut album, uses the hook.[60] In 2022, Ronald released a new duet version with Beyoncé, which is discussed in chapter 12. All the ballads on *The Heat Is On* place the woman on a high pedestal; there is barely a hint of bruising masculinity.[61] It's no surprise how well this album was received and praised.

Bob Palmer of *Rolling Stone* wrote, "*The Heat Is On* has some of the best body music around." Mark Anthony Neal of *Pop Matters* wrote, "Whereas the up-tempo workouts helped the Isleys reach new audiences, it was their balladry, courtesy of lead vocalist Ronald, that distinguished them among other soul/R&B/funk bands of the era."[62] Alex Henderson of AllMusic wrote that Ronald is as convincing on the funk tracks as he is on the ballads. He proclaims that *The Heat Is On* is superb from start to finish and is among The Isleys' most essential albums.[63] The year 1975 was good for The Isley Brothers and funk music artists in general.

As Rickey Vincent has noted, by 1975, real bands not only dominated Black music, they were challenging each other to even higher standards. Stevie Wonder's recordings remained the centerpiece of the fluid funk mix, as his classics "You Haven't Done Nothin'," "Boogie on Reggae Woman," and "Creepin'" dominated Black radio. *The Heat Is On* featuring "Fight the Power" was The Isley Brothers' attempt to keep up with Stevie's flare for social commentary and smooth sentiments. Earth, Wind & Fire's "Shining Star" and "Sing a Song" were also causing a major sensation. Other bands, such as Rufus, The Ohio Players, Kool & the Gang, and Parliament, were also redefining the hit-making tradition to reflect their own approach to the music—a synthesis of the entire African American musical experience.[64] The following year would be just as good for The Isleys, if not better.

The first major task of business for The Isley Brothers in 1976 was staging a revue on February 6 at the International Amphitheatre in Chicago, with Millie Jackson introducing the entire performance. At that time, The Isleys were in constant demand as they had several hit songs in their catalog. Many of those songs entered the charts as soon as they were released. At the Amphitheatre, The Isleys performed old and contemporary songs.[65] A compilation album was published in March of that year.

The Best . . . Isley Brothers

The Best . . . Isley Brothers features a total of twenty songs. The first album contains ten tracks: "It's Your Thing," "Love the One You're With," "I Know Who You Been Socking It To," "Get Into Something," "Shout," "Work to Do," "Give the Women What They Want," "The Blacker the Berrie," "I Turned You On," and "Put a Little Love in Your Heart." The second album also has ten tracks: "Pop That Thang," "Lay Lady Lay," "Spill the Wine," "Fire and Rain," "Freedom," "Ohio/Machine Gun," "Nothing to Do But Today," "Lay Away," "Brother, Brother," and "It's Too Late." The cover photo shows the brothers onstage in funky seventies fashion.[66]

The Best . . . Isley Brothers did not make much noise when it was released. It peaked at number forty-nine on the *Billboard* Top Soul Albums chart on April 3, 1976.[67] It failed to reach *Billboard*'s pop albums chart. Although the reception was not grand, this compilation contains great records and is a welcome addition to the collection of any Isley Brothers fan. After this compilation, The Isleys decided to publish new studio material, which they had been working on since the previous year.

The cover for *The Best . . . Isley Brothers* is a photo of the brothers onstage in concert.

Harvest for the World

The Isley Brothers released "Who Loves You Better" in early May. In this song, the singer asks a rhetorical question, implying that no one loves his woman better than he does. Ronald's aggressive delivery blends well with Ernie's guitar solos.[68] "Who Loves You Better" climbed to number three on the *Billboard* Hot Soul Singles chart on June 12 and peaked at number forty-seven on the *Billboard* Hot 100 Songs chart on June 19.[69] In the latter part of May, *Harvest for the World* was published.

Harvest for the World is the fourteenth studio album by The Isley Brothers. It contains eight tracks: "Harvest for the World (Prelude)," "Harvest for the World," "People of Today," "Who Loves You Better," "(At Your Best) You Are Love," "Let Me Down Easy," "So You Wanna Stay Down," and "You Still Feel

The *Harvest for the World* cover features the brothers in bold 1970s fashion.

the Need." This album was reissued in 2001 with the bonus track "Summer Breeze (Live)." Like previous album covers, the cover for this album shows the brothers clad in freaked-out seventies fashion.[70] *Harvest for the World* was swiftly considered one of the best albums of that year.

Journalist Frederick Douglass of the *Afro-American* wrote, "The sweltering heat that has been bearing down on Baltimore has not been caused by Mother Nature—it's The Isley Brothers that are causing the tropical heat with their blistering hot new LP titled *Harvest for the World*." Douglass claimed that one could count on The Isleys to come through every summer with a thriller killer jam that is a real gas for partying through June, July, and August. He stated. "Well some of the music on the album is so scorching hot that winter might even be moved back a couple of months."[71] The public also felt good about this album.

Harvest for the World swiftly sold more than five hundred thousand units after its release and was certified gold on June 3.[72] The album soared to number one on the *Billboard* Top Soul Albums chart on June 26. This is The Isleys' third consecutive album to top that chart. *Harvest for the World* also climbed to number nine on the *Billboard* 200 Albums chart on July 4.[73] On that same date, America celebrated its bicentennial.

While America celebrated its bicentennial, many African Americans did not perceive America as the "land of the free," nor had they realized the American dream. A series of inconceivable blows to the urban industrial economy caused the nation to collapse into a stagflation nightmare. Racial tension continued to erupt, as the long-fought battle for school desegregation through integrated busing sparked unjustifiable hostility and violence toward African Americans. White flight was on the rise, leaving devastated cities to fall into further decline and governmental neglect.[74] In response to the hostile conditions in America and around the world, The Isley Brothers released the politically charged "Harvest for the World" in August of that year.

"Harvest for the World" was written by The Isley Brothers as a group effort. This song is an open-hearted call for equality across the world. Principle lyricist Ernie declared, "'Harvest for the World' refers to a peaceful gathering where every human being is invited, and where no one will be hindered in any way from participating."[75]

> Gather every man, gather every woman
> Celebrate your lives, give thanks for your children
> Gather everyone, gather all together
> Overlooking none, hopin' life gets better for the world[76]

When Ernie presented the song to the three older brothers, their reaction was pretty much, "Wow! This record will be great." Ronald declared, "The song had a super meaning, which was inspiring as a vocalist, because you want to deliver the message as best you can."

"Harvest for the World" was recorded at The Record Plant in Los Angeles, the same studio Stevie Wonder used. The Isleys also used his engineer-producer Malcolm Cecil, who did incredible things in the studio. He made the group record the drums all over again because he said there was something missing because of the position of the microphones. Ronald stated, "We tried all sorts of things. I think Marvin and Kelly may have done the handclaps.

At first, I sang 'Harvest for the World' much higher. But once it was ready, I laid down a guide vocal, and then recorded the one on the finished record the following day in the first take. You go in the vocal booth and call on a gift from God."[77] "Harvest for the World" is introduced with a prelude.

"Harvest for the World (Prelude)" starts the album. It was concocted by keyboardist Chris Jasper in the studio. Chris told *Uncut*, "After we recorded 'Harvest for the World,' I remember saying, 'This is a great message here—it would be nice if there was a setup.' So "Harvest for the World (Prelude)" was done on the spot in the studio. I just took some motifs from "Let Me Down Easy" and "Harvest for the World" and did it in half an hour."[78] The Isleys have always been conscious of the type of songs they produced.

Ronald declared that Stevie Wonder and The Beatles had made records about social issues, and The Isley Brothers were trying to have a political song on every album. He explained the importance of "Harvest for the World":

> We'd lived through the assassination of Martin Luther King and Bobby Kennedy and wondered what was going to happen next. "Harvest for the World" was a ballad for the fallen soldiers, but the lyric is about what could be possible. The world today is at least as turbulent as when we recorded it. There's a great amount of fear. The only way things will change is if people come together in peace instead of war. That's what we try to do with the music. When we play the song in concert, you see smiles on people's faces, like the harvest for the world is something they're waiting for.[79]

Chris also spoke about the relevance of "Harvest for the world."

> At that time, Vietnam had just ended, and a lot of people were still missing in action, the economy wasn't great. It was like it is now, there was a big difference between the "haves" and the "have-nots." That's kind of what this song is talking about, asking a rhetorical question, "When will there be a harvest for the world?" When will there be a time that people have an equal share of what's going on, when will they have equality in their lives? Basically, we know—the return of Christ, that's when it's going to be, because he's a God of equality. So, that's when it will ultimately occur. But the song is just asking that question.[80]

"Harvest for the World" was well received by the public and did well on the music charts.

"Harvest for the World" climbed to number nine on the *Billboard* Hot Soul Singles chart on October 2 and peaked at number sixty-three on the Hot 100 Songs chart on the same date.[81] "Harvest for the World" was covered by English band The Christians as a charity song. It reached number eight on the UK chart in 1988.[82] When the song was released by The Isleys, they began performing around the country.

In late August, The Isley Brothers began headlining a concert series titled Great Soul Revue. Other performers included The Dynamic Superiors, Black Smoke, and Wild Cherry. On one occasion, The Bar-Kays substituted for Wild Cherry.[83] On a different occasion, The Stylistics substituted for The Dynamic Superiors. Marie Moore wrote in *New York Amsterdam News* that The Isleys began their performance with white smoke surging up and surrounding them while they sang "Fight the Power" as the audience roared at Madison Square Garden. The sparks attributed to the show were produced mainly by Ronald's smooth voice and Ernie's slick guitar playing.[84] The brothers continued to perform through the fall of 1976. They also began working on their follow-up to *Harvest for the World*.

Harvest for the World is considered one of the best albums by The Isley Brothers. Although only two singles were released from the album, every track on the album is worthy of attention. "Harvest for the World (Prelude)," "Harvest for the World," "People of Today," and "Who Loves You Better" make up a funky, danceable side one. Each song has a deep and solid message as The Isleys continue to demonstrate that they can say something meaningful and still sound good. On side two, the Brothers get smooth and mellow as they get into "(At Your Best) You Are Love" and "Let Me Down Easy." They go back upbeat on "So You Wanna Stay Down" and "You Still Feel the Need." Ronald soothes the listener with his soul-steering voice as he glides along with the music.[85] *Harvest for the World* was eventually certified platinum on October 19, 2001, after selling more than one million units.[86] As expected, the album was affirmed by music critics.

Robert Christgau declares that on *Harvest for the World*, Ronald croons and Ernie zooms.[87] Daryl Easlea of the BBC wrote that *Harvest for the World* serves as a fantastic snapshot of The Isleys at their career peak.[88] Craig Lytle of AllMusic states that Ronald changes his tone on some of the songs by adding a roughness to his smooth tenor. On ballads, he sweetly caresses the lyric with compassion and agility.[89]

Songs from *Harvest for the World* have been heavily covered or sampled by other artists. In addition to The Christians, the title track has been covered by Vanessa Wiliams, Jewel, The Power Station, and others. That song has also been sampled by Paul Johnson and Mo Kolours. "(At Your Best) You Are Love" was covered by Aaliyah, Frank Ocean, and Sinead Harnett. "Let Me Down Easy" has been sampled by Tracey Lee and Devin the Dude. Ronnie Laws covered the entire album when he recorded *Portrait of The Isley Brothers' Harvest for the World*. These covers and samples exemplify the impact The Isleys have had on popular music. The year 1976 was another good time for Black music.

Each succeeding generation of African Americans contributed to the musical heritage of America, and for more than four centuries, they have fused America with songs. Their creative genius transcends sacred, popular, folk, and classical styles, but their idioms are strongly etched within the musical structure. The bicentennial year of the United States of America heard the sound waves of African Americans stretching from coast to coast. With creative vitality, they sing, dance, and make music. Along with The Isley Brothers, the year 1976 saw the brilliance of Black music superstars, including Stevie Wonder, Earth, Wind & Fire, The Jacksons, Aretha Franklin, Minnie Riperton, and many others.[90] By this time, Black music was in popular demand and would always be.

Chapter 5
Keep On Doin'

The year 1977 was a special time for pop culture. The first Apple II computers went on sale and Elvis Presley died at the age of forty-two. Two iconic films, *Star Wars* and *Saturday Night Fever*, premiered in theaters. In January of that year, the popular miniseries *Roots* aired on ABC. This is a saga about an African American family from slavery to freedom that urged people in America to examine race relations and racism. In the following month, The Isley Brothers received the good news they had anticipated for eight years.

On February 23, the long and drawn-out court case between The Isley Brothers and Motown Records over who owns the rights to the smash hit "It's Your Thing" was finally settled by a federal court jury in New York. The jury ruled that The Isley Brothers recorded the song after leaving Motown and the label was not entitled to any royalties.[1] This was a huge win for the group, and they moved forward with their next studio album.

Go for Your Guns

In March, The Isley Brothers released the first single from their upcoming album, titled "The Pride (Parts 1 & 2)." This is a funky track that serves as a warning to politicians to be the leaders that people need. It also speaks to people who want to change, reminding them that it is the pride that keeps them strong and makes them want to belong. "The Pride" peaked at number thirty on the *Billboard* Disco Action chart on April 16. It also rose to number one on the *Billboard* Hot Soul Singles chart on April 23. Surprisingly, it stalled

The *Go for Your Guns* cover is a photo of The Isleys in concert.

at number sixty-three on the *Billboard* Hot 100 on May 28.[2] This song is the lead track for *Go for Your Guns*.

Go for Your Guns is the fifteenth studio album by The Isley Brothers. After recording four albums that were assisted by producers Malcolm Cecil and Robert Maugouleff, The Isleys decided to stay on the East Coast and record at Bearsville Studios in upstate New York, not too far from the T-Neck label in New Jersey.[3] *Go for Your Guns* was released on April 16. It features seven tracks: "The Pride (Parts 1 & 2)," "Footsteps in the Dark (Parts 1 & 2)," "Tell Me When You Need It Again (Parts 1 & 2)," "Climbin' Up the Ladder (Parts 1 & 2)," "Voyage to Atlantis," "Livin' in the Life," and "Go for Your Guns," which is basically an instrumental extension of the preceding track. The 2011 reissue features three bonus tracks: "Voyage to Atlantis (Alternate Version)," "The Pride (Part

1) (Single Version)," and "Voyage to Atlantis (Single Version)." The front cover is a photo taken of the group onstage during an arena concert.[4] This album gives every indication that The Isley Brothers would be on top for a long time.

On *Go for Your Guns*, The Isley Brothers mix their material up very well with hardcore funk in dominating Isley style. Then they drop a smooth, mellow ballad on each side to change up the groove. The brothers wrote, produced, and arranged all the material, and again they displayed that they are some of the best writers in the music business with unique lyrics on all the songs. "Voyage to Atlantis" is one of their most beautiful songs, but it is not much above the rest of the album tracks, which all add up to another classic for The Isleys.[5] This is proven by the album's sales.

Go for Your Guns sold more than five hundred thousand copies in the first week of its release. It was certified gold by the RIAA on April 19. In less than two months after its release, the album sold more than one million units and was certified platinum by the RIAA on June 2. It would eventually be certified double platinum on August 17, 1999.[6] *Go for Your Guns* shot to number one on the *Billboard* Top Soul Albums chart on May 14 and remained there for two weeks. The album also rose to number six on the *Billboard* 200 Albums chart on May 21.[7]

If anything seemed to best qualify The Isley Brothers' annual recording proclivity, it was the group's attitude that there could be change in continuity. Ernie explained the production of *Go for Your Guns* when he declared, "We're using the same basic instrumentations on all our albums, with a different makeup each time, so that each one is individual and different, yet part of an overall musical picture that is totally and completely our own."[8] By spring 1977, The Isley Brothers were touring with Parliament-Funkadelic.

The popularity attained by The Isley Brothers made it possible for them to be considered a headlining act. Seldom did they appear on dates they did not headline, as they did with the Parliament-Funkadelic tour, in which P-Funk headlined. The Isleys also limited their concerts to primarily weekends, which were first reserved when the younger brothers joined the group because they were finishing their college studies. By this time, according to Marvin, they spent a major portion of their time in the studio. They preferred the studio to the tour because creating music is their first love.[9] The Isleys also preferred to protect their image.

Reaching millions of music lovers placed The Isley Brothers on a plane where they were constantly being watched. So, they felt obligated to have a good reputation. When asked if they feel obligated to maintain a certain image, Marvin replied, "Yes, definitely. It's in our music. We say a lot of things about the way we feel, the way we live." Chris added, "Have you ever heard anything about The Isleys being busted somewhere or having a run-in with the law? We don't ever become involved in any kind of crime. We are straight all the way and don't deal with anything illegal." Ernie stated, "We are constantly trying to achieve something positive in life—whatever it may be. We try to project something positive always, whether it be good musicians, good businessmen, good people with good personalities."[10] The next single released by The Isleys hinted at them protecting their image and business.

In late June, "Livin' in the Life" was released. This is the second single from *Go for Your Guns*. This is a popular funk track that encourages prying people to stop assuming and stay out of other folks' business.

> Somebody said, I was living in the life
> Somebody told me, I was living in the life
> Think that you might know, you find that you're readin' me wrong
> My pictures come and go, but my life has got to go on[11]

"Livin' in the Life" rose to number four on the *Billboard* Hot Soul Singles chart on June 23 and peaked at number forty on the Hot 100 songs chart on August 6.[12] With two hit songs from *Go for Your Guns*, The Isleys performed in major cities across America.

On Friday, August 25, The Isley Brothers headlined at Madison Square Garden. According to Marie Moore of *New York Amsterdam News*, it was their best performance. Moore wrote that The Isleys were more in the pocket than they were out. It was a sellout concert, and everyone enjoyed every minute of the performance.[13] On Saturday, September 10, The Isley Brothers performed at the Soul Explosion in the Oakland Coliseum. Other acts on the bill were Hamilton Bohannon and Graham Central Station.[14] The Isley Brothers performed in Cleveland, Ohio, on Saturday, October 8, with Maze and Mass Production on the bill.[15] In late October, they traveled to Atlanta, Georgia.

There was a saying in the music business that goes "people live off familiarity," and that was the case for The Isley Brothers' concert at the Omni in Atlanta. With so many hits, all the brothers had to do with their songs was come close to the record to turn on the crowd, which is exactly what they did, come close. According to Prentis Rogers of the *Atlanta Daily World*, with each song The Isleys performed, the crowd could be seen rising to their feet with roars of approval, and from that standpoint alone, the show had to be considered a success.[16] A short time after this concert, The Isleys issued a new single in November.

"Voyage to Atlantis" is an extraordinary soul rock ballad that features unforgettable guitar riffs by Ernie.[17] Ron's soulful voice and the song's mesmerizing sound help the listener believe the mythical Atlantis really did exist. Surprisingly, "Voyage to Atlantis" peaked at number fifty on the *Billboard* Hot Soul Singles chart on December 3. Many believe this may be the strongest track on *Go for Your Guns*. Robert Christgau described it as the most hard-edged song they had recorded since moving T-Neck to CBS in 1973.[18] The album itself also received positive reviews from music critics.

According to Andresmusictalk, the one quality that defines *Go for Your Guns* is confidence. Moreover, on both the instrumental and vocal levels, the album comes at the listener with the passion of a sociopolitical musical preacher.[19] Andrew Hamilton of AllMusic declares that *Go for Your Guns* is not dull, and there are no fillers.[20] According to Dustygroove, *Go for Your Guns* was recorded at the height of The Isley Brothers' glory days, when their sound was completely on the money. The entire album is great—in the best Isley Brothers seventies way.[21] *Go for Your Guns* is not the only album published by The Isleys in 1977.

Forever Gold

In August, The Isley Brothers released a compilation album titled *Forever Gold*. It contains ten tracks released in the mid-1970s. Those tracks include "That Lady (Parts 1 & 2)," "Live It Up (Parts 1 & 2)," "Hello It's Me," "(At Your Best) You Are Love," "Fight the Power (Parts 1 & 2)," "For the Love of You (Parts 1 & 2)," "Hope You Feel Better Love (Parts 1 & 2)," "The Highways of My Life," "Harvest for the World," and "Summer Breeze."[22] *Forever Gold* peaked at number fifty-eight on the *Billboard* 200 Albums chart on October 1 and reached number forty on the Top Soul Albums chart on November 12.[23] With two more albums in their catalogue, The Isley Brothers were looking forward to publishing new music in the following year.

Showdown

Since the mid-1970s, the music tracks of The Isley Brothers were created by the three younger members. Usually, a track began with Chris and Ernie (on drums) laying down the rhythm track. That's how "Take Me to the Next Phase" was created. Chris played synth bass while Ernie played the rhythm. The song has the sound of a live stadium recording, though it was recorded in a studio. Chris, Ernie, and Marvin laid the stomps and some of the crowd noises across twenty-four recording tracks.[24] This was the first single from The Isleys' next album.

"Take Me to the Next Phase (Parts 1 & 2)" was released in March 1978. This funky track is sure to make the listener feel like moving.[25] It rose to number one on the *Billboard* Hot Soul Singles chart on May 13 and remained in that spot for two weeks. However, it did not make it to the *Billboard* pop chart. The studio album featuring "Take Me to the Next Phase" was released in April.

Showdown contains eight tracks: "Showdown (Parts 1 & 2)," "Groove with You," "Ain't Givin' Up No Love," "Rockin' with Fire (Parts 1 & 2)," "Take Me to the Next Phase (Parts 1 & 2)," "Coolin' Me Out (Parts 1 & 2)," "Fun and Games," and "Love Fever (Parts 1 & 2)." Like the previous album, it was recorded at Bearsville Studios. The front cover shows a group photo of the brothers dressed in vibrant seventies fashion. The back cover shows the brothers posing individually.[26]

Showdown was assured to be another successful album for The Isley Brothers. It quickly sold more than five hundred thousand units and was certified gold by the RIAA on April 10. Less than a month later, on May 3, it was certified platinum after selling more than one million copies.[27] *Showdown* quickly soared to number one on the *Billboard* Top Soul Albums chart on May 13 and stayed in that position for three weeks. The album also rose to number four on the *Billboard* 200 Albums chart on June 4.[28] This was the fifth consecutive platinum album by The Isley Brothers. So, what is the key to The Isleys' success?

Chris explained, "If there is any such thing as a secret or formula to our success, it would mainly have to be objectivity. We try not to get carried away by things. We'll come up with some material, pick it apart, and work on them. The songs we put on our albums are done by a step-by-step process." The Isley Brothers' catalogue proves this process to be effective. The Isleys' only

The front of the *Showdown* cover displays the brothers in vibrant 1970s fashion.

The back of the *Showdown* cover shows the brothers posing individually.

problem was figuring out what songs to play in concert, since the demand was so great, and the time was so little to meet that demand. Chris declared, "We might have four or five basic numbers we do, but we try to pick out the hit singles, the ones that did extremely well in the R&B and Top 40 market. We also depend on a lot of feedback we get from what records the different cities have been playing and which ones have been getting the best reaction."[29] With a new hit album and hefty catalogue, The Isleys were ready for a new tour.

The Isley Brothers began their national tour in May 1978. Teddy Pendergrass performed on some dates. This same team had a sellout performance in Madison Square Garden during the summer of 1977.[30] The band Brainstorm also performed on this 1978 tour. The tour produced nothing less than sold-out arenas everywhere they performed.[31] While on tour, The Isleys released "Groove with You" in July.

"Groove with You" is another consoling ballad from The Isley Brothers.

> Oh, I've been thinking of you
> And you've been thinking of me
> Oh, I'll give all that I have
> If you give all that I need[32]

"Groove with You" reached number sixteen on the *Billboard* Hot Soul Singles chart on August 5.[33] Surprisingly, it didn't place on the pop chart. No other singles were released from *Showdown*, but the smooth funk jam "Coolin' Me Out" became a popular tune. With *Showdown*, The Isley Brothers continued to integrate rock with funk and falsetto vocals with guitar curvature. This album ranks among The Isleys' best.

According to Alex Henderson of AllMusic, when *Showdown* was released in 1978, The Isley Brothers hadn't lost any of their freshness. He believes this album is generally excellent. Henderson writes, "The Isleys bring a great deal of passion to funk/rock scorchers like 'Rockin' with Fire,' 'Love Forever,' and the number one hit 'Take Me to the Next Phase,' and they are equally appealing on the smooth caressing slow jam 'Groove with You.' Meanwhile, the slow-burning 'Ain't Givin' Up No Love' is one of the most bluesy things that the 3 + 3 sextet recorded." *Go for Your Guns* was a tough act to follow, and Henderson believes *Showdown* comes impressively close.[34] Marvin gave insight to the quality of The Isleys' music.

Marvin declared, "Our music is about a positive message. It sometimes comes out as a political statement or sometimes as a philosophical statement. I think that because our music is serious to us, it means something to other people. We don't tell you to go out and do a thing because it's the thing to do—but rather we just try to translate what's happening." Marvin actually wrote "Groove with You." He explained, "We try to write universally—to write songs that will appeal to you whoever you are. I was just fooling around when I wrote the lyrics for 'Groove with You.' I wrote it in about five minutes. I was just singing and about to stop when I asked one of my brothers to listen to the words. He said, 'Don't stop' and that's how 'Groove with You' happened."

Durability is the word that may best describe the lyrics of The Isley Brothers' songs. The words are saturated with emotion, with a depth that ranges from the heartbreak felt over the loss of a lover to the triumph one feels when he reaches a personal achievement. This lyric durability has marked The Isleys' career, and it is one that has been triumphantly recognized by their millions of listeners.[35] A testament to this was a Madison Square Garden filled to the rafters with fans on August 10, 1978. The Isley Brothers managed to find a niche that sells and evokes the kind of stuff that had hordes of people dancing in the aisles.[36] With so many hits behind them, The Isleys decided to publish another compilation album in October.

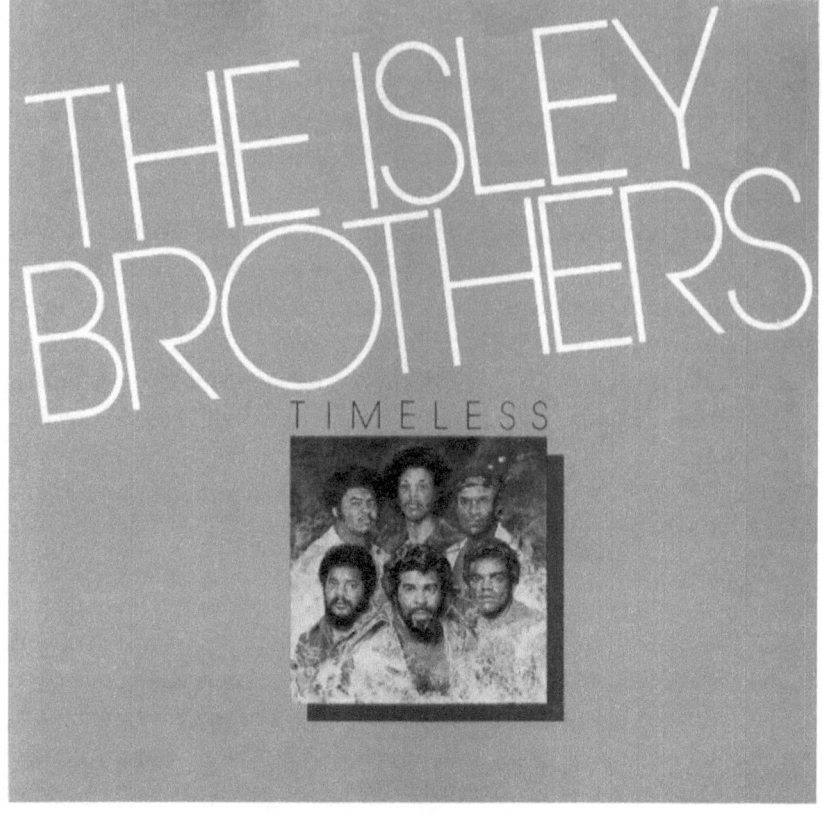

The *Timeless* cover features a portrait of The Isleys.

Timeless

Timeless is a double album that contains their pre-1973 hits associated with Buddah Records. The first album features ten tracks: "It's Your Thing," "Love the One You're With," "I Know Who You Been Socking It To," "Get Into Something," "I Need You So," "Work to Do," "Brother, Brother," "Keep On Doin'," "I Turned You On," and "Put a Little Love in Your Heart." The second album also features ten tracks: "Pop That Thang," "Lay Lady Lay," "Spill the Wine," "Fire and Rain," "Freedom," "Ohio/Machine Gun," "Nothing to Do But Today," "Lay Away," "If He Can, You Can," and "It's Too Late."[37] *Timeless* stalled at number seventy on the *Billboard* Top Soul Albums chart on November 25, 1978.[38] This compilation helped solidify another successful year for The Isley Brothers. This year was also special for many other Black recording artists.

The year 1978 could be described as "the year of the great crossover" for Black music. It was a time of great achievement for unknowns, such as Cheryl Lynn, who, by year's end, had gone from obscurity to number two on the music chart. It was a year for rapidly developing artists, such as Melba Moore, to reach totally new audiences by moving from the pop arena to the fast-growing disco market. It was a year in which Earth, Wind & Fire skyrocketed toward double platinum with a "best of" compilation. Furthermore, it was a year in which the final charts reflected 25 percent of the top one hundred albums in America were Black oriented. More Black-oriented albums were RIAA certified platinum in gold in 1978 than in any preceding year. As stated previously, platinum success was found with The Isley Brothers' *Showdown*. Other platinum albums were The O'Jays' *So Full of Love*, Heatwave's *Central Heating*, Teddy Pendergrass's debut album *Teddy Pendergrass*, as well as his *Life Is a Song Worth Singing*, and Johnny Mathis's *You Light Up My Life*.[39] The 1970s were coming close to an end, and The Isleys were ready to close out another decade.

At this place in their career, The Isley Brothers were reaping the benefits of their work. In the spring of 1979, marketing biggies argued that The Isleys had reached the point in their career where they didn't have to work the concert trail anymore. The experts declared that good investments and vast real estate holdings in New Jersey and New York City had made The Isleys millionaires.[40] In the same season, disco music was at its peak, and some of the songs on The Isley Brothers' upcoming album would contribute to the genre.

Winner Takes All

In April 1979, The Isley Brothers released "I Wanna Be with You." In addition to funk, this song also has a disco rhythm.[41] Disco is a genre of dance music and a subculture that emerged in America in the mid-1970s from the urban nightlife scene. The sound of disco is characterized by four-on-the-floor beats, syncopated bass lines, string sections, horns, electric piano, synthesizers, and electric rhythm guitars. Initially ignored by radio, disco received its first significant exposure in deejay-based underground clubs that catered to Black, Latino, and gay dancers.

Deejays were a major creative force for disco, helping to establish hit songs and encouraging a focus on singles. A new subindustry of extended twelve-inch singles evolved to meet specific needs of club deejays. While most disco artists were African American, the genre's popularity crossed over racial lines.⁴² The disco element helped "I Wanna Be with You" shoot to number one on the *Billboard* Hot Soul Singles chart on May 26. However, this song did not make it to the pop songs chart.⁴³ Also, in the spring of 1979, The Isleys were selected to be a part of the Kool Jazz Festivals.

The Kool Jazz Festivals tour featured fifteen dates in major cities across America. There were ten stadium festivals and five arena events. The stadium festivals included improved color televisions, and all events used new giant stages. In addition to The Isley Brothers, other artists who performed were Teddy Pendergrass, George Benson, Ashford & Simpson, The O'Jays, The Bar-Kays, Rose Royce, Peabo Bryson, and B. B. King. The tour began on May 26 in Washington, DC, and ended in New York City on August 11.⁴⁴ Shortly after the tour began, The Isley Brothers published their seventeenth studio album in mid-June.

Winner Takes All is a double album that contains fourteen tracks: "I Wanna Be with You (Parts 1 & 2)," "Liquid Love (Parts 1 & 2)," "Winner Takes All," "Life in the City (Parts 1 & 2)," "It's a Disco Night (Rock Don't Stop) (Parts 1 & 2)," "(Can't You See) What You Do to Me?," "Let's Fall in Love (Parts 1 & 2)," "How Lucky I Am (Parts 1 & 2)," "You're the Key to My Heart," "You're Beside Me (Parts 1 & 2)," "Let Me into Your Life (Parts 1 & 2)," "Love Comes and Goes (Parts 1 & 2)," "Go for What You Know," and "Mind Over Matter (Parts 1 & 2)." The 2013 reissue features the bonus track "It's a Disco Night (Rock Don't Stop) (12" Disco Version)." The cover displays photos of the brothers dressed in casual seventies attire.⁴⁵

Winner Takes All had a good reception. Shortly after its release, the album was certified gold by the RIAA on June 7, after selling more than five hundred thousand copies.⁴⁶ *Winner Takes All* climbed to number three on the *Billboard* Top Soul Albums chart on July 7, and it reached number fourteen on *Billboard*'s 200 Albums chart on the same date.⁴⁷

The second single and title track from *Winner Takes All* was released in July 1979. "Winner Takes All" is a funky disco tune that celebrates confidence and enterprise.

> Come on and make your play
> You'll be a winner in my game
> Come on and make your play
> You just remember that the winner takes it all⁴⁸

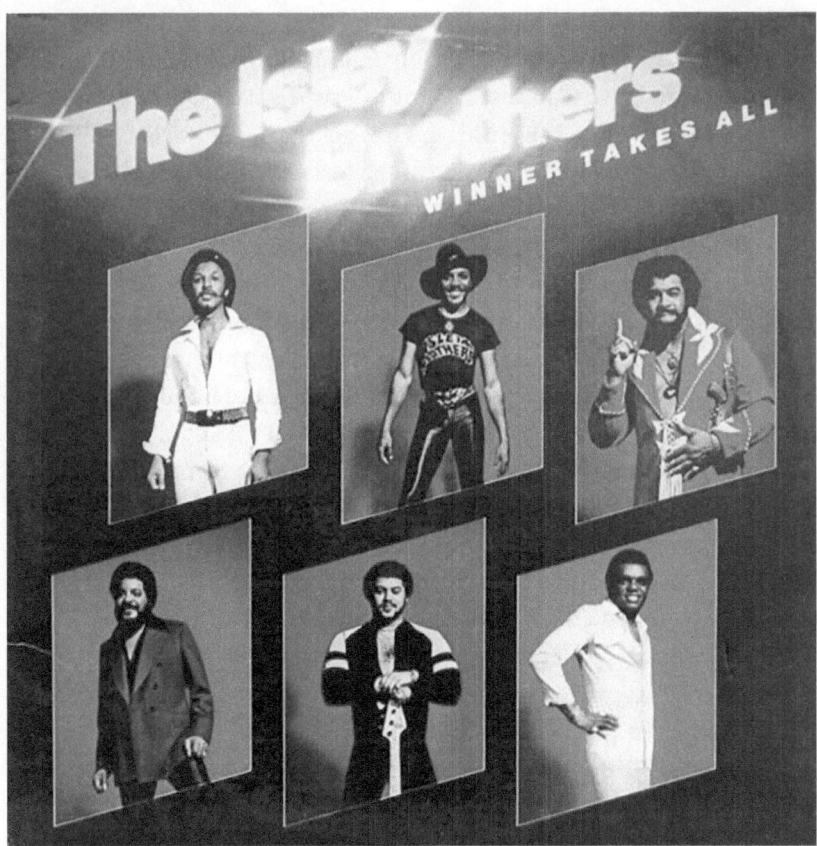

The *Winner Takes All* cover features photos of the brothers dressed in casual late 1970s fashion.

This song reached number thirty-eight on the *Billboard* Hot Soul Singles chart on August 18, but it did not make it to the pop songs chart.[49] Ironically, this song was released when some people were frustrated with disco music.

By the summer of 1979, disco had taken over the airwaves. Donna Summer, Gloria Gaynor, and Chic were at the top of the charts. Steve Dahl, a twenty-four-year-old disc jockey in Chicago was upset. He had been fired from a radio station when it went all-disco. In his new job at a rival rock music station, he took out his frustration by destroying disco records on the air. Soon after, station reps and Chicago White Sox promotors got the idea of actually blowing up disco records. The team was willing to do anything to fill Comiskey Park. So, on July 12, at a muggy Thursday night doubleheader with the Detroit Tigers, fans could bring a disco record and get in for less than a dollar. There were more than fifty thousand rowdy fans in attendance. Some of the fans started using records as Frisbees. Also at the game was a teenager named Vince Lawrence who was an aspiring musician.

Vince Lawrence says he was one of the few African Americans in attendance that night. He was saving up money for a synthesizer and hoped to snag some disco records to take home. Vince noticed something about the records some people were bringing. They were records by Tyrone Davis, Curtis Mayfield, and Otis Clay. Many of the records were not disco records but were just records by Black artists. After the first game, a giant crate full of records was placed in the outfield. Steve Dahl led chants of "disco sucks," and the crate was blown up. The explosion scattered records all over the field. This event became known as Disco Demolition. The demolition has been considered an overt attack against disco's early adopters: Blacks, Latinos, and gays. July 12, 1979, has been dubbed "the night disco died."[50] But it hadn't died just yet. While disco was a problem for some people, The Isley Brothers were dealing with their own problems.

In August 1979, the Internal Revenue Service (IRS) charged The Isley Brothers with failure to pay more than $63,000 in federal taxes due from a $25,000 health spa and restaurant they owned in Mt. Kisco, New York. According to IRS spokesman Milton Waldman, the taxes were deducted from employees' wages dating to January 1977. He stated that $59,000 was due from the Northern Westchester Health Club and $13,000 from the Peppertree Restaurant and Lounge located inside the club. The Isleys had acquired the business in 1976 from the Manhattan Savings Bank after the former owner went into bankruptcy.[51]

In early September, the IRS seized all of The Isleys' property it could find in New York and New Jersey. This was done to satisfy an alleged tax deficit of $650,000. According to IRS records, this tax due situation was a family affair with a combined debt of $660,731. The alleged tax bill included all members of the group, except Chris Jasper.[52] Within a few years, this type of financial issue would have a permanent effect on the dynamic of the group. But The Isley Brothers persevered.

Furthermore, in early September, The Isley Brothers released the third single from *Winner Takes All*, titled "It's a Disco Night (Rock Don't Stop) (Parts 1 & 2)." This is an upbeat disco track, notable for being one of the few disco-based tunes released by The Isleys. The title alone confirms its contribution to the disco genre.⁵³ "It's a Disco Night" peaked at number forty-four on the *Billboard* National Disco Action chart on September 22, and it reached number twenty-seven on the *Billboard* Hot Soul Singles chart on October 6. This song stalled at number ninety on the *Billboard* Hot 100 Songs chart on October 27. "It's a Disco Night" was the final single released from *Winner Takes All*, which features eighteen superb tracks. The Isley Brothers had built a repertoire of groove songs celebrating joy, courage, and dreamy love.

Winner Takes All is no different, but it is cleaner and fiercer than most of the previous albums. Mike Freedberg wrote in the *Bay State Banner*, "'Life in the City' is similar to 'Live It Up,' and its bass riff, very like classic Stax R&B, is played with delicious sourness. 'It's a Disco Night' is 'Who's That Lady' again, with a new harmonic and speedier beat." Freedberg adds, "'I Want to Be with You' is angry love funk. 'Winner Takes All' is a celebration of confidence and enterprise." Side three features love ballads with Ronald's unique vocals complemented with elegant instrumentals. Freedberg declared, "Side four is a mixture of less captivating styles, but the economy of means by which The Isleys state their contrast of softs and hards on the other three sides makes the album more than worth your money."⁵⁴

George Lane, who also wrote for the *Bay State Banner*, declared, "*Winner Takes All* does not represent a drop in the usual Isleys' quality, but it does show a desire to remain stationary in terms of thematic development. Every song is done in the charismatic two-part formula, with high energy levels and the familiar funk-rock synthesis." Lane added, "Ernie takes his one customary son-of-Hendrix guitar solo, and the singing remains entertaining. Side 3 is the strong side, but everything else is well-done."⁵⁵ The Isley Brothers completed the 1970s with another successful album and established themselves as one of the most successful artists of that decade.

To some, the 1970s is considered the golden era of Black music. This was the period of the musicians. They moved from the background to equal status with the vocalists. Most singles and albums released during the 1970s were either one half or more composed of musical leads. The psychedelic era and the disco era both had musicians as the main force in the music. Even when the musicians remained in the background publicity wise, in most cases, they still dominated. This brought out the popularity of self-composed groups.

Instead of just backing stand-up vocal groups and individual singers, musicians joined together and did their own vocal work. Thus came the birth of super groups/bands, such as Earth, Wind & Fire, Ohio Players, Rufus,

Parliament-Funkadelic, The Commodores, Kool & the Gang, and many others. The Isley Brothers went from stand-up to self-composed. The self-composed group/band became the dominant force along with session musicians, those who formerly backed individual artists and groups. This is where the writers, arrangers, and producers displayed their genius. They beautifully fused jazz, soul, pop, rock, psychedelic, disco, gospel, and funk into whatever they wanted.

The 1970s saw the gradual decline of rock and blues, and the birth of psychedelic during the early years and disco in the latter years. But the love ballad continued to flow smoothly through all years as funk kept everyone partying throughout the decade while prolonging both popular music styles.[56] The Isley Brothers definitely had their share of funk jams and love ballads during the 1970s and would produce more of the same in the 1980s.

Go All the Way

The Isley Brothers published their next single, titled "Don't Say Goodnight (It's Time for Love)," in March 1980. This is a smooth slow groove that embodies romance.[57] When asked if there's a different feeling when writing love songs, Ernie declared that all the brothers collaborate on all the songs, but he, Marvin, and Chris do most of the writing. Ernie revealed that "Don't Say Goodnight" started out as Chris's idea. "The three of us were fooling around with some musical ideas and we came up with the title. Chris snatched down on a piece of paper: 'I want to love you over and over again.' I said it sounded a bit strange, but we threw the line in anyway."[58] A string synthesizer was used to get the string sound. Chris explained, "I was thinking about the stage performance, the rhythmic breaks in the song and everything. It was approached in that direction, a slow song to get a stage reaction."[59] This is one of The Isley Brothers' most memorable songs.

"Don't Say Goodnight" climbed to number one on the *Billboard* Hot Soul Singles chart on April 19, 1980, and remained in that position for four weeks. It also reached number thirty-nine on the *Billboard* Hot 100 Songs chart on May 24.[60] This song was covered by Natalie Cole and R&B group Vertical Hold, featuring Angie Stone on lead vocals. Soon after releasing this single, The Isleys used their popularity for civic engagement.

The Isley Brothers, along with other CBS artists, including The O'Jays, Barry White, George Duke, Cheryl Lynn, and many others, voluntarily taped

The *Go All the Way* cover shows the members dressed in furs and winter clothing.

spots for the 1980 Census. The key phrase implemented in the campaign was "Support the 1980 Census . . . We're Counting On You." The communications industry developed a package of ten-, thirty-, and sixty-second public service announcements recorded by top artists that were broadcast by over 250 Black-owned radio stations around the country. The public service announcements had a positive and tremendous impact in the African American community.[61] The brothers also published their next album on April 19.

Go All the Way features only six tracks: "Go All the Way (Parts 1 & 2)," "Say You Will (Parts 1 & 2)," "Pass It On (Parts 1 & 2)," "Here We Go Again (Parts 1 & 2)," "Don't Say Goodnight (It's Time for Love) (Parts 1 & 2)," and "The Belly Dancer (Parts 1 & 2)." The album cover displays The Isley Brothers neatly dressed in country western–styled winter clothing.[62]

Within two weeks of its release, *Go All the Way* soared to number one on *Billboard*'s Top Soul Albums chart on May 3 and remained in that spot for five weeks. The album also made it to number eight on the *Billboard* 200 Albums chart on May 17.[63] In less than two months after its release, *Go All the Way* was certified platinum by the RIAA on June 4, after selling more than a million copies.[64] One could assume Isley fans were expecting another great album after "Don't Say Goodnight" became a number one R&B hit for four weeks. The second single from *Go All the Way* was the title track.

"Go All the Way" was released in late April. The upbeat funky track may remind some listeners of "It's a Disco Night." This song did not make it to *Billboard*'s R&B and pop songs charts. However, it did make it to number forty on the Disco Action chart on June 14.[65] Before the next single was published, The Isley Brothers returned to Madison Square Garden.

The Isley Brothers performed at Madison Square Garden on the weekend of June 6 and 7. Stephanie Mills and The S.O.S. Band appeared with them. The S.O.S Band was touring with The Isleys during the summer. They received the Garden Gold Ticket for having their fourth sellout concert at Madison Square Garden. Among the others in that select company who attracted more than one hundred thousand are Earth, Wind & Fire, N. Y. Salsa, Fania All-Stars, The Bee Gees, and Bob Dylan.[66] The Isley Brothers and The S.O.S Band also performed at Chicago Stadium on June 19. This was The Isleys' first Chicago appearance in two years.[67]

In late June, it was announced that The Isley Brothers would replace Barry White for the Ohio Kool Jazz Festival in Cincinnati, Ohio, on August 2 at Riverfront Stadium. Since the brothers were born and attended school there, the festival and the city of Cincinnati would engage in a giant welcome-home celebration for the group. Performing on the same day as The Isley Brothers were Chic, Kool & the Gang, Angela Bofill, and The Gap Band.[68] The Isley Brothers also performed at Richfield Coliseum in Cleveland, Ohio, on August 10 for their first appearance there in two years. Funk group Cameo also appeared.[69] In the midst of performing during the summer, The Isleys published another single in mid-June.

"Here We Go Again" has a moderate tempo with a strong bass by Marvin, a tight guitar from Ernie, and delightful keyboards by Chris. The vocals of the three older brothers are on point. "Here We Go Again" reached number 11 on the *Billboard* Hot Soul Singles chart on August 2 but failed to reach the pop chart.⁷⁰ This is the last single released from *Go All the Way*, which features six noteworthy tracks.

The *Call and Post* of Cincinnati, Ohio, examined every track of *Go All the Way*. The title track is a "catchy tune, bolstered by heroic handclaps and the Brothers' 'talkin' about the real deal.'" "Say You Will" is a "hypnotic track highlighted by the funky, fluid guitar of Ernie Isley." "Pass It On" has a "sledgehammer beat and the instant groove of Marvin Isley's booming bass." "Here We Go Again" proves that Ronald "breathes better than most singers sing." "Don't Say Goodnight" suggests that "sex is not everything; it's the only thing" because "Ronald wants to check out his new woman in bed." He says he wants to do it "over and over." "The Belly Dancer" is a hot "dance track with lyrics as torrid as Chris Jasper's synthesized keyboards."⁷¹

The *Los Angeles Sentinel* also praised the album, describing it as a "platinum package of funky sophistication shimmering with passion, precision, and pure sex. In the United States of Love, the title track could be the national anthem."⁷² This was the sixth platinum album by The Isley Brothers. It seemed as if The Isleys were on the right path to have the same kind of success in the 1980s as they did in the '70s. Their next album was just a few months away.

Chapter 6
Fire and Rain

In 1981, significant events were taking place around the world. Former movie star Ronald Reagan was inaugurated as the fortieth president of the United States after he defeated Jimmy Carter in the 1980 presidential election. In April, NASA launched the first space shuttle mission. President Reagan appointed Sandra Day O'Connor as the first woman to the US Supreme Court, and IBM launched its first PC. At the beginning of the year, The Isley Brothers already had a new single on the charts.

Grand Slam

"Who Said?" had been released at the very end of 1980. This is a funky dance track about rumors that sounds like "The Pride" with a faster tempo.

> Who said I was shacking up
> Who's makin' all these rumors up now
> Yea . . . hea . . . hea[1]

"Who Said?" peaked at number seventy-one on the *Billboard* Disco Action chart on January 31, 1981. It also reached number twenty on the *Billboard* Hot Soul Singles chart on February 21.[2] A month later, on March 21, *Grand Slam* was published.

Grand Slam is The Isley Brothers' nineteenth studio album. It features seven tracks: "Tonight Is the Night (If I Had You)," "I Once Had Your Love

The cover for *Grand Slam* is a group headshot.

(And I Can't Let Go)," "Hurry Up and Wait," "Young Girls," "Party Night," "Don't Let Up," and "Who Said?" For the first time since 1972, outside musicians were used. Everett Collins played drums, Kevin Jones played congas, and Eve Otto played the harp. The album cover shows a collective headshot of all the brothers.[3]

Less than a month after *Grand Slam* was published, The Isley Brothers released "Hurry Up and Wait" in mid-April. This is another funky dance track that could make any listener want to move.[4] "Hurry Up and Wait" peaked at number fifty-eight on *Billboard*'s Hot 100 Songs chart on May 16 and reached number seventeen on the Hot Soul Singles chart on May 30.[5] Right after this song was released, *Grand Slam* peaked on the music charts.

On April 18, *Grand Slam* soared to number three on the *Billboard* Top Soul Albums chart. The album also reached number twenty-eight on *Billboard*'s 200 Albums chart on April 25.[6] Less than two weeks later, on May 5, *Grand Slam* was certified gold by the RIAA for selling more than five hundred thousand units.[7] During the spring and summer, The Isleys were involved in another Kool Jazz Festivals series.

The annual Kool Jazz Festivals tour began May 30 at the Oakland Stadium in Oakland, California. Artists included in the festivals were Aretha Franklin, James Brown, Kool & the Gang, The Temptations, and a few others. The tour ended on August 29 at the Masonic Auditorium in Detroit, Michigan.[8] In addition to the Kool Jazz Festivals, The Isleys made other performances throughout the summer.

The Isley Brothers performed six concerts at the Mill Run Theatre in Chicago, Illinois, from Friday, June 26, through Sunday, June 28. Two shows were done each day.[9] The brothers were at the Holiday Star Theatre in Merrillville, Indiana, on August 7.[10] They were also in concert for the third annual Reggae Sunsplash at Jarrett Park in Montego Bay, Jamaica, which was held from August 4 through 8.[11] In the midst of traveling, "I Once Had Your Love (And I Can't Let Go)" was released in early July.

"I Once Had Your Love" is the third and final single from *Grand Slam*. This mellow, mid-tempo ballad features Ron's smooth vocals.[12] "I Once Had Your Love" peaked at number fifty-seven on the *Billboard* Hot Soul Songs chart on July 25, but it failed to reach the pop songs chart.[13] This final single is part of a decent album with only seven tracks. The Isleys had proven they didn't always need many tracks to produce a superb album. It is obvious they considered quality over quantity. *Grand Slam* received mix reviews from critics.

Wilson and Alroy describe *Grand Slam* as being as good as its predecessor, with solid ballads and funk jams.[14] Ron Wynn stated that "the bloom was definitely off The Isleys' rose," and "the innocent, energetic air that sparked their '70s albums was gone."[15] Philip Harrigan of the *New Pittsburgh Courier* declared that the upbeat songs on *Grand Slam* are terrible, but the slower ones are nicely done.[16] Nevertheless, *Grand Slam* is an album that will be enjoyed by any Isley Brothers fan or anyone who loves good R&B music. Before the year was out, another studio album was published.

Inside You

On October 3, The Isley Brothers released "Inside You (Parts 1 & 2)." This was the first single from their next album. "Inside You" is a provocative, funky dance track that is over nine minutes long.

> Baby, just stay with me a little longer
> Baby, I'll guarantee we'll get it on
> Read my mind and I know you'll find
> I wanna be inside you, baby[17]

This song climbed to number ten on the *Billboard* Hot Soul Singles chart on November 21 and to number eighteen on the Disco Action chart on December 12.[18] "Inside You" is also the title track for The Isleys' twentieth studio album.

Inside You was released near the end of October. It features seven tracks: "Inside You (Parts 1 & 2)," "Baby Hold On," "Don't Hold Back Your Love (Parts 1 & 2)," "First Love," "Love Merry-Go-Round," "Welcome to My Heart," and "Love Zone." More than twenty guest musicians appear on this album. The album cover shows the brothers dressed as cowboys.[19] What is inside you is the basis for continued inspiration and artistic or entertainment expressions. Earl Calloway of the *Chicago Defender* believed this is what The Isley Brothers were expressing when they titled the album *Inside You*. The same musical vitality and melodic invention that made The Isleys a viable legend in soul music for nearly three decades is apparent in this album.[20]

Inside You did not sell as well as The Isley Brothers' previous album and didn't even reach gold status. The album had peaked at number forty-five on the *Billboard* 200 Albums chart on November 21. However, it climbed to number eight on the *Billboard* Top Soul Albums chart on November 28.[21] The second single, "Welcome to My Heart," was released on February 20, 1982.

"Welcome to My Heart" is a ballad that doesn't sound like an Isley song from the early 1980s. Instead, it sounds like a tune from one of the vocal soul groups of the early 1970s, like Blue Magic or The Delfonics.[22] "Welcome to My Heart" peaked at number forty-five on *Billboard*'s Hot Soul Singles Chart on March 27, but it failed to reach the pop songs chart.[23] This was the final single from *Inside You*. It is evident to the listener The Isleys decided to change their sound for this album.

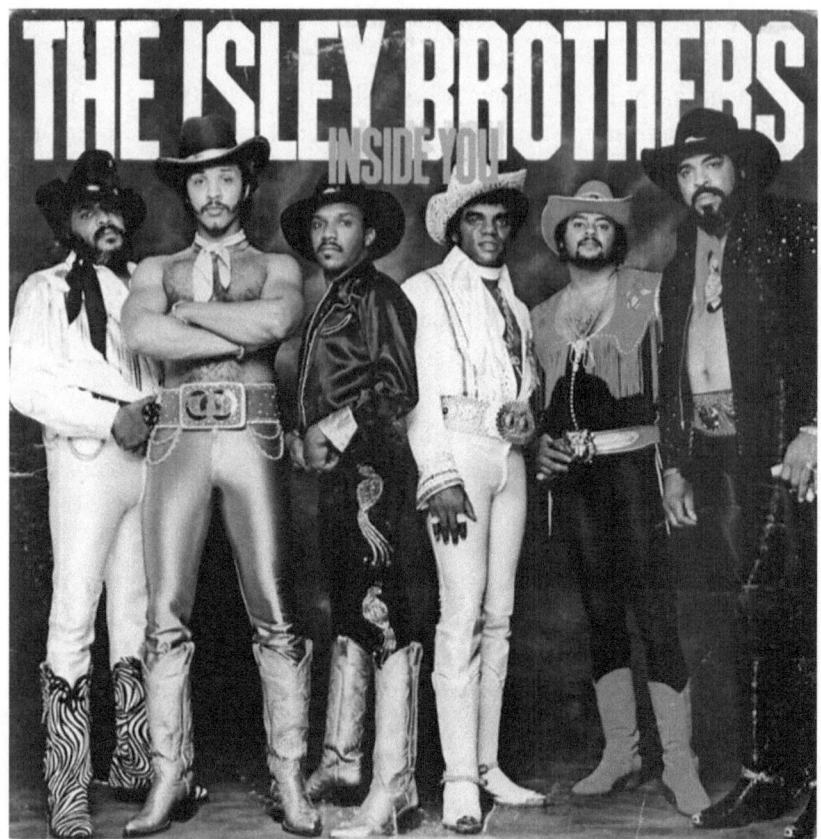

The *Inside You* cover features the group dressed in country western attire.

Stephen Holden of the *New York Times* claims that *Inside You* demonstrates The Isleys' affinity for a pop style that's reminiscent of The Doobie Brothers. Holden believes that style, though pleasant, isn't as interesting as the mixture of Motown, folk-rock, and hard rock that was exemplified in the mid-1970s.[24] John Rockwell, also of the *New York Times*, wrote, "The Isley Brothers are a more rock-oriented band, but their *Inside You* lacks the focus and energy of the best rock, opting instead for a lazy collection of funk wallpaper music and anonymous ballads over a subdued funk beat."[25]

Wilson and Alroy also described the album as a "temporary change of direction." The title track is up-tempo funk while most of the songs are lush ballads that seem to be a tribute to early 1970s smooth R&B groups. "Don't Hold Back Your Love" sounds like The Stylistics. "Baby Hold On" and "First

Love" sound like Earth, Wind & Fire. There is a heavy use of strings, which overwhelms almost every song. Wilson and Alroy believe this album was a low point in The Isleys' career.[26] This left some people wondering how the next album would sound. The Isleys saw themselves as visionaries and had every right to change or reinvent themselves. By the spring of 1982, The Isley Brothers were already working on another album.

The Real Deal

In late June, The Isley Brothers released the first single from their next album, titled "The Real Deal (Parts 1 & 2)." This is a funky party song that makes a comparison of life and gambling at a casino. It sounds similar to other funk artists of the early 1980s, including The Gap Band and Rick James. Yet it still has that Isley Brothers flair.[27] "The Real Deal" climbed to number fourteen on the *Billboard* Hot Black Singles chart on August 21, but it did not make it to the pop songs chart.[28] This song is the title track for the album that was published on August 7.

The Real Deal is the twenty-first studio album from The Isley Brothers. Like the two previous albums, this one contains seven tracks: "The Real Deal (Parts 1 & 2)," "Are You with Me?," "Stone Cold Lover," "It's Alright with Me," "All in My Lover's Eyes," "I'll Do It All for You," and "Under the Influence." The cover displays a photo of the brothers standing beside a gambling table in a casino.[29]

The Real Deal soon climbed to number nine on the *Billboard* Top Black Albums chart on September 11. However, the album stalled at number eighty-seven on the *Billboard* 200 Albums chart on September 18.[30] Like its predecessor, *The Real Deal* did not reach gold status. This was surprising for many Isley fans. They believe this album is underrated and ranks among their best. The second single from *The Real Deal*, titled "It's Alright with Me," was released in mid-October.

"It's Alright with Me" is an upbeat love song with strings and the signature keyboard style of Chris Jasper. Chris is also featured on lead vocals with Ronald.[31] This song peaked at number fifty-nine on the *Billboard* Hot Black Singles chart on October 30, 1982, but it did not reach the Hot 100 Songs chart.[32] The third and final single, "All in My Lover's Eyes," was released on Christmas day.

The cover for *The Real Deal* is a photo of the brothers in a casino.

"All in My Lover's Eyes" is a smooth ballad with a mesmerizing bass and Ernie's slick guitar work.³³ This song stalled at number sixty-seven on *Billboard*'s Hot Black Singles chart on January 22, 1983. And like the previous single, it failed to reach the pop songs chart.³⁴ Of the three songs released from *The Real Deal*, none of them reached the *Billboard* 100 Songs chart, and "The Real Deal" is the only one to reach the top twenty of the Black Singles chart. Album sales were not good. This caused concern for The Isleys, their fans, and critics.

Andy Kellman of AllMusic argues that *The Real Deal* is satisfactory, but by The Isley Brothers' standard, only serious fans would find it interesting.³⁵ Wilson and Alroy claim that The Isleys used this album to bid farewell to the styles that had carried them to multiplatinum success. They describe the title track as a "fun, punchy electrofunk track that sounds more like Prince than anything they ever recorded before." "Stone Cold Lover" is described as "vintage power-funk." "Under the Influence" is considered The Isleys' first take on the twelve-bar blues, and the deep pocket combined with Ernie's guitar makes it one of their best songs. The lack of sales prompted a major rethink for the next album.[36]

Between the Sheets

By late fall 1982, The Isley Brothers had begun recording another album. The first single from the album is the title track. "Between the Sheets" was released in early April 1983. This is a provocative song with mellow lyrics about making love. It has been described as one of the sexiest songs ever made and is known for the climaxing synth chords.

> Hey, girl, ain't no mystery
> At least as far as I can see
> I wanna keep you here layin' next to me
> Sharin' our love between the sheets[37]

The song was so sensual that someone felt it should be rated with a big red "R."

A citizen of Columbus, Ohio, wrote to the *Call and Post* newspaper in Cleveland, Ohio, to express concern. The citizen believed that responsible adults and leaders of the community should be more cognizant of the effects certain trends that can be viewed through dress, television, recreation, and music can have on children. The citizen argued that for children and young teenagers, "Between the Sheets" could be a dangerous and suggestive means of encouraging them to engage in sex and foreplay that could result in situations they are not prepared to handle. The citizen also claimed that there is nothing discreet about the song, writing that the singer blatantly expresses his desire to have sex, to stop singing and make love, and he even goes as far as to describe the act as it progresses to orgasm.[38] While that is true, many will argue that Ronald's words were chosen wisely, and many young people didn't even understand exactly what he was singing about. The reaction to "Between the Sheets" was similar in Philadelphia, Pennsylvania.

W. Cody Anderson, general manager for WDAS in Philadelphia, banned "Between the Sheets" from the playlists. He declared that the community expected WDAS to maintain not just a high standard of commitment, but of morality, of family values. Anderson stated, "I refuse to play it. I know for a fact that the community would never allow us to get away with it."[39] In spite of the objections and criticism, the song became a hit.

"Between the Sheets" soared to number three on the *Billboard* Hot Black Singles chart on May 14. Surprisingly, it did not reach the *Billboard* 100 songs chart.[40] This song was eventually certified gold by the RIAA on June 14, 2006, after selling over half a million copies.[41] "Between the Sheets" is a classic and has been sampled by a long list of artists, including Notorious B.I.G. for "Big Poppa," Gwen Stefani for "Luxurious," Whitney Houston for "One of These Days," and several others. Less than a month after the song peaked as an R&B hit, The Isleys published their twenty-second studio album in early June.

Between the Sheets features ten tracks: "Choosey Lover," "Touch Me," "I Need Your Body," "Between the Sheets," "Let's Make Love Tonight," "Ballad for the Fallen Soldier," "Slow Down Children," "Way Out Love," "Gettin' Over," and "Rock You Good." The second edition, released in 2011, includes five bonus tracks: "Between the Sheets (Instrumental Version)," "Choosey Lover (Instrumental Version)," "I Need Your Body (Instrumental Version)," "Let's Make Love Tonight (Instrumental Version)," and "Between the Sheets (Single Version)." The album cover displays a red rose on silky bedclothes, letting listeners know that romance is a major theme.[42]

Between the Sheets was a bounce back for The Isley Brothers after the two previous albums had disappointing sales numbers. *Between the Sheets* climbed to number nineteen on the *Billboard* 200 Albums chart on July 9. It did even better on the Top Black Albums chart when it rose to number one on July 23.[43] The album was certified gold by the RIAA on July 18 after selling more than five hundred thousand copies. It eventually reached platinum status on September 12, 1995, after selling more than one million units.[44] The high album sales can be attributed to the title track and the second single, titled "Choosey Lover."

"Choosey Lover" was released in early June 1983. This is another romantic song with bold lead vocals from Ron and a fierce guitar solo by Ernie. It actually sounds like it was recorded in the 1970s.[45] "Choosey Lover" rose to number six on the *Billboard* Hot Black Singles chart on August 13, but it did

The *Between the Sheets* cover art is a red rose on silky bedclothes.

not reach the Hot 100 Songs chart.[46] This is a favorite among many and was covered by R&B singer Aaliyah. It has also been sampled by Bone Thugs-N-Harmony for "Buddah Lovaz" and by Nas for the remix to "Street Dreams," featuring R. Kelly. No other songs from *Between the Sheets* made it to the music charts, but one track got special attention.

The Isley Brothers produced a music video for "Ballad for the Fallen Soldier." Videos became popular for music artists in the early 1980s, especially in 1981, when Music Television (MTV) was created. But when MTV began business, it refused to show videos by Black artists. Black artists' videos could primarily be seen on the Black Entertainment Network (BET)'s *Video Soul*. Prince was the first Black artist to appear on MTV, and Michael Jackson was the first Black artist to have his videos appear on that network regularly.

A music video not only spreads the music; it almost universally represents and circulates the performer. Although the image track may include narrative, graphic, or documentary visuals, it usually (even if sometimes briefly or intermittently) shows the performer performing. The music thus gains narrative status and appears to come from the world the video depicts.[47] The purpose of music videos and all forms of advertisement is to attract the attention of viewers and make them interested in a product or service. Artists found videos to be a viable marketing tool, especially if the song conveys a special message or deals with a serious matter.

"Ballad for the Fallen Soldier" is a funky rock tune that features a guitar solo by Ernie. It is a tribute to the many American war casualties, especially those from the Vietnam War.

> His country wanted him to fight
> For the things they thought were right
> And he tried to give his all
> In DC, his name is on the wall[48]

The video for this song features The Isley Brothers in camouflage, scenes of war, a boy studying his relative's uniform, and a young man preparing to go to war.[49] Like "Fight the Power" and "Harvest for the World," "Ballad for the Fallen Soldier," shows how socially conscious The Isleys' music can be. This song helped make *Between the Sheets* a superb album.

Dustygroove claims *Between the Sheets* is a departure from The Isley Brothers' funkier sound of the 1970s. The entire album is great, and it has the group operating in a wonderful smooth soul mode.[50] According to Wilson and Alroy, The Isley Brothers were smart musicians: "As soon as the small band guitar-clavinet sound stopped selling, The Isleys shifted to a lush, synth-heavy sound with electronic percussion alongside Ernie's guitar work." It sounded like they had been working on this style for a decade. The melody of "Choosey Lover" sounds like "Devotion" by Earth, Wind & Fire, but the other tunes are clever and original.[51] With another great album, it seemed The Isleys had gotten their groove back. They were nominated for an American Music Award in the category of Favorite Soul/R&B Band, Duo, or Group. By the time *Between the Sheets* was released, it had been almost twenty-five years since the release of The Isley Brothers' first single, "Shout."

If longevity is a testimony to greatness in the music business, The Isley Brothers had stayed at the top for nearly a quarter of a century. Since the hit song "Shout" in 1959, The Isleys accumulated three gold singles, ten gold albums, and three platinum albums. A few of those gold albums reached platinum status years later. To commemorate their twenty-fifth year, The Isley Brothers established the Twenty-Fifth Anniversary Tour, which kicked off October 8, 1983, at the Fox Theatre in Atlanta, Georgia. Chris was thrilled about performing in Atlanta. Although The Isleys had prior performances at Fulton County Stadium and the Omni, that was their first performance at the Fox Theatre. Chris stated, "We love Atlanta. This is one of our biggest markets. They have given us tremendous support. I would like to thank the people there."[52] Atlanta is considered the "Cradle of the Civil Rights Movement" and the "Black Mecca." To close out 1983, The Isley Brothers celebrated the festivities of New Year's Eve with Chicago fans with the help of the soul group Enchantment at the Arie Crown Theater on December 31 at 8:00 p.m. and 11:00 p.m.[53]

By 1984, tension between the older brothers and the younger brothers had been mounting. As Chris recalled, O'Kelly, Rudolph, and Ronald had accumulated too much debt, especially with the IRS. The way they wanted to solve the problem would not have been fair for Ernie, Chris, and Marvin. The Isleys could not have maintained their lifestyles if they had continued as the six-member group. They were trying to cover the problem with more debt. It was impossible for the six of them to continue. The older brothers wanted to get out of the CBS contract by filing for bankruptcy. Chris believed the three younger brothers didn't have to file for bankruptcy because they didn't have much debt. This created a conflict, and the three younger brothers wanted to produce their own album. The older brothers didn't like the idea and sued the younger brothers, but the younger brothers prevailed.[54] In the midst of this conflict, a compilation album was published in March 1984.

Greatest Hits, Vol. 1

Greatest Hits, Vol. 1 contains eight tracks: "That Lady (Parts 1 & 2)," "Groove with You," "For the Love of You (Parts 1 & 2)," "Footsteps in the Dark (Parts 1 & 2)," "Between the Sheets," "It's Your Thing," "Fight the Power (Parts 1 & 2)," and "Live It Up." The album cover displays the six brothers in unique poses between the moniker.[55] *Greatest Hits, Vol. 1* turned out to be another top

The cover for *Greatest Hits, Vol. 1* is an animated display of the brothers posing individually.

seller for The Isley Brothers. The album was certified gold by the RIAA on August 11, 1992. It was certified platinum on September 11, 1995, and eventually reached double platinum status on August 17, 1999.[56] After this album, there would be no more studio albums featuring all six members that fans had come to love since 1973.

One of the main reasons for the band's transformation and newfound success in the 1970s was the only member not bearing The Isleys' name: Chris Jasper. The brother-in-law of Rudolph Isley, Chris brought to the group a classic knowledge of music that the brothers did not have. In fact, Chris was sometimes solely responsible for their biggest hits. It may have been Ron's voice and face that became symbols of the group, but it was Chris's creativity that gave them songs like "For the Love of You" and "Between the Sheets." And despite the record label credits, Chris has declared that he wrote, produced, and played all the instruments on "Between the Sheets," a song that has since become one of the most sampled tunes in hip-hop history.

That music was the kind of magic Chris created with The Isley Brothers from 1973's 3 + 3 to 1983's *Between the Sheets*. That ten-year period is known as their golden age. During that time, The Isleys released at least one album every year, sometimes two. Seven of those albums reached number one on the *Billboard* R&B chart, with several going top-ten pop as well. Many of them went platinum or double platinum, and they generated timeless classics that have been R&B staples for decades.[57] After the golden age, a splinter group was formed.

Broadway's Closer to Sunset Blvd (Isley-Jasper-Isley)

Because of the tension with the three older brothers, in mid-1984, the three younger brothers of the group, Ernie Isley, Chris Jasper, and Marvin Isley, formed their own group titled Isley-Jasper-Isley. Their first album, *Broadway's Closer to Sunset Blvd*, was released in the fall of 1984. This album contains eight tracks: "Sex Drive," "Serve You Right," "I Can't Get Over Losin' You," "Kiss and Tell," "Love Is Gonna Last Forever," "Broadway's Closer to Sunset Blvd," "Look the Other Way," and "Break the Chain."[58] The group did not rule out the possibility of recording again with The Isley Brothers. Marvin stated, "This is basically a separate project from The Isley Brothers. So, I wouldn't really say that we've broken up in the sense that we would never record with them again." The new group said they wanted to take on a new challenge and move in another direction. The album includes a mixture of funk, rock, and adult contemporary.[59]

The first single from *Broadway's Closer to Sunset Blvd* is "Look the Other Way." This is a funky rock tune, featuring Ernie on lead vocals.[60] The video for this song shows the brothers performing and women dancing with a computerized background.[61] This song became an R&B hit, reaching number fourteen on the *Billboard* Hot Black Singles chart. The second single, "Kiss and Tell," is another funky rock jam that features Marvin on lead vocals.[62] This song peaked at number fifty-two on the same chart.[63] The video for the song shows the brothers having fun on the beach, receiving readings from a fortune teller, and finding their mates.[64] Sales of *Broadway's Closer to Sunset*

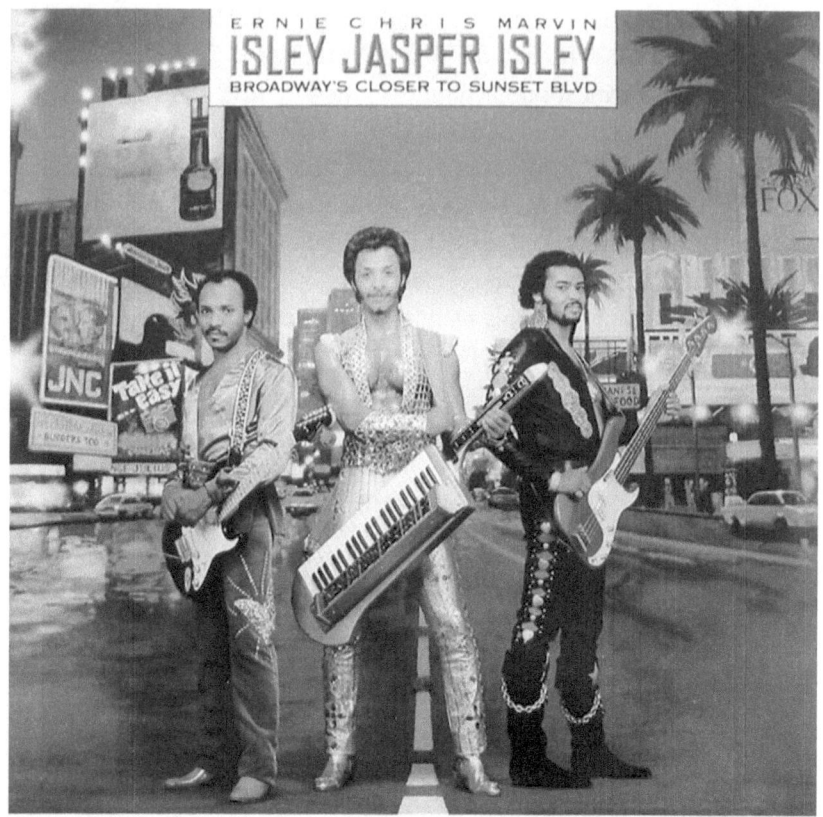

The cover for *Broadway's Closer to Sunset Blvd* features the three musicians standing in a vibrant thoroughfare.

Blvd were relatively poor. The album reflected the rock style of the brothers and was rejected by some R&B fans. Not long after this album's release, the three older brothers released an album.

Masterpiece

Nearly a year after the separation, O'Kelly, Rudolph, and Ronald signed another record contract, this time with Warner Brothers. To compensate for losing the young musicians, they hired session musicians to round out their sound. They also used outside writers, giving their material a new color, variety, and dimension.[65] Their Warner Brothers debut, *Masterpiece*, was released in the spring of 1985.

The *Masterpiece* cover displays the three brothers dressed in tuxedos.

Masterpiece consists of nine songs: "May I?," "My Best Was Good Enough," "If Leaving Me Is Easy," "You Never Know When You're Gonna Fall in Love," "Stay Gold," "Colder Are My Nights," "Come to Me," "Release Your Love," and "The Most Beautiful Girl." For this album, more emphasis is placed on the brothers' superb vocals instead of the instrumentation. *Masterpiece* is dedicated to their brother Vernon Isley and their parents, Sally and O'Kelly Isley Sr. The liner notes were written by Elaine Isley, wife of Rudolph and sister to Chris Jasper. The album cover displays the brothers dressed in black tuxedos.[66]

The first single from *Masterpiece*, "Colder Are My Nights," was released in the fall of 1985. This is an upbeat song about a man feeling lonely with no one to keep him warm at night.[67] "Colder Are My Nights" climbed to number 12 on the *Billboard* Hot Black Singles chart on January 18, 1986.[68] While this single was on the music chart, *Masterpiece* reached number 19 on *Billboard*'s

Top Black Albums chart on December 28, 1985. The album also peaked at number 140 on the *Billboard* 200 Albums chart on January 11, 1986.[69] The second and final single from *Masterpiece* is "May I?"

"May I?" was released in March 1986. This is a ballad in which the singer is yearning for affection. The song has a groove that sounds similar to the ending of "Between the Sheets."

> May I beg you
> Out of some lovin'?
> One more time
> Please, baby[70]

"May I?" peaked at number forty-two on the *Billboard* Hot Black Singles chart on April 12, 1986.[71] *Masterpiece* was a decent revamp for The Isley Brothers.

Masterpiece is virtually all ballads. Richard Defendorf of the *Orlando Sentinel* wrote, "The funk that dominated The Isleys' records during the 1970s faded in favor of a safe but pleasurable excursion into the lushly orchestrated realm of middle-of-the-road arrangements and satin smooth vocals." There are only three songs that sound like the old Isley R&B: "May I?," "Colder Are My Nights," and "Release Your Love." The other six songs consist of romance. The choruses flow along with horns, strings, and synthesizers.[72]

Most of the songs on *Masterpiece* are covers, and according to Wilson and Alroy, "Ronald sings so convincingly that he sells mediocre tracks like Phil Collins's 'If Leaving Me Is Easy.'" These music critics believe The Isleys pulled quite a trick with their version of "The Most Beautiful Girl" in which they reshape the melody so well that it sounds original and familiar at the same time.[73] Jason Elias of AllMusic wrote that "what typified *Masterpiece* was a few choice ballads." "You Never Know When You're Gonna Fall in Love" and "Stay Gold" have poignant and reserve vocals from Ronald." Elias believes The Isleys' mature approach worked for *Masterpiece*.[74] While the three older Isleys were having a decent run with *Masterpiece*, the three younger brothers made a conscious effort to add more soul to their follow-up album.[75]

Caravan of Love (Isley-Jasper-Isley)

Caravan of Love was released in 1985. It features seven tracks: "Dancin' Around the World," "Insatiable Woman," "I Can Hardly Wait," "Liberation,"

The *Caravan of Love* cover is a photo of the three musicians dressed in Eastern-style clothing with two horses.

"Caravan of Love," "If You Believe in Love," and "High Heel Syndrome."[76] The first single from the album is the title track. "Caravan of Love" is a smooth, soulful tune that became a global anthem of peace and brotherhood.[77] Marc Taylor described the song as a beautiful, melodic, and lyrically powerful gem.[78] The music video shows the brothers performing in a park and features scenes of people from various ethnicities. At the end of the video, a diverse group of people sing with the group.[79] The video helped the song become Isley-Jasper-Isley's biggest hit.

"Caravan of Love" topped the *Billboard* Hot Black Singles chart for three weeks. Chris explained, "I had been looking at the world scene quite a bit, and I wasn't pleased with what I was seeing. I just felt that we all needed a positive message. I had the melody in my head for about four months before I put pen to paper. When I did, I wrote the song in 20 minutes and those lyrics just poured out." In the following year, the British group The Housemartins recorded an a cappella version of the song that topped the UK charts over Christmas 1986.[80] An additional single came from *Caravan of Love*.

"Insatiable Woman" was released in 1986. This is a ballad that features Chris on lead vocals.[81] The video for this song primarily shows intimate moments of Chris and his beautiful love interest. It also shows the group performing.[82] "Insatiable Woman" is dedicated to Chris's wife, Margie Jasper. The song peaked at number thirteen on the *Billboard* Hot Black Singles chart in early 1986. The two singles helped *Caravan of Love* climb to number three on the *Billboard* Top Black Albums chart.[83] In early 1986, the group went on their first national tour.

When Isley-Jasper-Isley released their first album, *Broadway's Closer to Sunset Blvd*, they decided not to tour because they felt they did not have enough material of their own to put on a show that would be distinct from The Isley Brothers shows. After acquiring the hit single "Look the Other Way" from the first album and the two hit songs from *Caravan of Love*, the group decided to tour with Starpoint and Luther Vandross.[84] In the spring, tragedy struck the Isley family again.

On March 31, 1986, O'Kelly Isley Jr. suffered a heart attack at his home in Alpine, New Jersey, and was declared dead of a cerebral hemorrhage at Englewood Hospital. He was forty-eight years old.[85] In addition to four brothers, O'Kelly was survived by mother Sallye and his two sons, Frank and Doug.[86] It seemed death struck at those times when the brothers had undergone decisions to make momentous change. When Vernon was killed as a teenager, the brothers were heading toward a promising career as a family gospel act. When O'Kelly Sr. died, the group was deciding if they should stay in Ohio or move to New York City. And when O'Kelly Jr. died, he, Rudolph, and Ronald had reinvented themselves and started a new phase in their career. Each time death occurred in the family, the surviving members were devastated, and each time they composed themselves and persevered.[87]

Chapter 7
The Next Phase

In 1987, hip-hop music was becoming mainstream, and the funk and soul bands who came of age during the seventies were becoming less popular. Additionally, The Isley Brothers had lost the oldest member, O'Kelly, the previous year. O'Kelly's passing caused uncertainty about the future of the group. Fortunately, Rudolph and Ronald decided to continue as a duo. Ronald declared, "People wondered whether we'd go on after that, especially when we didn't go into the studio right away. But we couldn't quit. We're not ready yet. Music has been our life and it still is. Rudolph and I had to go on without Kelly."[1] To carry on their work, The Isley Brothers were joined in the studio by multitalented Angela Winbush for their next album, *Smooth Sailin'*.

Angela Winbush was born and grew up in St. Louis, Missouri. She was grounded in gospel and attended Howard University in Washington, DC. At Howard, Angela took lessons from the same vocal coach who had instructed Roberta Flack and Donny Hathaway. In the late 1970s, she began singing with Stevie Wonder's Wonderlove and other artists, including Lenny Williams, Jean Carn, and Dolly Parton. In 1980, Angela joined René Moore and formed the R&B duo René and Angela. In 1985, they released *A Streetcar Named Desire*. Four singles from the album made it into the top ten of the R&B chart.

In 1987, Angela began her solo career and released *Sharp*, which included the number one R&B hit "Angel" and the number two song "Run to Me." Her other albums include *The Real Thing* (1989) and *Angela Winbush* (1994). Angela established Angela Winbush Productions, a production company and rigorous training ground for musical talent. She has written, arranged, and produced for several artists, including Janet Jackson, Sheena Easton, Stephanie Mills, and Lalah Hathaway.[2]

Smooth Sailin'

Angela Winbush coproduced and cowrote The Isley Brothers' *Smooth Sailin'*. She had been invited to work on the album by Warner Brothers executive Benny Medina, and it worked out for all parties involved. Ronald was so appreciative of Angela's talent that he soon took her under his wing and became her manager.[3] Within a short time, the relationship between Angela and Ronald went beyond business. The first single from *Smooth Sailin'* was "Smooth Sailin' Tonight."

"Smooth Sailin' Tonight" was released in May 1987. This is a mellow ballad written by Angela Winbush.[4] "Smooth Sailin' Tonight" rose to number three on the *Billboard* Hot Black Singles chart on July 11.[5] In June, The Isley Brothers released their twenty-fourth studio album, *Smooth Sailin'*. It contains eight songs: "Everything Is Alright," "Dish It Out," "It Takes a Good Woman," "Send a Message," "Smooth Sailin' Tonight," "Somebody I Used to Know," "Come My Way," and "I Wish." The album cover shows Rudolph and Ronald dressed in white with a serene background.[6] At the same time of this album's release, The Isleys' music was selected for a soundtrack.

In July, a soundtrack was released for *Moonlighting*. *Moonlighting* was an American comedy drama television series that aired from March 1985 until May 1989. Cybill Shepherd and Bruce Willis starred in the series. The soundtrack featured tunes that appeared in original episodes of the show. The Isley Brothers' Motown hit "This Old Heart of Mine" is featured. Other highlights include "The Moonlighting Theme" by Al Jarreau (the first single), "Stormy Weather" by Lena Horne, and "Someone to Watch Over Me" by Linda Ronstadt.[7] Also during the summer, rumors were still buzzing about the breakup of The Isley Brothers.

There were many versions about the group's split. Although the split happened more than three years prior, it became a hot gossip topic in music circles again. The older brothers were considered the villains. Supposedly, they repressed the younger brothers, driving them to form another act. During a break in a recording session one night in a West Hollywood studio, in a rare interview with the *Los Angeles Times*, Ronald gave the older brothers' side

The *Smooth Sailin'* cover shows the brothers in white sunshine suits with a serene background.

of what happened. Ronald cautioned, "Don't believe everything you hear on the street. If people are saying the split was nasty and it caused bad blood in the family, they're wrong. We talk. We always did. In fact, I talked to my younger brothers earlier today." So, what really happened?

According to Ronald, it all started in 1984, when CBS record executives wanted two Isleys albums: one featuring all six members and one with the three younger brothers. Ronald explained, "It was the wrong time for two Isley albums. It seemed like too much product at one time. We thought it would hurt our career to flood the market with Isley records. We really wanted the younger members to record a separate album. I don't care what you've heard. But we didn't want to do it then." Ronald was asked if part of the problem was that the younger members were simply fed up with being background figures. He answered, "They probably couldn't do—do what they wanted musically with us. The group wasn't structured for that. And I was probably guilty of being too bossy to them—too much like a father, saying 'Do this and that but not this.' Eventually, they were going to go off and do what they wanted. They had things they had to get out of their system. But when they left to form their own group, it was all very friendly."[8] The second single from *Smooth Sailin'* is "Come My Way."

"Come My Way" was released in September 1987. This is a cover of a tune by René & Angela. It is a smooth ballad that makes a perfect wedding song.[9] "Come My Way" stalled at number seventy-one on *Billboard*'s Hot Black Singles chart on October 17.[10] A third single was published from *Smooth Sailin'*, titled "I Wish" in January 1988.

"I Wish" is another sensual ballad that was written by Raymond Reeder. Ronald sings about his desire to touch and hold his lover when feeling lonely.[11] Like the previous single, it did not climb high on the chart. It stalled at number seventy-four on the *Billboard* Hot Black Singles chart on January 30, 1988.[12] With one R&B hit, and two other songs that reached the R&B chart, *Smooth Sailin'* proved to be a decent production for The Isley Brothers.

Ron Wynn of AllMusic described *Smooth Sailin'* as "both painful and poignant." The album is painful because it is the first album after the death of O'Kelly Jr. It is poignant because of Ronald's soulful vocals that have been showcased on many ballads.[13] Entertainment journalist Derrick Dunn claims, "*Smooth Sailin'* is a weaker entry in The Isley Brothers' catalog. However, it was the start of a tremendous fourteen-year musical chemistry run with Angela Winbush. There is strength in the ballads, but the first half is forgettable." As far as the title track, Dunn declared that it "puts to shame some artists whose careers started after The Isley Brothers."[14]

It was interesting that The Isley Brothers and Isley-Jasper-Isley both had albums circulating in 1987. The Isley Brothers' *Smooth Sailin'* peaked at number sixty-four on the *Billboard* 200 Albums chart on July 18 and climbed to number five on the *Billboard* Top Black Albums chart on August 8.[15] However, Isley-Jasper-Isley's third album, *Different Drummer*, was not successful.

Different Drummer (Isley-Jasper-Isley)

Different Drummer was released in the first half of 1987. It contains nine songs: "Different Drummer," "8th Wonder of the World," "Blue Rose," "Do

The cover for *Different Drummer* is a portrait of a drummer with various faces in the background.

It Right," "Givin' You Back the Love," "A Once in a Lifetime Lady," "For the Sake of Love," "Brother to Brother," and "I Wanna Be Yours."[16] The techno-funk jam "8th Wonder of the World" entered the top twenty of *Billboard*'s Hot Black Singles chart in the spring of 1987. The sweet, mid-tempo "Givin' You Back the Love" also entered the top twenty on the same chart in the summer of 1987.[17] *Different Drummer* was not a success. When describing the album, Ron Wynn of AllMusic wrote, "The singing was perfunctory, the production and arrangements routine, and they got little mileage from any of the material."[18] After this album, the group broke up and Chris began a solo career.

In the fall of 1987, Chris Jasper formed an independent record label and production company called Gold City Records. He released his first solo album in 1988, titled *Superbad*. *Superbad* contains eight songs: "Superbad,"

"Givin' My All," "One Time Love," "Earthquake," "Like I Do," "Dance for the Dollar," "The Son of Man," and "My Soul Train."[19] The title track is about the importance of education.[20] The music video for "Superbad" shows Chris performing, surrounded by young dancers and scenes of youth activity.[21] This debut single rose to number one on the *Billboard* Hot Black Singles chart. Since then, Chris recorded seventeen albums, including four urban contemporary gospel CDs. He also produced music for other artists for his label, including Chaka Khan, Average White Band, and his son Michael Jasper.[22] While Chris pursued a solo career, Ernie and Marvin rejoined The Isley Brothers in the early 1990s.

The Isley Brothers' next album was released more than two years after *Smooth Sailin'*. Before recording the album, in early 1989, Ronald Isley and Angela Winbush put big money on the line to take over total ownership of some valuable property on Sunset Boulevard in Los Angeles, California. The venture housed the Golden Lady Studios, in which they could record music together.[23] By then, Angela was Ronald's girlfriend, and they seemed to be a match made for good music.

Spend the Night

The first single from The Isley Brothers' next album is "Spend the Night," which is also the title track. The music of this song is similar to Angela's 1987 hit "Angel."[24] The video shows Ronald singing and romantic scenes of couples in love.[25] "Spend the Night" was released in June 1989 and soared to number three on the *Billboard* Hot Black Singles chart on August 26.[26] The full album was released in early September.

Spend the Night is credited as The Isley Brothers featuring Ronald Isley. It contains eight tracks: "Spend the Night (Ce Soir)," "You'll Never Walk Alone," "One of a Kind," "Real Woman," "Come Together (featuring Kool Moe Dee)," "If You Ever Need Somebody," "Baby Come Back Home," and "One of a Kind (Reprise)." This album is the last official recording that features original member Rudolph Isley. The cover features a photo of Ronald only.[27]

Ronald is the only brother shown on the album cover because Rudolph left the group shortly after the album was recorded. In response to O'Kelly's passing, Rudolph left the music industry to become a minister. He explained, "When my brother died in his sleep of a heart attack, the same way our

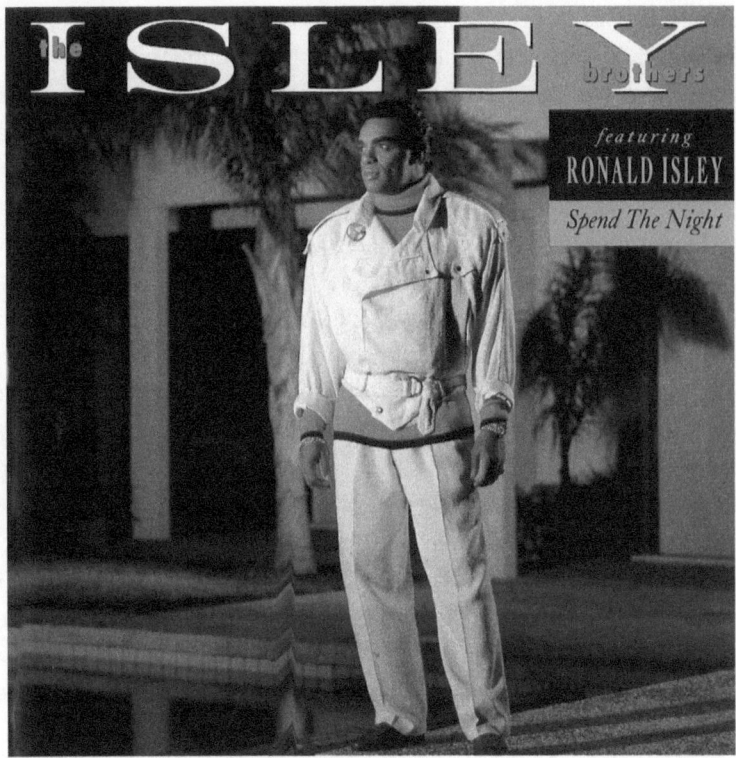

Only Ronald is featured on the cover of *Spend the Night*.

father did, I knew I had to make a change away from show business. Now I have a new king, and I'm singing about a new kind of truth, the truth about Jesus Christ."[28] Although Ronald lost his group partner, he sang a duet with another top recording artist.

In the fall of 1989, Ronald joined Rod Stewart in the studio to do a remake of The Isley Brothers' Holland-Dozier-Holland classic, "This Old Heart of Mine." The song was originally released by The Isleys in 1966 on Motown. This remake did even better than the original. It eventually reached number ten on the *Billboard* pop songs chart, two spaces higher than in the spring of 1966.[29] Ronald released his second single from *Spend the Night* in October, titled "You'll Never Walk Alone."

"You'll Never Walk Alone" is another smooth R&B tune produced by Angela Winbush.[30] The video for this song shows Ronald singing to his love interest in different environments, including a ranch, a hilltop, a lake, and a residence. Horses are seen galloping, and Ronald is riding a horse at the end of the film.[31] "You'll Never Walk Alone" reached number twenty-five on the *Billboard* Hot Black Singles chart on December 16.[32] A new year was right around the corner, and Ronald was going into his fifth decade of making hit music. He had acquired hits in the 1950s, '60s, '70s, and '80s, and he would gain more in the following decades.

In March 1990, the final single from *Spend the Night* was released, titled "One of a Kind." This tune has a moderate tempo with the signature Angela Winbush style, and she provides background vocals.[33] "One of a Kind" reached number thirty-eight on *Billboard*'s Hot Black Singles chart on April 7.[34] This was the third R&B hit from *Spend the Night*, which proved the name "Isley" was still relevant in the music business.

Ron Wynn declared that Ronald, the featured vocalist for *Spend the Night*, "still had a soaring and dynamic sound."[35] Wilson and Alroy wrote that the album "is produced and written in Angela Winbush's elegant, synth-heavy style, and the ballads are pleasant but lack individuality."[36] *Spend the Night* provides another distinct style for the Isley catalogue. In early 1990, Ernie Isley published a solo album.

Ernie Isley's solo project is titled *High Wire*. This album contains twelve tracks: "Song for the Muses," "High Wire," "Love Situation," "Diamond in the Rough," "Deal With It," "In Deep," "She Takes Me Up," "Fare Thee Well, Fair-Weather Friend," "Rising From the Ashes," "Deep Water," "Back to Square One," and "The Muses."[37] The title track was the album's first single. "High Wire" does not subscribe to any specific music genre. It's hip, not hip-hop. It's funky, not funk. It's homey, not house.[38]

Throughout *High Wire*, Ernie acts as a one-man band and delivers a sleek, punchy collection of hard-rock R&B, with plenty of six-string pyrotechnics and solid songs that both soul crooners and rock bands would love to have. Since the music was neither straightforward rock nor soul, it was not played by radio stations and, unfortunately, became a lost treasure. *Entertainment Weekly* considered it the ninth-best album of 1990.[39] The *New York Times* called *High Wire* "the surprise pop album of the year."[40] *High Wire* is proof that Ernie has the talent to do his own thing. In the spring, Ronald and Angela began touring in America and Canada.

By early 1990, Ronald was basically a solo act, and his key collaborator, Angela, was the opening act for his shows. Ronald declared, "Balancing a personal and professional relationship like that isn't hard. It's fun. We're so amazingly in the same frame of mind musically. Angela is a genius. As a songwriter, she's on a level with somebody like Stevie Wonder. In the next couple of years, that will be brought out so everybody will know it."[41]

At that time, ballads were The Isleys' thing. Mike Boehm of the *Los Angeles Times* described one of Ronald and Angela's concerts: "His 65-minute set went from sigh to swoon, from coo to croon, with only marginal contrast in between. For most of the audience, however, all this prelude-to-a-kiss stuff seemed to be just the thing. As Isley and his well-tempered band swung from one smooth number to the next, a cheer would greet each selection. Isley executed his smoothfest well, singing near the top of his range for much of the show in a reedy, mellifluous voice, and doing it with believable ardor." Boehm also praised the opening act for her live vocals. Angela Winbush's "opening set also was heavily slanted toward the elegant, shimmering romantic balladry of what is known as the 'Quiet Storm' approach to R&B. Thanks to Winbush's exceptional voice, her version of the quiet storm was no dull drizzle. She was able to dip down to a deep, husky timbre not far removed from a blues singer's lowdown snarl, or swoop up to stratospheric passages that resembled the line of an alternately darting and gliding soprano saxophone." Angela's set included three duets with Ronald.[42] While they were on tour, Ronald and Angela had a hit song on the airwaves.

In May 1990, Angela released "Lay Your Troubles Down" from her 1989 album titled *The Real Thing*. This is a duet with Ronald.[43] Jazzy with soul, this performance between Angela and Ronald served as an ideal pick-me-up song as both singers brought forth a memorable presentation with their rhythmic vocals and sultry play of the saxophone in the background. "Lay Your Troubles Down" eventually reached number ten on *Billboard*'s Hot Black Singles Chart.[44] The video for the song shows the two vocalists happily singing onstage with a band, which features famed saxophonist Gerald Albright.[45] With this hit record, it was obvious the duo made good music partners, and they continued to perform together throughout the year.

Ronald and Angela closed the year with a New Year's Eve concert. The Front Row Productions New Year's Eve Show featuring The Isley Brothers, Angela Winbush, and Marcia Griffith was held at the International Amphitheatre in Chicago, Illinois, on December 31, 1990. The show was originally scheduled at the University of Illinois Chicago Pavilion. By moving the show to the International Amphitheatre, the promoters hoped the event could be transformed into a fantastic gala evening.[46] As stated previously, Ronald was in his fifth decade in the music business, and by 1991, The Isley Brothers had amassed dozens of quality albums and hit records.

In March 1991, Rhino Records released two volumes of a compilation for The Isley Brothers. The first collection is titled *The Isley Brothers Story, Vol. 1: Rockin' Soul (1969–68)*. This volume contains twenty songs on one compact disc:

1. "Shout (Parts 1 & 2)"
2. "Respectable"
3. "Rock Around the Clock"
4. "Open Up Your Heart"
5. "Your Old Lady"
6. "Twist and Shout"
7. "Twistin' with Linda"
8. "Nobody but Me"
9. "She's Gone"
10. "You'll Never Leave Him"
11. "Who's That Lady"
12. "Testify (Parts 1 & 2)"
13. "The Last Girl"
14. "Move Over and Let Me Dance"
15. "This Old Heart of Mine (Is Weak for You)"
16. "Take Some Time Out for Love"
17. "I Guess I'll Always Love You"
18. "Got to Have You Back"
19. "Take Me in Your Arms (Rock Me a Little While)"
20. "Behind a Painted Smile"[47]

The second collection is titled *The Isley Brothers Story, Vol. 2: The T-Neck Years (1969–85)*. This volume has a total of twenty-eight songs on two compact discs.

Disc One:
1. "It's Your Thing"
2. "I Turned You On"
3. "Love the One You're With"
4. "Spill the Wine"
5. "Lay-A-Way"
6. "Pop That Thang"
7. "Work to Do"
8. "That Lady"
9. "If You Were There"
10. "What It Comes Down To"
11. "Summer Breeze"
12. "Live It Up (Parts 1 & 2)"
13. "Midnight Sky (Parts 1 & 2)"
14. "Fight the Power (Parts 1 & 2)"
15. "For the Love of You"

Disc Two:
1. "Harvest for the World"
2. "Who Loves You Better"
3. "The Pride (Parts 1 & 2)"
4. "Footsteps in the Dark (Parts 1 & 2)"
5. "Livin' in the Life"
6. "Take Me to the Next Phase (Parts 1 & 2)"
7. "Groove with You"
8. "I Wanna Be with You (Parts 1 & 2)"
9. "Don't Say Goodnight (Parts 1 & 2)"
10. "Inside You"
11. "Between the Sheets"
12. "Choosey Lover"
13. "Caravan of Love" (Isley-Jasper-Isley)[48]

The Isley Brothers Story was the largest compilation of Isley music to date.

Later that year, the personnel of The Isley Brothers changed again. Since Rudolph had decided to leave show business, younger brothers Ernie and Marvin rejoined Ronald to make the group a trio again. Ronald explained, "We'd been wanting to work together again for a long time. Marvin, Ernie and I see ourselves as king of the next generation of Isley Brothers, in touch with the past but looking forward to the future."[49] In the fall, they began working on another album, and it was announced that The Isley Brothers would be inducted into the Rock & Roll Hall of Fame the following year.[50]

On January 21, 1992, the Seventh Rock & Roll Hall of Fame Induction Ceremony was held at the Waldorf-Astoria Hotel in New York City. The Class of 1992 Inductees are Bobby Bland, Booker T and the MG's, Johnny Cash, Sam & Dave, The Yardbirds, Elmore James, Professor Longhair, Leo Fender, Bill Graham, Doc Pomus, The Jimi Hendrix Experience, and of course, The Isley Brothers.[51] Little Richard inducted The Isleys into the Hall of Fame. Ronald, Chris, Ernie, and Marvin attended the ceremony. On February 26, the Grammy Awards ceremony was held.

At the Thirty-Fourth Annual Grammy Awards ceremony, Michael Bolton won the Grammy for Best Pop Vocal Performance, Male. The day before, The Isley Brothers filed a copyright infringement action against Bolton. Bolton gained popularity in the late 1980s and early '90s by covering songs by soul music artists, such as Percy Sledge's "When a Man Loves a Woman" and Otis Redding's "(Sittin' On) the Dock of the Bay." He also wrote his own hit songs, including "Love Is a Wonderful Thing," which is cowritten by Andrew Goldmark.[52] This song is very similar to a song recorded by The Isleys, but Bolton has denied ever hearing The Isleys' version.

As mentioned in chapter 2, The Isley Brothers recorded a song titled "Love Is a Wonderful Thing," which was released as a single on United Artists' Veep label in June 1966. This song was included on a compilation CD titled *The Isley Brothers: The Complete UA Sessions*. It was released in the UK in 1991. Bolton's song appeared on his quintuple platinum album *Time, Love & Tenderness*. It reached number four on the *Billboard* Hot 100 Singles chart in June 1991. As to why the suit was filed, Ronald explained, "He added some words, but it's the same hook, the same melody. I'm totally shocked that he went this far in claiming that song as his own. I have met him before. I like his singing, but because of this, I have lost all respect for him." Bolton was determined to challenge the suit.

Louis Levin, Michael Bolton's longtime manager, believed the lawsuit was ludicrous. He issued a statement saying, "The song is an original song. We view the claim to be without merit and are vigorously defending the matter." The suit was filed on behalf of The Isleys' Three Boys Music Corporation by attorney Karen A. Breslow of the Los Angeles firm of Gang, Tyre, Ramer & Brown against Michael Bolton, Andrew Goldmark, their publishing companies, Nonpareil Music, Warner/Chappell Music, and WB Music, as well as Sony Music Entertainment, the parent company of Columbia Records. In May of that year, Bolton and Goldmark received songwriting awards from BMI and ASCAP for "Love Is a Wonderful Thing." Ronald urged Bolton to return the awards and decided to publicize the lawsuit.[53] The case would not go to trial until 1994.

Tracks of Life

In early May 1992, The Isley Brothers released the first single from their next album, titled "Sensitive Lover." This is a ballad produced by Angela Winbush that features Ronald's smooth vocals and Ernie's distinctive guitar work.[54] The video for the song shows all three brothers displaying their skills and also features a beautiful model.[55] "Sensitive Lover" reached number twenty-four on *Billboard*'s Hot R&B Singles chart on June 6.[56] At the end of May, The Isleys released their twenty-sixth studio album, titled *Tracks of Life*.

Tracks of Life contains fourteen songs: "Get My Licks In," "No Axe to Grind," "Searching for a Miracle," "Sensitive Lover," "Bedroom Eyes," "Lost in Your Love," "Whatever Turns You On," "Morning Love," "Dedicate This Song," "Red Hot," "Koolin' Out," "Brazilian Wedding Song," "I'll Be There 4 U," and "Turn on the Demon." The album cover features the three brothers dressed in black.[57] *Tracks of Life* stalled at number 140 on *Billboard*'s 200 Albums chart on June 13 and peaked at number 49 on the Top R&B Albums chart on August 8.[58] The second single from the album, "Whatever Turns You On," was released in August.

"Whatever Turns You On" is a moderate groove with subtle references to bondage in which Ronald croons to let his woman know he is willing to do almost anything to make her feel good romantically. Angela's piano work shines in this song, which exemplifies the "baby-making" music of

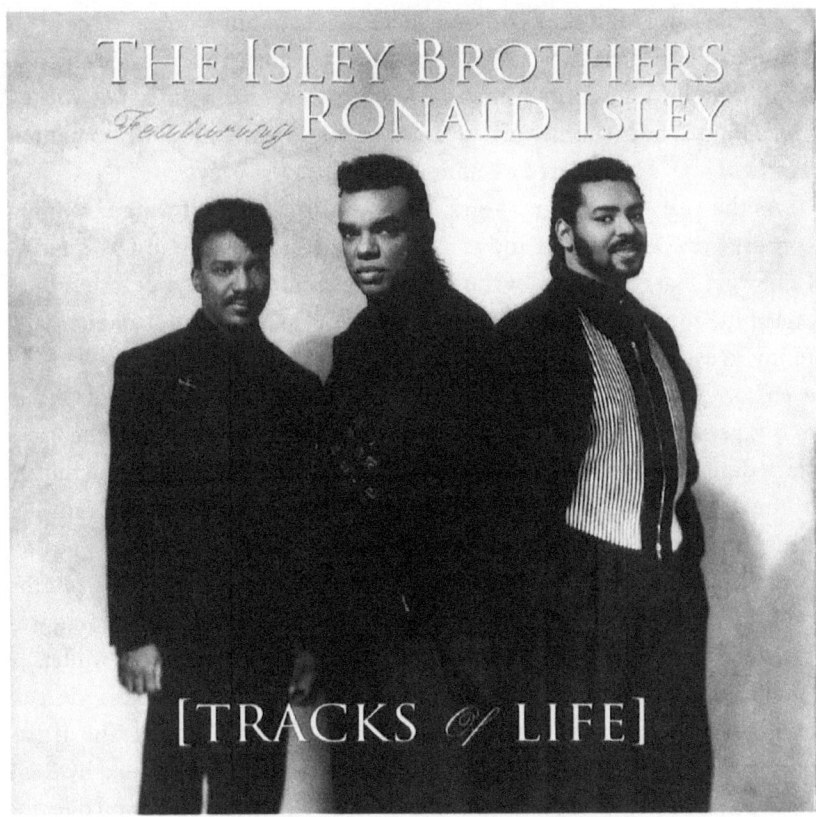

The *Tracks of Life* cover shows the three brothers dressed in black.

the 1990s.[59] "Whatever Turns You On" peaked at number forty-six on the *Billboard* Hot R&B Singles chart on September 5.[60] No other singles were released from this album.

Tracks of Life is considered another decent album that came after The Isleys' heyday. Scott Goldfine of Funknstuff describes it as a "hearty helping of silky, sensual soul music."[61] Alex Henderson of AllMusic claims, "*Tracks of Life* is a solid and respectable collection that benefits greatly from Angela's contribution to the songwriting." He adds, "Ron sounds genuinely inspired on all tracks, from the synth-funk to the sexy ballads. The album makes it clear that even in the '90s, the Isleys could still captivate."[62] For *Tracks of Life*, the brothers were more involved, being credited as producers and contributing some of the tunes. Wilson and Alroy believe the best song on the album is "Lost in Love," the slow jam on which Angela did not appear or cowrite. These two critics claim that "his impending marriage to Angela seemed to have brought out a more romantic, Marvin Gaye–like tone in his vocals." The album is over seventy minutes and has several memorable moments.⁶³ *Tracks of Life* is considered a reunion album for The Isleys.

As the year came near its end, The Isley Brothers performed "reunion concerts" on December 11 and 12 at the Strand Supper Club in Los Angeles, California. Barry Jackson of the *Los Angeles Sentinel* gave a description of one of the concerts. The opening act, comedian T. K. Carter, was raunchy and funny, as usual. The sold-out audience comprised young people who were not even born when some of The Isleys' songs were originally released and fans up to two generations older. The crowd really jumped to its feet when The Isleys started performing the songs from their 3 + 3 years. One of the highlights of the concert is when Ronald invited his then-fiancée Angela and funkster Rick James to join him onstage. Angela's four-octave vocal range was a perfect complement to Ronald's sexy bedroom tenor. Ernie's guitar playing put the capacity crowd on its feet, especially on "Who's That Lady." The evening was a joyful event.⁶⁴ The Isleys performed at two more concerts in the winter.

On Saturday, February 20, 1993, The Isley Brothers joined Meli'sa Morgan in a soul revue at the Arie Crown Theater in Chicago, Illinois. The artists performed two shows at 7:30 p.m. and 11:00 p.m. They were joined by R&B vocal group After 7. The event was sponsored by writer, producer, and director Shelly Garrett.⁶⁵ Shelly was married to Meli'sa for a brief time. A few months later, wedding bells rang for Ronald and Angela.

On June 26, Ronald Isley married Angela Winbush at Apostolic Faith Home Assembly Church in Los Angeles, California. The singing lovebirds exchanged wedding vows in a traditional ceremony before approximately four hundred guests. Friends and musical colleagues congratulated the newlyweds at a gala reception at the Four Seasons Hotel in Beverly Hills, California.⁶⁶ A month later, The Isley Brothers could be seen in a documentary.

During the summer, the Museum of African-American History & Arts in New York City exhibited Black films. On Saturday, July 24, *Soul Brothers of Rock 'N' Roll* was shown at 3:05 and 6:05 p.m. The documentary showcases several Black music legends, including The Temptations, Little Richard, The Four Tops, Chuck Berry, Chubby Checker, and The Isley Brothers.⁶⁷ Because of their longevity, The Isleys are among the most recognized names in rock 'n' roll, and that longevity encouraged them to record another live album.

Live!

The Isley Brothers released *Live!* in late August 1993. This album contains twelve tracks: "Here We Go Again," "Between the Sheets," "Smooth Sailin' Tonight," "Voyage to Atlantis," "Take Me to the Next Phase," "Medley—Choosey Lover/Footsteps in the Dark/Groove with You/Hello It's Me/Don't Say Goodnight (It's Time for Love)/Spend the Night (Ce Soir)," "That Lady," "It's Your Thing," "Shout," "For the Love of You," "Fight the Power," and "Make Me Say It Again."[68] Bruce Elder of AllMusic declares that the entire album has a warm, nostalgic tone to it, coupled with state-of-the-art recording.[69] *Live!* reached number thirty-four on the *Billboard* Top R&B Albums chart on October 9.[70]

The Isley Brothers used their talent to promote *Live!* by going on tour around the world for eight months. After the tour, the plan was to return to the studio and chart the next phase of their ever-developing careers. Ronald explained the group's longevity: "We try to keep our ears on the street. Our main secret is our faith in God, but beyond that, we try to keep real close in touch with what direction music is going—and what direction it should go in."[71] The Isley Brothers also appeared on a special Warner Brothers album.

In the winter of 1994, in tribute to Curtis Mayfield, Warner Brothers released *A Tribute to Curtis Mayfield*. A few years prior, while performing in Brooklyn, Curtis was seriously injured when a lighting rig hit him, making him permanently paralyzed. The tribute album contains seventeen tracks. It features "I'm So Proud" by The Isley Brothers, "People Get Ready" by Rod Stewart, "Choice of Colors" by Gladys Knight, "Gypsy Woman" by Whitney Houston, and other Curtis Mayfield hit songs performed by popular artists.[72] The Isleys' "I'm So Proud" did justice to the original, and it was released as a single.[73] The song peaked at number sixty-six on *Billboard*'s Hot R&B Singles chart on June 18, 1994, and reached number thirty-six on the Adult R&B Airplay chart on July 9.[74] In the spring of that year, The Isleys' case against Michael Bolton went to trial.

On Monday, April 25, a federal jury ruled that Michael Bolton's "Love Is a Wonderful Thing" is basically the same as the song of the same name released by The Isley Brothers in 1966. The jury reached the decision after about two and a half days of deliberations. Earlier that day, the eight-member jury announced that it was deadlocked, but US District Judge Lourdes Baird ordered them to continue deliberating. The jury agreed with The Isleys and Three Boys Music Corporation that crucial elements of The Isleys' "Love

Is a Wonderful Thing" were present in Bolton's song, which helped sell ten million copies of his 1991 *Time, Love & Tenderness*. Bolton's attorney, Robert Sugarman, and Andrew Goldmark had argued that the two songs "look different and they sound different."[75] The jury also decided how much The Isleys should be awarded.

On April 30, the jury decided that Bolton's "Love Is a Wonderful Thing" accounted for 28 percent of the profits from *Time, Love & Tenderness*. They also found that 66 percent of the profits from commercial uses of the song could be attributed to the inclusion of infringing elements. On May 9, the district court entered judgment in favor of The Isley Brothers based on the jury decisions. The defendants filed motions for a new trial, but they were dismissed by the district court. The allocation of damages would not be decided until late 1996.[76] In June, The Isley Brothers began touring with Bobby Womack and Angela Winbush, and a unique compilation project was published in August.

Beautiful Ballads

The compilation *Beautiful Ballads* consists of fourteen songs: "Brown Eyed Girl," "Hello It's Me," "Let's Fall in Love (Parts 1 & 2)," "You're the Key to My Heart," "You're Beside Me (Parts 1 & 2)," "I Once Had Your Love (And I Can't Let Go)," "Caravan of Love," "All in My Lover's Eyes," "Don't Let Me Be Lonely Tonight," "Make Me Say It Again, Girl (Parts 1 & 2)," "Voyage to Atlantis," "Choosey Lover," "Lay Lady Lay," and "Don't Say Goodnight (It's Time for Love) (Parts 1 & 2)."[77] Many Isley fans would be surprised "Sensuality" and "Between the Sheets" are not on this compilation. *Beautiful Ballads* peaked at number sixty-seven on the *Billboard* Top R&B Albums chart on September 3.[78] It was eventually certified gold by the RIAA on November 6, 2001, after selling more than half a million copies.[79] During the fall, The Isleys continued touring with Angela Winbush.

In late October, The Isley Brothers serenaded a sold-out audience at the Trump Plaza Hotel and Casino in Atlantic City, New Jersey. In fact, so many people attended that some had to sit in chairs along the walls because all the table seats were occupied. The Isleys sang many of their hits and a popular tune by Rufus and Chaka Khan titled "Sweet Thing." Special guest Angela Winbush opened with a duet with Ronald. They sang the Marvin Gaye classic

"Inner City Blues." The remainder of Angela's appearance was filled with gospel tunes.[80] On Friday, December 30, The Isley Brothers were back by popular demand at the Playhouse Square Center in Cleveland, Ohio. Special guests were Angela Winbush and Johnny "Guitar" Watson.[81] On the following day, The Isleys brought in the new year at the United Center in Chicago, Illinois. This was the first New Year's Eve celebration at the arena. Other performers included Angela Winbush, The O'Jays, The Whispers, El DeBarge, and comedians Sinbad and Dawn Keith.[82]

In February 1995, two compilations featuring The Isley Brothers were released. On February 14, Rhino Records released *Smooth Grooves: A Sensual Collection*.[83] This is a five-volume set of R&B ballads. The Isley Brothers' "Voyage to Atlantis" is featured on volume 3, and "Between the Sheets" is featured on volume 5.[84] The Isleys have been admired for their smooth, sultry ballads, as well as their messages of social uplift. On February 21, a compilation of various artists was released by The Right Stuff label. *Movin' On Up, Vol. 2* is an all-star sequel to the previous year's compilation of 1960s-era songs tracing the civil rights movement. This second volume embraces the '70s with songs focused on Black pride and self-empowerment.[85] The CD features "Fight the Power" by The Isley Brothers, "Inner City Blues" by Marvin Gaye, "The World Is a Ghetto" by War, "People Hold On" by Eddie Kendricks, and nine other tracks.[86] The Isley Brothers were soon featured on a motion picture soundtrack.

In April 1995, the comedy *Friday* was released in theaters. This film was written by DJ Pooh and rapper Ice Cube. For the soundtrack, The Isley Brothers provided the song titled "Tryin' to See Another Day." It samples music from The Isleys' "Coolin' Me Out," which is featured on *Showdown* (1978).[87] Ice Cube had proven himself a fan of The Isley Brothers when he sampled "Footsteps in the Dark" for his 1992 hit "It Was a Good Day." In addition to The Isley Brothers, the *Friday* soundtrack features music from other soul music legends, including Bootsy Collins, Rick James, Rose Royce, Zapp, and various hip-hop artists.[88] Tony Green, music critic for the *St. Petersburg Times*, stated that half of this hip-hop album doesn't groove as hard as the track by The Isley Brothers.[89] The track helped expose The Isleys to hip-hop fans, and songs on new compilations exposed them to younger R&B music fans.

In the summer, The Isley Brothers went on tour with the newly formed R&B girl group Brownstone.[90] Also, young R&B superstar R. Kelly took time to write and produce songs for The Isley Brothers' next studio album.[91] Ernie declared, "R. Kelly, being a big fan, was doing songs for us for the *Mission to Please* album." R. Kelly was recording in Florida when The Isleys went down to Miami. R. Kelly stated, "Oh, by the way guys, I'm doing a session tonight of my own stuff. I got this idea for a song, 'Down Low,' and Ronald, I'd like you, if you would, to sing on it, and Ernie, if you would, to play some lead guitar on it." And The Isleys said, "No problem."[92]

According to Richard Harrington, "No one has benefited more from the Isley influence than Kelly. Kelly might have gotten the Bolton treatment when his 'Your Body's Callin'' bore a strong resemblance to The Isleys' 'Groove with You,' with Kelly's phrasing also similar to Ronald's." Ronald stated, "I had a few phone calls in which he said, 'I bit off a bit of this song or that song on "Body's Callin',"' and he was trying not to be sued. That's how we began to work together on 'Down Low,' and from that day on, it's like he's been a member of the family. He knows what the Brothers know, and he's a genius in doing what he does."[93] Ronald and R. Kelly also worked with Quincy Jones.

In the fall, Quincy Jones released *Q's Jook Joint*. This album has fifteen tracks with several guest vocalists, including Stevie Wonder, Ray Charles, and Barry White. Ronald Isley and R. Kelly appear on the track titled "Heaven's Girl" with Aaron Hall and Charlie Wilson. This is a jazzy ballad with all four crooners providing quality vocals. Ronald's voice sounds unique and is the most recognizable.[94]

In December 1995, R. Kelly released "Down Low (Nobody Has to Know)," featuring The Isley Brothers. The song is about a man having an affair with another man's lover and wanting her to keep it a secret (down low).[95] In the video for the song, Ronald Isley portrays a mob boss named Mr. Biggs. Mr. Biggs leaves town and instructs his employee Kelly (R. Kelly) to take care of his wife Lila (Garcelle Beauvais) and warns him to never touch her. The two have an affair and are found in bed by Mr. Biggs. Mr. Biggs's bodyguards get revenge on Kelly and Lila.[96] Ronald would reprise the role of Mr. Biggs in music videos for other artists. "Down Low" soared to number one on *Billboard*'s Hot R&B singles chart on March 9, 1996, and stayed in that position for seven weeks. It also climbed to number four on the *Billboard* Hot 100 Songs chart on March 30, 1996.[97] "Down Low" became one of the best-selling singles of 1996 and reached platinum status for selling more than one million copies.[98] This collaboration with R. Kelly was a good move for The Isleys and was an indication of how well their next album would be received.

Chapter 8

Brother, Brother

The year 1996 was a special time in world history. Taiwan held its first presidential election. The United Nations adopted the Comprehensive Nuclear-Test-Ban Treaty. Major League Soccer had its first season. Mad cow disease hit Britain, and America hosted the Centennial Olympic Games in Atlanta, Georgia. The Isley Brothers played a part in the opening ceremony, and it was a prosperous year for them.

In January, *Don't Be a Menace to South Central While Drinking Your Juice in the Hood* was released, and "Let's Lay Together" by The Isley Brothers was featured on the soundtrack. This is a ballad written and produced by R. Kelly.[1] *Don't Be a Menace* is a comedy that spoofs Black coming-of-age hood films, such as *Menace to Society*, *South Central*, *Juice*, and *Boyz n the Hood*. The Isleys' feature on this soundtrack is an indication of the younger generation's appreciation for the legendary artists.

On February 29, the Rhythm and Blues Foundation's Pioneer Awards ceremony was held at the Hollywood Palladium in Los Angeles, California. The organization was started by music industry veterans and provides honors and cash awards to deserving, and often overlooked, musicians. The ceremony was hosted by past inductees Darlene Love and Mavis Staples. The 1996 honorees include Jay McShann, Dave Bartholomew, The Cadillacs, Eddie Floyd, Johnny Taylor, Bobby Womack, Doris Troy, Betty Everett, and The Isley Brothers. Bo Diddley received the Lifetime Achievement Award. All the honorees, except The Isley Brothers, performed. Ronald and Rudolph, the two surviving members of the original Isley recording trio, were there to receive the award but chose not to

The *Mission to Please* cover features the members in suits sitting on a Mercedes.

perform.² In the latter half of March, The Isleys released the first single from their next studio album.

"Let's Lay Together" is a romantic ballad sounds similar to some of The Isleys' slow jams of the 1970s.³ As stated previously, this song is featured on the soundtrack for *Don't Be a Menace to South Central While Drinking Your Juice in the Hood*. "Let's Lay Together" stalled at number ninety-three on the *Billboard* Hot 100 Songs chart on May 25, but it reached number twenty-four on the Hot R&B Singles chart on June 1. The song also climbed to number four on the Adult R&B Airplay chart on June 15.⁴ On May 14, The Isleys released their twenty-seventh studio album, titled *Mission to Please*.

Mission to Please contains ten songs: "Floatin' On Your Love (Featuring Angela Winbush)," "Whenever You're Ready," "Let's Lay Together," "Tears," "Can

I Have a Kiss (For Old Times Sake)?," "Mission to Please You," "Holding Back the Years," "Make Your Body Sing," "Let's Get Intimate," and "Slow Is the Way." The cover art shows the brothers in debonair fashion beside a luxury vehicle.[5]

Working with R. Kelly, Babyface, Keith Sweat, and Angela Winbush (who coproduced seven of the tracks with Ronald), The Isley Brothers created an album that married their unique soulful sound with the 1990s' beats and slow jam grooves. According to Ronald, the brothers plotted and planned this album. He declared, "We took time off after touring in 1994 and 1995 to come up with an album that could take us to another level. Knowing that our music is being sampled and featured on so many old school compilations, we wanted to come up with new songs that would have the same feel as our older material and yet have a 90s flavor." Ronald added, "The vocals for the song 'Let's Lay Together' were completed within half-an-hour, right there in the studio . . . the same thing with 'Can I Have a Kiss.' R. Kelly and Angela were writing the words as I was singing. That's how many of our sessions went in the 70s and 80s—and this album has the same kind of passion and spontaneity."[6] *Mission to Please* swiftly climbed the *Billboard* music charts. On June 1, it reached number thirty-one on the 200 Albums chart and rose to number two on the Top R&B Albums chart.[7] Shortly after, The Isleys were guests at the White House.

On Friday, June 14, President Bill Clinton invited The Isley Brothers to the White House for ceremonies marking Black Music Month.[8] Ernie brought along one of his guitars, a royal blue Stratocaster, as a gift for President Clinton. Ernie recalled the experience:

> It was in its case, and that caused quite a stir with the Secret Service people. They wanted to know what it was, and I told them it was a guitar. Well, there were dogs sniffing at it and I was told it would have to be X-rayed. Five minutes later, they brought the guitar back and told me that it would be better if they took it into the Oval Office instead of having me walk in with it. Can you believe that? So, we finally went in. I picked up the guitar case and presented it to the President. He seemed to really like it. He said it would be a perfect addition to the music room. I'll tell you, that was a humbling experience.[9]

Moreover, The Isleys received two prestigious awards.

On the same day as The Isley Brothers' White House visit, the International Association of African-American Music (IAAM) began its sixth annual celebration, which commemorated the seventeenth anniversary of Black Music Month. Scheduled for June 14–16 in Washington, DC, the celebration attracted members of the music industry, including music executives, recording artists, radio disc jockeys, retailers, and those who simply loved music. There were workshops and symposiums as well as artist showcases and tributes to music legends. One highlight of the celebration was the Diamond Award for Excellence ceremony, which occurred Saturday, June 15. Some of the honorees were Earth, Wind & Fire, Gladys Knight, and The Isley Brothers.[10] A week later, The Isleys were honored by *Vibe*.

On June 22, *Vibe* magazine presented its first Vibe Props Legend Award to The Isley Brothers at Pleasure Island/Disney World in honor of their forty-plus years in the music business. *Vibe* president Keith Clinkscales declared, "Without The Isley Brothers, there would be no R. Kelly, Annie Lennox or Teddy Riley. Pop music would be . . . something much less compelling." Ernie Isley agreed. He stated, "There's not another group whose resume starts with early rock, goes through the twist, the British Invasion, psychedelic stuff, soul, funk, disco and rap eras." Later that day, The Isleys headlined the Vibe Magazine Black Music Month Celebration at Pleasure Island.[11] A day before receiving the award from *Vibe*, they performed at the Hampton Jazz Festival.

The twenty-ninth Hampton Jazz Festival was held from Thursday, June 20 to Sunday, June 23, in Hampton, Virginia. Opening night was R&B Roots Night, which featured performances by artists who were instrumental in giving R&B music and the Hampton tradition their enduring names. Opening night artists included Millie Jackson, Isaac Hayes, Harold Melvin & The Blue Notes, and of course, The Isley Brothers. The legendary weekend-long concert series is sponsored jointly by the City of Hampton, Hampton University, and jazz impresario George Wein's Festival Productions Inc.[12] Within three weeks, *Mission to Please* was certified gold by the RIAA on July 16.[13] The Isleys soon traveled to Atlanta, Georgia, to begin their Mission to Please Tour.

Atlanta hosted the 1996 Summer Olympics from July 19 until August 4. Around that time, an eighteen-night concert series was held at Underground Atlanta to provide entertainment near the Olympic venues. On Wednesday, July 24, The Isley Brothers headlined a concert with the band War. The audience consisted of more than 1,500 fans during the standing room–only performance.[14] The Isleys performed with a new background singer. Kelly Price is a singer/songwriter who had done studio work with Ronald. He was so impressed with her that he asked her to fill in at the last minute when one of his background singers was not able to perform.[15] Two days later, they traveled to Boston, Massachusetts.

The Isley Brothers performed at the Berklee Performance Center in Boston on Friday, July 26. Patricia Smith of the *Boston Globe* was fortunate to attend the concert and described the performance. She claimed The Isleys proved they could still wring sweat out of a love ballad, and the funk was definitely in the house. The audience was a mixture of baby boomers and young people who got on the Isley train only after Ice Cube sampled their hit "Footsteps in the Dark." Everyone knew all the words to the songs, and the first strains of recognized classics caused the crowd to jump out their seats.

They Isley Brothers kicked off the set with the pounding "Fight the Power," sliding right into a steamy medley of "For the Love of You" and "Between the Sheets." Dancing throughout were four graceful, attractive dancers. Backup singers refused to be relegated to the background, with the dynamic Angela Winbush as part of the trio. She later brought the house down in a too-short duet with Ronald of "Summer Breeze." Although Ronald sang a couple of songs from *Mission to Please*, he wisely chose to sing old classics, such as "Work to Do," "Groove with You," "Hello It's Me," "It's Your Thing," and others. Ernie wailed on guitar with his teeth, behind his back, over his head, and between his legs on a romping "That Lady." By the time the group went all the way back with "Shout," middle-agers had gone wild. Sweat was dripping, and the solemn Berklee had already soaked up more than its share of soul. The group's final song was "Voyage to Atlantis." Ernie's opening guitar licks rattled the rafters, and the audience screamed and sang along. According to Smith, it was the best concert to hit Boston that year.[16] At the end of the show, Ronald gave Kelly Price the opportunity to shine.

Ronald began to croon, "You abandoned me. Love don't live here anymore." He then said, "Ladies and gentlemen, I want you to meet somebody. Come here, Kelly. Kelly, come here." Kelly moved forward. Ronald told Kelly's background and how he met her. He declared that her name is one that would be heard for decades. He stated that she would be a household word and be mentioned in sentences with Gladys, Aretha, and Patti. Ronald started singing "Love Don't Live Here Anymore" again. He gave Kelly the mic and told her to sing. She closed her eyes and sang. When she opened her eyes, the entire crowd was standing screaming. Ronald added, "You will be hearing from her soon, everybody. This is my new artist, Kelly Price." Kelly was on the road with The Isleys for nine months, and she finished her deal with

T-Neck Records while touring.[17] She is now recognized among the great soul music vocalists. The Mission to Please Tour continued through September.[18]

In September, The Isley Brothers released the second single from *Mission to Please*, titled "Floatin' On Your Love (Featuring Angela Winbush)." This is one of the songs that has a nineties hip-hop groove.[19] In fact, hip-hop artists Sean Combs, Lil' Kim, and Luther Campbell appear in the music video. In the video, Mr. Biggs (Ronald) is onstage singing while Angela's character walks in on the arm of her lover. Soon, Angela begins to sing back to Mr. Biggs and they come together to sing to each other. After that, Lil' Kim jumps out of a cake and has a few rap lyrics for Mr. Biggs.[20] *Floatin' On Your Love* climbed to number eleven on the *Billboard* Adult R&B Airplay chart on September 14, but it peaked at number forty-seven on the Hot 100 Songs chart on November 2. The song also reached number fourteen on the Top R&B Songs chart on November 11.[21] At the time, there were lots of references to the no-nonsense gangster Mr. Biggs.

When the Mission to Please Tour stopped at Constitution Hall in Washington, DC, on Friday, September 20, Mr. Biggs's mob image was at odds with Ronald's status as legendary soul man. Ronald showed that ruthlessness has nothing to do with the heart necessary for a fifty-five-year-old man to get on his knees in his good suit and sing some of the steamiest love songs ever written, such as "Hello It's Me," "Between the Sheets," or "Mission to Please You." Mr. Biggs gets mucked up as soon as Ronald pours on his hot chocolate tenor and a falsetto that trails to a whisper. The concert fused slick 1990s marketing and '70s showmanship. Trench-coated dancers carried plastic machine guns that parodied mob life. Mr. Biggs is a powerful image that draws young fans attracted to wealth and power and older fans who simply like to see a man dressing sharp.

Ronald changed his suits three times, going from bright red to bright yellow to candy green, and offered the audience the improbable vision of Mr. Biggs singing the 1970s anthem "Fight the Power." At another point, he was suddenly transformed into a slick preacher, raising the audience to its feet for the 1959 classic "Shout." For that number, dancers first donned choir robes, then stripped to spandex lace for a wayward-woman look. When the spotlight wasn't on Ronald, it often fell on Ernie, who showed his ferocity on lead guitar, taking extended solos that alternated between his trademark wails and recognizable funky expressions. At the end of the show, Ronald strode onstage for his finale, "Down Low." The band played the intro, which is reminiscent of *The Godfather* soundtrack. Ronald poured his voice into the lyrics. Then, he jolted the audience, raising his hands as if in victory, asking, "How y'all like Mr. Biggs?"²² Mr. Biggs helped The Isley Brothers remain popular throughout the 1990s. Because of their popularity, they performed a new single from *Mission to Please* titled "Tears" at the Second Annual Soul Train Lady of Soul Awards, which aired on September 9.

"Tears" is a smooth ballad written by Babyface. It is about a man crying tears of gratitude for his love interest.²³ In the music video, Angela Winbush portrays Ronald's wife who has lapsed into a coma after a car accident. Ronald comes to the hospital and expresses his undying love for her while singing.²⁴ "Tears" eventually reached number twelve on the *Billboard* Hot R&B Songs chart on February 1, 1997, and it peaked at number fifty-five on the Hot 100 songs chart on February 15. "Tears" also rose to number one on the Adult R&B Airplay chart on February 22. It was in that position for two weeks.²⁵ This was the last single from *Mission to Please*, and critics affirmed the album's gold status.

Stephen Thomas Erlewine of AllMusic declares that *Mission to Please* is one of The Isley Brothers' "strongest efforts of the latter part of their career." He wrote, "The majority of the songs on the album are first-rate '90s contemporary R&B, and those that aren't quite as strong make for pleasing fillers. As a result, *Mission to Please* is a testament to the talents of not only The Isleys, but also their far-reaching influence." They are fortunate to have given inspiration to such gifted songwriters and musicians who worked on the album.²⁶ Lemon Wire wrote, "With the support of some of the hottest R&B producers available, including R. Kelly, Babyface, and Keith Sweat, The Isleys step into the present with an LP filled with lyrics reminiscent of their classic hits and a sound that brings them into the '90s."²⁷ The Isley Brothers also showcased their talents on a Christmas CD.

In mid-November, Island Records released *Special Gift*. This twelve-track holiday album features traditional Christmas carols done with a nineties flair. The songs are performed by Island Black Music recording artists, including The Isley Brothers, who perform the title track. Other artists on the CD include Angela Winbush, Will Downing, Dru Hill, and Kurtis Blow. The renditions range from R&B to rap to bass style.²⁸ Ronald also introduced a new character on *The Steve Harvey Show*.

The Steve Harvey Show is an American sitcom that aired on the WB network from 1996 until 2002. In the sitcom, Steve Harvey portrays Steve

Hightower, a 1970s funk music legend who has become a high school music teacher. In the "High Top Reunion" episode, Steve reunites with his group, Steve Hightower and The Hightops. Ronald portrays a member named Pretty Tony. This was a recurring role for him until 2001. In December, The Isleys received good news about their lawsuit against Michael Bolton.

On December 5, the district court adopted the findings of the Special Master's Amended Report about the allocation of damages. In the final judgment entered against Michael Bolton and his associates, the district court ordered Sony Music to pay $4,218,838, Bolton to pay $932,924, Goldmark to pay $220,785, and their music publishing companies to pay $75,900. The defendants would soon appeal this decision.[29] This case would not be completely settled until 2001.

Later in December, The Isley Brothers donated memorabilia to the Hollywood Hard Rock Café. They donated two signature stage costumes designed by Georgia O'Dell and one of Ernie's guitars for display at the restaurant. The memorabilia donation followed the presentation of The Isleys' gold album *Mission to Please*. By that time, the album had sold over 760,000 units.[30] *Mission to Please* was certified platinum by the RIAA on January 23, 1997.[31] In early winter, The Isleys were in the latter part of their Mission to Please Tour.

On the third weekend of January, The Isley Brothers traveled to Atlantic City, New Jersey. They performed at the Tropicana Casino and Resort for two shows on Saturday, January 18, and one show on Sunday, January 19. On Monday, January 20, The Isleys returned to Washington, DC, for President Clinton's second inauguration.

For the inauguration, The Isley Brothers performed in the Ohio-Pennsylvania Ball at the National Building Museum. The Isleys shared the stage with Angela Winbush and The Coasters as they sang "This Old Heart of Mine" while the Clintons danced. This song has the popular lyric "I love you." The singers and the crowd proclaimed to the Clintons, "We love you. We love you." The Isleys continued their tour in major cities, such as Houston, Cincinnati, and New York. And on March 7, the brothers performed "Tears" at the Eleventh Annual Soul Train Music Awards, at which *Mission to Please* was nominated for Best R&B/Soul Album by a Group, Band or Duo.[32] After their successful album, The Isleys stayed in demand.

The Isley Brothers performed at several music festivals during the summer. On Memorial Day weekend, they performed at Sinbad's 70s Soul Music

Festival: Funk Part III in Oranjestad, Aruba.³³ The brothers also performed at the Muskegon Summer Celebration at the end of June in Muskegon, Michigan.³⁴ On July 3, Ihe Isleys performed at the Third Annual Essence Music Fest in New Orleans, Louisiana.³⁵ On July 19, they performed at the Coors Light Festival in Cincinnati, Ohio.³⁶ Soon, classic music by the group was reissued.

In early August, four classic albums were released for the first time on CD by Columbia/Legacy. Those albums are *The Brothers: Isley*, *Get Into Something*, *Givin' It Back*, and *Brother, Brother, Brother*. These four albums produced fifteen hits by The Isley Brothers. They succeeded whether doing their own compositions ("It's Your Thing," "Get Into Something," "Work to Do") or covers of well-known tunes ("Love the One You're With," "Spill the Wine," "Lay Lady Lay"). It never mattered. Ronald's sensual tenor and the group's blistering funk imbued any song they did with a sound that was distinctly Isley. *The Brothers: Isley* is notable as the first album on which the three younger brothers provided instrumentation.³⁷ In addition, a compilation published.

Greatest Hits

Epic Records released a compilation in Europe simply titled *Greatest Hits*. This CD contains thirteen tracks: "Summer Breeze," "That Lady," "Harvest for the World (Prelude)," "Harvest for the World," "Hope You Feel Better Love," "Highways of My Life," "Caravan of Love," "Between the Sheets," "Don't Let Me Be Lonely Tonight," "Who Loves You Better," "The Pride," "Love the One You're With," and "It's a Disco Night (Rock Don't Stop)."³⁸ This CD is another indication of the quality of The Isleys' catalogue. A solo album had also been published.

In 1997, Rudolph Isley released his only solo album, titled *Shouting for Jesus*. This is a gospel album written and produced by Rudolph and his wife, Elaine Jasper Isley. *Shouting for Jesus* features Clarence MacDonald on keys and Paul Jackson on guitar.³⁹ As stated previously, Rudolph became a minister of the gospel after leaving the group. While Rudolph was charting new territory, misfortune fell on his youngest brother, Marvin.

In 1997, Marvin Isley was forced to leave The Isley Brothers because of diabetes. He was diagnosed with the disease in 1990. Marvin soon had to have both of his legs amputated.[40] He would no longer be seen at special appearances such as award shows and interviews. From that point onward, Ronald and Ernie would be the only members of the group. In mid-autumn, Ronald and Ernie traveled overseas for another music festival.

The Second Annual Air Jamaica Jazz and Blues Festival took place from Friday, November 7, through Sunday, November 9. It was held at the Great Lawn of the Rose Hall Great House in Montego Bay, Jamaica. The Isley Brothers demonstrated why they were able to maintain their relevance in pop music by adapting to the changing times without sacrificing typical soul ballads. Other soul music artists performed, including George Duke, Regina Bell, and Eyrkah Badu.[41] This was a busy time for the brothers and the second consecutive year in which they appeared on a Christmas CD.

In late autumn, *The Soul Train Christmas Starfest Album* was released. This collection features veteran R&B acts (The Isley Brothers, James Brown, Stevie Wonder) alongside younger artists (Boyz II Men, New Edition, En Vogue). The Isleys' "Special Gift" is featured. The seasoned artists fare well, bringing some depth to their performances. But the young singers here frequently settle in timid arrangements.[42] "Special Gift" peaked at number thirty-one on the *Billboard* Adult R&B Airplay chart on January 10, 1998.[43] In the beginning of the new year, Ronald could be seen in a different acting role.

On January 18, 1998, Ronald appeared in an episode of *The Jamie Foxx Show*, an American sitcom that aired on the WB network from 1996 until 2001. In the sitcom, Jamie Foxx portrays Jamie King, a young man who moved from Texas to Los Angeles to pursue a music career. While in the big city, he works at his aunt and uncle's hotel. In the "Papa Don't Preach" episode, Ronald portrays an overprotective preacher father who won't allow his daughter Oda Mae (Mary J. Blige) to sing secular music. No matter what type of character he portrays, there is no mistaking the voice of Ronald Isley. Acting is just another phase in Ronald's constantly evolving career, and he showed no signs of slowing down.[44]

Ernie gave insight when he was asked how a group that began in the 1950s managed to stay current and record chart-topping songs in the late 1990s. He declared, "That's a blessing. That's ordained from on high. We thrive on competition. We love the music. We'd hear something from Philly Int'l. We'd hear something from Stevie Wonder. We'd hear something from Earth, Wind & Fire and say 'Alright, you hear how strong these guys are. What are WE going to do?' We've always been willing to change."[45] That willingness to change kept The Isley Brothers on the road. They performed two shows per day in the Superstar Theater at Resorts Casino Hotel in Atlantic City on Friday, January 23, and Saturday, January 24.[46] Because of their success and longevity, The Isleys were honored by the NAACP.

The twenty-ninth NAACP Image Awards ceremony was held on February 14, 1998, at the Pasadena Civic Auditorium in Pasadena, California. The Isley Brothers were inducted into the Image Awards Hall of Fame by Gregory Hines. Before the induction, Steve Harvey played a game called "Name that Groove," in which he selected audience members to name the song after hearing a snippet. Ronald and Ernie were present for the induction and gave acceptance speeches. The program aired March 5 on the Fox Network.[47] The Isleys continued to perform at select venues throughout the spring.

In August, The Isley Brothers joined Earth, Wind & Fire for the Sweet Sounds of Soul Tour. It was the first time these legendary soul acts toured together. Honey Nut Cheerios, made by Minneapolis-based General Mills, sponsored the tour and featured a $3.99 CD offer on the back of packages. The CD featured three hit songs from each of the three groups. David Dix, director of communications for General Mills, stated, "The music created by these groups is beloved the world over, and Honey Nut Cheerios is extremely proud to be bringing these legendary music groups to cities all across America." The tour endured through October with stops in New York, Los Angeles, and major cities in between.[48] With Honey Nut Cheerios as the sponsor, the tour attracted a diverse crowd. After the tour, Ronald was honored for his stability in the music business.

The first WGCI-AM/FM Urban Awards occurred Saturday, November 14, at the Chicago Theatre. The program was hosted by Steve Harvey, who once served as host of the WGCI-FM morning show. The Lifetime Achievement Award was bestowed on Ronald Isley. Mary Dyson, president of WGCI, exclaimed, "Ronald Isley has been the catalyst for keeping The Isley Brothers at the forefront of urban music for four decades. We couldn't have chosen a more worthy musical pioneer."[49] Ronald had earned his place in music history and finished the year in old-school style.

The Isley Brothers performed at the Star Plaza Theatre in Merrillville, Indiana, on Saturday, December 26. After more than forty years in entertainment, Ronald proved he hadn't lost his touch. He drove the crowd wild as he stepped out "sharp as a tack" in a gold suit with matching coat and his famous cane, working his Mr. Biggs/old-school "playa" persona. He later changed into a blue "playa" suit. Ronald had the crowd cheering as he sang such hits as "Summer Breeze," "Harvest for the World," Footsteps in the Dark," and many more. He also sang a little bit from "Friend of Mine" remix. Not forgetting his roots, Ronald performed vintage hits "Shout," "Twist and Shout," and "It's Your Thing."[50] No matter what decade Ronald pulls his songs from, fans are likely to be satisfied.

In the spring of 1999, The Isley Brothers were back in Atlantic City. They performed in the Tropicana Showroom at the Tropicana Casino and Resort for one show on Friday, March 26, and two shows on Saturday, March 27.[51] The Isleys also performed at the Thirtieth Anniversary New Orleans Jazz & Heritage Festival, which occurred Friday, April 23, until Sunday, May 2.[52] In the summer, The Isley Brothers were a part of the Jammin' Tour 1999. This soul music tour included other legendary bands: The Gap Band, Kool & the Gang, and Morris Day and the Time.[53]

Steve Morse of the *Boston Globe* wrote about one concert that occurred at the BankBoston Pavilion in Boston, Massachusetts:

> The Isley Brothers headlined and were a still-potent combination of earthy R&B music, erotic guitar solos, and a timeless showmanship right from the start, when Ronald came out in a bright yellow suit and floor-length yellow jacket that summoned near-acid flashbacks. . . . The Isleys pumped out the funky grit of "It's Your Thing" and the all-time classic "Shout," while inducing a party atmosphere throughout. Ernie emphasized the Hendrix influence by playing the guitar over his head, under his legs, and even under the legs of one of the two female dancers who gyrated suggestively during some songs. . . . The Isleys caught fire quickly with "Fight the Power" and built a classics-filled, groove-brimming set that included a reworking of Seals & Crofts's "Summer Breeze," which a had passionate Ernie Isley solo at the end. And brothers weren't the only story in the show, since it also featured a new group of young, backup-singing sisters: Kim, Krystal, and Kandy Johnson, who were discovered in Los Angeles. The result was nostalgic nirvana with a contemporary twist.[54]

During the tour, a movie soundtrack featuring The Isley Brothers was published.

On July 14, *Muppets from Space* was released. This is a family movie packed with stars, both Muppet and human. "It's Your Thing" by The Isley Brothers is featured on the soundtrack titled *Muppets from Space: The Ultimate Muppet Trip*. The album also features songs from The O'Jays, The Commodores, James Brown, and other soul artists, which makes for a funky soundtrack.[55] A new anthology was also published.

It's Your Thing: The Story of The Isley Brothers

On August 24, Sony Legacy's "Rhythm & Soul" Series released the three-CD box set titled *It's Your Thing: The Story of The Isley Brothers*.[56] The Isley story was first captured on *The Isley Brothers Story*, the 1991 three-CD, forty-eight-track series from Rhino. The same tale is told in a little more detail on *It's Your Thing: The Story of the Isley Brothers*. This anthology offers more of the rare 1957–59 singles (including a crazed novelty number, "Rockin' McDonald" (based on the nursery rhyme), but fewer of the 1960–65 singles on RCA, Atlantic, and United Artists. The Rhino set ends with the 1985 Isley/Jasper/Isley hit "Caravan of Love," but this set goes on, including The Isleys' version of "I'm So Proud" from *A Tribute to Curtis Mayfield*.[57]

Volume one contains twenty tracks:

1. "Building Up to Shout (Live, Yankee Stad.)"
2. "Shout (Parts 1 & 2)"
3. "Shout (Live from the TV Show Shindig)"
4. "Twist and Shout"
5. "Who's That Lady"
6. "Time After Time"
7. "Move Over and Let Me Dance"
8. "Testify (Parts 1 & 2)"
9. "This Old Heart of Mine (Is Weak for You)"
10. "Take Me In Your Arms"
11. "It's Your Thing"
12. "I Turned You On"
13. "Get Into Something"
14. "Freedom"
15. "Keep On Doin'"
16. "The Blacker the Berrie"
17. "Rockin' McDonald"
18. "Don't Be Jealous"
19. "Angels Cried"
20. "It's Your Thing (Live at Yankee Stad.)"

Volume two contains fifteen tracks:

1. "That Lady (Parts 1 & 2)"
2. "Don't Let Me Be Lonely Tonight"
3. "For the Love of You (Parts 1 & 2)"
4. "Brother, Brother"
5. "Work to Do"
6. "Lay Away"
7. "Cold Bologna"
8. "Midnight Sky (Parts 1 & 2)"
9. "Hello It's Me"
10. "Make Me Say It Again, Girl (Pts 1 & 2)"
11. "Summer Breeze"
12. "Live It Up (Parts 1 & 2)"
13. "Fight the Power (Parts 1 & 2)"
14. "Fire and Rain"
15. "Love the One You're With"

Volume three contains fifteen tracks:

1. "Harvest for the World (Prelude)"
2. "Harvest for the World"
3. "Groove with You"
4. "For the Love of You"
5. "Mission to Please You"
6. "Between the Sheets"
7. "Caravan of Love"
8. "I'm So Proud"
9. "Smooth Sailin' Tonight"
10. "Voyage to Atlantis"
11. "Take Me to the Next Phase (Parts 1 & 2)"
12. "The Pride (Parts 1 & 2)"
13. "(At Your Best) You Are Love"
14. "Footsteps in the Dark (Parts 1 & 2)"
15. "Don't Say Goodnight (It's Time for Love)"[58]

The biggest difference between this anthology and other compilations is the generous liner notes and photos in the fifty-two-page booklet. Commentary by poet Nikki Giovanni, the *New York Times*'s William Rhoden, Aaron Neville, Bobby Womack, and The Isley Brothers themselves provides a rich context for the reinventions repeatedly pulled off by these talented siblings.[59] The Isley Brothers continued to perform throughout 1999 as the world looked forward to the new year.

The year 1999 was the last year of the decade, the last year of the century, and the last year of the millennium. Throughout the year, Prince's 1982 hit "1999" was playing constantly over the airwaves and was often played on television programs. Some people believed the world was about to end, and many prepared for a possible cataclysmic computer and internet crash called Y2K. Aside from that, what did the future hold for The Isley Brothers? There were only two brothers left in the group. Ernie was approaching the age of fifty, and Ronald was approaching sixty. How much longer could they keep going? Only time could tell.

Chapter 9

Winner Takes All

As the year 1999 came to an end, people all around the world were planning extravagant celebrations for the new millennium. Prince's 1982 hit song "1999" was being played on the airwaves and at social events. While many people were excited about the turn of the millennium, others were worried about the Y2K hysteria. Y2K is short for year 2000, and the problem was with computers. Computer programmers had long been rendering years with the last two digits only. For example, "89" was used in place of 1989. It was a way of saving bits on the computer. So, what would happen when 1999 clicked over into 2000? Would computers think we were moving back in time to 1900? Then anything electronic might go crazy! There could be massive power failures. Financial records could disappear. Planes might fall from the sky, and missiles could be launched by mistake.[1] So, what would happen at the turn of the millennium? Would the computer systems crash? Those questions were soon answered.

On December 31, 1999, people around the world were celebrating to bring in the new year, the new decade, the new century, and the new millennium. In their specific time zones, citizens of the world counted down Five . . . Four . . . Three . . . Two . . . One . . . Happy New Year! Happy New Century! Happy New Millennium! There were no catastrophes. Any Y2K problems that occurred were minor.[2]

Ronald's first priority of the new millennium was taking care of his finances. He had filed for chapter 7 bankruptcy in 1997, due in large part to an Internal Revenue Service claim of nearly $5 million. His assets were scheduled to be auctioned January 18 at bankruptcy court in Los Angeles.

The most valuable property was his one-third interest in The Isley Brothers' music catalogue. Ronald and his brothers, Rudolph and the late O'Kelly, had written more than two hundred songs, including "Twist and Shout," "It's Your Thing," and "That Lady." EMI Recorded Music put in a bid of $4.1 million to acquire Ronald's portion of songwriter and publishing rights.[3]

Later in the month, The Isley Brothers' music catalogue was pulled from the auction block after an investment group proposed a $6.5 million deal that would let Ronald retain his share of the rights to his songs. US Bankruptcy Court in Los Angeles postponed the auction until February 23 after the proposed deal was reached on January 18 by the Pullman Group, EMI (one of The Isleys' former record companies), Ronald, and his bankruptcy trustee. The Pullman Group invented the so-called Bowie bonds, named after rock music artist David Bowie, in which music assets are pledged to secure bonds and the debt is repaid from royalties. The Pullman Group would issue fifteen- to twenty-year bonds to cover Ronald's debt. Ronald or his heirs would resume receiving profits from the song copyrights after the bonds expire.[4]

Surprisingly, in February, singer Michael Bolton attempted to buy the assets of Ronald Isley. Bolton had offered $5.3 million for Ronald's estate, including the right to receive royalties from Ronald's songs. Some music industry observers saw Bolton's offer as an ironic turnaround, given that The Isleys and their record company had successfully sued Bolton in 1994 for copyright infringement. Among the assets Bolton sought in the bankruptcy case was Ronald's portion of the 1994 jury award. Bolton was still appealing that judgment, claiming that he and his cowriter never heard The Isleys' song. Bolton's offer was declined in the final week of February, when federal judge Kathleen March accepted a $4.8 million bid for Ronald's assets from the Pullman Group. That bid had the blessing of EMI and Ronald Isley, Chris Jasper, and Marvin Isley.

Although the Pullman Group's bid was less than Bolton's, the lawyers said, judge Kathleen March ruled that Pullman Group's was superior because Bolton's was still contingent on raising financing and legally problematic, considering Bolton had no agreement with EMI, the Pullman Group, or Ronald, Chris, and Marvin. Lee Bogdanoff, an attorney for the Pullman Group, compared Bolton to a guest who shows up at a wedding offering to marry the bride. "It's possible," said *Pollstar* magazine editor Gary Bongiovanni, "that Michael Bolton was motivated by a little revenge.[5]

This was a satisfying time for The Isley Brothers. Because of the agreement with the Pullman Group, Ronald was able to take care of most of his debt, and a blow was dealt to Michael Bolton. The deal allowed The Isleys to continue with their career. In fact, on Valentine's Day, The Isley Brothers headlined a concert with Mint Condition at the Orpheum Theatre in Minneapolis, Minnesota. The Isleys continued to prove they were still relevant and just as popular as younger artists in the music business. But their issue with Michael Bolton was not over yet.

In early May, the Ninth US Circuit Court of Appeals upheld a $5.4 million verdict against Michael Bolton. A three-judge panel said a jury had sufficient evidence to reach its decision in 1994. The panel awarded The Isley Brothers 66 percent of all past and future royalties from the single and 28 percent of past and future royalties from Bolton's *Time, Love & Tenderness*. "It's a wonderful, wonderful victory for the jury system," said lawyer John McNicholas, who represented The Isleys.[6] Bolton was determined to take this case all the way to the Supreme Court, but The Isleys received more good news.

Near the end of June, David Pullman proudly announced the completion of the Pullman Bond music securitization with Rudolph Isley, Ronald Isley, and the estate of O'Kelly Isley. This completed $10 million deal joined the famous series of Pullman bonds, which includes the $55 million Bowie bonds, the $30 million Holland-Dozier-Holland (Motown hit machine) bonds, the $30 million James Brown bonds, and an eight-figure deal with Ashford & Simpson. At the time, there were over three hundred songs in the Isley catalogue, including fifty *Billboard* hits. The Isley Pullman Bond transaction was rated at the single-A level by two nationally recognized rating agencies.

Rudolph and Ronald were the founders, creators, and 100 percent owners of The Isley Brothers' catalogue and co-owners of the estate of O'Kelly, the third founder and equal member of their companies Three Boys Music Group and Triple Three Music. David Pullman stated, "Never have I seen such a bond among brothers as between Rudolph and Ronald Isley, who for six decades as hit makers have proven over and over they stick together through thick and thin. Their bond is unbreakable." Rudolph and Ronald declared that David Pullman and the Pullman Group embody the hit song they wrote, "Fight the Power."[7] After securing such a lucrative deal, The Isley Brothers performed in various cities throughout the summer and fall, and a compilation CD was published.

The Ultimate Isley Brothers

On October 17, Epic/Legacy released *The Ultimate Isley Brothers*. This CD contains seventeen songs: "It's Your Thing," "That Lady (Parts 1 & 2)," "Harvest for the World," "Work to Do," "Spill the Wine," "Summer Breeze," "Caravan of Love," "For the Love of You (Parts 1 & 2)," "Groove with You," "Twist and Shout," "Live It Up (Part 1)," "Fight the Power (Part 1)," "The Pride (Part 1)," "Shout (Parts 1 & 2)," "Love the One You're With," "Between the Sheets," and "Don't Say Goodnight (It's Time for Love) (Part 1)."[8] Richie Unterberger of AllMusic wrote that The Isley Brothers have had such a long and varied career that trying to sum up their highlights in a best-of package is bound to fall short of the mark. Although every song on this anthology was a hit, it short-changes their vital (and extensive) pre-1970 output.[9] Liner notes for this addition to Legacy's "Rhythm & Soul Series" were written by Elvis Mitchell, film critic for the *New York Times* and a commentator on National Public Radio.[10] The Isleys are featured on two other projects released later in the year.

In November 2000, Hip-O Records released the box set *The Funk Box*. Covering 1970–1980, this four-disc, fifty-five-song set features The Isleys' "Fight the Power" and juicy fatback grooves from the regal likes of James Brown, Parliament, Slave, Brass Construction, The New Birth, and many more.[11] In December, Harmless Records released *Stand Up and Be Counted: Soul, Funk and Jazz from a Revolutionary Era, Vol. 2*. Like its predecessor, this CD is a compelling portrait of the years of Black Power in America, an age of extravagant afros and flamboyant political rhetoric. The Isleys' "Fight the Power" is also on this project, which features songs from the early 1970s. Other artists featured are James Brown, Nikki Giovanni, The Watts Poets, and The Voices of East Harlem.[12] In the new year, a romantic compilation CD was published.

Love Songs

On January 9, 2001, Sony Legacy released collections of love songs by music legends Duke Ellington, Aretha Franklin, Patti LaBelle, Frank Sinatra, and The Isley Brothers for romantics who tried to get a jump on Valentine's Day.[13] The Isley CD, simply titled *Love Songs*, contains thirteen songs: "Hello It's Me," "Groove with You," "For the Love of You (Parts 1 & 2)," "All in My Lover's

Eyes," "Voyage to Atlantis," "I Once Had Your Love (And I Can't Let Go)," "Footsteps in the Dark (Parts 1 & 2)," "Sensuality (Parts 1 & 2)," "Make Me Say It Again, Girl (Parts 1 & 2)," "Summer Breeze," "Between the Sheets," "(At Your Best) You Are Love (Parts 1 & 2)," and "How Lucky I Am (Parts 1 & 2)."[14] This album actually charted on the *Billboard* Top R&B Albums chart and peaked at ninety-one on April 21.[15] Less than two weeks after the release of *Love Songs*, The Isleys received celebratory news.

On January 22, 2001, the US Supreme Court refused to hear Michael Bolton's appeal of the May 2000 decision by the Ninth US Circuit Court of Appeals in San Francisco. Because of this, the case was closed permanently, and Bolton had to pay. The battle was over, and The Isley Brothers felt vindicated. In an interview with *Billboard*, Ronald stated, "He could have settled the case for way less money, rightful money, and he didn't want to do it. And then he got into this kind of contest thing with us: I'm going to show you. And that's what it turned out to be. I lost a lot of respect that I had for him as an artist. But we just went all the way with it."

Ronald always felt he had a solid case against Bolton. When asked if he had met Bolton before the case, Ronald replied, "Angela was performing on the Lou Rawls' annual UNCF telethon. And so was Bolton. She was going to introduce me to him and he said, 'Hey, you don't have to introduce me to him. I know all of his stuff from a kid on up.' And I didn't forget that he said that." Ronald stated that in the courtroom, Bolton forgot Lou Rawls's name. He even forgot the show. Bolton declared, "Well, I've played so many shows." Ronald described Bolton as a connoisseur of Black music, but on the witness stand, Bolton told people he didn't know who The Isley Brothers were. He was told that they are the same group who sang "Twist and Shout." Bolton responded by saying, "I thought that was The Beatles." When Bolton was asked about "For the Love of You," he replied, "I thought that was Whitney Houston." When asked about "Summer Breeze," he responded, "I thought that I heard Ernie play on that but I thought it was somebody else." Ernie declared, "He told one lie after another. He made himself look real stupid."[16] It appeared to be an open-and-shut case. This issue was finally put to rest. In the following month, The Isleys received an overdue honor.

The Fifteenth Annual Soul Train Music Awards was held at the Shrine Auditorium in Los Angeles on February 28. The Isley Brothers received the Quincy Jones Award for "Outstanding Career Achievements." By this time, The Isleys had been in the music business over forty years and had a staggering fifty singles on the *Billboard* charts. Hits such as "That Lady," "Fight the Power," "Footsteps in the Dark," and "For the Love of You" remain standards on Urban Adult Contemporary and "Jammin' Gold" playlists.[17] Ronald and Ernie were working on their next studio album while Marvin was informing people about the effects and severity of diabetes.

After moving from Los Angeles to metro Atlanta, Georgia, Marvin and his wife Sheila had taken up diabetes awareness as unofficial spokesmen for the American Diabetes Association, including appearing at African American outreach programs and on educational videos and public service announcements. Since his diagnosis, he had his legs amputated, underwent a kidney transplant, and lost movement in his left hand. Marvin told *The Atlanta Constitution*, "It's a sneaky disease. It's silent. Diabetes is a very serious disease with a lot of devastating effects. Finally, I'm doing it right—no sugar, no salt. But I could have done it right years ago." Marvin and Sheila learned how to juggle their cause while raising their two young daughters, Jalen and Sydney, and their son Cory. Marvin's mission was about helping others. He declared, "I'm going to tell as many people as possible. That's what's important to me now."[18] While Marvin informed people about diabetes, Ronald and Ernie continued to work.

As the summertime approached, The Isley Brothers were scheduled to appear at several music festivals across the country. Those festivals included the Montreux Music Festival in Atlanta, Georgia; the Soul Beach Music Festival in Miami, Florida; the Ford Detroit Music Festival in Detroit, Michigan; and the Indy Jazz Festival in Indianapolis, Indiana. The Isleys were also scheduled to perform at the Taste of Cincinnati Festival in Cincinnati, Ohio, on May 26.

The Isley Brothers and Midnight Star withdrew from the festival in Cincinnati because a coalition of clergymen called for a boycott due to the unrest in the city after the fatal shooting of an unarmed nineteen-year-old Black man. Timothy Thomas was killed by policeman Steven Roach on April 7. Even before the shooting, the American Civil Liberties Union had joined Black civil rights groups in filing suit in a federal court in Cleveland, pointing to a longtime pattern of racial profiling by Cincinnati police officers. From 1995 to 2000, the suit pointed out, Cincinnati officers had killed thirteen suspects, all of them Black.[19] The Isleys grew up in Cincinnati, and they have always felt compelled to take a stand for social justice. In June of that summer, the brothers released the single "Contagious."

Eternal

"Contagious" was written and produced by R. Kelly. In this song, Ronald a.k.a. Mr. Biggs catches his wife with another man. The singer is accompanied by R. Kelly and R&B singer Chanté Moore. Mr. Biggs goes down memory lane after singing "The down low happened to me all over again" during the middle of the second verse. He is referencing R Kelly's 1996 hit single, "Down Low (Nobody Has to Know)." During the third verse, Mr. Biggs confronts the cheating couple. The song concludes with Mr. Biggs warning the cheating couple, "Now, I think you all better leave this place. Cause I'm about to catch a case." Ronald admitted that he didn't know what "catch a case" meant. He recalled, "I would do it on the stage and everyone would scream. I was saying 'what are you talking about catch a case?' Then, I realized, someone told me you catch a case in jail. Catch a case means you're going to jail—you caught this case.' Maybe that's something I shouldn't even tell. R. Kelly just laughed his head, just fell on the floor laughing at me."[20] The saga of the song is played out in the music video, which features all three singers.

"Contagious" rose to number three on the *Billboard* Hot R&B/Hip-Hop Songs chart on June 23, 2001. It also reached number nineteen on the Hot 100 Songs chart and number twenty-two on the Rhythmic Airplay chart on September 8. On September 15, the song rose to number one on the *Billboard* Adult R&B Airplay chart and remained there for two weeks.[21] "Contagious" returned The Isley Brothers to the top forty of the pop singles charts after a four-year gap. Its rise to number nineteen meant that The Isleys became the first group to score a top-fifty hit in six consecutive decades on *Billboard*'s Hot 100. They started with "Shout," which reached number forty-seven in 1959. "Contagious" won the 2002 Soul Train Music Award for Best R&B/Soul Single by a Group, Band or Duo.[22] It was also nominated for a Grammy Award in the category of Best R&B Performance by a Duo or Group with Vocal.[23] The video was nominated for Outstanding Music Video by the NAACP Image Awards. "Contagious" proved to be a good lead single for the new studio album.

On August 7, The Isley Brothers released their twenty-eighth studio album, *Eternal*. This CD contains fourteen songs: "Move Your Body," "Contagious," "Warm Summer Night," "You Deserve Better," "Just Like This," "Secret Lover," "You're All I Need," "Settle Down," "Eternal," "If You Leave Me Now," "Said Enough (Featuring Jill Scott)," "You Didn't See Me," "Ernie's Jam," and "Think." The cover art shows the two brothers with an alluring maidservant.[24] Ronald

The *Eternal* cover features The Isleys with an alluring maidservant.

declared, "We wanted to make a record that was worthy of our entire career. We're at a point in our lives where we're doing the best work we've ever done. This is The Isley Brothers' Super Bowl record."

Eternal features an all-star lineup of contributors, including R. Kelly, Jill Scott, Jimmy Jam and Terry Lewis (writers of "You're All I Need," "Settling Down," and "Eternal"), Raphael Saadiq, Steve "Stone" Huff, and singer-songwriter Avant. Angela Winbush is the cowriter of "Move Your Body" and the coproducer of "Warm Summer Night." Ronald stated, "Everyone involved with the record knew one thing coming in: Ernie and I wanted the very best, and that's just what they gave us. We all had something to prove to each other and to ourselves. We accomplished our goals, and the process was truly inspirational."[25] A month after its release, *Eternal* was certified platinum by the RIAA on September 10, 2001.²⁶ At the end of August, The Isleys and America mourned the loss of a young talent the brothers admired.

On August 25, twenty-two-year-old singer Aaliyah Haughton, commonly known as Aaliyah, was killed along with eight others when a small plane carrying them back from a video shoot in the Bahamas crashed shortly after takeoff. According to Ronald, Aaliyah and The Isley Brothers had discussed a possible collaboration before her death. Ronald told the Associated Press, "We were going to do a duet together, so I was looking forward to that. She was a beautiful lady."

Aaliyah had already performed covers of Isley classics on her first two albums. Her cover of "(At Your Best) You Are Love" was one of her early hits. Ronald declared that the song will be forever identified with Aaliyah. "I was so hurt over the thing that happened to her, and in our concerts, we turn that [song] over to her—that is her song forever," he stated.²⁷ In the middle of September, Americans were faced with a more devastating tragedy.

On the morning of September 11, 2001, four coordinated suicide terrorist attacks were carried out by Al-Qaeda against the United States. Nineteen terrorists hijacked four commercial airplanes that were traveling from the northeast region of the country to California. The first two planes crashed into the Twin Towers of the World Trade Center in New York City. The third plane crashed into the Pentagon in Arlington County, Virginia. The fourth plane was intended to hit a federal building in Washington, DC, but crashed into a field after passengers revolted. The attacks, commonly referred to as 9/11, killed nearly three thousand people. Americans were on high alert as new federal guidelines for air travel were implemented.

The Isley Brothers were scheduled to appear in concert at the Southern Heritage Classic in Memphis, Tennessee, on September 13, but the concert was canceled because grounding of airlines made it impossible for entertainers to get flights to Memphis.²⁸ The Isleys were also scheduled to perform at a John Lennon tribute concert at Radio City Music Hall in New York City, which was originally scheduled for September 20, but not all of the entertainers could get to NYC in time due to the terrorist attacks. Because of that, the concert was postponed to October 9, and this rescheduled date forced The Isleys to drop out because of a conflict.²⁹ In spite of the tragedies, it was a prosperous year for the brothers.

With a hit album and hit single, The Isley Brothers began a two-month nationwide tour on Friday, October 5. As stated previously, "Contagious" gave the brothers the distinction of being the act with the longest chart span on *Billboard*'s Hot 100 Songs chart at forty-two years. "If you count from '59 till now, you'll get the six decades. No group since the microphone has been invented has done that, black or white, single group or duet, whatever. No one in the history of the business has done that. So that's a gift to us, to be able to say, 'Hey we were there at the end of '59, and we're No. 1 today,'" said Ronald, who turned sixty that year. "This is turning out to be our year," said forty-nine-year-old Ernie. The Isleys found themselves competing with artists like Alicia Keys, Usher, and OutKast, some of whom weren't even born when the brothers posted some of their biggest hits, such as "Twist and Shout" and "It's Your Thing."

The hip-hop generation became familiar with The Isleys' catalog of hits; their songs have been heavily sampled by rap artists, including Ice Cube and the Notorious B.I.G.[30] At a concert in St. Louis, Missouri, Ronald honored the Notorious B.I.G. during "Between the Sheets," by singing a line from B.I.G.'s "Big Poppa." The slain rapper used "Between the Sheets" as the backdrop to "Big Poppa." Ronald also paid tribute to Aaliyah, whom he met through R. Kelly when she was fifteen years old. He dedicated "(At Your Best) You Are Love" to her and was visibly choked up performing the song.[31]

While on tour, The Isley Brothers released "Secret Lover," the second and final single from *Eternal*. This is a smooth, mid-groove tune, which features R&B singer Avant on the chorus. His vocals provide a nice contrast to Ronald's lead vocals.[32] Surprisingly, "Secret Lover" peaked at number sixty on the *Billboard* Hot R&B/Hip-Hop Songs chart on December 1, 2001, but it reached number twelve on the Adult R&B Airplay chart on February 16, 2002.[33] The music video shows Mr. Biggs courting his lover, who is another man's woman, on a yacht. The man is portrayed by actor Shemar Moore. Ernie is shown playing his guitar, and the group JS are shown as background singers.[34]

JS stands for Johnson Sisters. The trio consisted of Kandy Johnson, Kim Johnson, and Krystal Johnson. The Johnson sisters grew up in Los Angeles and began singing gospel music in church as youngsters. They were afforded the opportunity to sing alongside such popular gospel artists as Andre Crouch and Shirley Caesar. The group began to pick up steam after appearing on television shows, including *The Oprah Winfrey Show* and *Ally McBeal*. When the sisters met Ronald, he became their manager. He was so impressed with their talents that he invited them to work on *Eternal*. They would also work on The Isleys' next studio album.[35] Krystal Johnson left the group in 2002 when she married Philip Bailey of Earth, Wind & Fire. Ronald introduced Kim and Kandy to R. Kelly, who immediately agreed to work with the duo.

Signing a recording contract with DreamWorks Records, JS worked on their debut album. Ronald and R. Kelly served as the album's executive producers. The resulting album, *Ice Cream*, was issued during the summer of 2003, and the title track was a hit single.[36] Krystal and Kim became background vocalists for Earth, Wind & Fire in 2004.

By the end of 2002, it seemed the Mr. Biggs character had taken on a life of his own. Ronald explained, "The hip-hop players in the business kind of look up to me because of my longevity in the industry." He pointed out that, along with James Brown and George Clinton, The Isley Brothers are the most sampled in hip-hop. Ronald declared, "Mr. Biggs was sort of the unspoken title that was given to me, so we just put it on a record." Ronald and R. Kelly had finished writing the screenplay for a full-length feature that Kelly planned to direct, with both artists contributing songs. "We hope to have it out next year," said Ronald, who also wanted to take Mr. Biggs to Broadway. "We have so much fun with it."

According to Ernie, there was a slight downside to the Mr. Biggs character. Mr. Biggs became synonymous with Ronald, at times threatening to overshadow him. For instance, *Eternal* is credited to "The Isley Brothers featuring Ronald Isley a.k.a. Mr. Biggs." Ernie noted, "There are a lot of young people who relate to my brother as Mr. Biggs, and they're really not aware of 'Shout' or 'Twist and Shout' or 'It's Your Thing,' and all of the history that's involved in The Isley Brothers and the musical changes that we participated in and thrived on, so that virtually everybody has copied or sampled our stuff and been very successful with it. But all they know is Mr. Biggs because that's when they came on board."[37] Overall, the character was a nice gimmick for The Isleys, and *Eternal* was a successful project.

Eternal soared to number one on the *Billboard* Top R&B/Hip-Hop Albums chart on August 25, 2001, for two weeks. The album also rose to number three on the *Billboard* 200 Albums chart on the same date. It remained in that position for three weeks.[38] *Eternal* won the Soul Train Award for Best R&B/Soul Album by a Group, Band or Duo.[39] It earned The Isleys an American Music Award nomination in the category of Favorite Soul/R&B Band, Group or Duo. Music critics explained the rationale for the album's success.

Liana Jonas of AllMusic argues that after hearing the upbeat opening track, "Move Your Body," listeners will agree that The Isley Brothers still have it. Jonas also claims Ronald's falsetto is unwavering. and Ernie soars on guitar, especially on "Ernie's Jam."[40] Mark Anthony Neal wrote in PopMatters, "Many of the Jam and Lewis produced tracks, in particular 'You're All I Need,' 'Settle Down' and the title track 'Eternal' evoke 'vintage' Isley ballads like 'Voyage to Atlantis,' 'Make Me Say It Again,' and '(At Your Best) You Are Love.'" Neal believes *Eternal* is a testament to the longevity of a group that has endured many challenges.[41]

Surprisingly, for *Eternal*, Angela Winbush had only cowritten one song and only coproduced one other. In 2001, Ronald and Angela's marriage began to cool down, and they quietly divorced in early 2002. Angela decided to go in a new direction and sing gospel music.[42] She later became an ordained minister.[43] Ronald soon began dating Kandy Johnson of JS, and The Isleys added more awards to their collection.

On Thursday, January 10, 2002, The Isley Brothers were inducted into the Hollywood RockWalk at 7425 Sunset Blvd in Hollywood, California. Ronald's and Ernie's handprints reside alongside those of a host of music legends. The RockWalk is the only sidewalk gallery dedicated to honoring artists who have made a significant contribution to the evolution of rock 'n' roll.[44] On March 30, The Isleys won a total of three awards at the Sixteenth Annual Soul Train Music Awards ceremony held at the Los Angeles Sports Arena. In addition to the awards for Best R&B/Soul Single and Album by a Group or Duo, The Isleys were also named Entertainer of the Year for male artists. Young newcomer artist Alicia Keys also won three awards, including Entertainer of the Year for female artists.[45] It is worth noting that The Isley Brothers and Keys had a forty-year difference between them in the music business, and The Isleys proved that time was on their side.

As the summer approached, The Isley Brothers were booked for several concerts around the country. They returned to New Orleans for the eighth annual Essence Music Festival. The Isleys performed at the Beale Street Music Festival in Memphis, Tennessee; the Soul Festival in Cincinnati, Ohio; the Seventeenth Annual Mango Festival in Deerfield Beach, Florida; and others.[46] The Isleys also provided entertainment for the Ninety-Third Annual NAACP Convention in Houston, Texas.[47] On August 9, the Second Annual Billboard Music Awards were staged at Miami's Billboardlive, and The Isleys were awarded the inaugural Founder's Award for their indelible contributions to R&B music.[48] The group soon began working on their twenty-ninth studio album.

Body Kiss

In February 2003, The Isley Brothers released "What Would You Do? (featuring The Pied Piper)" amid a cross-country tour. This single is the precursor to their LP *Body Kiss*.⁴⁹ The Pied Piper in the title is R. Kelly, who wrote and produced this seductive song.⁵⁰ The music video was filmed in front of a live audience at Chicago's Congress Theater. Ronald appears as Mr. Biggs, joined by Ernie onstage. R. Kelly makes a guest appearance.⁵¹ "What Would You Do?" debuted as the most added song on urban radio during the week of March 3. This song rose to number two on the *Billboard* Adult R&B Airplay chart on May 17. It reached number fourteen on the *Billboard* Hot R&B/Hip-Hop Songs chart on May 31 and peaked at number forty-nine on the Hot 100 Songs chart on the same date.⁵² Earlier in the month, *Body Kiss* was released on May 6.

Body Kiss features twelve tracks: "Superstar," "Lucky Charm," "What Would You Do (featuring The Pied Piper)," "Body Kiss (featuring Lil' Kim)," "Busted (featuring JS)," "Showdown, Vol. 1," "Keep It Flowin," "Prize Possession," "Take a Ride," "I Want That," "I Like (featuring The Pied Piper and Snoop Dogg)," and "What Would You Do Part 2 (featuring The Pied Piper)." R. Kelly produced eleven of the tracks. "I Want That" was produced by Tim & Bob. The cover shows The Isley Brothers dressed in white.⁵³ According to record executives, the album promised to be one of the biggest hits of The Isleys' career, following the platinum success of *Eternal*.⁵⁴

Body Kiss became the first Isley Brothers album to hit number one on the *Billboard* 200 Albums chart since *The Heat Is On* (1975). *Body Kiss* debuted at number one on the 200 Albums Chart and Top R&B/Hip-Hop Albums chart on May 24, 2003. It remained at number one on the Top R&B/Hip-Hop Albums chart for three weeks.⁵⁵ A month after its release, *Body Kiss* was certified platinum by the RIAA on June 9.⁵⁶ It was also nominated for a Grammy Award in the category of Best R&B Album.⁵⁷ The album's second and final single, "Busted," was released in July.

"Busted" is a song in which Mr. Biggs and his lover, Asia, have a conversation after she comes home late and lies about where she has been.⁵⁸ The music video follows the storyline of the lyrics. It opens with Asia (Kim Johnson) being dropped off in the driveway by her alleged boyfriend (R. Kelly). She then creeps into the house at 2:00 a.m. Asia and Mr. Biggs argue, and she makes up lies about where she's been all night. Mr. Biggs tells Asia to go upstairs and pack her bags, and she keeps begging and promising to tell the truth. The video concludes with Mr. Biggs telling his brother (Ernie) to watch surveillance from that night, and they find Asia creeping with R. Kelly in the car. After saying she's "innocent," Asia gets kicked out of the house.⁵⁹ "Busted" reached number fifteen on the *Billboard* Adult R&B Airplay chart on September 13 and peaked at number thirty-five on the Hot R&B/Hip-Hop

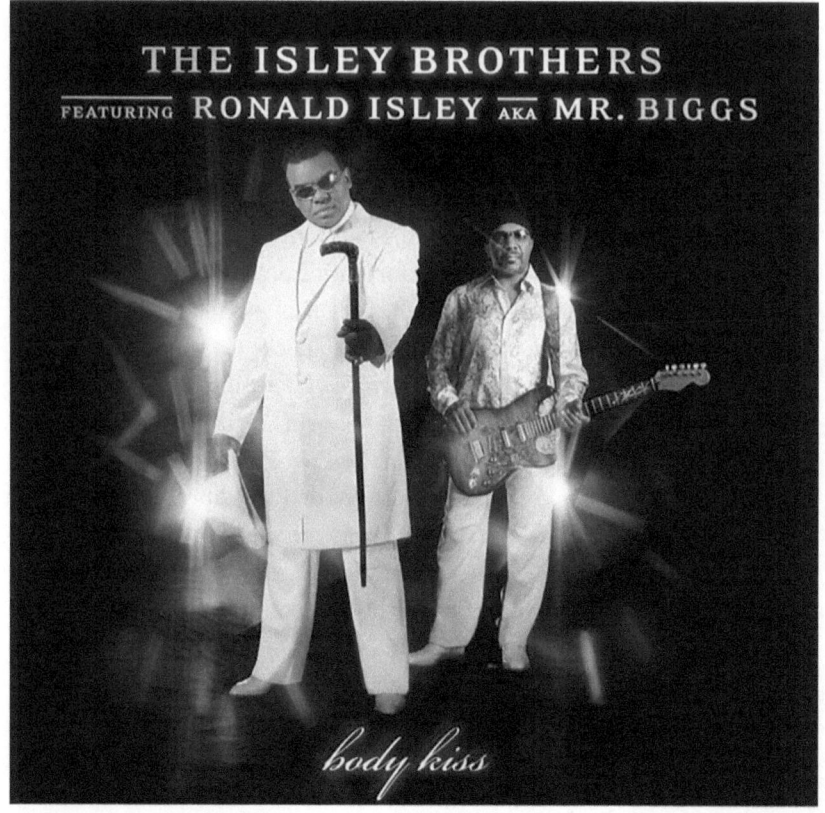

The *Body Kiss* cover shows The Isleys dressed in white.

Songs chart on November 8.⁶⁰ It was nominated for a Soul Train Music Award in the category of Best R&B/Soul Single by a Group, Band or Duo. Near the end of the year, "Prize Possession" was released.

"Prize Possession" is a mellow groove produced by R. Kelly.⁶¹ This song made it to the *Billboard* Adult R&B Airplay chart and peaked at number forty on January 24, 2004.⁶² "Prize Possession" and other quality tracks helped *Body Kiss* receive a Soul Train Music Award nomination in the category of Best R&B/Soul Album by a Duo or Group. The album also earned The Isley Brothers an American Music Award for Favorite Soul/R&B Band, Duo, or Group and received high praise from some critics.

Thom Jurek of AllMusic wrote, "Feeling more like a return to the T-Neck years than anything else, *Body Kiss* is an album of the prime seductive variety harking back in terms of tempo, song structure, production, and pace to releases like *The Heat Is On* and *Harvest for the World*."⁶³ Jim Fusilli told National Public Radio (NPR) that producer R. Kelly "places the brothers in a lush, romantic, and fairly contemporary setting." Fusilli claims the album is not perfect but gorgeous.⁶⁴ However, Mark Anthony Neal wrote, "Unfortunately, too much of the songwriting and production on *Body Kiss* is focused on the drama of Mr. Biggs and rightfully so, since it is the *only* reason why the 60-plus year old Ronald has any commercial cachet."⁶⁵ Ernie gave an explanation for Mr. Biggs and The Isleys' success.

"Anytime you get The Isleys and R. Kelly together, there's bound to be some sparks flying," said Ernie. "And Lil' Kim and Snoop Dogg, they're all right. They were fans of ours before they got involved in the business. It was an excellent opportunity for us to do some music together." Ernie said joining forces with R. Kelly resulted in a collection of songs he describes as hip, seductive, and often theatrical. Like "Busted," "Showdown, Vol. 1" tells the tale of a jilted husband and his thirst for vengeance on his wife's lover. "All these rap and hip-hop guys grew up listening to us and they wanted to be Mr. Biggs," said Ernie. "So, my brother has to make some sort of representation as to what being Mr. Biggs means in the current marketplace. He's sort of created a character out of himself just like all the rap guys are doing."

Regardless of how hard The Isley Brothers work to maintain their popularity, both Ernie and Ronald believe it wouldn't be possible without help from a higher power. They consider music their divine calling and are thankful for all the souls they continue to have the opportunity to reach. "My mother was a pianist in the church, and the foundation of what we do comes from a church background," said Ernie. "The idea of our longevity is under divine power, not under human power at all. That's why we look at what we do as a calling and a great blessing."⁶⁶ Ronald was blessed to record a solo album.

On November 11, 2003, Ronald released *Here I Am: Isley Meets Bacharach*. For this album, Ronald covers songs arranged by renowned musician Burt Bacharach. Bacharach was an American composer, songwriter, record producer, and pianist who composed hundreds of pop songs from the 1950s through the 1980s. Several of his hit songs were written specifically for and performed by Dionne Warwick during the early years of her career.

Here I Am: Isley Meets Bacharach contains thirteen songs. It features eleven classics: "Alfie," "Raindrops Keep Fallin' on My Head," "In Between the Heartaches," "Make It Easy on Yourself," "A House Is Not a Home," "The Look of Love," "This Guy's in Love with You," "Close to You," "Anyone Who Had a Heart,"

"Here I Am," and "Windows of the World." The two new songs are "Count on Me" and "Love's (Still) the Answer."[67] Ronald put his own style into the classics.

For Ronald's takes on "Alfie" and "Close to You," Bacharach put the instrumental focus on a full orchestra. Jim Farber wrote in the *New York Daily News*, "The pop perk of such hits as 'Raindrops Keep Fallin' on My Head' or 'Anyone Who Had a Heart' gives way to slower, lusher readings. Accordingly, Isley isolates the syllables of the words into their own hooks." Farber believes Ronald's style is far different from Dionne Warwick's. He declared, "She took a blithe approach to the material, matching the chiffon melodies to vocals as chic as her cheekbones. The depth came from the emotions she kept at bay rather than from the feelings she showed. Her poise communicated its own sad power." Ronald has stated that he was jealous of Dionne Warwick getting to sing those Bacharach songs.[68] In fact, The Isley Brothers almost recorded with Burt Bacharach in the early 1960s.

"The Isley Brothers had a recording session in 1962," Ernie stated. "They were supposed to do a song called 'Make It Easy on Yourself' by Burt Bacharach and Hal David. And there was an A&R person at the record company who changed the title of the song to 'Are You Lonely By Yourself.' Burt Bacharach and the A&R guy had a major falling out because Bacharach was like, 'That's not my song. It's not gonna go down like that. It's not gonna be recorded.' So, The Isleys had to do another song." The song they recorded is "Twist and Shout." Ernie added, "That's kind of weird, but you know. It shows you that's the way your destiny is intended to go because 'Twist and Shout' is one of those songs, if you don't know that song, it's like not knowing 'Jingle Bells.'"[69] The Isleys almost went down a different path.

In the early 1960s, The Isley Brothers' label was considering molding Ronald into another Johnny Mathis. Four decades later, he finally got to play the part. His style is smooth enough for it, and his falsetto has the androgynous quality for Bacharach, who always preferred female voices over male. Jim Farber stated, "Bacharach's arrangements gave Ronald plenty of room for improvisation. His patience with the leisurely arrangements gives these classics new density and meaning."[70] *Here I Am* stalled at number seventy-three on the *Billboard* 200 Albums chart on November 29, but it reached number twenty-two on the Top R&B/Hip-Hop Albums chart on the same date.[71] It had been a good year for The Isley Brothers, and a major milestone was at hand.

The year 2004 marked the fiftieth anniversary of the formation of The Isley Brothers and the forty-fifth anniversary of their first hit song, "Shout." Ronald had been carrying the Isley name in music for fifty years. Ronald and Ernie continued to perform around the country, and in this golden anniversary year, Steve Harvey presented The Isley Brothers a lifetime achievement award at the Fourth BET Awards ceremony, which was held at the Kodak Theatre in Los Angeles, California, on June 29, 2004. Ronald and Ernie performed the standards "Fight the Power," "Between the Sheets," "For the Love of You," "Contagious," and "It's Your Thing." Rudolph joined the brothers to perform the classic "Shout." They gave acceptance speeches after performing.

In July, The Isley Brothers headlined The Good Thang Man Tour, which also featured Keith Sweat and Klymaxx. While walking in London, England, on Friday, July 30, Ronald suffered a minor stroke. He checked himself into a hospital and soon returned to his home in St. Louis, Missouri, to recover.[72] The tour had to be canceled. Ronald's ex-wife Angela Winbush rushed to be by his side as they had remained friends after their divorce.[73] While Ronald recovered, a compilation was published.

The Essential Isley Brothers

On August 3, *The Essential Isley Brothers* was released by Epic Records. This compilation contains two compact discs and covers the group's hits from the early 1960s to their collaborative work with R. Kelly in the 2000s. The cover art is a group photo from the golden age.

Disc one contains eighteen tracks:

1. "Twist and Shout"
2. "That Lady (Parts 1 & 2)"
3. "What It Comes Down To"
4. "Brown Eyed Girl"
5. "For the Love of You (Parts 1 & 2)"
6. "Groove With You"
7. "Brother, Brother"
8. "Work to Do"
9. "Harvest for the World"
10. "Summer Breeze"
11. "Make Me Say It Again, Girl (Parts 1 & 2)"
12. "Live It Up (Parts 1 & 2)"
13. "Fight the Power (Parts 1 & 2)"
14. "Freedom"
15. "Keep On Doin'"
16. "This Old Heart of Mine (Is Weak for You)"
17. "Move Over and Let Me Dance"
18. "Shout (Parts 1 & 2)"

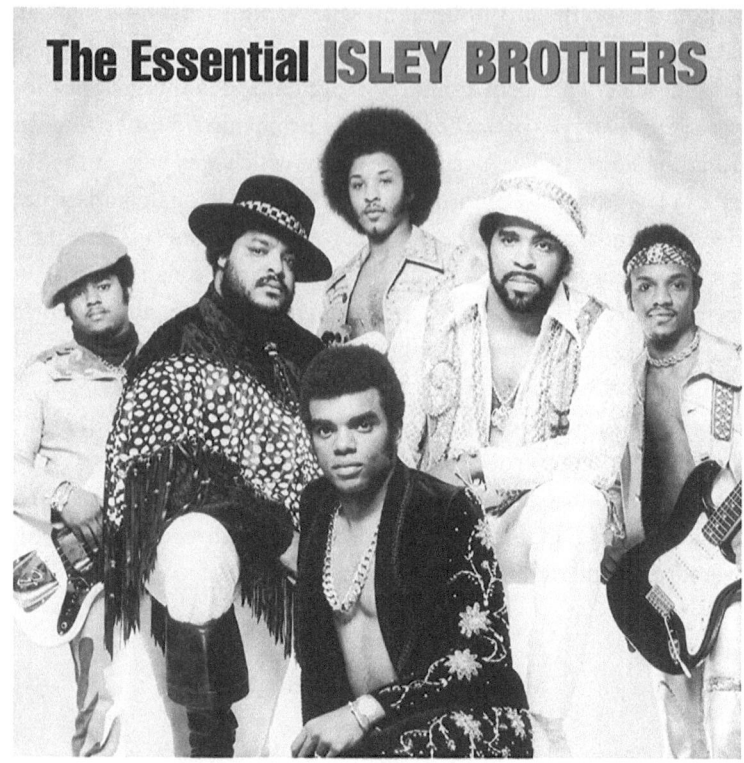

The cover for *The Essential Isley Brothers* is a group photo from the 1970s.

Disc two contains sixteen tracks:

1. "It's Your Thing"
2. "I Turned You On"
3. "Lay Away"
4. "Love the One You're With"
5. "Pop That Thang"
6. "Spill the Wine"
7. "Take Me to the Next Phase (Parts 1 & 2)"
8. "I Wanna Be with You (Parts 1 & 2)"
9. "The Pride (Parts 1 & 2)"
10. "Footsteps in the Dark (Parts 1 & 2)"
11. "Voyage to Atlantis"
12. "Don't Say Goodnight (It's Time for Love)"
13. "Between the Sheets"
14. "Caravan of Love"
15. "Mission to Please You"
16. "Down Low (Nobody Has to Know)"[74]

According to Rob Theakston of AllMusic, it is nearly impossible to include The Isley Brothers' best music on one disc, and most two-disc sets tend to have too many fillers. This compilation is no exception to the rule and is the most accessible when measured against some previous Isley compilations. Including the final two songs gives the listeners a comprehensive survey of the group's evolution over five decades. Theakston wrote, "This is a first-class compilation that casual listeners and loyal devotees will be more than satisfied with."[75]

Taken to the Next Phase

On August 24, a compilation of Isley songs remixed by younger artists was released by Epic Records. *Taken to the Next Phase* features ten tracks on one disc: "Tell of Tales (Tell Me When You Need It Again) (featuring will.i.am)," "Take Me to the Next Phase (Parts 1 & 2) (featuring Ignorants, Dead Rabbits)," "That Lady (Parts 1 & 2) (featuring Questlove)," "Tonight Is the Night (If I Had You) (featuring Stuart Matthewman)," "Summer Breeze (featuring Esthero, Onda)," "Between the Sheets (featuring Steven "Lenky" Marsden)," "Footsteps in the Dark (featuring Gabriel Rene)," "It's a New Thing (It's Your Thing) (featuring Onda, De la Soul)," "Harvest for the World (featuring Raphael Saadiq, Kevin Wooten)," and "Beauty in the Dark (Groove with You) (featuring Mos Def)." The cover art shows someone floating above the clouds.[76] This CD made it onto the *Billboard* charts. It reached number 26 on the Top R&B/Hip-Hop Albums chart and stalled at number 135 on the 200 Albums chart on September 11, 2004.[77] According to one critic, these remixes are superb.

David Jeffries of AllMusic declares, "The idea of remixing The Isley Brothers is hardly the stunning part; it's the excellent and tasteful selection of remixes on *Taken to the Next Phase*, an unnecessary but incredibly fun reworking of The Isley Brothers' deepest moments. None of the producers here mishandle these Isleys, but they aren't afraid to attack these tracks with an unexpected attitude either." Jeffries added, "The rap world has mined The Isleys' back catalog for their own use plenty of times, and this payback shows how much these artists appreciated it."[78] Within two months of this compilation's release, Ronald found himself in trouble with the IRS again.

The cover for *Taken to the Next Phase* is a depiction of someone floating above the clouds.

On Wednesday, October 13, Ronald was charged with tax evasion and could face twenty-six years in jail. A US federal grand jury ruled that he should face five offenses of tax evasion and one of failing to file a tax return. He was accused of buying personal cars with a business account and depositing royalty checks for his own use that had been issued to other group members, including his deceased brother O'Kelly. He allegedly required that half of his guaranteed tour fees be paid in cash on the day of each performance. He then paid musicians in cash to keep payments off the books. Ronald avoided paying taxes numerous times and declared bankruptcy after the IRS seized his yacht, cars, and other property in 1997. He was discharged from bankruptcy in 2001, but allegedly didn't file tax returns for the years 1997 to 2001. In 2002, he didn't sign his return and failed to pay all taxes due.[79] This was surprising for someone who had been in show business for so long.

After fifty years, The Isley Brothers were still relevant in pop culture. They had acquired awards among artists who were much younger, and Ronald proved he could sing any style of music. After working for so many years, many wondered how much longer could they continue. At that time, Ernie was fifty-two years old, and sixty-three-year-old Ronald had suffered a stroke. The Isleys had faced challenges before, and they could face more, but they always found a way to keep on moving.

Chapter 10
The Heat Is On

In 2005, prominent events were occurring around the world. The video-sharing website YouTube was founded, and Ellen Johnson Sirleaf was elected president of Liberia, becoming the first woman president of an African nation. Hurricane Katrina struck the American Gulf Coast, devastating New Orleans, Louisiana, and killing more than 1,600 people. At the beginning of the year, Ronald was still recovering from a stroke while he was in conflict with the IRS.

On Monday, January 10, Ronald pleaded not guilty to charges of tax evasion and was ordered to stand trial on March 8 before US District Judge Dean D. Pregerson in Los Angeles, California.[1] By May, his health had improved, and he was confident enough to resume performing. The Isley Brothers opened a show for Alicia Keys in Los Angeles.[2] They also performed at the Black Expo Summer Celebration in Indianapolis, Indiana, on July 17, along with Chaka Khan, Cameo, Babyface, and others.[3] In late July, the compilation *Summer Breeze* was published in Europe.

Summer Breeze: Greatest Hits

Summer Breeze: Greatest Hits was released by Epic Records. This CD features seventeen Isley classics: "Summer Breeze," "Harvest for the World," "That Lady (Parts 1 & 2)," "Between the Sheets," "The Highways of My Life," "Caravan of Love," "It's a Disco Night (Rock Don't Stop) (Parts 1 & 2)," "Love the One You're With," "For the Love of You (Parts 1 & 2)," "Don't Let Me Be Lonely Tonight," "Take Me in Your Arms (Rock Me a Little While)," "This Old Heart of Mine

(Is Weak for You)," "Behind a Painted Smile," "I Guess I'll Always Love You," "If You Were There," "Footsteps in the Dark," and "It's a New Thing (It's Your Thing)."[4] *Summer Breeze* peaked at number sixty-nine on the UK Albums chart on July 30, 2005.[5] Two weeks later, wedding bells rang for Ronald.

On August 14, 2005, Ronald Isley married Kandy Johnson after a six-month engagement. The garden wedding ceremony was held in front of 350 guests at the Beverly Hills Hotel in Beverly Hills, California. Kandy's father, Pastor Robert B. Johnson Jr., officiated the ceremony and her brother, Robert Johnson IV, walked her down the aisle. Philip Bailey of Earth, Wind & Fire, Kandy's brother-in-law, sang a rendition of "The Lord's Prayer," and served as a groomsman. Rudolph Isley was the best man and Ernie was a groomsman. Krystal Johnson Bailey served as the matron of honor, and Kimberley Johnson was the maid of honor. The newlyweds shared their first dance to "You Help Me Write This Song," which Ronald sang as they danced. At that time, Ronald was sixty-three and Kandy was twenty-eight.

When asked about their age difference, Ronald declared that love is not about their age, but their hearts.[6] Kandy stated, "Age is nothing but a number. The most important thing is love. He's a charming, loving, romantic, supportive man. He's every woman's dream."[7] In October, The Isley Brothers released the smooth romantic ballad "You Help Me Write This Song" as a CD single with three different mixes.[8] Footage from the wedding was supposed to be used for a video that was never released.[9] The single never charted, and Ronald soon found himself in a troubling situation that could affect his marriage.

On October 12, Ronald went on trial in Los Angeles on tax evasion charges. The main prosecution witness was his former tour manager, Ruby Martin, who worked with him for eight years and who testified under immunity from charges that she did not file her own income taxes on time for four years.[10] On October 31, a federal grand jury convicted Ronald of five counts of tax evasion and one count of willful failure to file a tax return for concealing millions of dollars of income from the Internal Revenue Service. He was scheduled to be sentenced by United States District Judge Dean D. Pregerson in January 2006. Ronald was facing a maximum possible sentence of twenty-six years in federal prison.[11] As a result of the conviction, the "Getting Back to the Family" hurricane relief benefit concert scheduled for November 6 had been indefinitely postponed. The concert would feature The Isley Brothers, Bobby Valentino, Teairra Mari, and Chris Brown.[12] Despite Ronald's conviction, The Isleys published new music.

Baby Makin' Music

In January 2006, The Isley Brothers released the second single from their next album and the only one to chart, titled "Just Came Here to Chill." This is a mellow R&B groove with a contemporary sound.[13] In the video, Mr. Biggs and Lady Biggs host a party at their mansion. Actor Idris Elba portrays a thief who plans to rob Mr. Biggs, but a beautiful woman is aware of his intentions. She seduces him and handcuffs him to the bed and notifies Lady Biggs. Mr. Biggs finds out and walks to the bedroom with his bodyguards. This story is "to be continued."[14] "Just Came Here to Chill" reached number twenty-five on the *Billboard* Hot R&B/Hip-Hop Songs chart on April 15, and it rose to number three on the Adult R&B Airplay chart on April 22.[15] While this song was on the charts, The Isleys performed around the country and soon published a new album.

On May 9, after a several-month delay, The Isley Brothers released their thirtieth studio album, titled *Baby Makin' Music*. This CD features eleven songs: "You're My Star," "Blast Off (featuring R. Kelly)," "Just Came Here to Chill," "Gotta Be with You," "Pretty Woman," "Forever Mackin'," "Show Me," "Give It to You," "Beautiful," "Heaven Hooked Us Up," and "You Help Me Write This Song." The album is credited to The Isley Brothers Featuring Ronald Isley a.k.a. Mr. Biggs, and the cover art displays the two brothers dressed in white on a ship.[16] Each song on this project is worthy of attention.

Baby Makin' Music features production by a slew of the hottest R&B producers, including Jermaine Dupri, mega producer for multiplatinum artists such as Mariah Carey and Usher. Producers Tim & Bob are the masterminds behind R&B sensation Bobby Valentino. Manuel Seal Jr. produced Mariah Carey's "We Belong Together" and Usher's smash hit "My Boo" with Alicia Keys.[17] "Blast Off," the only track produced by R. Kelly, was released as a CD single with three mixes, but it did not chart.

Baby Makin' Music is described as "vintage Isley" and "hip-hop soul." This CD debuted at number five on *Billboard*'s 200 Albums chart on May 27, 2006. It also debuted at number one on the Top R&B/Hip-Hop Albums chart on the same date and remained in the position for two weeks.[18] *Baby Makin' Music* earned The Isley Brothers a Soul Train Music Award for Best R&B/Soul Album by a Group, Band or Duo. The album received positive reviews from critics.

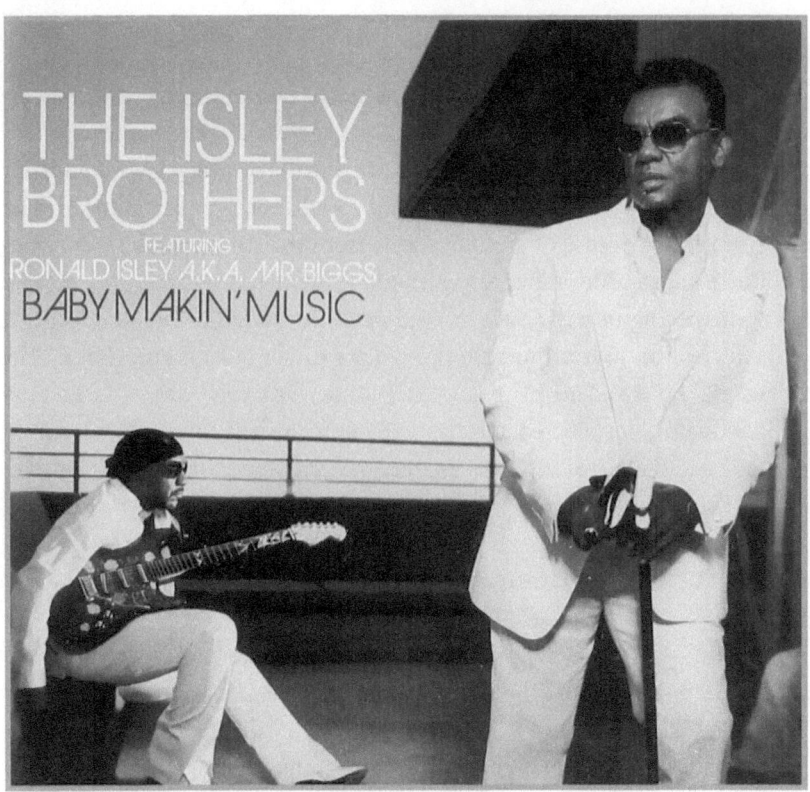

The cover for *Baby Makin' Music* is a photo of The Isleys dressed in white on a yacht.

Andy Kellman of AllMusic described *Baby Makin' Music* as "a remarkably tight album filled with songs that deliver on the promise of its title, and the songs that aren't immediately memorable at least make for fitting mood music."[19] According to David Weigel of PopMatters, *Baby Makin' Music* boils down to Ronald's formula of letting the ballads take center stage, and it was the best Isley album since *Mission to Please* (1996).[20] Wilson and Alroy wrote, "Ron's voice is still silk-smooth, and Ernie's magic guitar tone—when you can hear him—is unchanged."[21]

Although The Isley Brothers boasted a new number one album, time was running out for Ronald. His sentencing date was rescheduled for August 21. He was facing up to twenty-six years in jail. The judge ruled that this would be the last continuance in his case. He was supposed to be sentenced in

January, then in the beginning of May. Would Mr. Biggs wind up in jail?[22] He soon received some unwanted news.

On Friday, September 1, Ronald was sentenced to three years and one month in prison for tax evasion. The sixty-five-year-old was also ordered to pay $3.1 million in back taxes to the IRS. During the hearing, defense attorney Anthony Alexander argued that Ronald should receive probation instead of prison time because of complications from the stroke and a recent bout of kidney cancer. Alexander also pleaded for leniency because Ronald had been attempting to pay down his IRS debt. But Judge Pregerson declined to sentence him to less time than called for under federal guidelines. "The term serial tax avoider has been used. I think that's appropriate," Pregerson said.[23] Ronald was expected to be sent to a Bureau of Prisons hospital facility. He appealed the decision, and a second compilation of ballads was issued.

Beautiful Ballads, Vol. 2

At the end of December, Epic's Legacy Records began releasing a series of soulful recordings called *Beautiful Ballads*. This series features five classic R&B compilations from the romantic side of Earth, Wind & Fire, Gladys Knight and the Pips, Patti Labelle, The O'Jays, and The Isley Brothers. Every disc contains at least a dozen or more of each group's coziest cuts. It's all about love. These jams are for those nights when you want to turn the lights down low. This is old-school soul with no rap or samples anywhere in sight.[24] This compilation by The Isleys is actually the second volume.

Beautiful Ballads, Vol. 2 contains twelve songs: "For the Love of You," "Groove with You," "Between the Sheets," "Here We Go Again (Parts 1 & 2)," "I Need Your Body," "Love Put Me on the Corner," "It's Too Late," "Footsteps in the Dark (Parts 1 & 2)," "Lover's Eve," "Let Me Down Easy," "Sensuality (Parts 1 & 2)," and "Insatiable Woman (Isley-Jasper-Isley)."[25] The Isley Brothers' secret strength is their niche for slow love ballads, and this second volume is another nice taste of the gentle and sentimental side of the group.[26] This CD was released just in time for Valentine's Day in mid-February.

At the time, Ronald was confident his appeal would be successful. Despite receiving a thirty-seven-month prison sentence, he and Ernie were scheduled to embark on the Fan Appreciation Tour in America. When he appeared on the *Tom Joyner Morning Show*, he gave listeners an update on his highly publicized legal woes. Ronald stated, "It's on appeal, and I don't know what date the appeal is going to come up, but it looks like it's going to turn around for me." He believed he would not have to go to prison.

While Ronald waited for more information on his appeal, the twenty-nine-city tour began on March 14 in Las Vegas, Nevada, at the Rio Hotel and Casino. Other stops on the tour included Phoenix, San Diego, Denver, and Dallas. The tour concluded on April 28 at the Tower Theater in Philadelphia. In various cities, guest artists joined The Isley Brothers. Some of the dates were with The O'Jays, some with Frankie Beverly, and some with Stephanie Mills. The tour was a family affair, with Ronald's wife Kandy and his two-month-old son Ronald Isley Jr. joining him on the road.[27]

Ronald's ex-wife Angela Winbush also joined him on the road when she opened a concert during the tour at the Fox Theatre in St. Louis, Missouri. Angela sang a few of her hits, and announced she was a four-year cancer survivor. She closed her set with "I've Learned to Respect the Power of Love" and a gospel number. The Isleys performed several of their classics, including "That Lady," "Groove with You," and "Between the Sheets." They also performed their hits from the 2000s: "Just Came Here to Chill," "What Would You Do?," and "Contagious," which was partially acted out in dramatic fashion much like its video. Angela joined Ronald for "Don't Say Goodnight." Making this event more of a family affair were the two Johnson sisters, Kandy and Kim, singing background. Some people mistakenly referred to this tour as a farewell tour for The Isleys because of Ronald's legal woes, but he never suggested that notion.[28]

During the tour, The Isley Brothers began working on a new album. Ronald declared, "We're just doing it on the road, in the times that we have off." Each brother had been writing songs and planned to keep the next album more self-contained than the previous few, which included collaborations with R. Kelly, Jermaine Dupri, and Bryan-Michael Cox. Ronald explained, "We're gonna try to produce the majority of this album or at least half of the album ourselves. All the albums that we had that were really, really successful, we try to write the majority of the songs ourselves. We take a lot of pride in that. When someone else is writing music for you, you say 'I like it' or 'I don't like it.' But in doing your own, you have to really concentrate. You want to make sure everything is exactly right." The brothers were hoping to have the album finished within two months and ready for a fall release. They were also taping and filming shows on the tour for a possible live album on DVD.[29] The final night of the tour was an emotional one in Philadelphia.

According to Kimberly Roberts of the *Philadelphia Tribune*, the mood was bittersweet at the Tower Theater on April 28, when The Isley Brothers thanked fans for their unfailing support throughout their fifty-year career. Fans shouted out encouragement. Ronald rallied for what could have been his final performance before beginning a thirty-seven-month prison sentence. The evening featured four costume changes. Ronald began the show in a red three-piece suit, with his signature "Mr. Biggs" hat and cane. He started the set with "Who's That Lady," which shifted into "It's Your Thing" and "Take Me to the Next Phase." During this up-tempo segment, three seductive, scantily clad dancers made the first of many appearances, and many of the middle-aged men in the audience were pleased. Ronald sounded "just like the record" as he delivered the classic songs "Groove with You," "Hello It's Me," "Don't Say Goodnight," "Choosey Lover," and several other standards. They ended the show with James Brown's "I Got the Feeling," before bringing out the real star of the show, the cute little Ronald Isley Jr. The fans were treated to an evening of romance, soul, and rock 'n' roll that could only be delivered by The Isley Brothers.[30] There were no plans of slowing down in the near future.

The Isley Brothers returned to New Orleans to perform at the Thirteenth Annual Essence Music Festival, which occurred July 5 through 7. Several top music acts appeared, including The O'Jays, Frankie Beverly & Maze, Vanessa Bell Armstrong, Kelly Rowland, and more. Senator Barack Obama also spoke.[31] The Isleys also performed at Artscape 2007. Artscape is one of the largest outdoor festivals of the arts, which is held in Baltimore, Maryland. The event occurred July 20 through 22 at the Maryland Institute of Art, the Lyric Opera House, and the University of Baltimore. Among the music artists were Keyshia Cole, Lupe Fiasco, Burning Spear, and Ryan Shaw.[32] A couple weeks later, Ronald's world was turned upside down.

On August 7, Ronald began serving his three-year sentence at the Federal Correctional Institution's hospital facility in Terre Haute, Indiana.[33] Def Jam released a statement asking fans to lend their support to an executive presidential pardon, which could have kept Ronald out of prison. He had no prior criminal record, and there were concerns about his health. Ronald suffered a stroke in 2004 and was diagnosed with kidney cancer in 2006. Without proper care, his health could have declined further, and there was genuine concern as to whether he could survive a lengthy incarceration.[34] During his time in prison, it was imperative for Ronald to hold on to his faith.

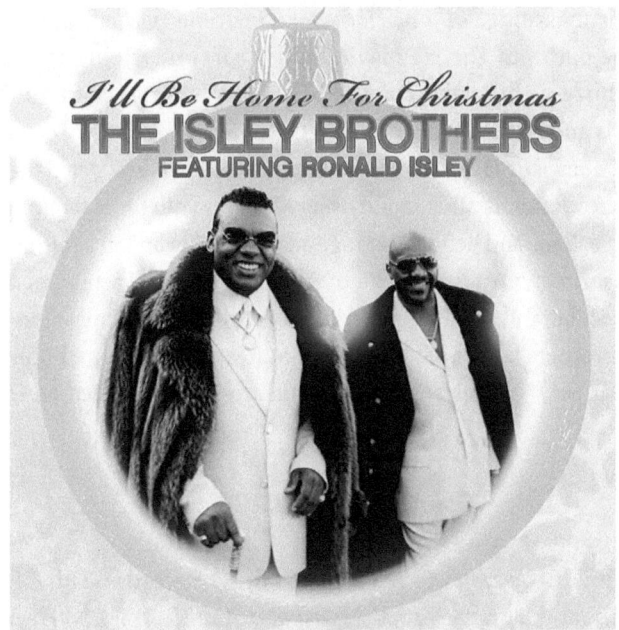

The cover for this Christmas CD features The Isleys elegantly dressed inside a Christmas ornament.

I'll Be Home for Christmas

Before Ronald began serving his sentence, The Isley Brothers completed a Christmas album. *I'll Be Home for Christmas* was released October 9.[35] This CD features ten songs: "Winter Wonderland," "I'll Be Home for Christmas," "I'm in Love," "Have Yourself a Merry Little Christmas," "Santa Clause Is Coming to Town," "Isley Christmas Medley," "What Can I Buy You?," "The Christmas Song," "White Christmas," and "Silent Night." The front cover shows a photo of the brothers inside a Christmas tree ornament.[36] The album was recorded by producers Jimmy Jam and Terry Lewis at their Flyte Tyme Studios in Santa Monica, California.

Terry Lewis claimed it took some doing to get The Isley Brothers in the Christmas spirit in the middle of August, but the project turned out well. *I'll Be Home for Christmas* is the first holiday album by The Isleys. Ronald wanted to do something "very serene and really warm and comfortable." The producers wrote "I'm in Love" and "What Can I Buy You?" for the album, which includes eight Christmas classics. Jazz guitarist Doc Powell is featured on Mel Torme's

"The Christmas Song."[37] *I'll Be Home for Christmas* peaked at number forty-one on the *Billboard* Top Holiday Albums chart on October 27 and reached number thirty-eight on the Top R&B/Hip-Hop Albums chart on December 22.[38] This is another superb studio album added to The Isleys' catalogue.

To describe *I'll Be Home for Christmas*, Wilson and Alroy stated that The Isley Brothers "create a captivating mood using Moog-y synth tones reminiscent of the classic '70s ballads and deftly rearrange a few tunes, bringing a fresh perspective to the most tired."[39] Andy Kellman of AllMusic wrote, "There's a good balance between secular and spiritual material, so the disc should appeal to just about any Isley Brothers fan who doesn't want to hear the same tired holiday music year in, year out."[40] A collection of Isley hits was also published on October 9.

The Definitive Collection

The Definitive Collection was released by Hip-O Records.[41] This CD contains seventeen songs: "Shout (Part 1)," "Twist and Shout," "This Old Heart of Mine (Is Weak for You)," "I Guess I'll Always Love You," "Take Me in Your Arms (Rock Me a Little While)," "Fight the Power," "Don't Say Goodnight (It's Time for Love) (Parts 1 & 2)," "Smooth Sailin' Tonight," "Spend the Night," "Lay Your Troubles Down (Angela Winbush Featuring Ronald Isley)," "Down Low (Nobody Has to Know) (R. Kelly Featuring The Isley Brothers)," "Floatin' On Your Love (Featuring Angela Winbush)," "Let's Lay Together," "Contagious," "What Would You Do?," "Busted (Featuring JS)," and "Just Came Here to Chill."[42] This compilation is distinguished by the inclusion of the recent hits: the final three tracks. *The Definitive Collection* reached number twenty-nine on the *Billboard* Top R&B/Hip-Hop Albums chart on October 27.[43] Unfortunately, Ronald would be away from the public for a while.

In mid-February 2008, a three-judge panel of the Ninth Circuit Court of Appeals rejected Ronald's argument that his sentence was unreasonable due to his age, poor health, and lack of proof that the federal prison system could provide him adequate health care. The panel unanimously upheld Ronald's sentence, noting that US District Judge Dean Pregerson correctly concluded that thirty-seven months in federal prison "best balanced the need to sanction Mr. Isley's 'pathological' tax evasion against the need to accommodate Mr. Isley's poor health."[44] This was a tough situation for both Ronald and Ernie and their fans. The Isley Brothers would not be able to perform for a few years. Many were left wondering about the future of The Isleys.

Original Album Classics

Later that year, *Original Album Classics* was released in Europe by Legacy Records. This is a five-CD box set of Isley albums released in the late 1960s and early '70s. Those albums are *The Brothers: Isley* (1969), *Get Into Something* (1970), *Givin' It Back* (1971), *Brother, Brother, Brother* (1972), and *3 + 3* (1973).[45] The albums, which range from decent to excellent, contain several of The Isley Brothers' Top Ten R&B singles, such as "I Turned You On," "Love the One You're With," "Pop That Thang," and "What It Comes Down To." When this box set was released, it sold for roughly the same amount as two full-price CDs.[46] In the following year, another box set was issued.

The Motown Anthology

In celebration of Motown Record's fiftieth anniversary, Universal Music released *The Motown Anthology* of The Isley Brothers in Europe. This double CD collects almost everything the three older brothers recorded while they were with Tamla Motown between 1965 and 1968. The cover art is a photo of the three older brothers from their time at Motown.

Disc one contains twenty-six tracks:

1. "Nowhere to Run"
2. "Stop in the Name of Love"
3. "This Old Heart of Mine (Is Weak for You)"
4. "Take Some Time Out for Love"
5. "I Guess I'll Always Love You"
6. "Baby Don't You Do It"
7. "Who Could Ever Doubt My Love"
8. "Put Yourself in My Place"
9. "I Hear a Symphony"
10. "Just Ain't Enough Love"
11. "There's No Love Left"
12. "Seek and You Shall Find"
13. "Got to Have You Back"
14. "That's the Way Love Is"
15. "Whispers (Getting Louder)"
16. "Tell Me It's Just a Rumor (Baby)"
17. "One Too Many Heartaches"
18. "It's Out of the Question"
19. "Why When Love Is Gone"
20. "Save Me from This Misery"
21. "Little Miss Sweetness"
22. "Good Things"
23. "Catching Up on Time"
24. "Behind a Painted Smile"
25. "Take Me in Your Arms (Rock Me a Little While)"
26. "All Because I Love You"

Disc two also contains twenty-six tracks:

1. "Ain't That Real Satisfaction"
2. "It Moves Me to Tears"
3. "What Becomes of the Broken Hearted (Smile)"
4. "Greetings (This Is Uncle Sam)"
5. "Leaving Here"
6. "How Sweet It Is (To Be Loved By You)"
7. "A Weakspot in My Heart"
8. "Sure Is a Whole Lotta Woman"
9. "You've Got So Much to Shout About"
10. "Trouble"
11. "Nevermore"
12. "No Good Without You"
13. "My Love Is Your Love (Forever) (Mono Version)"
14. "Born to Love You"
15. "Sad Souvenirs"
16. "Share a Little Love with Me (Somebody)"
17. "I Can't Help It (I Love You)"
18. "I Can't Go On Sharing Your Love"
19. "This Old Heart of Mine (Mono Version)"
20. "I Guess I'll Always Love You (Mono Version)"
21. "Tell Me It's Just a Rumor (Mono Version)"
22. "I Guess I'll Always Love You (Stereo Version)"
23. "My Love Is Your Love (Forever) (Stereo Version)"
24. "Greetings (This Is Uncle Sam) (Stereo Version)"
25. "Take Me in Your Arms (Stereo Version)"
26. "All Because I Love You (Stereo Version)"[47]

With several B-sides, mono versions, and covers, there are plenty of up-tempo Motown sound nuggets to be discovered in this set.

While The Isley Brothers were taking a break from performing and recording new music, they received an honor from the Grammy Awards. In January 2010, "Twist and Shout" was inducted into the Grammy Hall of Fame. The Grammy Hall of Fame was established in 1973 to honor recordings released before the Grammy Awards began in 1958. Now, it is open to any recording that's been out for at least twenty-five years. "Twist and Shout" is a part of the permanent landscape at the Grammy Museum in downtown Los Angeles.[48] In the spring, Ernie went on tour with other guitarists.

In March, the Experience Hendrix Tour began. The tour consisted of twenty dates in nineteen cities, with a changing ensemble of up to ten guitarists, including Ernie Isley, and a rhythm section playing music written and inspired by Jimi Hendrix. Along with the tour, Jimi's classic studio albums

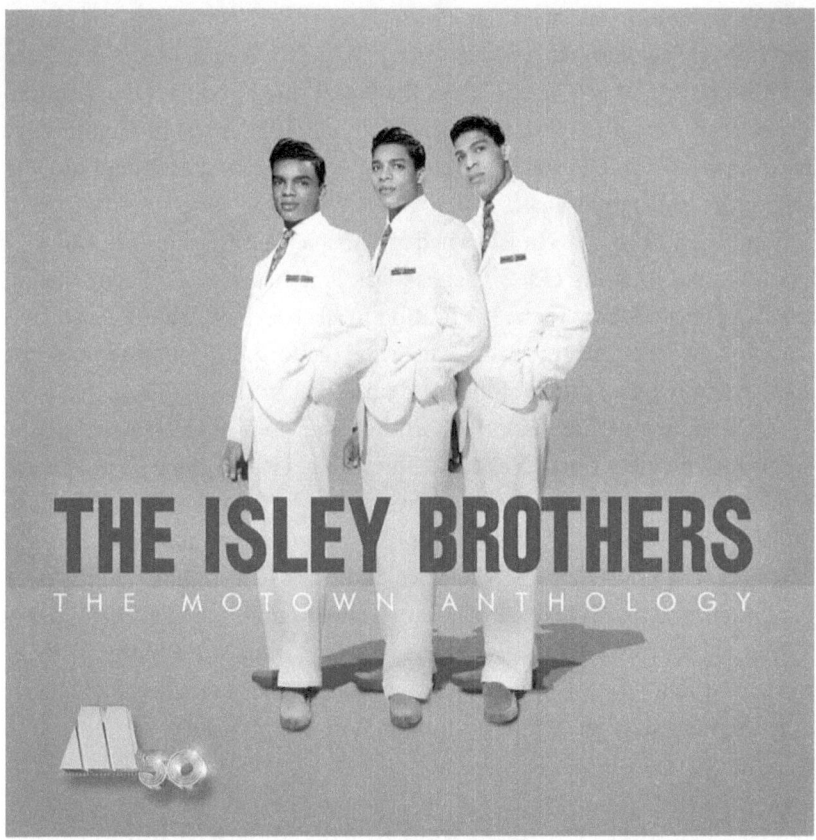

The cover for this anthology is a photo of the three older brothers from their Motown years.

were re-released, and a CD titled *Valleys of Neptune*, featuring unreleased studio recordings, was released. To describe Jimi Hendrix, Ernie stated, "Like Louis Armstrong and Miles Davis are to the trumpet, Jimi is to the electric guitar. America has George Washington, and rock has Jimi Hendrix."[49] In the following month, Ronald was given a reason to "shout."

On April 13, Ronald was released from jail after serving more than two and a half years and soon began work on his second solo album. In a radio interview, Ronald said that his next album would be an "all-star" effort, featuring current popular acts and veteran artists. His time behind bars was challenging. Ronald stated, "I was talking to young people and crying with them and people that were gonna be in there some years and that part really hurts. They looked up to me." Ronald was able to keep his spirits high by participating in music activities. He declared, "I was working at the chapel and I did gospel shows every week. That kept me up."[50] Ronald soon returned to the stage. On May 8, The Isley Brothers headlined a concert that featured Teena Marie and The Whispers at the Mother's Day Festival in Atlantic City, New Jersey.[51] While Ronald was enjoying his newfound freedom, tragedy struck the Isley family again.

On June 6, 2010, Marvin Isley died at a hospice near his home in Chicago. He was fifty-six years old. The cause was diabetes. He had been battling the disease for twenty years. In addition to his brothers Ernie, Ronald, and Rudolph, Marvin was survived by his wife, the former Sheila Felton; a son, Corey; and two daughters, Sidney and Jalen.[52]

After mourning the loss of his brother Marvin, Ronald released a new single in September titled "No More." This a ballad with a guitar complementing Ronald's smooth voice.[53] Though he's singing to his woman when he says, "Like a timeless record, you never get old," he could have just as easily been talking about himself. In the video, Ronald sings in a studio and images of soul music icons are shown, including Aretha Franklin, Chaka Khan, Barry White, Nina Simone, Patti LaBelle, and Don Cornelius.[54] "No More" stalled at number seventy on the *Billboard* Hot R&B/Hip-Hop Songs chart on October 2, 2010. A few days later, an Isley compilation was published.

Playlist: The Very Best of The Isley Brothers

Playlist: The Very Best of the Isley Brothers was released by Epic Records. This CD contains fourteen songs: "Love the One You're With," "Listen to the Music," "Need a Little Taste of Love," "For the Love of You (Parts 1 & 2)," "That Lady (Parts 1 & 2)," "Spill the Wine," "Who Loves You Better," "Summer Breeze," "Between the Sheets," "Voyage to Atlantis," "Hello It's Me," "Let's Fall in Love (Parts 1 & 2)," "Winner Takes All," and "Here We Go Again (Parts 1 & 2)."[55] Some may feel this CD is not titled properly because some of The Isleys' biggest hits are excluded. The classics "It's Your Thing," "Fight the Power," and "Don't Say Goodnight (It's Time for love)" should be included. The voice that made these classics was honored again by the Soul Train Music Awards in November.

Ronald was the only original member of The Isley Brothers who was still in the group; he had been carrying the Isley name in show business for more than fifty years. His status earned him the Legend Award for Male at the 2010 Soul Train Music Awards. Anita Baker won the Legend Award for Female. For Ronald's tribute, Eric Benet, Bilal, Tank, Freddie Jackson, and Jeffrey Osborne performed Isley classics. While Ronald was getting back into the limelight, Ernie was on tour again.

The Experience Hendrix Tour made a second 2010 run. This tour visited nineteen venues throughout the US and Canada. The October–November run marked the first time the tour had been organized twice in one concert year, and it also included the tour's first Canadian dates. The run started in Pittsburgh on October 26, then moved on to four dates in Canada, followed by a round of US dates, and ended in Indianapolis on November 20.[56] On November 30, Ronald released his second solo album, titled *Mr. I*.

Mr. I contains ten songs: "Take It How You Want," "No More," "If I Lose My Woman," "Put Your Money On Me," "Supposed to Do," "Dance for Me," "What I Miss the Most," "I Need You," "You've Got a Friend," and "You Had Me at Hello."[57] Ronald plotted *Mr. I* while he was in prison. During that time, he discovered another purpose for his "gift from God." "People looked up to me, and I taught them things they didn't know about," he said. "The shows I did there were the best of my life. People were crying, it was me crying, the audience was crying. I couldn't believe how much love was there. I will never forget that." For this album, Ronald enlisted all-star producers, including Greg Curtis, Sound Dynasty, Kajun, and Tricky Stewart. Among guests singing with him are Aretha Franklin, Lauryn Hill, and T.I.

After the album's release, Ronald began planning a tour. But his first priority was spending time with his wife Kandy and his son Ronald Jr., who was only eight months old when his father went to prison. "He is my strength," Ronald stated. "He's a singer now—all the songs from the Disney programs. I was like that when I was young. It's like seeing myself all over again." Ronald hoped that a track from *Mr. I* or from a future release would extend his distinction of having had a pop or R&B hit in every decade since the 1950s. "That would be great," he said. "I watched Sinatra, and he was doing it all the way up until his end. I'm going to do it until the Lord comes back."[58]

In December, the second single from *Mr. I* was released. "What I Miss the Most" is a slow, romantic ballad written and composed by Gregory G. Curtis Sr.[59] This song stalled at number seventy-nine on the *Billboard* Hot R&B/Hip-Hop Songs chart on January 29, 2011.[60] "What I Miss the Most" was the final single released from *Mr. I*, an album in which Ronald contemporizes his style with twenty-first-century producers.

On *Mr. I*, Ronald's distinctive, still-vibrant tenor and passion for sultry ballads keep him in touch with the fans he earned long before millennials knew about him. His duet with Aretha Franklin on "You've Got a Friend" makes people wonder what took them so long to collaborate.[61] "She's one of my best friends," Ronald said of Franklin. "We've been talking about doing a song for 40 years and we've finally done it." He believes the song is proof that there's always something new to do to keep life interesting. It is the last song Aretha recorded before her cancer diagnosis.[62] "You've Got a Friend" earned the two singers a Grammy nomination in the category of Best Performance by a Group or Duo with Vocals.[63] In the spring of 2011, The Isleys began performing together again.

On March 20, The Isley Brothers performed at the annual Jazz in the Gardens concert at the Sun Life Stadium in Miami, Florida. Lauryn Hill, Charlie Wilson, En Vogue, Gladys Knight, and others also performed.[64] On May 14, The Isleys opened for Gladys Knight at the Fox Theatre in Detroit, Michigan.[65] On June 11, the brothers kicked off the summer concert series at the Country Club Hills Theater in Country Club Hills, Illinois, located outside Chicago. Music stars of the series included Kem, Erykah Badu, Charlie Wilson, and others.[66]

On September 3, The Isley Brothers headlined a concert at Chastain Park in Atlanta, Georgia, dubbed "The Reunion." They shared the bill with El DeBarge and Carl Thomas. Ronald wasn't sure why the show was deemed a "reunion" since he was performing frequently with Ernie. But he assumed it was because Ernie joined the "Experience Hendrix Tour" the previous year, so casual fans might not have realized they were still a unit. As for the other performers, Ronald declared, "I know El very good. I've been knowing him at least 10 years; he's been a good friend of mine. . . . Carl, I met once. We talked for a while, but I haven't seen him in a long time."[67]

On September 17, The Isley Brothers headlined the Superstars of Soul concert at Chaifetz Arena in St. Lous, Missouri, which featured El DeBarge and After 7. They performed their standards, including the hits of Mr. Biggs. In a change of pace, Ron Isley told the crowd one song in particular, "Falling in Love with Jesus," kept him going during the couple of years he was "away." Aldermanic President Lewis Reed, accompanied by Alderman Marlene Davis and St. Louis rapper Yung Ro, stopped the show to issue a resolution from the Board of Aldermen thanking The Isley Brothers for their contributions to the music industry.[68]

Though Ronald is revered for his contributions to the R&B canon, he had weathered his share of complications. After being released from prison, Ronald said he made plans to travel extensively for a couple of years, with Africa, where he's never performed, at the top of the list. Throughout his career, Ronald worked with artists ranging from Burt Bacharach to R. Kelly to Aretha Franklin. But there were still a couple of names on his collaboration list. "I'll probably do something with Alicia Keys and I've always wanted to do something with Al Green—that would be nice," he said. "Alicia has talked to me several times, we just haven't found the time to get together. Oh yeah, and Beyoncé. She wanted me to do a duet with her three years ago, so I'm sure we'll wind up doing something."[69] Ronald's travel plans came to pass as he and Ernie continued to perform across America.

In February 2012, The Isley Brothers were in concert at the Chicago Theatre, which featured Chrisette Michele.[70] In March, they performed at the Smooth Grooves Music Fest at Save Mart Center in Fresno, California, with Keith Sweat.[71] In June, The Isleys took their talents to the Arena at Golden Moon Hotel and Casino in Choctaw, Mississippi.[72] In July, The Isley Brothers and Bobby Womack performed at Chene Park (now Aretha Franklin Amphitheatre) in Detroit.[73] They also headlined a concert at the twenty-fifth Long Beach Jazz Festival at the Rainbow Lagoon Park in Long Beach, California.[74] The brothers were seen at other venues throughout the year, and on December 21, they concluded their 2012 performances with their "Christmas Show" at the Durham Performing Arts Center in Durham, North Carolina.[75] In 2012, Ronald turned seventy-one years old, and Ernie turned sixty, but each brother showed no signs of slowing down.

Chapter 11
Forever Gold

Near the end of 2012, rumors about the end of the world began to resurface. Some scholars believed the calendar of the ancient Mayan civilization predicted the world to end on December 31. Also, American radio personality Dick Clark had died on April 18. Clark's name had been attached to NBC's *New Year's Rockin' Eve* for several years. Some people believed his death was a sign that there wouldn't be any more "new years" on Earth. However, there was a smooth transition from 2012 to 2013, and the rumors became a distant memory.

In 2013, President Barack Obama was inaugurated for his second term on January 21. New words "twerk" and "selfie" were added to the dictionary. Taking "selfies" and posting them to social media was all the rage that year. Social media became a major player during moments of crisis. Former South African president and leader of the anti-apartheid movement Nelson Mandela died on December 5, and Ronald Isley released another solo album.

Before Ronald's album was released, The Isley Brothers performed in various locations. On April 12, they performed at the Arizona Jazz Festival in Phoenix.[1] On May 16, they performed at the Daughters of the American Revolution (DAR) Constitution Hall in Washington, DC.[2] On May 18, The Isleys provided entertainment for Clark Atlanta University's Spirit of Greatness Gala at the Hyatt Regency Hotel in Atlanta, Georgia. The event raises funds for deserving Clark Atlanta University students and honors alumni and community members for their achievements in diverse fields of endeavor.[3] In early May, Ronald released the first single from his upcoming album, titled "Dinner and a Movie."

"Dinner and a Movie" is a song in which Ronald sings about meeting a beautiful woman and asking her for a date.[4] The music video demonstrates the lyrics of the song. Ronald's wife, Kandy, portrays his love interest.[5] "Dinner and a Movie" scaled to number nine on the *Billboard* Adult R&B Airplay chart on August 31. It also reached number thirty-five on the R&B/Hip-Hop Airplay chart on the same date.[6] On July 13, Ronald released his third solo album, three years after his second.

Ronald knows his previous album, 2010's *Mr. I*, wasn't Ronald Isley at his tip-top best, unlike this 2013 project, *This Song Is for You*. "It was rushed," he says. "I didn't have the time to really sit down and get it right. I had deadlines. I was trying to get some music out there right away, and I had certain shows I wanted to do and I wanted to do this and do that." But Ronald makes up for *Mr. I* with *This Song Is for You*, which was released by MNRK Music (formerly eOne Music)/Notifi Records. Notifi Records head Ira DeWitt, who has overseen albums from Johnny Gill and Ginuwine, executive produced this album. Ronald co-owns the studio with DeWitt, and eight of the songs on *This Song Is for You* were recorded at Notifi in St. Louis, Missouri.[7]

This Song Is for You consists of thirteen tracks: "This Song Is For You," "Dinner and a Movie," "My Favorite Thing (featuring Kem)," "The Boss," "Bed Time," "Another Night," "Lay You Down (Intro)," "Lay You Down (featuring Trey Songz)," "Reunion," "He Won't Ever Love You," "Better or Worse," "Let's Be Alone," and "Make Love to Your Soul."[8] Ronald wanted to educate younger audiences with this album. "I'm trying to show the young people where music is supposed to be, and at the same time show them what I know," he said. Ronald also wanted listeners to know an album can be listened to from beginning to end; it does not just have to be a collection of a couple of singles.

What's remarkable about *This Song Is for You* is how current it sounds. It feels fresh and modern and could have been released by an artist half his age.[9] This album made it to number nine on the *Billboard* Top R&B/Hip-Hop Albums chart on August 3. It also reached number twenty-seven on the 200 Albums chart the same date.[10] After the release of the album, The Isley Brothers were on the road again. On July 26, The Isleys began a summer tour with Maze featuring Frankie Beverly and Kem.[11] The second single from Ronald's third album is actually a duet with Kem titled "My Favorite Thing."

"My Favorite Thing" was released in November. Ronald and Kem began talking about recording a song together about eighteen months before the album's release, but they both agreed it had to be the right song. "It had to be the perfect thing for us," Ronald said. "We would talk every month and he came up with a song nine months later. He's so particular, just like Luther Vandross. He wants everything to be just right."[12] With Ronald and Kem, this song is the epitome of old school and new school blending in perfect harmony.[13] The video shows the singers harmonizing. Their love interests are also shown. Once again, Kandy portrays Ronald's significant other.[14] "My Favorite Thing" climbed to number five on the *Billboard* Adult R&B Airplay chart on February 1, 2014. It also reached number twenty-three on the R&B/Hip-Hop Airplay chart on February 22.[15] The Isleys and Kem performed at Alabama State University (ASU).

On Wednesday, November 27, The Isley Brothers headlined the ASU homecoming concert with Kem as special guest. Danielle Kennedy, ASU vice president for university relations and longtime Isley Brothers fan, believes their music is timeless. She declared that there had been "tons" of excitement surrounding the show, both from folks older than forty, who probably can point to a favorite Isley Brothers tune—or a couple dozen of them—and from younger generations. She also stated that Kem plays some of the most romantic music and has an uplifting backstory, having hit rock bottom as a homeless addict and then climbing out to embark on a successful music career.[16] In the first week of December, one of the Isleys purchased R. Kelly's former mansion.

Rudolph and his wife Elaine purchased the property in Olympia Fields, Illinois, for $587,000. R. Kelly had owned the 14,525-square-foot mansion that sits on a little more than three acres from 1997 until he lost it to foreclosure in March 2013. Rudolph and Elaine, longtime residents of Otisville, New York, really liked the place because it was fenced in and knew it was coming on the market before it was listed. They wanted to move to metro Chicago because they have children and grandchildren there. Kelly built the sixteen-room mansion in 1997. Features include five bedrooms, an indoor pool, and a six-car garage.[17] This was a great Christmas present for the couple. In early 2014, The Isleys received a present that was long overdue.

The year 2014 marked the sixtieth anniversary for The Isley Brothers, and it seemed the Grammys had been a little stingy when it came to the group. A group as legendary as The Isley Brothers should have a closet full of Grammy Awards. But there was only one, a single trophy won in 1969 for "It's Your Thing." The Isley Brothers missed out on Grammys for "Shout," "Twist and Shout," "Between the Sheets," "This Old Heart of Mine," "Fight the Power,"

"Summer Breeze," and "Harvest for the World." None of their albums have won Grammys either. "I don't know what to call it," said Ronald. "Can you imagine not having a Grammy for 'Between the Sheets,' the biggest record by anybody?" The song has been heavily sampled by many other artists over the years, including the Notorious B.I.G. and Gwen Stefani. "I've been nominated so many times I stopped going, like 'hey man, I ain't going to that junk,'" he stated. "It didn't mean that much to me at one time until people would say they had this many Grammys."

The Fifty-Sixth Annual Grammy Awards presentation was held Sunday, January 26. On the previous night, the Recording Academy took action to rectify the situation by giving The Isley Brothers the Lifetime Achievement Grammy in a special ceremony. Other lifetime achievement award recipients include The Beatles, Kraftwerk, and Kris Kristofferson. Ronald accepted the award along with Ernie and Chris. Rudolph did not attend. Ronald revealed that he was certain he would win a Grammy when he teamed up with Burt Bacharach for *Here I Am*. He also thought his duet with Aretha Franklin of "You've Got a Friend" was a contender, though neither work yielded a Grammy. *This Song Is for You* was not nominated either.

Though some artists downplay the Grammys, Ronald declared, "It means everything because it means something to the people, like 'oh, you got the Lifetime Achievement Award.'" To Ronald, that award, in particular, is a big deal. He stated, "I talked to the president of the Grammys, and he explained how important it was. I know it will be important to our fans. It's one of the biggest deals we've ever been involved with. Everyone is excited." Paul McCartney and Ringo Starr of The Beatles performed during the Grammy ceremony, but The Isleys did not. Ronald would have liked to perform "Twist and Shout" with Paul, but for some reason, the Grammy producers did not ask. He believed if Paul had suggested it, it would have happened. But Ronald was still grateful. He claimed, "The Lord has been the best with us and I'm still doing it. We've been blessed. We accomplished the hopes and prayers our mother and father had from the beginning. They wanted us to last as long as the Mills Brothers. We've lasted as long as anything."[18] And Ronald and Ernie continued to prolong the Isley legacy.

Throughout the spring, The Isley Brothers performed at concerts and special events. On April 6, they were at the Thirty-fifth Annual UNCF: An Evening of Stars, which took place at the Atlanta Civic Center.[19] Younger artists included Jill Scott, Sevyn Streeter, Tye Tribbett, and others. This event is a scholarship-based telethon for the United Negro College Fund, which encourages and entertains viewers by joining together the hottest stars with the next generation of excellence. It spotlights students in the African American community and the celebrities who support them by providing scholarship opportunities that would not otherwise be accessible to them.[20] On May 2, The Isleys performed at the Grand Gala for the Kentucky Derby in Louisville. Other performers included Peabo Bryson, Regina Bell, and The Jacksons.[21] On May 14, The Isley Brothers were featured at Funk Fest 2014 in Atlanta, Georgia, with Musiq Soulchild, Monica, Doug E. Fresh, Slick Rick, and others.[22] On June 10, a celebration was held for the eightieth anniversary of the Apollo Theater. The program was titled "Don't Stop 'Til You Get Enough" and hosted by Wayne Brady. Special guests included Gladys Knight, Natalie Cole, Joss Stone, Savion Glover, and The Isley Brothers. The event was the institution's most successful gala ever, raising $2.3 million.[23] The Isleys continued working throughout the year.

On August 23, The Isley Brothers were in concert at the Grand Theater at the Foxwoods Casino in Ladyard, Connecticut. David Goodson of the *New York Amsterdam News* attended the concert and explained why The Isleys were still a force of reckoning. According to Goodson, several artists have heard "I grew up with your music" and a few have heard "I made some babies to your music." Leading the league in receiving both these respectful, although cliché, compliments hands down has to be The Isley Brothers. With acts that have been around for at least a decade, there are many fans who support only either the older or the newer material. This audience was able to groove to hit songs throughout the 120-minute-plus journey over their sixty-year-plus music career. They couldn't help but do so, especially when Ronald's silky voice crooned through songs like "Footsteps in the Dark," "Between the Sheets," or "Groove with You." When The Isleys performed "Hello It's Me" and "For the Love of You," the deal was sealed.

The Isley Brothers were not confined to mid-tempo jams and ballads. Their set included "Fight the Power" and the rock-infused "Who's That Lady." They also gave an ode to funk with "It's Your Thing," while also strolling down memory lane with their early singles, such as "Shout," "Twist and Shout," and "This Old Heart of Mine" to remind everyone what set their career in motion. While it's easy to get caught up in the signature voice of The Isley Brothers, seeing them perform live dispels the notion that they are a one-man show. Ernie Isley is definitely a force in his own right, and he taught himself how to do it, as a drummer and on acoustic and electric guitar. "Summer Breeze" and "Voyage to Atlantis" allowed Ernie to have his moment in the spotlight and show his skills on the guitar. Putting in that kind of work brought home the fact that their spot in the Rock & Roll Hall of Fame was well deserved.[24] A week later, The Isleys were in Detroit.

On August 31, The Isley Brothers headlined the last concert of the season at Chene Park, which has since been renamed the Aretha Franklin Amphitheatre. This was a star-studded concert featuring En Vogue, the all-female nineties R&B group, and the eighties British R&B act Loose Ends.[25] There were more performances during the holiday season.

On November 27, Thanksgiving Day, The Isley Brothers entertained young and old at the Macy's Great Tree Lighting at Lenox Square in Atlanta, Georgia. Music was also provided by the Macy's All-Star Holiday Choir, Pentatonix, and Toby Miller of the Atlanta Opera.[26] On December 26, The Isleys and Angie Stone provided holiday soul at the CFE Arena in Orlando, Florida, located at the University of Central Florida.[27] On December 31, at the Philips Arena in Atlanta, The Isley Brothers rang in the new year with Morris Day, Mint Condition, Jeffrey Osborne, Dru Hill, and Griffy.[28] The Isleys were frequently seen in concert with artists several years their junior. They proved that time was on their side and they had not lost their edge. Ronald had been performing for sixty years and the brothers would be around for several more.

In early 2015, The Isley Brothers were awarded once again for their illustrious career. On January 23, they were honored at the twenty-third Trumpet Awards. The ceremony was held at the Cobb Energy Performing Arts Centre in Atlanta, Georgia. The Trumpet Awards were created by Xernona Clayton to celebrate and honor African American achievers and those who support the African American experience.

This annual event salutes accomplishments in law, medicine, business, politics, the arts, civil rights, sports, entrepreneurship, entertainment, and other fields. Other honorees included actor Jamie Foxx, singer Janelle Monae, designer Tommy Hilfiger, Major League Baseball Hall of Famer Lou Brock, Carnival Corp. president and CEO Arnold W. Donald, Morehouse School of Medicine president and dean Dr. Valerie Montgomery Rice, and Sunshine Holdings chairman Franklin R. Wilson. Xernona Clayton stated, "I'm hoping that through this program, we can continue to inspire young people to do better, to make their moments count, to make their future bright, to instill in them the need to be somebody."[29] Throughout their legendary career,

The Isley Brothers have inspired several young artists, including Whitney Houston, R. Kelly, and Aaliyah, and throughout the year, they sporadically shared venues with younger artists.

On February 13, The Isley Brothers headlined the Zulu Coronation Ball for the Mardi Gras carnival at the Ernest N. Morial Convention Center in New Orleans, Louisiana. They were joined by Fantasia, Juvenile, and DJ Captain Charles.[30] Mardi Gras is a Christian holiday and popular cultural phenomenon that dates back thousands of years to pagan spring and fertility rites. Also known as Carnival or Carnaval, it's celebrated in many countries around the world—mainly those with large Roman Catholic populations—on the day before the religious season of Lent begins.[31] The Zulu Ball is an annual black-tie event known for its top-notch funk, soul, and R&B musical talent.[32] A month later, The Isleys traveled to South Georgia.

On March 15, The Isley Brothers joined Fantasia again for the sixth annual Soulfest celebration at the Civic Center in Albany, Georgia. Other performers were the Atlanta Pleasure Band, MC Lighfoot, and the Trap Girls. This was The Isleys' first appearance in Albany, where they have familial ties. They were still influential after more than six decades in the business. Ernie declared, "It's an amazing thing that we've been embraced by an audience that spans across generations." Much of that is due to being sampled by other artists. Ernie added, "We're expecting a Grammy any day for Kendrick Lamar's song ['i,' which samples 'That Lady']. Everyone says, 'That's Kendrick Lamar,' and it is. But it's The Isleys, too. That's something that's been constant throughout our career."[33] Ronald made an appearance in the music video, and Lamar won Grammys in the categories of Best Rap Performance and Best Rap Song.[34] The Isleys did not receive Grammys for the song, but they were not deterred.

On May 10, The Isley Brothers performed at the Performing Arts Center in Durham, North Carolina.[35] On June 13, they headlined the Urban Expo Music Fest at the KFC Yum! Center in Louisville, Kentucky, which featured Johnny Gill, Kelly Price, and Tom Browne.[36] On June 19, The Isleys performed at Arena Theatre in Houston, Texas.[37] On July 18, they were onstage at the Indiana Black Expo Summer Celebration, along with Patti LaBelle and El DeBarge, at Bankers Life Fieldhouse in Indianapolis, Indiana.[38] In midsummer, The Isleys took another stroll down memory lane.

The RCA Victor and T-Neck Album Masters (1959–1983)

On August 21, Sony's Legacy Recordings released *The RCA Victor and T-Neck Album Masters (1959–1983)*, a twenty-three-CD compilation. The cover art for this anthology is a vintage photo of The Isley Brothers recording in a studio. This is the largest product ever released by The Isley Brothers. The box set traces the group's evolution across four decades.[39] This anthology was compiled and produced by Grammy Award–winner Leo Sacks, coproduced by Jeffrey James and Jeremy Holiday, and mastered from the original analog tapes by Grammy Award–winner Mark Wilder at Battery Studios. The CDs feature newly remastered versions of The Isley Brothers' twenty-one albums released for both labels, nearly all of which are expanded, with rare mixes and tracks making their CD and digital debuts. The collection includes eighty-four rare and previously unreleased bonus tracks.

One of the most significant inclusions is the "Great Lost Isley Brothers Album" *Wild in Woodstock: The Isley Brothers Live at Bearsville Sound Studio 1980*. First conceived as a "live" double album (with overdubbed crowd noise), this newly restored performance offers an immersive look at a crucial chapter in The Isley Brothers' history, a pivotal moment in the fusion of rock and funk music in an era fueled by the sound of The Isleys.[40]

The compilation begins with the original recording trio of Ronald, O'Kelly, and Rudolph and "Shout," includes 1960s and '70s soul hits "It's Your Thing," "That Lady," and "Fight the Power," then continues to early '80s "quiet storm" ballads, such as "Between the Sheets." Ernie stated, "In listening to all of it, you'll hear that we didn't have any master plan or road map, but we were in pursuit of the music, whatever music we were doing."

While most early rock 'n' roll acts who came up with The Isley Brothers during the late 1950s saw their popularity wane after just a few years, especially once The Beatles came along, The Isleys managed to stick around for the long haul. After a brief stint with Motown Records, the group began putting out records on its own T-Neck Records, releasing crossover psychedelic-soul hits "It's Your Thing" and "I Turned You On" in 1969. When Ernie, Marvin, and Chris entered the fold, The Isleys became a self-contained, six-piece band with 3+3, which featured another massive crossover hit, "That Lady." "Things were changing pretty quickly, musically," Chris stated. "If you wanted to remain relevant, you had to realize the music was changing and you needed to adapt."

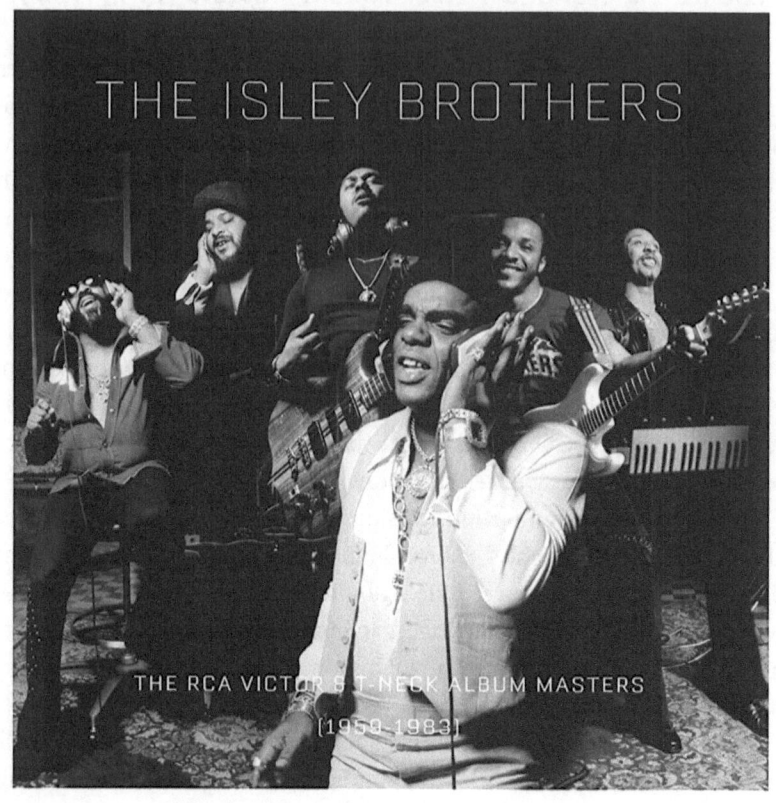

The cover for this anthology is a vintage photo of The Isleys in the studio.

Ernie's distinctive guitar sound, introduced on "That Lady" and "Summer Breeze," and Chris's expertise in composition and arranging took The Isley Brothers in yet another direction. Chris declared, "When we added what we added, we extended what the group could do. If you listen to the albums before *3+3*, they have a certain sound. That's something that jumped out at me, when I listened to the box set. The sound changed, from the almost Southern soul the group was into and changed into a whole 'nother thing." Music critic Eric Weisbard claims the group's reinvention gave its career an impressive second act. "They were part of the crossover era of Top 40 and rock 'n' roll, and they flourished equally well when soul was becoming a major-label music aimed at a black audience."[41] Having an extensive catalogue with so many hit records, there is no wonder why so many people love The Isley Brothers.

Also, in August, the White House decided to have President Barack Obama kick off its launch of an official channel on Spotify, the music streaming service, by creating two summer playlists. "Handpicked" by President Obama during his vacation in Martha's Vineyard, the day and night playlists last for about ninety minutes each and have a distinctly relaxing, summertime vibe. During the day, President Obama preferred the likes of Aretha Franklin, The Temptations, and "Live It Up" by The Isley Brothers. At night, he switched to more low-key tunes from John Coltrane, Al Green, and Joni Mitchell.[42] On August 22, two of President Obama's favorite artists, The Isley Brothers and Aretha Franklin, performed at Detroit's Chene Park (now Aretha Franklin Amphitheatre) to celebrate the venue's thirtieth anniversary.[43] The Isley Brothers remained busy throughout the fall.

In October, the Oprah Winfrey Network (OWN) began taping its series *Legends: OWN at the Apollo*. Filmed at the world-famous Apollo Theater, the four-part primetime special featured musical performances and intimate reflections by some of the biggest artists in music history. The first episode (October 24) featured seven-time Grammy Award-winner Gladys Knight. The second episode (October 31) featured Grammy Living Legend Recipient and Rock & Roll Hall of Famer Smokey Robinson. The third episode (November 7) featured Grammy Award-winning and *Billboard* powerhouse The Isley Brothers. The final episode (November 14) featured Grammy Award-winning and Rock & Roll Hall of Fame recipients Earth, Wind & Fire.[44] In late November, one particular Isley album was published in a special format.

Groove with You . . . Live!

On Black Friday, November 27, Legacy Recordings issued a limited edition exclusive for *Groove with You . . . Live!* This is the "Great Lost Album" renamed. As stated previously, this is a previously unreleased double album recorded for release in 1980. This newly restored project offers an immersive listen into a crucial chapter in The Isley Brothers' history, a pivotal moment in the fusion of rock and funk music in an era fueled by the sound of The Isleys. Featuring new cover art, evocative of the era, *Groove with You . . . Live!* is a two-LP set pressed on 180-gram gold (LP1) and blue (LP2) vinyl, designed to look like a classic release from The Isley Brothers' T-Neck discography.[45] *Groove with You . . . Live* features eleven tracks: "That Lady," "Here We Go

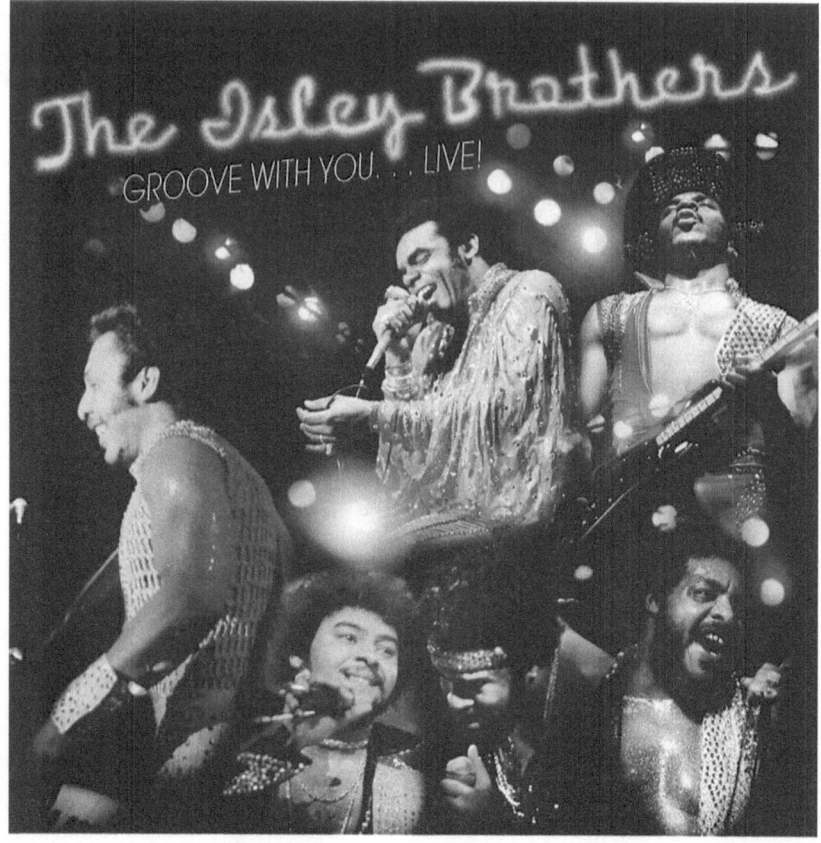

The cover for *Groove With You... Live!* is a collage of photos of the brothers in concert.

Again," "Don't Say Goodnight (It's Time for Love)," "Medley: Hello It's Me/ Footsteps in the Dark/For the Love of You/Take Me to the Next Phase," "Fight the Power," "Groove with You," "Summer Breeze," "Say You Will," "Voyage to Atlantis," "It's a Disco Night (Rock Don't Stop)," and "Livin' in the Life/Go For Your Guns." The cover art is a collage of photos of The Isley Brothers in concert. The CD version has an introduction and an outro.[46]

This had been a productive year for The Isley Brothers. They received a Trumpet Award, performed at special events, and released a twenty-three-disc anthology and a "lost" album that should have been released in 1980. In addition to all of this, they were nominated for induction into the Songwriters Hall of Fame for 2016.[47] With such a great catalogue, the brothers went into the new year with high expectations of being inducted.

The first point of business for The Isley Brothers in 2016 was performing at the Zora Neale Hurston Festival of the Arts and Humanities in Eatonville, Florida. The festival is named after the famous author and folklorist who became a key figure of the Harlem Renaissance. It explores both Hurston's and Eatonville's influences on culture with events about music, art, gardening, and more.[48] The Isleys could be seen in other various locations throughout the winter and spring, and Ronald had the privilege of appearing on another artist's album.

In April, American Latin rock band Santana released their twenty-fourth studio album titled *Santana IV*. Ronald appears on two songs from the album. His vocals highlight the eagerly impassioned Latin-rock workout "Love Makes the World Go Round" and the hard-edged and funky "Freedom in Your Mind."[49] Ronald's association with Santana would lead to a greater collaboration between the two artists the following year. But in a few weeks, The Isleys received honorary degrees.

On May 7, more than nine hundred graduates from sixty-eight countries received degrees at Berklee College of Music's commencement ceremony. Berklee President Roger H. Brown presented honorary doctor of music degrees to four music legends: The Isley Brothers, Lucian Grainge, Milton Nascimento, and Rita Moreno. Moreno delivered the commencement address to the graduating class and an estimated audience of nearly seven thousand guests at the Agganis Arena. The annual commencement concert, held the previous evening at the same venue, featured some of the college's most accomplished students paying tribute to the honorees with performances of music associated with their careers. Ernie was obviously moved by the tribute concert. In his acceptance speech, he stated, "Berklee, I want you to know, last night, you outdid yourselves. You're professionals. Ronald and I, and in the spirit of all the brothers, appreciate it beyond words, and appreciate you. And I'm fully confident that the future of music rests in good hands because of Berklee."[50] After receiving their doctorates, the brothers traveled abroad.

On Friday, May 27, during Memorial Day weekend, The Isley Brothers performed at the Sixteenth Annual Soul Beach Music Festival in Aruba. They mesmerized festivalgoers at the Soul Beach Harbor Arena with their timeless musical repertoire. The concert was hosted by comedian Chris Spencer. Other artists included Miguel, Fantasia, and Jazmine Sullivan.[51] The Isleys were continuing their practice of holding their own against much younger artists.

On July 16, The Isley Brothers headlined a concert with Sheila E. for the Taste of Chicago Festival at the Petrillo Music Shell in Chicago, Illinois.[52] On July 31, they were in concert with American Idol Ruben Studdard at the Portsmouth Pavilion in Portsmouth, Virginia.[53] On August 20, The Isleys participated in a Night of Soul, an "All White Affair" themed concert at the Wolf Creek Amphitheater in Atlanta, Georgia. The musical menu also included soul music legend Freddie Jackson, award-winning songbird Chanté Moore, and the Velvet Teddy Bear Ruben Studdard. The seventy-five-year-old Ronald took care of business and definitely owned the stage while Ernie continuously captivated the audience with his noted guitar skills.[54] Like his brother, Ernie managed to keep himself busy.

On Thursday, November 24, during Thanksgiving weekend, Ernie was a special guest when the Apollo Theater celebrated his mentor Jimi Hendrix, the most influential guitarist in rock music history. Other guests included singer/songwriter Nona Hendryx, poet Saul Williams, and more. The concert sailed through Hendrix's reservoir of early R&B influences that eventually led to his explorations of rock. As mentioned in chapter 2, Hendrix toured with The Isleys during 1964 and briefly resided with them in their home in Englewood, New Jersey, where the young Ernie first met the guitarist. The Apollo celebrated the fiftieth anniversary of the Jimi Hendrix Experience and what would have been his seventy-fourth birthday. Johnny Allen Hendrix was born November 27, 1942, in Seattle, Washington. He died September 18, 1970.[55] Within two months, Ernie returned to NYC with Ronald.

At the beginning of 2017, The Isley Brothers performed over a three-day weekend. On Friday, January 13, they were at the Twin River Event Center in Lincoln, Rhode Island.[56] On Saturday, the fourteenth, The Isleys performed at B. B. King Blues Club and Grill in New York City. And on the following day, they were at the NYCB Theatre in Westbury, New York.[57] The brothers appeared in multiple cities across America, and they were on the West Coast for Memorial Day weekend.

On May 27, The Isley Brothers headlined a concert at the ever-popular KBLX Stone Soul Concert, held at the Pavilion in Concord, California. Other artists who took the stage were Joe, Cameo, Doug E. Fresh, Lalah Hathaway, Average White Band, and Rick & Russ.[58] At seventy-six, Ronald, a.k.a. Mr. Biggs, still had the seductive voice and debonair presence, and Ernie played thrilling guitar on hits like "That Lady," "Summer Breeze," and "Voyage to Atlantis." Their extensive catalogue kept them in demand. After pleasing their fans on the road, The Isleys published their next album, which had been recorded in 2016.

Power of Peace

On July 28, The Isley Brothers and Santana released *Power of Peace*. At this time, Santana consisted of Carlos Santana and his wife Cindy Blackman Santana. The album is the fulfillment of a dream, a musical studio collaboration connecting Santana and The Isleys on a mind-bending journey through some of the enduring soul, funk, blues, rock, jazz, and pop songs that have inspired them.[59] *Power of Peace* features twelve cover songs and one new song: "Are You Ready (Chamber Brothers)," "Total Destruction to Your Mind (Swamp Dogg)," "Higher Ground (Stevie Wonder)," "God Bless the Child (Billie Holiday)," "I Remember," "Body Talk (Eddie Kendricks)," "Gypsy Woman (Curtis Mayfield)," "I Just Want to Make Love to You (Muddy Water/Willie Dixon)," "Love, Peace, Happiness (Chambers Brothers)," "What the World Needs Now Is Love Sweet Love (Dionne Warwick/Jackie DeShannon)," "Mercy Mercy Me—The Ecology (Marvin Gaye)," "Let the Rain Fall on You (Leon Thomas)," and "Let There Be Peace on Earth (Sy Miller and Jill Jackson)." On the front cover of the album is a dove, which usually symbolizes peace.[60]

When speaking about *Power of Peace*, Carlos Santana stated, "I feel a deep sense of gratitude, appreciation, and thankfulness. There is a spirit of creativity that came knocking and presented itself as a golden opportunity to do something with and for a supreme musician, who I consider to be the best in the world. Brother Ronnie Isley has been in the center of collective unity and harmony on the radio around the world since 1962 with 'Twist and Shout,' the song that the Beatles chose to invade America with." He added, "Like Michael Jackson, John Lennon, and Bob Marley, he's an iconic supreme of the highest order. Cindy and I feel very blessed to offer him this gift. From God, through us to you, for the world . . . Mr. Ronnie Isley." In return, Ronald stated, "It was an absolute joy working on this album with Carlos! I hope this record carries the spirit of hope, love, and peace to the world that it brought to me, my brother and Carlos!" Ernie shared his brother's sentiments, saying, "Doing this project with Carlos Santana was fun and illuminating. I hope all music lovers enjoy what we have done."

The *Power of Peace* cover displays a dove.

Power of Peace is led by Ronald on lead vocals and its main producer/arranger Carlos Santana on lead guitar, rhythm guitar, percussion, and background vocals. The new song, "I Remember," was written and sung by Cindy Blackman Santana. Cindy, who plays drums on the album, produced and arranged "Higher Ground" (along with Carlos). *Power of Peace* is a family affair featuring two Santanas, Carlos and Cindy, and four Isleys, Ronald, Ernie, Kandy Johnson Isley (Ronald's wife), and Tracy Isley (Ernie's wife). Kandy sings background on "God Bless the Child," "Body Talk," and "Gypsy Woman." Tracy also sings background on "God Bless the Child."[61]

Although no singles were released from *Power of Peace*, it did well on the music charts. On August 19, the album peaked at number sixty-four on *Billboard*'s 200 Albums chart and climbed to number seven on the Top R&B Albums chart. It also reached number twelve on *Billboard*'s Top Rock Albums chart on the same date.[62] *Power of Peace* received positive feedback from music critics.

Thom Jurek of AllMusic declared, "*Power of Peace* is loose, but everyone brought their chops to the party. This is what happens when great musicians gather simply to see what happens and enjoy one another's company."[63] Tristan Kneschke of PopMatters wrote, "The musicians clearly care about their chosen source material, and as a result, the album features faithful recreations of stirring originals. It actually picks up energy as it goes along, cresting on 'I Just Want to Make Love to You' and the cleansing 'Love, Peace, Happiness.' The album connects us with the expression of love across 20th century songwriting."[64] Doug Heselgrave of *Paste* magazine describes the songs as "well arranged, creatively charted, and, for the most part, beautifully performed. The vocals are generally stunning. Santana's unmistakable tone and unique approach to the guitar also remain intact."[65] A few weeks after the release of *Power of Peace*, The Isleys linked up with another powerhouse group.

On October 7, The Isley Brothers and The Commodores converged for a night of funky hits at Fantasy Springs Resort Casino in Indio, California. Like The Isleys, The Commodores had numerous chart-topping songs, many awards, and music that is embedded in sonic history. It's hard to flip through the radio dial and not hear a song by either group on a regular basis.[66] The Isleys' last performance of 2017 was in Memphis, Tennessee.

The Isley Brothers were selected as the recipient of the 2017 AutoZone Liberty Bowl Outstanding Achievement Award. Each year, the award is presented in recognition of excellence in the field of music and entertainment. The Isleys received their award on Friday, December 29, at the President's Gala, which was held at the Peabody Hotel in Memphis. On the following day, The Isley Brothers performed for the AutoZone Liberty Bowl's halftime spectacular.[67] They thrilled the Southern crowd with their classics "Twist and Shout" and "Shout." The brothers continued to perform throughout 2018.

By this time, it became increasingly rare to find groups who have been playing shows since the 1950s, but Ronald was still leading a group with his fine voice after more than six decades. Because of their success and longevity, The Isley Brothers received another honor while performing in Mableton, Georgia, a suburb of Atlanta.

On Saturday, July 14, The Isley Brothers performed at the Mable House Barnes Amphitheatre in Mableton and received a proclamation onstage. The Fulton County Board of Commissioners declared July 14 "The Isley Brothers Day" in metro Atlanta. Commissioner Natalie Hall said the honor was in recognition of the group's more than six-decade-long musical career.[68] After so many years, hits, and awards, the brothers appeared to be on cloud nine. But four weeks later, they had to deal with the loss of another loved one.

On August 16, The Isleys' good friend Aretha Franklin died from pancreatic cancer at the age of seventy-six. She was known as the "Queen of Soul." Franklin's funeral was held at Greater Grace Temple on the outskirts of her hometown, Detroit, Michigan. Many celebrities and preachers were in attendance. After giving words of expression, Ronald performed an emotional rendition of "His Eye Is on the Sparrow." It was obvious to everyone how much he missed his dear friend. In the meantime, Ronald composed himself, and he and Ernie went back on the road. They remained focused on their career as they looked forward to more productive years.

Chapter 12
Eternal

The year 2019 marked the sixtieth anniversary of The Isley Brothers' first hit tune, "Shout." This song is often played at parties, wedding receptions, and sporting events. Since 1959, The Isleys have inspired The Beatles, Ice Cube, R. Kelly, and countless others. They became one of the few music acts who had charted new music in six different decades: from the 1950s to the 2000s. Because of their prolific career, The Isleys were invited to participate in the Super Bowl festivities.

Super Bowl LIII was played on February 3 at Mercedes Benz Stadium in Atlanta, Georgia. The Big Game Weekend kicked off on Friday, February 1, with the "Legends Live Atlanta" concert at the Georgia International Convention Center. The Isley Brothers performed at the concert along with Maze featuring Frankie Beverly and Keke Wyatt. Melissa Sessoms, the concert's organizer, explained, "We wanted to produce an amazing live concert experience inspired by the rich history of Atlanta for music lovers and fans that want to share in the ambiance and excitement of the Big Game."[1] As time has shown, there is never a dull moment when The Isleys are onstage. A month later, Ernie again paid tribute to his mentor Jimi Hendrix.

On March 3, the critically acclaimed Experience Hendrix Tour returned for its biggest tour ever with thirty dates through the East Coast, South, and Midwest. This latest edition of the much-anticipated tour once again emphasized the influence Hendrix made on a diverse group of artists. The concerts brought together artists as contrasting as Ernie Isley, Billy Cox, and Taj Mahal. The tour began at the Pompano Beach Amphitheatre in Pompano Beach, Florida, and ended on April 6 at the Oakdale Theater in Wallingford,

Connecticut.² In late April, Ronald and Ernie were honored by the city of St. Louis, Missouri.

On April 24, The Isley Brothers were inducted into the St. Louis Walk of Fame at 6161 Delmar Boulevard. Ronald believes the inclusion was special, considering all the great acts with St. Louis roots. "We were from St. Louis at the time, and that part is great," he says. "Tina Turner, Miles Davis, Donny Hathaway, Chuck Berry, quite a few have been inducted, and I'm glad to be among them." At the time of the induction, the brothers had lived in the St. Louis area for twenty-two years.

Ronald moved to the St. Louis area when he was married to Angela Winbush, who is a native of the city. He had visited St. Louis with her, and they moved from Los Angeles and bought a house there. Ernie also moved; wherever his brother lived was where he wanted to be. Ronald still has a home in California. But what helped keep him and his wife Kandy in St. Louis were the educational offerings for son Ronald Jr., who attended a Christian school. Ernie and his wife, Tracy, love Missouri, except for the cold weather—though the barbecue options somewhat make up for it. He also enjoys the relative quiet, compared to the noise of Los Angeles and New York City.³ After their induction into the St. Louis Walk of Fame, The Isleys announced plans for another tour.

The Isley Brothers released their classic "Shout" on September 21, 1959. To celebrate its sixtieth anniversary, they organized the You Make Me Wanna Shout—Sixtieth Anniversary Tour. The tour started on July 6 at the Black Oak Casino in Tuolumne, California, and took the brothers across the country, hitting Biloxi, Mississippi, Wilmington, North Carolina, Reno, Nevada, and more. Ten additional dates were added to the original schedule, prompting them to be busy during the summer and on the road through the end of fall. The added dates included stops in Atlanta, Atlantic City, Albuquerque, and Los Angeles, where they played the famed Greek Theatre on August 24. The tour did not end until December 20, when The Isleys performed at the Kravis Center in West Palm Beach, Florida.⁴ One of the highlights of the tour was their July 20 performance at the three-day Pitchfork Music Fest in Chicago.

Pitchfork has a knack for incorporating music royalty in their eclectic three-day festival weekend lineups. The Isley Brothers unleashed their musical mojo that set fire to the 1960s and '70s soul era and solidified them as household names. Their hour-and-a-half-long set on the Pitchfork mainstage boasted hits spanning over four decades, including the reimagining of classics like "Footsteps in the Dark," "That Lady," "It's Your Thing" and "Fight the Power." Tributes were paid to legends who had transitioned. Ernie incorporated a soul-searing, electric tribute to Prince in their cover of "Summer Breeze." "If you love Prince like we do, I wanna hear you!" Ronald encouraged the crowd, backing up his brother. A powerful tribute was paid to Aretha Franklin as Ronald somberly reminisced on their friendship, which he said spanned from the early 1960s through her unfortunate passing in 2018. "I talked to her every day," he recalled. "She was one of my best friends."

The Isley Brothers were accompanied onstage by background vocalists, including Kandy Isley, and a line of vibrantly dressed background dancers, proving they still had the ability to move crowds even several generations removed from their work. Making sure to keep the ear of younger festival goers who may not have been as familiar with the group's decades-long accolades, songs like "Between the Sheets," most notably sampled in the Notorious B.I.G.'s breakout hit "Big Poppa," was remixed to include song and rapper vocals in their set. An ode was also given to Ice Cube during their performance of "Footsteps in the Dark," famously sampled on his 1992 classic "It Was a Good Day." Ronald's alter ego Mr. Biggs also made an appearance, as he arrived with jeweled-out chalice and cane, donning a stark white suit that appeared to be sprinkled with diamonds. To end the night, The Isleys closed their set with a high-octane performance of their first gold single, "Shout," demonstrating that they still had what it takes to rock a crowd.[5] In the midst of the tour, The Isleys received a special proclamation.

On Saturday, October 26, The Isley Brothers stopped in Cleveland, Ohio, for a concert with The O'Jays at the Playhouse Square. At the concert, City of Cleveland Ward 6 Councilman Blaine Griffin, along with Larry Wallace, presented the legendary group with a proclamation celebrating sixty years in the music industry.[6] After a successful sixtieth anniversary tour in America, The Isleys planned a 2020 tour for the United Kingdom.

In mid-December, The Isley Brothers announced a return to the UK after more than a decade away for their You Make Me Wanna Shout—Sixtieth Anniversary Tour. The tour was scheduled for six dates, beginning on June 24, 2020, at the Royal Concert Hall in Glasgow and ending on July 3 at the 02 Apollo in Manchester.[7] The brothers were optimistic for the new year, but neither could predict what would happen in 2020.

The year 2020 started nicely for The Isley Brothers. On January 16, the coveted Songwriters Hall of Fame Class of 2020 inductees were announced on

CBS This Morning. The Isley Brothers, along with Mariah Carey, Eurythmics, Rick Nowels, The Neptunes, William "Mickey" Stevenson, and Steve Miller, were scheduled to be celebrated for their legendary contributions in the art form of songwriting on Thursday, June 11, in New York City.[8] Songwriters are eligible for induction after writing hit songs for at least twenty years. New annual slates are voted on by the membership.[9] While 2020 was shaping up to be another good year for The Isleys, sinister events were taking place around the world.

On the same day the Songwriters Hall of Fame Class of 2020 inductees were announced, the impeachment trial of President Donald Trump began. On January 21, the first case of COVID-19 in the United States was confirmed by the CDC. On January 26, basketball superstar Kobe Bryant and his daughter Gianna Bryant were killed in a helicopter crash in Calabasas, California, along with seven others. Within a few weeks, the world would shut down.

On March 11, the World Health Organization (WHO) declared the coronavirus disease COVID-19 a global pandemic. Because of this, many countries around the world ordered their citizens to shelter in place and wear masks. In the United States, millions of people became unemployed as many businesses shut down, and thousands of people died. Schools switched to online learning, churches closed, and sporting events, conventions, and concerts were canceled.

On March 31, the Songwriters Hall of Fame (SHOF) rescheduled their Fifty-First Annual Induction and Awards Gala originally set for June 11, 2020, to June 10, 2021, at the Marriott Marquis New York. In making the announcement, SHOF president and CEO Linda Moran stated, "Although sad and very disappointing, it seemed to be more prudent and in the best interests and well-being of everyone, especially our inductees, honorees, and guests to move the 2020 class of inductees and honorees in its entirety to next year's gala when they can be truly celebrated." SHOF Chairman Nile Rodgers said, "The wonderful songs that members of the Songwriters Hall of Fame have created are currently bringing comfort to billions of people all over the world in their time of uncertainty and need, and that is something I believe we can all find gratitude in. We are family, please be safe."[10]

In addition to the pandemic, America was dealing with its perpetual problem of racism. All over the country, unarmed innocent African Americans were being murdered senselessly. On February 23, Ahmaud Arbery was murdered by three White men during a racially motivated hate crime in Brunswick, Georgia. On March 13, Breonna Taylor was fatally shot at her home in Louisville, Kentucky, when seven cops forcibly entered. On May 25, George Floyd was murdered by a racist cop in Minneapolis, Minnesota. After these murders and other racially motivated tragedies, The Isley Brothers' background singers, Kandy Isley and her sister Kim Johnson, decided to release a new single titled "Free."

Kandy and Kim had been sitting on "Free" since 2016, waiting to figure out what to do with it. As a new era of the civil rights movement began taking over the world, they knew it was time to release their anti-hate song.

> I believe the day will come
> No one's gonna hate no one and this broken world will see
> Only love can set us free

The country-soul song, credited to Kim & Kandy, was cowritten and coproduced by the sisters with Doug Johnson (no relation) and Robin Ruddy of Nashville, Tennessee. It speaks to peace, healing, reconciliation, and love and was timelier in 2020. "My heart was hurting," Kandy says of the recent deaths. "I literally couldn't stop crying. We said, 'OK, it's time to release the song.' So, I pushed the button."

During the first week of June, Kandy called her sister and said it was time to release "Free." They initially had planned to put out the song in 2016; with Donald Trump on his way into the White House, the vibe of the country was changing. But, Kandy said, they ultimately decided the timing wasn't right. Kim declared that Black Americans were seeing some of the same things happening in the world that earlier generations saw. "It's just a different time," she says. "There's still lynching right in the street.... We're not going to put up with discrimination and systemic racism. I feel there's a change coming in ways we would have never thought."

The reception to the song was warm. "We're grateful, thankful and in awe of just being able to give this song as a gift to the world and seeing people coming together like the song says," Kim stated. "We're seeing again in our lifetime this huge revival happening all over the world. People are being healed, and it's a healing experience for everybody. We're happy to be a part of the moment.... God gave us this divine song." "Free" is available on all streaming platforms.[11] Kim and Kandy also released Christmas music that year.

For years, Kim and Kandy had lent their voices, either together or separately, to Christmas projects by artists, including The Isley Brothers, Christina

Aguilera, Yolanda Adams, Andrae Crouch, and CeeLo featuring Rod Stewart. In the fall of 2020, they came up with their own Christmas project titled *Christmas with Kim & Kandy*. The EP includes their harmonious takes on three classics: "Have Yourself a Merry Little Christmas," "Santa Baby," and "Away in a Manger." Kim and Kandy decided in November to record the EP, which meant the project would require a quick turnaround. Kim, who arranged the songs, traveled to Nashville, Tennessee, to oversee the musicians' recording at Parlour Studios on Music Row. Those tracks were brought back to St. Louis so the sisters could record vocals. The Isleys have a studio at home. Because of the time constraints, they were only able to record three songs, which made song selection all the more crucial. The songs range from country to timeless pop to music geared toward the Christian market. *Christmas with Kim & Kandy* is also available on streaming platforms.[12]

At the turn of the new year, the world was still dealing with the pandemic, and many public spaces were still shut down. Since concerts were canceled, Americans were able to enjoy music from some of their favorite artists virtually. One popular form of online entertainment is the Verzuz battle. This live show consists of two challengers in the music industry who compete with their best hit records. The Verzuz battle may consist of up to twenty rounds of hit songs to go head-to-head against each other. During the battle, the artist will play each song one after another, through audio sound systems via computer or recording studio equipment. People could watch via Instagram, Twitter, or YouTube. There are no official winners chosen. It's just a means to entertain people and spread joy and positivity during a time of uncertainty.

After the esteemed pairings of Snoop Dogg and DMX, and Alicia Keys and John Legend, The Isley Brothers and Earth, Wind & Fire (EWF) appeared in the next round of the beloved series on Easter Sunday, April 4, 2021, the first time two bands bumped heads on Verzuz. The battle was hosted by Steve Harvey, and music was provided by veteran DJ D-Nice. D-Nice spun 1980s classics from Stevie Wonder and Chaka Khan before Harvey introduced himself, offered a prayer for Verzuz veteran DMX, and raved about the formative importance of the two groups in his own life: "These groups made me. This music shaped me." The Isleys and EWF battled for twenty-five rounds. It was a mutual celebration of their respective catalogue of classics.

Earth, Wind & Fire showed why they're still one of popular music's greatest institutions and will be a major live draw until the day they (or we) turn to dust. But even on the verge of his eightieth birthday, Ronald just has that inextinguishable star power that makes him transfixing whenever he's on the screen and the voice that has made him a music icon. He hadn't been a pop fixture for over sixty years now by accident. EWF came with hits like "Shining Star," "Reasons," and "Fantasy." The Isleys used their classics, such as "It's Your Thing," "Harvest for the World," and "Voyage to Atlantis." There are no official winners for Verzuz battles, but *Billboard* magazine scored this battle 16-10-4 in The Isley Brothers' favor.[13]

After their epic battle with Earth, Wind & Fire, The Isley Brothers released a new single titled "Friends and Family," which is considered an anthem for cookouts and family reunions. This is a step jam featuring a rap from Snoop Dogg.[14] It is the lead single for their album released in 2022. The music video shows Ronald and Kandy with Ernie and Tracy hosting a party with family and friends in a mansion situated high on a hill.[15] "Friends and Family" peaked at number forty-five on *Billboard*'s R&B/Hip-Hop Airplay chart on July 31, and it reached number thirteen on the Adult R&B Airplay chart on September 11.[16] In early summer, The Isleys traveled to New Jersey for more honors.

On Thursday, June 24, echoes of "It's Your Thing," "Shout," and other hits by The Isley Brothers punctuated as more than five hundred people were in attendance for back-to-back ceremonies to rename Van Arsdale Place and Van Cortlandt Terrace in Teaneck and Liberty Road in Englewood. Included in the audience were Ronald and Ernie, Englewood Mayor Michael Wildes, Councilman-at-Large Charles Cobb, and Bergen County Sheriff Anthony Cureton. Both towns now have streets named The Isley Brothers Way. The group's lengthy musical career has strong roots in Englewood and Teaneck. The family lived in Englewood, and Ronald and Rudolph eventually moved to Teaneck. Their record label, T-Neck Records, was named for the city. "This is the biggest thing since the pandemic," said Darryl Greene, a Teaneck Planning Board member who helped the day come to pass.

The Isley Brothers had another reason to be in Teaneck; they were attending the Isleys' grandchildren's graduation from Dwight Morrow High School. "Thank you, thank you, thank you," Ronald told the crowd in Teaneck. "It's a really special moment to be honored this way," said VeRon Garrison, grandson of Ronald and a graduate of Dwight Morrow. Letters of resolution from Governor Phil Murphy recognized The Isley Brothers for their achievements and were read by Englewood Mayor Wildes. "The Isley Brothers' music, it teaches you how to act, how to be kind, and how to treat others," Wildes said. "We want this next generation to uphold that." A proclamation was read stating that every June 24 in Englewood and Teaneck will be recognized as The Isley Brothers Day. Ronald and Ernie were also presented with keys to the city of Englewood.[17] By this time, pandemic restrictions had begun to ease, but some events were still put on hold.

The Songwriters Hall of Fame had originally postponed its 2020 induction ceremony for June 10, 2021, but The Isley Brothers and others had to wait another year to be inducted because the SHOF rescheduled the induction for June 16, 2022.[18] But the world slowly began to reopen. Because of this, a few concerts and music festivals began to take place.

On July 23, The Isley Brothers performed at Cross Pointe Park in Hazel Crest, Illinois, a suburb of Chicago. They were joined by Carl Thomas, Kindred the Family Soul, Chantay Savage, Sandy Redd, Nathan Palmer, and Uneqka.[19] On July 24, The Isleys headlined the Cincy Soul Fest at Sawyer Point Park in Cincinnati, Ohio. Other musical guests included Ari Lennox and SWV.[20] While the brothers were in Cincinnati, they were inducted into the Cincinnati Black Music Walk of Fame.

The Cincinnati Black Music Walk of Fame was officially slated to open in the summer of 2022. At the time, the future walkway was a pile of gravel in front of the Andrew J. Brady ICON Music Center. Plans for the interactive park and star-studded path were unveiled July 24 during an induction ceremony. The first four inductees to receive stars on the Walk of Fame were Bootsy Collins, King Records icon Otis Williams, late gospel singer Dr. Charles Fold, and of course, The Isley Brothers. Through a video, Ronald and Ernie expressed their gratitude for receiving a star on the Black Music Walk of Fame.[21] In the meantime, the delta variant of COVID-19 was spreading and became the dominant strain in America by late summer. Consequently, concerts were still few and far between.

In the fall, The Isley brothers gave Ernie's daughter, Alexandra Isley, also known as Alex Isley, the opportunity to showcase her talent. On Saturday, September 25, The Isleys performed at the KFC Yum! Center in Louisville, Kentucky, with Charlie Wilson, Stokely, and Alex Isley.[22] On the following day, the same lineup performed at the Chaifetz Arena in St. Louis, Missouri.[23] As the daughter of Ernie and the niece of Ronald, one could argue that Alex's musical path is her birthright.

Alex Isley was born in Westwood, New Jersey, but is a longtime resident of Los Angeles, California. Classically trained by her maternal grandmother, an opera singer, Alex studied jazz theory and performance at Los Angeles

County High School for the Arts and continued at UCLA, where she graduated with a degree in jazz studies. In 2012, Alex debuted with *Love/Art Memoirs*, an EP that introduced her mellow approach to R&B. The following year, she released the full-length *Dreams in Analog*. Alex released two more albums: *LUXURY* (2015) and *Marigold* (with Jack Dine) (2022). She has worked with several artists, including Robin Thicke, Scarface, Kendrick Lamar, and PJ Morton.[24] Alex also makes random appearances with The Isley Brothers at special events. For the remainder of 2021, the brothers could be seen in various cities across America.

On October 10, The Isley Brothers headlined a concert with Lil Wayne and Burna Boy at One Music Fest, held at Centennial Olympic Park in Atlanta, Georgia. Some of the other artists at the festival were Lucky Daye, Ari Lennox, and H.E.R.[25] On November 6, The Isleys were in concert with Maze Featuring Frankie Beverly, Joe, and comedian Buck Wild at Boardwalk Hall in Atlantic City, New Jersey.[26] The Isley Brothers were scheduled to perform at the Once Upon a Time in LA Music Festival, which occurred December 18 at Banc of California Stadium and Exposition Park in Los Angeles. Unfortunately, around 8:36 p.m., a fight broke out behind the main stage.

During the altercation, rapper Drakeo was severely injured by a man wielding an edged weapon. He was rushed to the hospital, where he later died. Out of respect for those involved and in coordination with local authorities and artists, the organizers decided not to move forward with remaining sets so the festival was ended an hour early. The Isleys were not able to perform. Other artists who were unable to perform were Al Green, Snoop Dogg, 50 Cent, Ice Cube, and Cypress Hill.[27] By this time, a new variant of the coronavirus had been discovered.

On November 4, scientists in South Africa discovered a second mutation for COVID-19. This mutation was named the omicron variant. It quickly began to spread around the globe. On Christmas Day, more than 4,500 flights worldwide were cancelled, and omicron caused much concern in the new year. As a precaution, some restrictions were still in place, and concerts were occurring sparsely. The Isleys' next major performance didn't occur until March the following year.

On the weekend of March 12 and 13, 2022, the popular Jazz in the Gardens Festival was held at the Hard Rock Stadium in Miami Gardens, Florida. Back in 2020, in the wake of the global pandemic, Jazz in the Gardens was forced to cancel just two days before the doors were slated to open. Almost two years later, the 2022 festival represented an impressive comeback as the City of Miami Gardens' signature event and was expected to be an even better experience for the thousands of loyal and eager ticket buyers who hail from all over the world. The organizers wanted to get the best acts in jazz and R&B music. In addition to The Isley Brothers, the lineup included H.E.R., The Roots, SWV, Mary J. Blige, Stokely, and others. Entrants were required to show a valid COVID-19 vaccination card or a negative COVID-19 test. Social distancing protocols were observed and face masks were strongly encouraged.[28] Almost two months later, The Isleys returned to Louisville, Kentucky, and Newark, New Jersey.

On May 4, the Louisville Urban League Derby Gala, a black-tie fundraiser, featured a performance by The Isley Brothers at Norton Healthcare Sports and Learning Center, marking the first concert ever held at the facility. This was one of several events leading up to the Kentucky Derby that was held on May 7.[29] On May 6, The Isleys performed for the Mother's Day Good Music Fest at Prudential Center in Newark, New Jersey. Other artists on the bill were Keith Sweat, Monica, and SWV.[30] After putting in a little work, The Isleys received a long-awaited honor.

Following a two-year postponement due to the pandemic, The Isley Brothers were inducted into the Songwriters Hall of Fame on June 16. Representing The Isley Brothers were Ernie, Ronald, and Elaine Isley Goodstone (Rudolph's daughter). Ernie reminded the guests that their early hit "Shout" was recorded sixty-three years prior and their music would go on for decades, prompting The Beatles to cover them. The two brothers then joined up for a medley of hits that included "That Lady," "It's Your Thing," and "Between the Sheets." They brought the crowd to its feet with the aforementioned classic "Shout." Other inductees were Mariah Carey, Eurythmics, The Neptunes, and Steve Miller.[31] During the same week, The Isleys participated in Juneteenth celebrations in Houston, Texas.

Juneteenth is a federal holiday commemorating the emancipation of enslaved African Americans. Every year since 1872, Black communities in the Houston area have gathered on June 19 at Emancipation Park in the sweltering heat to reminisce, roller-skate, and dance the evening away. On June 19, 1865, enslaved people in Galveston, Texas (forty-five miles outside Houston), first discovered they had been freed after troops arrived in Texas to deliver a general order. At the time, most enslaved people in Texas were unaware that President Abraham Lincoln's 1863 Emancipation Proclamation had freed them two years prior. Emancipation Park is where the first Freedom Day—now coined Juneteenth—public celebration took place in 1872. Before then, Juneteenth celebrations were hosted privately among close family and friends at home. The Juneteenth celebration in 2022 marked the 150th anniversary of Emancipation Park. To help the people in Houston celebrate, The Isley Brothers capped off Juneteenth festivities by headlining concerts with Maze Featuring Frankie Beverly on the weekend of June 18–19.[32] Two weeks later, The Isleys traveled to New Orleans, Louisiana, for the Essence Festival.

After being postponed in 2020 and virtual in 2021, the Essence Festival returned in 2022 as a virtual and in-person celebration from June 30 to July 3 at the Caesar's Superdome. The theme for the 2022 festival was "It's the Black Joy for Me," and Essence intentionally created the most diverse range of music from Afrobeats to R&B with unexpected additions of country music to be shared by all who ventured to New Orleans. Headliners included The Isley Brothers, New Edition, The Roots, Janet Jackson, and Jazmine Sullivan. Other performing artists were Wizkid, Beenie Man, country music sensation Mickey Guyton, and more.[33] A few days after Essence Fest, on July 9, The Isleys were back in Atlanta, Georgia, for a concert with Maze Featuring Frankie Beverly at the Cadence Bank Amphitheatre in Chastain Park.[34] During this time, the brothers were preparing to publish their thirty-third studio album.

Make Me Say It Again, Girl

On August 12, The Isley Brothers released the single "Make Me Say It Again, Girl," a duet featuring Ronald and Beyoncé. This is a remake of the song with the same name from *The Heat Is On*.[35] Ronald and Beyoncé exchange lines throughout this revamp. Beyoncé laid down her vocals remotely in the Hamptons in 2021, and Ronald tracked his vocals in Los Angeles. Ronald first met Beyoncé when she was with Destiny's Child. The group sampled "Make Me Say It Again, Girl" for the song "Second Nature" on their self-titled debut album. When The Isleys began recording their album in Los Angeles in 2021, the idea of working with Beyoncé was one of the first things that came to Ronald's mind. Beyoncé's mother, Tina Knowles, helped bring about the collaboration. "She has a love for The Isley Brothers and her daughter grew up listening to this type of music," Kandy Isley told *Billboard*.[36]

Ronald also shared a sweet story about everyone's reaction to the remake. "Beyoncé's mother texted us to say how much they were crying over the record when Beyoncé played it for them," he said before admitting that he also shed some tears, along with his wife Kandy and her sister. "Me, Kandy and her sister were together when we first heard it, and they were crying. Then, Ernie and his wife came over, and there was crying again. We hadn't done any crying over a record in years [laughs]," he stated.[37]

The second version of "Make Me Say It Again, Girl" rose to number one on *Billboard*'s Adult R&B Airplay chart on October 1 and remained there for five weeks. It also reached number twenty on the Hot R&B Songs chart on October 29.[38] "Make Me Say It Again, Girl" was The Isleys' first number one song since their 2001 hit "Contagious." It was named Best Collaboration at the 2022 Soul Train Awards ceremony.[39] The song is also the title track for the brothers' first album in five years.

Make Me Say It Again, Girl was released on September 30. It contains fourteen songs: "Make Me Say It Again, Girl (featuring Beyoncé)," "Long Voyage Home," "The Plug (featuring 2 Chainz)," "Sexy Face," "My Love Song," "Great Escape (featuring Trey Songz)," "Last Time," "Keys to My Mind (featuring Quavo and Takeoff)," "There'll Never Be (featuring Earth, Wind & Fire and El DeBarge)," "Disappear," "Consolidate," "Right Way," "Friends and Family (featuring Snoop Dogg)," and "Biggest Bosses." The album covers shows Ronald and Ernie dressed in green with a green background.[40] The color green often symbolizes wealth and prosperity. It is definitely a blessing for The Isley Brothers to have had such a long and illustrious career.

When speaking about *Make Me Say It Again, Girl*, Ronald told *Billboard*, "For me, this new album is almost like the beginning. I'm so happy about it. But I also want people to hear it and decide. I remember when I couldn't wait for people to hear 'That Lady' when we were mixing it. That's how excited we all were. You just want all of your fans to hear it too."[41] After the album's release, The Isley Brothers released "The Plug (featuring 2 Chainz)."

"The Plug" is a smooth R&B groove about a man who has the ability to obtain or supply hard-to-find items.

What you need, come get it
I'm your sole supplier
Let me lift you higher.[42]

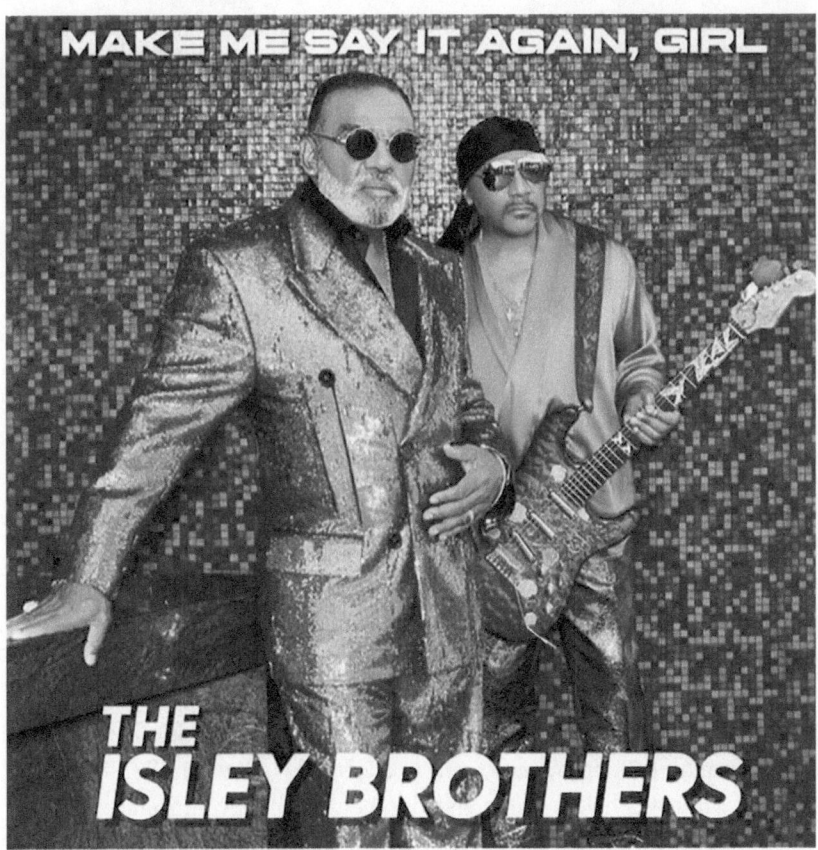

The cover for *Make Me Say It Again, Girl* features Ronald and Ernie dressed in green against a green background.

The video for "The Plug" follows The Isley Brothers into the studio to record the song. Filmed at the historical Jim Henson Studios, the producers wanted to give the space a modern look using dim neon lighting that also complemented the song's rhythm and groove.[43] "The Plug" eventually reached number twenty-four on *Billboard*'s Adult R&B Airplay chart on January 14, 2023.[44] Isley fans quickly took notice of the song and album.

Many fans were shocked at eighty-one-year-old Ronald's soulful spin on modern R&B music. On *Make Me Say It Again, Girl*, he sings sweet melodies, but it is surprising that he refers to himself as the "plug." Some fans also wonder who did the ghostwriting for The Isley Brothers in 2022. One fan jokingly questioned if it was the rapper Future. Other fans understand that The Isley Brothers have the unique star power, musical abilities, and adaptiveness to remain relevant throughout many decades. Several Isley lovers called the album "lit," claiming The Isley Brothers are responsible for making endless hits.[45] Songs such as "Long Voyage Home," "Sexy Face," and "Disappear" contain the smooth soul sounds Isley fans have come to love. But "Keys to My Mind" and especially "Biggest Bosses" may have some fans scratching their heads. Nevertheless, the album added three more hits to The Isleys' repertoire: "Friends and Family," "The Plug," and the title track.

The release of *Make Me Say It Again, Girl* was part of a fruitful year for The Isley Brothers. In addition to headlining Juneteenth concerts and performing at major music events, The Isleys were inducted into the Songwriters Hall of Fame. They also released two hit singles. The brothers closed the year by performing at the Fox Theatre in Detroit, Michigan, on December 31. The Isleys joined forces with Frankie Beverly and Maze to roll back the years and ring in the new year with silky soul music.[46] The groups joined forces again on January 13, 2023, for a concert at the H-E-B Center in Austin, Texas.[47] On February 3, The Isleys performed at the MusiCares's 2023 Person of the Year Gala.

The MusiCares's Person of the Year Gala is an annual pre-Grammy tradition from MusiCares, the charitable wing of the Recording Academy that raises money to help musicians in need. In 2023, Smokey Robinson and Berry Gordy, the visionary creative duo behind the revolutionary Motown Records, saw their legacy play out onstage at the gala honoring their life's work. The Isley Brothers reminisced over their days at Motown Records as they paid tribute to Gordy and Robinson. The star-studded event also included performances by Stevie Wonder, The Temptations, The Four Tops, and others.[48] Throughout the winter and spring, The Isleys continued performing at various events around the country. And in early spring, a sibling rivalry unfolded between Rudolph and Ronald in the Illinois court system.

On March 20, Rudolph filed a lawsuit against Ronald, accusing his younger brother of secretly and unfairly obtaining exclusive rights to the "Isley Brothers" trademark, which they had previously split. Rudolph requested a trial by jury in a bid to regain his "rightful 50 percent share" of The Isley Brothers empire. The United States Patent and Trademark Office approved Ronald's registration for sole ownership of The Isley Brothers brand in August 2022. Rudolph claimed that all profits and property accrued under The Isley Brothers trademark have been divided equally among the three founding members since the 1950s.

After O'Kelly died in March 1986, Rudolph and Ronald Isley agreed to 50/50 ownership of the band and trademark, the lawsuit states.

Rudolph Isley departed the group in 1989 while dealing with some health issues and mourning the loss of O'Kelly Isley, according to court documents. Though he had not recorded with the band since then, Rudolph argued he had "remained active in promoting and managing the group's properties" and deserved to keep his half of their earning. The court filing states, "Upon information and belief, Ronald Isley has within the past year offered goods and services in commerce to the public under the trademark within this judicial district and in other locations, without the authorization or approval of Rudolph Isley, and has failed to account to or make payment to Rudolph Isley in connection with such exploitation of the trademark." Ronald called the trademark case "an unfortunate family matter that will get resolved in litigation."[49] While the case lingered, The Isleys were still making appearances.

On March 24, The Isley Brothers appeared on *The Jennifer Hudson Show*. They discussed their longevity, Aretha Franklin, and *Make Me Say It Again, Girl* and performed "Shout" with the host. On May 5, The Isleys appeared on *Sherri*, hosted by Sherri Shepherd. The brothers discussed their catalogue, especially ballads, and their latest album. Ronald discussed his friendship with Aretha Franklin, and he announced his new Ronald Isley line of brandy. A week later, the brothers began a series of summer concert appearances.

On Friday, May 12, The Isley Brothers performed in front of screaming fans for the Peak House Festival at the Ventura County Fairgrounds in Ventura, California. Other artists there were Smokey Robinson and Anderson .Paak of Silk Sonic. The festival started in 2017 and raises money to support underserved youth through the Brandon Anderson Foundation, named after .Paak's birth name. It also featured hip-hop, rhythm and blues, and local marching band performances.[50] Three weeks later, the brothers were on the East Coast.

On Friday, June 3, The Isley Brothers performed for the Thirtieth Annual Capital Jazz Fest at the Merriweather Post Pavilion in Columbia, Maryland. Other musicians on the bill were George Benson, Corinne Bailey Rae, and Ne-Yo.[51] On the following day, The Isley Brothers performed for The Roots Picnic at the Mann Center. While drumming, Questlove introduced the group by saying: "On guitar, one of the greatest axemen of all time . . . Ernie Isley on guitar, and of course, the one and only, the legend, the smoothest . . . Mr. Biggs himself, Ronald Isley." The Isleys and The Roots opened with a soulful rendition of "Choosey Lover," followed by other hits like "For the Love of You" and "Footsteps in the Dark." It was hard to look away from Ernie's playing, and Ronald's personality easily showed through his captivating stage presence.⁵² The brothers also headlined a concert at the AFRAM Festival in Baltimore, Maryland, which occurred on Juneteenth weekend, June 17 and 18, at Druid Park. Ty Dolla $ign headlined Saturday, and The Isley Brothers headlined Sunday. The festival is for people of all ages to enjoy.⁵³ By that time, the brothers were due for a new single.

On July 7, The Isley Brothers released the fourth single from *Make Me Say It Again, Girl*, titled "Last Time." The single coincided with the album being available on vinyl and CD in the United States on the same date. *Make Me Say It Again, Girl* became available on vinyl and CD globally on July 21.⁵⁴ "Last Time" is a mellow ballad in which Ronald sings about reflecting on the last time he and his woman made love.⁵⁵ This song peaked at number twenty-seven on the *Billboard* R&B/Hip-Hop Airplay chart on November 11. It also climbed to number seven on *Billboard*'s Adult R&B Airplay chart on the same date.⁵⁶ While this song was on the charts, tragedy struck the Isley family again.

On October 11, Rudolph Isley died in his sleep of an apparent heart attack at his home in Chicago. He was eighty-four years old. Rudolph was a founding member of The Isley Brothers, who left the group in 1989 to become a Baptist minister. He once stated, "I may have stopped singing pop music, but I will always be an Isley Brother." In addition to brothers Ronald and Ernie, Rudolph's survivors include his wife Elaine Jasper, their children Rudy Jr., Elizabeth, Valerie, and Elaine, and several grandchildren.⁵⁷ Three weeks later, the surviving brothers performed in Chicago.

On Saturday, November 4, The Isley Brothers were the musical guests for the Chicago Urban League's Sixty-Second Annual Golden Fellowship Dinner, which raised nearly $2.4 million to support education, job training, housing, entrepreneurship, and leadership programs. The Isleys serenaded the audience with classic hits like "Between the Sheets," "Footsteps in the Dark," and a tribute to Tina Turner with "Proud Mary." The crowd lifted their phones, swung their hips, and sang along with the legendary group.⁵⁸ The legends also picked up two more award nominations.

On Sunday, November 26, the 2023 Soul Train Awards show was held in Los Angeles. The Isley Brothers were nominated in the category of Best Group, which was won by Maverick City. The Isleys were also nominated in the category of Certified Soul Award, which was won by Usher.⁵⁹ These nominations proved that the legends could still compete with artists who were several years their junior as they approached their seventieth anniversary in 2024.

The first point of business for The Isley Brothers in 2024 was the Beloved Community Awards in Atlanta, Georgia. The Martin Luther King Jr. Center for Nonviolent Social Change, commonly known as the King Center, in Atlanta held its annual Beloved Community Awards celebration on Saturday, January 13, 2024. The awards recognize national and international individuals and organizations that exemplify excellence in leadership and pursuit of social justice. The event was hosted by Essence Atkins and Dule Hill as part of the Center's King Holiday events. Honorees included Michael J. Fox, Deloris Jordan, and Spelman College. The Isleys provided a musical performance.[60] Three weeks later, The Isleys were on the West Coast.

The Sixty-Sixth Annual Grammy Awards ceremony was held Sunday, February 4, in Los Angeles. Every year, music mogul Clive Davis holds a Pre-Grammy Gala copresented by the Recording Academy. Performers for the 2024 gala included Public Enemy, Green Day, Josh Groban, and The Isley Brothers, who led the crowd through their 1959 call-and-response classic "Shout."[61] On Sunday, February 18, The Isleys performed for the Valentine's Super Love Jam at the Footprint Center in Phoenix, Arizona. Other hitmakers included Atlantic Starr, Peaches and Herb, GQ, All-4-One, and The Delfonics. It was an ideal concert for fans of old-school music.[62] Less than a month later, Ernie celebrated another birthday.

On March 7, Ernie turned seventy-two years old. By this time, he had been a professional musician for fifty-five years. His first professional gig was playing bass guitar on the smash hit "It's Your Thing." Ernie also played electric guitar, acoustic guitar, and drums on The Isley Brothers' early seventies albums before becoming an official member of the group in 1973. He cowrote some of their major hits, including "Fight the Power," "Harvest for the World," "Voyage to Atlantis," "Brown Eyed Girl," and "Between the Sheets."[63] In the spring, Ernie received a well-deserved honor.

On Thursday, April 4, the Guitar Center Music Foundation (GCMF) held its Third Annual Benefit Gala and Concert at the Hollywood Roosevelt Hotel in Los Angeles. The GCMF is a nonprofit organization that advances the healing transformative power of music by granting instruments to music education and music therapy programs in need. At this event, Ernie Isley was presented a Lifetime Achievement Award. Ernie amused the crowd with the tale of how he arrived at the iconic tone for his guitar solo on "That

Lady"—by testing gear (Electro-Harmonix Big Muff and a Maestro Phase Shifter) in a Guitar Center Store!

Before the award presentation, Ernie was celebrated musically by a diverse cast of musicians, accompanied by a band led by the program's musical director, Greg Phillinganes. Those musicians included Living Colour guitarist Vernon Reid, Ray Parker Jr., Melanie Faye, and Ernie's daughter, Alex Isley. Video tributes came from other artists, including Chaka Khan, Cheryl Crow, Nile Rodgers, Narada Michael Walden, Carlos Santana, and H.E.R. Ernie stated, "Many thanks to everyone involved with the Guitar Center for creating such a memorable evening. My sincere hopes and best wishes are with the future generations."[64] In the following month, older brother Ronald reached another milestone.

On May 21, Ronald celebrated his eighty-third birthday. By this time, he had been singing for seventy years. Ronald has been one of the most recognizable voices in R&B and funk music for six and a half decades, ever since the classic hit "Shout" in 1959. He is a true bridge between generations of music lovers and one of the most important singers of our time.[65] Ronald is sometimes dubbed the "King of R&B." In June, he reunited with ex-wife Angela Winbush.

On June 16, The Isley Brothers and Angela Winbush performed at the Aretha Franklin Amphitheatre in Detroit, Michigan, for a Father's Day concert. Angela's vocals were as powerful and captivating as ever, and she commanded the stage with an energy that defied her sixty-nine years. The Isleys delivered a stellar performance, blending their classic hits with a few surprises that had everyone on their feet. The backdrop imagery was filled with photos and videos showcasing their journey through the decades. It was a visual trip down memory lane, highlighting their evolution and enduring influence in the music industry. Ronald took a moment to thank the audience for rocking with them for sixty-five years, the time since their first hit, "Shout." The evening was about timeless music and the enduring talent of two iconic artists.[66] A week later, the brothers received what many consider a necessary and overdue honor.

On Monday, June 24, the Walk of Fame Selection Panel of the Hollywood Chamber of Commerce announced the artists chosen to receive stars on the Hollywood Walk of Fame in the class of 2025. The honorees were chosen from among hundreds of nominations to the committee at a meeting held on June 24 and ratified by the chamber's board of directors on the same day.

The Isley Brothers were selected in the category of Recording. Other artists in the same category include Fantasia, Prince, and War. Recipients have two years to schedule star ceremonies from the date of selection before they expire.[67] This is an appropriate honor for such a long and prosperous career.

When questioned about the secret to The Isley Brothers' longevity, Ernie stated, "I think the answer is that we've always loved all kinds of music and we changed with the musical terrain and climate. And as I said before, we also influenced many other bands like The Beatles and many others. I believe our influence has managed to cross generations too." By August, The Isleys were on a world tour, which included a scheduled appearance in Australia with The Beach Boys. Ernie added, "My greatest happiness comes from just being able to continue doing what I do and watching the joy it brings to people's faces. Not a lot of people can say that."[68] It is extremely rare for a music act to remain relevant after recording for more than half a century.

Ronald Isley has been the lead singer of The Isley Brothers for seventy years. His voice has carried the group through several genres of music and through major changes in the music industry. Ernie Isley has been a professional musician since 1969. Ronald's voice and Ernie's guitar work have become iconic in the world of pop music. Although they are mature musicians, The Isleys proved they can still bring joy and excitement to music lovers around the world. Their music is timeless and will be appreciated by many generations to come.

The Isley Brothers—Eternal

Afterword

The Isley Brothers began as a gospel quartet because their father and mother recognized their talent when they were very young. The brothers eventually moved to New York City to pursue their dreams of making it big in the recording industry. In 1959, The Isleys scored their first hit, the rock 'n' roll classic "Shout," which has become a party anthem. Their second rock 'n' roll classic is "Twist and Shout" from 1962.

Although they had two hit records, The Isley Brothers continued to struggle with recordings. They decided to move operations to New Jersey and formed T-Neck Records in 1964. During that time, famed guitarist Jimi Hendrix moved into their home and joined their band. His unique style eventually had a profound effect on their sound during their golden age, as Hendrix was a mentor to Ernie Isley. After Jimi Hendrix left, The Isley Brothers rode the Motown sound with their 1966 classic "This Old Heart of Mine."

The Isley Brothers' time at Motown Records was brief, and they decided to change their image and sound. "It's Your Thing" was the first of many funk tunes by the group. With this song, The Isleys earned their first Grammy Award. Their early 1970s albums covered songs by White rock artists, and when the three younger brothers joined, The Isleys' golden age began.

The Isley Brothers released 3 + 3 in 1973. This album features "That Lady," which showcases Ernie's powerful guitar work. Many consider this sound to be psychedelic or Black rock. This began a string of gold and mostly platinum albums that elevated The Isleys to the stratosphere of popular Black music, making them perhaps the quintessential soul group of the 1970s and the first to successfully merge the funk sounds of Sly and the Family Stone with the electric rock work of former Isley guitarist Jimi Hendrix.[1] During their golden age, The Isleys produced more funk standards, such as "Fight the Power," "Live It Up," and "Livin' in the Life." They also employed sultry R&B ballads, such as "Make Me Say It Again, Girl," "For the Love of You," and "(At Your Best) You Are Love." They also took a shot at disco with "Winner Takes All" and "It's a Disco Night (Rock Don't Stop)."

The golden age ended after the platinum-selling *Between the Sheets*. In 1984, the three younger brothers formed their splinter group and released a few singles, including the brotherhood anthem "Caravan of Love." The three older brothers returned to being a vocal trio. After the death of O'Kelly, the two older brothers produced more hits with the help of multitalented producer Angela Winbush. When Rudolph left the music business to become a full-time minister, Ronald carried The Isley Brothers moniker by himself for a brief time. Ernie and Marvin rejoined Ronald in 1991, making the group a trio again.

In the 1990s, hip-hop music began to dominate the airwaves. The Isley Brothers gained more popularity when their songs were being sampled by rappers such at Ice Cube and the Notorious B.I.G. The Isleys also gained more fans when they teamed up with R. Kelly and the Mr. Biggs character was born. The brothers remained relevant in the twenty-first century by continuing to work with Kelly and other major producers, including Jimmy Jam and Terry Lewis. They also worked with other popular artists, such as Santana and Beyoncé.

Throughout their illustrious career, The Isley Brothers have sold more than eighteen million units in America alone.[2] With their first major hit in 1959 ("Shout") and their last one in 2001 ("Contagious"), The Isleys are among the few groups to hit the *Billboard* Hot 100 (pop chart) with new music in six different decades. Sixteen of their albums charted in the top forty, and thirteen of those have been certified gold, platinum, or multiplatinum by the RIAA.[3] The Isley Brothers have received numerous awards and honors for their success. They have been inducted into the Rock & Roll Hall of Fame, the Hollywood RockWalk, the Vocal Group Hall of Fame, and the Grammy Hall of Fame. The Isleys have won several Soul Train Music Awards, a Grammy Award for "It's Your Thing," the Grammy Lifetime Achievement Award, and other awards.

The Isley Brothers have influenced various artists from different genres. Their songs have been covered by The Beatles, Rod Stewart, Whitney Houston, Vanessa Williams, Aaliyah, and others. The Isleys are one of the most sampled artists in music. Their music has been sampled by Nas, T-Pain,

Snoop Dogg, Lil Wayne, Kendrick Lamar, and many more. According to Ronald, the group has been sampled over nine hundred times. "It's very important to work with the new generation," said Ronald. "That's what keeps you up with the music and what's going on and what they're feeling, and you're writing about feelings, people, and actual things that are happening. It keeps us young and in the business and know where we are going with the business. We're here to show them the room. Follow the yellow brick road or The Isley Brothers road."[4] The Isley Brothers' music is sure to live forever by their own catalogue, through the many artists who admire them, and by the millions of fans who love them.

Notes

Introduction

1. RIAA, "Gold and Platinum: The Isley Brothers," https://www.riaa.com/gold-platinum/?tab_active=default-award&se=isley+brothers#search_section.
2. "The Isley Brothers," *Billboard*, https://www.billboard.com/artist/the-isley-brothers/chart-history/hsi/.
3. Andrew Winistorfer, "The Isley Brothers Are the Most Important Band of All Time," Vinyl Me Please, July 15, 2019, https://www.vinylmeplease.com/blogs/magazine/isley-brothers-liner-notes.
4. "The Isley Brothers Biography," Musician Guide, https://musicianguide.com/biographies/1608004017/The-Isley-Brothers.html.
5. "The Isley Brothers," *Billboard*, "This Old Heart of Mine," https://www.billboard.com/artist/the-isley-brothers/.
6. William C. Rhoden, "Pride, Power and Politics," *It's Your Thing: The Story of the Isley Brothers* (CD box set), Sony Music Entertainment, 1999, 27.
7. Teresa Reed, *The Holy Profane: Religion in Black Popular Music* (Lexington: University of Kentucky Press, 2003), 140–41.
8. RIAA, "Gold and Platinum."
9. Gold City Records, "Chris Jasper," https://goldcityrecords.com/chris-jasper/.
10. RIAA, "Gold and Platinum."

Chapter 1. Brother, Brother, Brother

1. Bob Gulla, *Icons of R&B and Soul: An Encyclopedia of the Artists Who Revolutionized Rhythm* Vol. 2 (Westport, CT: Greenwood, 2007), 192.
2. Leo Sacks, "Their Own Words," *It's Your Thing: The Story of the Isley Brothers* (CD box set), Sony Music Entertainment, 1999, 35.
3. Carlton Robert Collins, "Lincoln Heights: The Forgotten Black Wall Street," Medium, June 5, 2021, https://educ8drebel.medium.com/lincoln-heights-lessons-from-the-forgotten-black-wall-street-f670b2177c07.
4. Sacks, "Their Own Words," 33.

5. "Vernon Isley," Find A Grave, https://www.findagrave.com/memorial/106424018/vernon-isley.

6. Sacks, "Their Own Words," 33.

7. Elizabeth Isley Barkley, *One Isley Brother's Daughter* (Bloomington, IN: Xlibris, 2011), 23.

8. Sacks, "Their Own Words," 39.

9. William C. Rhoden, "Pride, Power and Politics," *It's Your Thing: The Story of the Isley Brothers* (CD box set), Sony Music Entertainment, 1999, 25.

10. Barkley, *One Isley Brother's Daughter*, 23.

11. Nikki Giovanni, "You See, Brother, Brother, Brother," *It's Your Thing: The Story of the Isley Brothers* (CD box set), Sony Music Entertainment, 1999, 6.

12. Sacks, "Their Own Words," 36.

13. Sacks, "Their Own Words," 33.

14. Barkley, *One Isley Brother's Daughter*, 24.

15. Sacks, "Their Own Words," 33, 35.

16. "Boy Singer Killed on Bike," *The Cincinnati Enquirer*, September 25, 1954, 3, https://www.newspapers.com/article/the-cincinnati-enquirer/148304318/.

17. Rhoden, "Pride, Power and Politics," 24.

18. Barkley, *One Isley Brother's Daughter*, 24.

19. Gulla, *Icons of R&B and Soul*, 194.

20. Brecht Stremes, "The Origin and Influence of Doo-Wop Music," *Bertolt Press*, April 24, 2020, https://bertoltpress.com/2020/04/24/doo-wop-music-history/.

21. Gulla, *Icons of R&B and Soul*, 194.

22. Barkley, *One Isley Brother's Daughter*, 24.

23. Sacks, "Their Own Words," 36.

24. Barkley, *One Isley Brother's Daughter*, 25.

25. Gulla, *Icons of R&B and Soul*, 194.

26. Barkley, *One Isley Brother's Daughter*, 26.

27. Gulla, *Icons of R&B and Soul*, 194.

28. "The Isley Brothers Biography."

29. Jeff Greenfield, "1959: The Year That Changed Everything," CBS News, January 3, 2010, https://www.cbsnews.com/news/1959-the-year-that-changed-everything/.

30. "Shout," The Isley Brothers, Songfacts, https://www.songfacts.com/facts/the-isley-brothers/shout.

31. "Shout," performed by The Isley Brothers, track no. 11, *Shout*, RCA Victor, 1959.

32. "Shout," Songfacts.

33. "The Isley Brothers," *Billboard*, "Shout," https://www.billboard.com/artist/the-isley-brothers/chart-history/bsi/.

34. Paul Wilner, "Isley Brothers: A Family Affair," *The New York Times*, March 13, 1977, 386.

35. "Shout," Songfacts.

36. The Isley Brothers, *Shout!*, RCA Victor, 1959.

37. "Shout," RateYourMusic, https://rateyourmusic.com/release/album/the-isley-brothers/shout/.

38. Gulla, *Icons of R&B and Soul*, 194.

39. "All-Star Stage Bill Rules Regal Stage: Isley Brothers, Bill Doggett and Will Gains Star," *The Chicago Defender*, January 16, 1960, 19.

40. Femi Lewis, "Black History Timeline: 1960–1964," ThoughtCo, https://www.thoughtco.com/african-american-history-timeline-1960-1964-45443.

41. Sacks, "Their Own Words," 36.
42. Lewis, "Black History Timeline."
43. Lewis, "Black History Timeline."
44. Gulla, *Icons of R&B and Soul*, 195.
45. The Isley Brothers, *Twist and Shout*, Wand, 1962.
46. The Isley Brothers, *Take Some Time Out for The Isley Brothers*, Scepter, 1966.
47. "Twist and Shout," The Isley Brothers, Songfacts, https://www.songfacts.com/facts/the-isley-brothers/twist-and-shout.
48. "Twist and Shout," performed by The Isley Brothers, track no. 1, *Twist and Shout*, Wand, 1962.
49. "The Isley Brothers," *Billboard*, "Twist and Shout," https://www.billboard.com/artist/the-isley-brothers/chart-history/bsi/.
50. "Gold in Them Discs," *The Baltimore Afro-American*, November 17, 1962, 11.
51. Gulla, *Icons of R&B and Soul*, 196.
52. Rhoden, "Pride, Power and Politics," 25.
53. "Twist and Shout," Songfacts.
54. "The Isley Brothers—Twistin' with Linda," Discogs, https://www.discogs.com/release/1106333-The-Isley-Brothers-Twistin-With-Linda.
55. "The Isley Brothers," *Billboard*, "Twistin' with Linda," https://www.billboard.com/artist/the-isley-brothers/chart-history/bsi/.
56. "Twist and Shout," The Isley Brothers, AllMusic, https://www.allmusic.com/album/twist-shout%21-mw0000099062.
57. "Record Details: The Isley Brothers," 45cat, http://www.45cat.com/record/131us2.
58. "3 Record Stars in Regal Show," *Chicago Daily Defender*, December 31, 1962, 16.
59. "Etta James, Isley Brothers, Miller Sisters Next at Apollo," *New Pittsburgh Courier*, February 9, 1963, 7.
60. The Isley Brothers, *Twisting and Shouting*, United Artists, 1963.
61. Virginia Prescott, "Stylin': Forty Years of Isley Fashion," *It's Your Thing: The Story of the Isley Brothers* (CD box set), Sony Music Entertainment, 1999, 44.
62. "Isley Brothers," Wilson and Alroy's Record Reviews, "The Famous Isley Bros. Twisting and Shouting," http://www.warr.org/isleys.html.
63. Lewis, "Black History Timeline."
64. Gulla, *Icons of R&B and Soul*, 196.

Chapter 2. Soul on the Rocks

1. Bob Gulla, *Icons of R&B and Soul: An Encyclopedia of the Artists Who Revolutionized Rhythm* Vol. 2 (Westport, CT: Greenwood, 2007), 196.
2. Steven Roby and Brad Schreiber, *Becoming Jimi Hendrix: The Untold Story of a Musical Genius* (Cambridge, MA: Da Capo Press, 2010), 78–79.
3. Roby and Schreiber, *Becoming Jimi Hendrix*, 79.
4. Roby and Schreiber, *Becoming Jimi Hendrix*, 81–82.
5. "Stars Will Entertain Montague at Rockland," *New Pittsburgh Courier*, June 13, 1964, 13.
6. "Disc Jockey Jamboree at Apollo," *New Pittsburgh Courier*, June 27, 1964, 16.
7. "Testify," performed by The Isley Brothers, T-Neck, 1964.
8. Roby and Schreiber, *Becoming Jimi Hendrix*, 82.

9. Gulla, *Icons of R&B and Soul*, 196.
10. William C. Rhoden, "Pride, Power and Politics," *It's Your Thing: The Story of the Isley Brothers* (CD box set), Sony Music Entertainment, 1999, 26.
11. Roby and Schreiber, *Becoming Jimi Hendrix*, 85.
12. "Honorary Brother Jimi: Memories of James Marshall Hendrix," *It's Your Thing: The Story of The Isley Brothers* (CD box set), Sony Music Entertainment, 1999.
13. Roby and Schreiber, *Becoming Jimi Hendrix*, 85–86.
14. "Apollo Re-Opens Friday with Top Holiday Fare," *New Pittsburgh Courier*, December 26, 1964, 16.
15. Gulla, *Icons of R&B and Soul*, 198.
16. Rickey Vincent, *Funk: The Music, the People, and the Rhythm of the One* (New York: St. Martins Griffin, 1996), 5.
17. Teresa Reed, *The Holy Profane: Religion in Black Popular Music* (Lexington: University of Kentucky Press, 2003), 140–41.
18. Tyler Golsen, "James Brown Explains the Origins of Funk," *Far Out*, November 24, 2021, https://faroutmagazine.co.uk/james-brown-origins-of-funk/.
19. Gulla, *Icons of R&B and Soul*, 198.
20. "This Old Heart of Mine (Is Weak for You)," performed by The Isley Brothers, track no. 3, *This Old Heart of Mine*, Tamla (Motown), 1966.
21. James Ferguson, "Life of a Song: This Old Heart of Mine (Is Weak for You)—How Motown Created the Perfect Pop Song," Financial Times, https://ig.ft.com/life-of-a-song/this-old-heart.html.
22. "This Old Heart of Mine (Is Weak for You)," The Isley Brothers, Songfacts, https://www.songfacts.com/facts/the-isley-brothers/this-old-heart-of-mine-is-weak-for-you.
23. Ferguson, "Life of a Song."
24. "The Isley Brothers," *Billboard*, "This Old Heart of Mine," https://www.billboard.com/artist/the-isley-brothers/chart-history/bsi/.
25. "The Isley Brothers," Classic Motown, https://classic.motown.com/artist/the-isley-brothers/.
26. Ferguson, "Life of a Song."
27. "The Isley Brothers," Songfacts, "This Old Heart of Mine (Is Weak for You)," https://www.songfacts.com/facts/the-isley-brothers/this-old-heart-of-mine-is-weak-for-you.
28. The Isley Brothers, *This Old Heart of Mine*, Tamla (Motown), 1966.
29. "The Isley Brothers," Classic Motown, https://classic.motown.com/artist/the-isley-brothers/.
30. "Take Some Time Out for Love," performed by The Isley Brothers, track no. 4, *This Old Heart of Mine*, Tamla (Motown), 1966.
31. "The Isley Brothers," *Billboard*, "Take Some Time Out for Love," https://www.billboard.com/artist/the-isley-brothers/chart-history/bsi/.
32. "Love Is a Wonderful Thing," performed by The Isley Brothers, United Artists, 1966.
33. Craig Allen Nard, Michael J. Madison, and Mark P. McKenna, *The Law of Intellectual Property* (New York: Aspen, 2017), 598.
34. "Isley Brothers at Apollo," *New York Amsterdam News*, July 2, 1966, 20.
35. "The Isley Brothers," *Billboard*, "I Guess I'll Always Love You," https://www.billboard.com/artist/the-isley-brothers/chart-history/bsi/.
36. "This Old Heart of Mine," The Isley Brothers, AllMusic, https://www.allmusic.com/album/this-old-heart-of-mine-mw0000198669.

37. "The Isley Brothers," *Billboard*, "This Old Heart of Mine," https://www.billboard.com/artist/the-isley-brothers/chart-history/bsi/.
38. "Display Ad 38," *New York Amsterdam News*, August 13, 1966, 18.
39. The Isley Brothers, *Soul on the Rocks*, Motown, 1967.
40. "Ali, Bond, Gregory Asked to Adam Bash," *New York Amsterdam News*, February 18, 1867, 40.
41. "Got to Have You Back," performed by The Isley Brothers, track no. 1, *Soul on the Rocks*, Motown, 1967.
42. "The Isley Brothers," *Billboard*, "Got to Have You Back," https://www.billboard.com/artist/the-isley-brothers/chart-history/bsi/.
43. Gulla, *Icons of R&B and Soul*, 198.
44. Farrell Evans, "The 1967 Riots: When Outrage Over Racial Injustice Boiled Over," History, June 21, 2021, https://www.history.com/news/1967-summer-riots-detroit-newark-kerner-commission.
45. Lorraine Boissoneault, "Martin Luther King, Jr.'s Assassination Sparked Uprisings in Cities Across America," *Smithsonian Magazine*, April 4, 1968, https://www.smithsonianmag.com/history/martin-luther-king-jrs-assassination-sparked-uprisings-cities-across-america-180968665/.
46. "Take Me in Your Arms (Rock Me a Little While)," performed by The Isley Brothers, Motown, 1968.
47. "The Isley Brothers," *Billboard*, "Take Me in Your Arms (Rock Me a Little While)," https://www.billboard.com/artist/the-isley-brothers/chart-history/bsi/.
48. Rhoden, "Pride, Power and Politics," 27.
49. Gulla, *Icons of R&B and Soul*, 198.

Chapter 3. Freedom

1. Eric Deggans, "'Summer of Soul' Celebrates a 1969 Black Cultural Festival Eclipsed by Woodstock," NPR, July 1, 2021, https://www.npr.org/2021/07/01/1010306918/summer-of-soul-questlove-movie-review-harlem-cultural-festival.
2. William C. Rhoden, "Pride, Power and Politics," *It's Your Thing: The Story of the Isley Brothers* (CD box set), Sony Music Entertainment, 1999, 27.
3. "It's Your Thing," The Isley Brothers, Songfacts, https://www.songfacts.com/facts/the-isley-brothers/its-your-thing.
4. "Its Your Thing," performed by The Isley Brothers, track no. 6, *It's Our Thing*, T-Neck, 1969.
5. "It's Your Thing," Songfacts.
6. "Isley Brothers Control Recording Company," *Chicago Daily Defender*, April 1, 1969, 10.
7. RIAA, "Gold and Platinum," "It's Your Thing."
8. "The Isley Brothers," *Billboard*, "It's Your Thing," https://www.billboard.com/artist/the-isley-brothers/chart-history/bsi/.
9. Grammy Awards, "Isley Brothers," https://www.grammy.com/artists/isley-brothers/14619.
10. Rhoden, "Pride, Power and Politics," 27.
11. "Isley Brothers Control Recording Company."
12. Leo Sacks, "Their Own Words," *It's Your Thing: The Story of The Isley Brothers* (CD box set), Sony Music Entertainment. 1999, 39.

13. The Isley Brothers, *It's Our Thing*, T-Neck, 1969.
14. "It's Our Thing," The Isley Brothers, AllMusic, https://www.allmusic.com/album/its-our-thing-mw0000075763.
15. "The Isley Brothers," *Billboard*, "It's Our Thing," https://www.billboard.com/artist/the-isley-brothers/.
16. The Isley Brothers, *Doin' Their Thing: Best of The Isley Brothers*, Tamla/Motown, 1969.
17. RateYourMusic, "Doin' Their Thing: Best of The Isley Brothers," https://rateyourmusic.com/release/comp/the-isley-brothers/doin-their-thing-best-of-the-isley-brothers/.
18. Official Charts, "Isley Brothers," https://www.officialcharts.com/artist/10762/isley-brothers/.
19. Graham Betts, *Motown Encyclopedia* (Scotts Valley, CA: CreateSpace, 2014).
20. "I Turned You On," performed by The Isley Brothers, track no. 1, *The Brothers Isley*, T-Neck, 1969.
21. "The Isley Brothers," *Billboard*, "I Turned You On," https://www.billboard.com/artist/the-isley-brothers/chart-history/bsi/.
22. "Isley Brothers Show Helps Bivins Fund," *New York Amsterdam News*, June 21, 1969, 35.
23. Reelblack One, "The Isley Brothers Live at Yankee Stadium (1969): It's Your Thing Movie Soundtrack," YouTube video. https://www.youtube.com/watch?v=JSMrM0SyxRU.
24. "Black Berries (AKA The Blacker the Berrie)," performed by The Isley Brothers, track no. 5, *The Brothers Isley*, T-Neck, 1969.
25. "The Isley Brothers," *Billboard*, "Black Berries-Pt 1," https://www.billboard.com/artist/the-isley-brothers/chart-history/bsi/.
26. "Was It Good to You?," performed by The Isley Brothers, track no. 4, *The Brothers: Isley*, T-Neck, 1969.
27. "The Isley Brothers," *Billboard*, "Was It Good to You?," https://www.billboard.com/artist/the-isley-brothers/chart-history/bsi/.
28. The Isley Brothers, *The Brothers: Isley*, T-Neck, 1969.
29. "The Brothers: Isley," The Isley Brothers, AllMusic, https://www.allmusic.com/album/the-brothers-isley-mw0000024667.
30. "The Isley Brothers," *Billboard*, "The Brothers: Isley," https://www.billboard.com/artist/the-isley-brothers/chart-history/bsi/.
31. The Isley Brothers, *Live at Yankee Stadium*, T-Neck, 1969.
32. "Entertainment Events," *New York Times*, November 15, 1969, 44.
33. "Bless Your Heart," performed by The Isley Brothers, track no. 10, *Get Into Something*, T-Neck, 1969.
34. "Isley Brothers Claim Faith Is Responsible," *New York Amsterdam News*, November 15, 1969, 32.
35. "Soul '70 at Cow Palace," *Sacramento Observer*, February 5, 1970, 15.
36. "Keep On Doin'," performed by The Isley Brothers, track no. 4, *Get Into Something*, T-Neck, 1969.
37. "The Isley Brothers," *Billboard*, "Keep On Doin'," https://www.billboard.com/artist/the-isley-brothers/chart-history/bsi/.
38. The Isley Brothers, *Get Into Something*, T-Neck, 1970.
39. "If He Can, You Can," performed by The Isley Brothers, track no. 7, *Get Into Something*, T-Neck, 1969.

40. "The Isley Brothers," *Billboard*, "If He Can, You Can," https://www.billboard.com/artist/the-isley-brothers/chart-history/bsi/.
41. "5th Dimension Dionne Sing 'Grammy' Hopefuls," *Afro-American*, May 9, 1970, 11.
42. "Girls Will Be Girls, Boys Will Be Boys," performed by The Isley Brothers, track no. 5, *Get Into Something*, T-Neck, 1969.
43. "The Isley Brothers," *Billboard*, "Girls Will Be Girls, Boys Will Be Boys," https://www.billboard.com/artist/the-isley-brothers/chart-history/bsi/.
44. Steven Roby and Brad Schreiber, *Becoming Jimi Hendrix: The Untold Story of a Musical Genius* (Cambridge, MA: Da Capo Press, 2010), 87.
45. "Honorary Brother Jimi: Memories of James Marshall Hendrix," *It's Your Thing: The Story of The Isley Brothers* (CD box set), Sony Music Entertainment, 1999.
46. "Get Into Something," performed by The Isley Brothers, track no. 1, *Get Into Something*, T-Neck, 1969.
47. "The Isley Brothers," *Billboard*, "Get Into Something," https://www.billboard.com/artist/the-isley-brothers/chart-history/bsi/.
48. "Freedom," The Isley Brothers, Songfacts, https://www.songfacts.com/facts/the-isley-brothers/freedom.
49. "The Isley Brothers," *Billboard*, "Freedom," https://www.billboard.com/artist/the-isley-brothers/chart-history/bsi/.
50. Mark Coleman, "The Isley Brothers," *Rolling Stone* (769), September 18, 1997, 106.
51. Richard Torres, "Sony Makes a Reissue Out of Isley Brothers," *Newsday*, September 14, 1997, D31.
52. "Get Into Something," The Isley Brothers, AllMusic, https://www.allmusic.com/album/get-into-something-mw0000594702.
53. Walter Moddy, "All That Jazz," *Sun Reporter*, January 23, 1971, 32.
54. The Isley Brothers and Jimi Hendrix, *In the Beginning . . .* , T-Neck, 1971.
55. Robert Christgau, "The Isley Brothers and Jimi Hendrix: *In the Beginning . . .* ," Consumer Guide Album, https://robertchristgau.com/get_album.php?id=7056.
56. Wieben, "In the Beginning . . . The Isley Brothers and Jimi Hendrix," Rate Your Music, https://rateyourmusic.com/release/comp/the-isley-brothers-jimi-hendrix/in-the-beginning-the-isley-brothers-and-jimi-hendrix/.
57. "Warpath," performed by The Isley Brothers, T-Neck, 1971.
58. "Love the One You're With," performed by The Isley Brothers, track no. 7, *Givin' It Back*, T-Neck, 1971.
59. "The Isley Brothers," *Billboard*, "Love the One You're With," https://www.billboard.com/artist/the-isley-brothers/chart-history/bsi/.
60. "Isley Bros. at Apollo," *New York Amsterdam News*, July 3, 1971, B10.
61. Bill Smallwood, "Bill Smallwood," *Oakland Post*, September 2, 1971, 15.
62. The Isley Brothers, *Givin' It Back*, T-Neck, 1971.
63. Steven E. Flemming Jr., "Eagles and Doves: With 'Givin' It Back,' The Isley Brothers Sang of Joy and Pain," Albumism, September 25, 2021, https://albumism.com/features/tribute-celebrating-50-years-of-isley-brothers-givin-it-back.
64. "Spill the Wine," performed by The Isley Brothers, track no. 4, *Givin' It Back*, T-Neck, 1971.
65. "The Isley Brothers," *Billboard*, "Spill the Wine," https://www.billboard.com/artist/the-isley-brothers/chart-history/bsi/.

66. "SCLC Announces First New York Black Expo," *New York Amsterdam News*, October 23, 1971, B12.

67. "5th Annual: Image Awards," *Sacramento Observer*, November 4, 1971.

68. "Lay Lady Lay," performed by The Isley Brothers, track no. 3, *Givin' It Back*, T-Neck, 1971.

69. "The Isley Brothers," *Billboard*, "Lay Lady Lay," https://www.billboard.com/artist/the-isley-brothers/chart-history/bsi/.

70. Numa La Guma, "The Most Creative Album of the Year," *Sun Reporter*, November 27, 1971, 20.

71. Kay Gibbs, "In the Cut," *Bay State Banner*, December 30, 1971, 10.

72. The Isley Brothers, *Billboard*, "Givin' It Back," https://www.billboard.com/artist/the-isley-brothers/chart-history/bsi/.

73. Flemming, "Eagles and Doves."

74. "Givin' It Back," The Isley Brothers, AllMusic, https://www.allmusic.com/album/givin-it-back-mw0000024635.

75. Bob Gulla, *Icons of R&B and Soul: An Encyclopedia of the Artists Who Revolutionized Rhythm* Vol. 2 (Westport, CT: Greenwood, 2007), 200.

76. The Isley Brothers, "Lay Away," *Billboard*, https://www.billboard.com/artist/the-isley-brothers/chart-history/bsi/.

77. The Isley Brothers, *Brother, Brother, Brother*, T-Neck, 1972.

78. "Pop That Thang," performed by The Isley Brothers, track no. 6, *Brother, Brother, Brother*, T-Neck, 1969.

79. The Isley Brothers, *Billboard*, "Pop That Thang," https://www.billboard.com/artist/the-isley-brothers/chart-history/hbu/.

80. "Theatrical Spotlight," *New York Amsterdam News*, August 26, 1972, D5.

81. "Soul Train Begins Second Season," *Bay State Banner*, September 14, 1972, 17.

82. Flemming, "Eagles and Doves."

83. "Work to Do," performed by The Isley Brothers, track no. 5, *Brother, Brother, Brother*, T-Neck, 1972.

84. "The Isley Brothers," *Billboard*, "Work to Do," https://www.billboard.com/artist/the-isley-brothers/chart-history/hsi/.

85. "The Isley Brothers," *Billboard*, "Brother, Brother, Brother," https://www.billboard.com/artist/the-isley-brothers/chart-history/hsi/.

86. Austin Saalman, "The Isley Brothers—Reflecting on the 50th Anniversary of 'Brother, Brother, Brother,'" *Under the Radar*, May 2, 2022, https://www.undertheradarmag.com/news/the_isley_brothers_reflecting_on_the_50th_anniversary_of_brother_brother_br.

Chapter 4. 3 + 3

1. The Isley Brothers, *The Isleys Live*, T-Neck/Rhino, 1973/1996.

2. "The Isley Brothers," *Billboard*, "The Isleys Live," https://www.billboard.com/artist/the-isley-brothers/chart-history/hsi/.

3. "It's Too Late," performed by The Isley Brothers, track no. 8, *Brother, Brother, Brother*, T-Neck, 1972.

4. The Isley Brothers, *Billboard*, "It's Too Late," https://www.billboard.com/artist/the-isley-brothers/chart-history/hsi/.

5. "Ernie Isley," En-Academic, https://en-academic.com/dic.nsf/enwiki/958208.
6. Dave Laing, "Marvin Isley Obituary," *The Guardian*, June 9, 2010, https://www.theguardian.com/music/2010/jun/09/marvin-isley-obituary.
7. "Introduction," Chris Jasper, Gold City Records, http://goldcityrecords.com/chris-jasper/.
8. "That Lady," performed by The Isley Brothers, track no. 1, 3 + 3, T-Neck, 1973.
9. Rickey Vincent, *Funk: The Music, the People, and the Rhythm of the One* (New York: St. Martins Griffin, 1996), 193.
10. "That Lady," The Isley Brothers, Songfacts, https://www.songfacts.com/facts/the-isley-brothers/that-lady.
11. "The Isley Brothers," *Billboard*, "That Lady," https://www.billboard.com/artist/the-isley-brothers/chart-history/hsi/.
12. RIAA, "Gold and Platinum," "That Lady."
13. "That Lady," Songfacts.
14. The Isley Brothers, 3 + 3, T-Neck/Legacy, 1973/2003.
15. "3 + 3," The Isley Brothers, Discogs, https://www.discogs.com/master/82584-The-Isley-Brothers-3-3.
16. Bob Gulla, *Icons of R&B and Soul: An Encyclopedia of the Artists Who Revolutionized Rhythm*, Vol. 2 (Westport, CT: Greenwood, 2007), 202.
17. "Isleys, Austin to Appear at Football Game," *Bay State Banner*, September 20, 1973, 10.
18. Soul Train, "The Isley Brothers—Who's That Lady," YouTube video, May 20, 2022, https://www.youtube.com/watch?v=BW8-BRnbV-Q.
19. RIAA, "Gold and Platinum," "3 + 3."
20. "The 500 Greatest Albums of All Time," *Rolling Stone*, September 22, 2020, https://www.rollingstone.com/music/music-lists/best-albums-of-all-time-1062063/.
21. "What It Comes Down To," performed by The Isley Brothers, track no. 6, 3 + 3, T-Neck, 1973.
22. "The Isley Brothers," *Billboard*, "What It Comes Down To," https://www.billboard.com/artist/the-isley-brothers/chart-history/hsi/.
23. The Isley Brothers, *Isleys' Greatest Hits*, T-Neck, 1973.
24. "The Isley Brothers," *Billboard*, "Isleys' Greatest Hits," https://www.billboard.com/artist/the-isley-brothers/chart-history/hsi/.
25. Frederick I. Douglass, "Black Experience: Isley Brothers," *Afro-American*, January 12, 1974, 11.
26. "The Isley Brothers," *Billboard*, "Summer Breeze," https://www.billboard.com/artist/the-isley-brothers/chart-history/hsi/.
27. "3 + 3," The Isley Brothers, AllMusic, https://www.allmusic.com/album/3-3-mw0000312124.
28. "Isleys Head Bill at Oakland Arena," *Oakland Post*, April 14, 1974, 3.
29. "Live It Up," performed by The Isley Brothers, track no. 1, *Live It Up*, T-Neck, 1974.
30. "The Isley Brothers," *Billboard*, "Live It Up," https://www.billboard.com/artist/the-isley-brothers/chart-history/hsi/.
31. RIAA, "Gold and Platinum," "Live It Up."
32. The Isley Brothers, *Live It Up*, T-Neck/Legacy, 1974/2004.
33. "The Isley Brothers," *Billboard*, "Live It Up (LP)," https://www.billboard.com/artist/the-isley-brothers/chart-history/hsi/.
34. RIAA, "Gold and Platinum," "Live It Up (LP)."

35. "Isley Brothers Rock the Garden," *New York Amsterdam News*, October 19, 1974, B16.
36. "The Isley Brothers on TV's Soul Train," *Tri-State Defender*, December 14, 1974, 10.
37. "Midnight Sky," performed by The Isley Brothers, track no. 5, *Live It Up*, T-Neck, 1974.
38. The Isley Brothers, *Billboard*, "Midnight Sky," https://www.billboard.com/artist/the-isley-brothers/chart-history/hsi/.
39. Wilson and Alroy's Record Reviews, "Isley Brothers," http://www.warr.org/isleys.html.
40. "Live It Up," The Isley Brothers, AllMusic, https://www.allmusic.com/album/live-it-up-mw0000327529.
41. "Fight the Power," performed by The Isley Brothers, track no. 1, *The Heat Is On*, T-Neck, 1975.
42. "Fight the Power," The Isley Brothers, Songfacts, https://www.songfacts.com/facts/the-isley-brothers/fight-the-power-part-i.
43. Gulla, *Icons of R&B and Soul*, 202.
44. "Funk My Soul—1975—The Heat Is On," FunkMySoul, https://www.funkmysoul.gr/the-isley-brothers-1975-the-heat-is-on/.
45. Todd Boyd, *The Notorious Ph.D.'s Guide to the Super Fly '70s: A Connoisseur's Journey Through the Fabulous Flix, Hip Sounds, and Cool Vibes That Defined a Decade* (New York: Crown, 2007), 146.
46. "Funk My Soul."
47. Boyd, *The Notorious Ph.D.'s Guide*, 146–47.
48. "The Isley Brothers," *Billboard*, "Fight the Power," https://www.billboard.com/artist/the-isley-brothers/chart-history/hsi/.
49. RIAA, "Gold and Platinum," "Fight the Power."
50. The Isley Brothers, *The Heat Is On*, T-Neck/Legacy, 1975/2001.
51. "Fight the Power," Songfacts.
52. Patrick Corcoran, "The Isley Brothers' 'The Heat Is On' Turns 45 | Anniversary Retrospective," Albumism, June 6, 2020, https://albumism.com/features/the-isley-brothers-the-heat-is-on-turns-45-anniversary-retrospective.
53. "George Wein Presents: On Tour . . . Kool Jazz Festivals," *Jet*, June 5, 1975, 61.
54. RIAA, "Gold and Platinum," "The Heat Is On."
55. "The Isley Brothers," *Billboard*, "The Heat Is On," https://www.billboard.com/artist/the-isley-brothers/chart-history/hsi/.
56. "Hear the Isley Brothers Do All Their Hits from Their Multi-Million Dollar LP," *Jet*, September 11, 1975, 12.
57. "For the Love of You," performed by The Isley Brothers, track no. 4, *The Heat Is On*, T-Neck, 1975.
58. "The Isley Brothers," *Billboard*, "For the Love of You," https://www.billboard.com/artist/the-isley-brothers/chart-history/hsi/.
59. "Make Me Say It Again, Girl," performed by The Isley Brothers, track no. 6, *The Heat Is On*, T-Neck, 1975.
60. "Make Me Say It Again, Girl," The Isley Brothers, Songfacts, https://www.songfacts.com/facts/the-isley-brothers/make-me-say-it-again-girl-part-1-2.
61. Corcoran, "The Isley Brothers' 'The Heat Is On' Turns 45."
62. "Funk My Soul."
63. "The Heat Is On," The Isley Brothers, Allmusic, https://www.allmusic.com/album/the-heat-is-on-mw0000203880.

64. Vincent, *Funk*, 195.
65. "Isley Bros. to Stage a Big Revue," *Chicago Defender*, January 27, 1976, 18.
66. The Isley Brothers, *The Best . . . Isley Brothers*, Buddah, 1976.
67. "The Isley Brothers," *Billboard*, "The Best . . . Isley Brothers," https://www.billboard.com/artist/the-isley-brothers/chart-history/hsi/.
68. "Who Loves You Better," performed by The Isley Brothers, track no. 4, *Harvest for the World*, T-Neck, 1976.
69. "The Isley Brothers," *Billboard*, "Who Loves You Better," https://www.billboard.com/artist/the-isley-brothers/chart-history/hsi/.
70. The Isley Brothers, *Harvest for the World*, T-Neck/Legacy, 1976/2001.
71. Frederick I. Douglass, "Isley Brothers Burn! *Afro-American*, July 10, 1976, 11.
72. RIAA, "Gold and Platinum," "Harvest for the World (LP)."
73. "The Isley Brothers," *Billboard*, "Harvest for the World (LP)," https://www.billboard.com/artist/the-isley-brothers/chart-history/bsi/.
74. Brandon Ousley, "Revisiting the Black Pop Liberation of Stevie Wonder and Earth, Wind & Fire, 40 Years Later," *Albumism*, September 26, 2016, https://www.albumism.com/features/revisiting-the-black-pop-liberation-of-stevie-wonder-and-earth-wind-and-fire.
75. "Harvest for the World," The Isley Brothers, Songfacts, https://www.songfacts.com/facts/the-isley-brothers/harvest-for-the-world.
76. "Harvest for the World," performed by The Isley Brothers, track no. 2, *Harvest for the World*, T-Neck, 1976.
77. Dave Simpson, "How The Isley Brothers Made Harvest for the World," *The Guardian*, July 6, 2020, https://www.theguardian.com/music/2020/jul/06/ernie-and-ron-isley-how-we-made-harvest-for-the-world-isley-brothers.
78. "Harvest for the World," Songfacts.
79. "Harvest for the World," Songfacts.
80. "Harvest for the World," Songfacts.
81. "The Isley Brothers," *Billboard*, "Harvest for the World," https://www.billboard.com/artist/the-isley-brothers/chart-history/hsi/.
82. "Harvest for the World," Songfacts.
83. Earl Calloway, "Bar-Kays Join Isley Brothers at Amphitheatre Saturday," *Chicago Defender*, August 25, 1976, 21.
84. Marie Moore, "Fiery Concerts: Black & White Smoke," *New York Amsterdam News*, October 9, 1976, 2.
85. Ulish Carter, "The Record Rack: Isley Brothers Continue Class Young at Heart," *New Pittsburgh Courier*, June 25, 1976, 21.
86. RIAA, "Gold and Platinum," "Harvest for the World (LP)."
87. Robert Christgau, "The Isley Brothers," https://www.robertchristgau.com/get_artist.php?name=The+Isley+Brothers.
88. BBC Review, Review of The Isley Brothers *Harvest for the World (LP)*, https://www.bbc.co.uk/music/reviews/fdfd/.
89. "Harvest for the World (LP)," The Isley Brothers, AllMusic, https://www.allmusic.com/album/harvest-for-the-world-mw0000318358.
90. Earl Calloway, "Black Stars Kept America Singing Jingling and Dancing in '76," *Chicago Defender*, January 1, 1977, a2.

Chapter 5. Keep On Doin'

1. "Music History Events: Legal Issues," Songfacts, https://calendar.songfacts.com/category/legal-issues/page-13.
2. "The Isley Brothers," *Billboard*, "The Pride," https://www.billboard.com/artist/the-isley-brothers/chart-history/bsi/.
3. The Isley Brothers, *Go for Your Guns*, T-Neck/Big Break, 1977/2011.
4. The Isley Brothers, *Go for Your Guns*.
5. Ulish Carter, "The Record Rack: Curtis' Latest Is a Downer," *New Pittsburgh Courier*, June 4, 1977, 15.
6. RIAA, "Gold and Platinum," "Go for Your Guns."
7. "The Isley Brothers," *Billboard*, "Go for Your Guns," https://www.billboard.com/artist/the-isley-brothers/chart-history/bsi/.
8. "The Isley Brothers," *Oakland Post*, June 19, 1977, 3.
9. Marie Moore, "The Institution Called the Isley Brothers: Mama Isley," *New York Amsterdam News*, August 27, 1977, b8.
10. Moore, "The Institution Called the Isley Brothers."
11. "Livin' in the Life," performed by The Isley Brothers, track now. 6, *Go for Your Guns*, T-Neck, 1977.
12. "The Isley Brothers," *Billboard*, "Livin' in the Life," https://www.billboard.com/artist/the-isley-brothers/.
13. Marie Moore, "Musical Potpourri," *New York Amsterdam News*, September 3, 1977, D14.
14. "Soul Explosion at the Oakland Coliseum," *Oakland Post*, September 4, 1977, 3.
15. "Isley Brothers to 'Go for Their Guns' Oct. 8 at Public Hall," *Call and Post*, October 1, 1977, 13A.
16. Prentis Rogers, "Isley Bros: Good Live but Better on Record," *Atlanta Daily World*, October 27, 1977, 6.
17. "Voyage to Atlantis," performed by The Isley Brothers, track no. 5, *Go for Your Guns*, T-Neck, 1977.
18. Robert Christgau, "Consumer Guide '70s: I," https://www.robertchristgau.com/get_chap.php?k=I&bk=70.
19. Dunderbeck1980, "Go for Your Guns: 40 Years of a Funky Voyage to Atlantis with The Isley Brothers," Andresmusictalk, https://andresmusictalk.wordpress.com/2017/05/16/go-for-your-guns-40-years-of-a-funky-voyage-to-atlantis-with-the-isley-brothers/.
20. "Go for Your Guns," The Isley Brothers, AllMusic, https://www.allmusic.com/album/go-for-your-guns-mw0000653379.
21. "The Isley Brothers, Go for Your Guns," Dustygroove, https://www.dustygroove.com/item/75774/Isley-Brothers:Go-For-Your-Guns.
22. The Isley Brothers, *Forever Gold*, T-Neck, 1977.
23. "The Isley Brothers," *Billboard*, "Forever Gold," https://www.billboard.com/artist/the-isley-brothers/chart-history/bsi/.
24. "Take Me to the Next Phase (Pts. 1 & 2)," The Isley Brothers, AllMusic, https://www.allmusic.com/song/take-me-to-the-next-phase-pts-1-2-mt0048480428.
25. "Take Me to the Next Phase," Performed by The Isley Brothers, track no. 5, *Showdown*, T-Neck, 1978.
26. The Isley Brothers, *Go for Your Guns*, T-Neck, 1978.
27. RIAA, "Gold and Platinum," "Showdown (LP)."

28. "The Isley Brothers," *Billboard*, "Showdown (LP)," https://www.billboard.com/artist/the-isley-brothers/chart-history/hsi/.
29. Prentis Rogers, "Objectivity Key to Success of The Isley Brothers," *Atlanta Daily World*, July 2, 1978, 10.
30. Gertrude Gipson, "Candid Comments: Nate Holden Party Sunday," *Los Angeles Sentinel*, May 18, 1978, B3A.
31. "Entertainment News," *Oakland Post*, July 30, 1978, 8.
32. "Groove with You," performed by The Isley Brothers, track no. 2, *Showdown*, T-Neck, 1978.
33. "The Isley Brothers," *Billboard*, "Groove with You," https://www.billboard.com/artist/the-isley-brothers/.
34. "Showdown (LP)," The Isley Brothers, AllMusic, https://www.allmusic.com/album/showdown-mw0000311455.
35. Kip Branch, "The Isley Brothers: They're Really Brothers!" *Afro-American*, August 19, 1978, A12.
36. Larry McKeithan, "The Showdown," *New York Amsterdam News*, August 12, 1978, D4.
37. The Isley Brothers, *Timeless*, T-Neck, 1978.
38. "The Isley Brothers," *Billboard*, "Timeless," https://www.billboard.com/artist/the-isley-brothers/chart-history/bsi/.
39. Vic Partipilo, "On Location," *Oakland Post*, February 23, 1979, 4.
40. "Charlie Cherokee," *Chicago Defender*, April 2, 1979, 14.
41. "I Wanna Be with You," performed by The Isley Brothers, track no. 1, *Winner Takes All*, T-Neck, 1979.
42. "Disco," Britannica, https://www.britannica.com/art/disco.
43. "The Isley Brothers," *Billboard*, "I Wanna Be with You," https://www.billboard.com/artist/the-isley-brothers/chart-history/bsi/.
44. "Kool Jazz Festivals: The Events of the Year," *Jet*, April 26, 1979, 62.
45. The Isley Brothers, *Winner Takes All*, T-Neck/Big Break, 1979/2013.
46. RIAA, "Gold and Platinum," "Winner Takes All."
47. "The Isley Brothers," *Billboard*, "Winner Takes All," https://www.billboard.com/artist/the-isley-brothers/chart-history/bsi/.
48. "Winner Takes All," performed by The Isley Brothers, track no. 3, *Winner Takes All*, T-Neck, 1979.
49. "The Isley Brothers," *Billboard*, "Winner Takes All," https://www.billboard.com/artist/the-isley-brothers/chart-history/bsi/.
50. Derek John, "July 12, 1979: 'The Night Disco Died'—Or Didn't," NPR, July 16, 2016, https://www.npr.org/2016/07/16/485873750/july-12-1979-the-night-disco-died-or-didnt.
51. Minor Roberts, "Jamaica Inn, Isley Bros. in $$$ Trouble," *New York Amsterdam News*, August 18, 1979, 4.
52. Billy Rowe, "Uncle Sam's Lien on Isley Bros.," *New York Amsterdam News*, September 8, 1979, 20.
53. "It's a Disco Night (Rock Don't Stop)," performed by The Isley Brothers, track no. 5, *Winner Takes All*, T-Neck, 1979.
54. Mike Freedberg, "Soul Dog," *Bay State Banner*, August 23, 1979, 22.
55. George Lane, "Shades of Blue," *Bay State Banner*, June 14, 1979, 16.
56. Ulish Carter, "1970's: Golden Era Musically but Not Lyrically," *New Pittsburgh Courier*, January 12, 1980, A5.

57. "Don't Say Goodnight (It's Time for Love)," performed by The Isley Brothers, track no. 5, *Go All the Way*, T-Neck, 1980.
58. Richard Mitchell, "Isley Brothers: Music, Family and Funk," *Chicago Defender*, June 11, 1980, 15wa.
59. "Don't Say Goodnight (It's Time for Love)," The Isley Brothers, Songfacts, https://www.songfacts.com/facts/the-isley-brothers/dont-say-goodnight-its-time-for-love.
60. "The Isley Brothers," *Billboard*, "Don't Say Goodnight (It's Time for Love)," https://www.billboard.com/artist/the-isley-brothers/chart-history/bsi/.
61. "CBS Stars Cut Tapes for Census Radio Spots," *Chicago Defender*, April 1, 1980, 16.
62. The Isley Brothers, *Go All the Way*, T-Neck, 1980.
63. "The Isley Brothers," *Billboard*, "Go All the Way," https://www.billboard.com/artist/the-isley-brothers/chart-history/bsi/.
64. RIAA, "Gold and Platinum," "Go All the Way (LP)."
65. "The Isley Brothers," *Billboard*, "Go All the Way," https://www.billboard.com/artist/the-isley-brothers/.
66. Mel Tapley, "About the Arts," *New York Amsterdam News*, June 7, 1980, 38.
67. "Isley Brothers Booked for Stadium," *Chicago Defender*, June 9, 1980, 17.
68. "Welcome Home Fete for Isley Bros. to Highlight Ohio Kool Jazz Festival," *Call and Post*, June 28, 1980, 3B.
69. "Isley Brothers Concert Is Set for Richfield Coliseum," *Call and Post*, July 26, 1980, 3A.
70. "The Isley Brothers," *Billboard*, "Here We Go Again," https://www.billboard.com/artist/the-isley-brothers/chart-history/bsi/.
71. "Isley Brothers Concert Is Set for Richfield Coliseum."
72. "Going All the Way Is a Way of Life," *Los Angeles Sentinel*, August 21, 1980, B8.

Chapter 6. Fire and Rain

1. "Who Said?" performed by The Isley Brothers, track no. 7, *Grand Slam*, T-Neck, 1981.
2. "The Isley Brothers," *Billboard*, "Who Said?," https://www.billboard.com/artist/the-isley-brothers/chart-history/bsi/.
3. The Isley Brothers, *Grand Slam*, T-Neck, 1981.
4. "Hurry Up and Wait," performed by The Isley Brothers, track no. 3, *Grand Slam*, T-Neck, 1981.
5. "The Isley Brothers," *Billboard*, "Hurry Up and Wait," https://www.billboard.com/artist/the-isley-brothers/chart-history/bsi/.
6. "The Isley Brothers," *Billboard*, "Grand Slam," https://www.billboard.com/artist/the-isley-brothers/chart-history/hbu/.
7. RIAA, "Gold and Platinum," "Grand Slam."
8. "Kool Jazz Festivals: The Only Way to Play It," *Jet*, April 30, 1981, 64.
9. "Isley Brothers Are Booked at Mill Run Theatre," *Weekend Chicago Defender*, June 20, 1981, 36.
10. "Solar Galaxy Stars to Sparkle at Holiday," *Weekend Chicago Defender*, July 25, 1981, 36.
11. Marie Moore, "Gil Scott Bringing Words of Wisdom," *New York Amsterdam News*, July 18, 1981, 36.
12. "I Once Had Your Love (And I Can't Let Go)," performed by The Isley Brothers, track no. 2, *Grand Slam*, T-Neck, 1981.

13. "The Isley Brothers," *Billboard*, "I Once Had Your Love (And I Can't Let Go)," https://www.billboard.com/artist/the-isley-brothers/chart-history/bsi/.

14. Wilson and Alroy's Record Reviews, "The Isley Brothers, Grand Slam," http://www.warr.org/isleys.html.

15. "Grand Slam," The Isley Brothers, AllMusic, https://www.allmusic.com/album/grand-slam-mw0000691059.

16. Philip Harrigan, "Funkadelic Leave Clinton, Lose Identity," *New Pittsburgh Courier*, April 4, 1981, A2.

17. "Inside You," performed by The Isley Brothers, track no. 1, *Inside You*, T-Neck, 1982.

18. "The Isley Brothers," *Billboard*, "Inside You," https://www.billboard.com/artist/the-isley-brothers/chart-history/bsi/.

19. The Isley Brothers, *Inside You*, T-Neck, 1971.

20. Earl Calloway, "Marvin Gaye Making Big Plans at CBS," *Chicago Defender*, December 28, 1981, 15.

21. "The Isley Brothers," *Billboard*, "Inside You (LP)," https://www.billboard.com/artist/the-isley-brothers/chart-history/bsi/.

22. "Welcome to My Heart," performed by The Isley Brothers, track no. 6, *Inside You*, T-Neck, 1981.

23. "The Isley Brothers," *Billboard*, "Welcome to My Heart," https://www.billboard.com/artist/the-isley-brothers/chart-history/bsi/.

24. Stephen Holden, "Music Noted in Brief; Durable Isley Brothers Play Date at the Savoy," *New York Times*, November 16, 1981, C18.

25. John Rockwell, "Big Black Pop Bands Have Lost Excitement and Adventure," *New York Times*, December 6, 1981, A 27.

26. Wilson and Alroy's Record Reviews, "The Isley Brothers, Inside You (LP)," http://www.warr.org/isleys.html.

27. "The Real Deal," performed by The Isley Brothers, track no. 1, *The Real Deal*, T-Neck, 1982.

28. "The Isley Brothers," *Billboard*, "The Real Deal," https://www.billboard.com/artist/the-isley-brothers/chart-history/bsi/.

29. The Isley Brothers, *The Real Deal*, T-Neck, 1982.

30. "The Isley Brothers," *Billboard*, "The Real Deal (LP)," https://www.billboard.com/artist/the-isley-brothers/chart-history/bsi/.

31. "It's Alright with Me," performed by The Isley Brothers, track no. 4, *The Real Deal*, T-Neck, 1982.

32. "The Isley Brothers," *Billboard*, "It's Alright with Me," https://www.billboard.com/artist/the-isley-brothers/chart-history/bsi/.

33. "All in My Lover's Eyes," performed by The Isley Brothers, track no. 5, *The Real Deal*, T-Neck, 1982.

34. "The Isley Brothers," *Billboard*, "All in My Lover's Eyes," https://www.billboard.com/artist/the-isley-brothers/chart-history/bsi/.

35. "Inside You/Real Deal," The Isley Brothers, AllMusic, https://www.allmusic.com/album/inside-you-real-deal-mw0000479767.

36. Wilson and Alroy's Record Reviews, "The Isley Brothers, The Real Deal (LP)," http://www.warr.org/isleys.html.

37. "Between the Sheets," performed by The Isley Brothers, track no. 4, *Between the Sheets*, T-Neck, 1983.

38. Susan Green, Donothea Bickell, and Shirley Smith, "Our Readers Write: Modern Day Pied Piper," *Call and Post*, July 14, 1983, 9A.

39. Harry Gould Jr., "The Power and the Juice," *Philadelphia Inquirer*, August 14, 1983, 13.

40. "The Isley Brothers," *Billboard*, "Between the Sheets," https://www.billboard.com/artist/the-isley-brothers/chart-history/bsi/.

41. RIAA, "Gold and Platinum," "Between the Sheets."

42. The Isley Brothers, *Between the Sheets*, T-Neck/Big Break, 1983/2011.

43. "The Isley Brothers," *Billboard*, "Between the Sheets (LP)," https://www.billboard.com/artist/the-isley-brothers/chart-history/bsi/.

44. RIAA, "Gold and Platinum," "Between the Sheets (LP)."

45. "Choosey Lover," performed by The Isley Brothers, track no. 1, *Between the Sheets*, T-Neck, 1983.

46. "The Isley Brothers," *Billboard*, "Choosey Lover," https://www.billboard.com/artist/the-isley-brothers/chart-history/bsi/.

47. Blaine Allan, "Musical Cinema, Music Video, Music Television," *Film Quarterly* 43, no. 3 (Spring 1990): 4.

48. "Ballad for the Fallen Soldier," performed by The Isley Brothers, track no. 6, *Between the Sheets*, T-Neck, 1983.

49. The Isley Brothers, *Ballad for the Fallen Soldier*, Sony Music Entertainment, https://www.youtube.com/watch?v=H7oeayNHeh4.

50. "Between the Sheets," The Isley Brothers, Dustygroove, https://www.dustygroove.com/item/5862/Isley-Brothers:Between-the-Sheets.

51. Wilson and Alroy's Record Reviews, "The Isley Brothers, Between the Sheets (LP)," http://www.warr.org/isleys.html.

52. Willliam Byrd, "Isley Brothers 25th Anniversary Tour Comes to the Fox," *Atlanta Daily World*, October 6, 1983, 7.

53. "Lou Rawls 'Parade of Stars' Airs on WGN-TV," *Chicago Defender*, December 29, 1983, 18.

54. Chris Jasper, interview with the author, Atlanta, GA, July 27, 2022.

55. The Isley Brothers, *Greatest Hits, Vol. 1*, T-Neck, 1984.

56. RIAA, "Gold and Platinum," "Greatest Hits, Vol. 1."

57. DJ Rob, "The Non-Isley Brother Who Made the Isleys Blow Up," *DJ Rob Blog*, September 19, 2016, https://djrobblog.com/archives/3515.

58. Isley-Jasper-Isley, *Broadway's Closer to Sunset Blvd*, CBS, 1984.

59. "Isley Brothers Split to Form New Group, Record New Album and Hit Single," *Jet*, November 12, 1984, 64.

60. "Look the Other Way," performed by Isley-Jasper-Isley, track no. 7, *Broadway's Closer to Sunset Blvd*, CBS, 1984.

61. Isley-Jasper-Isley, "Look the Other Way," Sony BMG Music Entertainment, https://www.youtube.com/watch?v=AyFvhd_242I.

62. "Kiss and Tell," performed by Isley-Jasper-Isley, track no. 4, *Broadway's Closer to Sunset Blvd*, CBS, 1984.

63. Marc Taylor, *A Touch of Classic Soul: Soul Singers of the Early 1970s* (Ann Arbor: University of Michigan Press, 1996), 172.

64. Isley-Jasper-Isley, "Kiss and Tell," Sony BMG Music Entertainment, https://www.youtube.com/watch?v=VeIqQ9bg2L8.

65. Bob Gulla, *Icons of R&B and Soul: An Encyclopedia of the Artists Who Revolutionized Rhythm* Vol. 2 (Westport, CT: Greenwood, 2007), 204.

66. The Isley Brothers, *Masterpiece*, Warner Brothers, 1985.

67. "Colder Are My Nights," performed by The Isley Brothers, track no. 6, *Masterpiece*, Warner Brothers, 1985.

68. "The Isley Brothers," *Billboard*, "Colder Are My Nights," https://www.billboard.com/artist/the-isley-brothers/chart-history/bsi/.

69. "The Isley Brothers," *Billboard*, "Masterpiece," https://www.billboard.com/artist/the-isley-brothers/.

70. "May I?," performed by The Isley Brothers, track no. 1, *Masterpiece*, Warner Brothers, 1985.

71. "The Isley Brothers," *Billboard*, "May I?," https://www.billboard.com/artist/the-isley-brothers/chart-history/bsi/.

72. Richard Defendorf, "The Isley Brothers (3 Star Edition)," *Orlando Sentinel*, December 1, 1985, 6.

73. Wilson and Alroy's Record Reviews, "The Isley Brothers, Masterpiece," http://www.warr.org/isleys.html.

74. "Masterpiece," The Isley Brothers, AllMusic, https://www.allmusic.com/album/masterpiece-mw0000714585.

75. Taylor, *A Touch of Classic Soul*, 172.

76. Isley-Jasper-Isley, *Caravan of Love*, CBS, 1985.

77. "Caravan of Love," performed by Isley-Jasper-Isley, track no. 5, *Caravan of Love*, CBS, 1985.

78. Taylor, *A Touch of Classic Soul*, 173.

79. Isley-Jasper-Isley, "Caravan of Love," Sony BMG Music Entertainment, https://www.youtube.com/watch?v=foFK6q7kF9Y.

80. "Caravan of Love by Isley-Jasper-Isley," Songfacts, https://www.songfacts.com/facts/isley-jasper-isley/caravan-of-love.

81. "Insatiable Woman," performed by Isley-Jasper-Isley, track no. 2, *Caravan of Love*, CBS, 1985.

82. Isley-Jasper-Isley, "Insatiable Woman," Sony BMG Music Entertainment, https://www.youtube.com/watch?v=aTTYalYGXvY.

83. Taylor, *A Touch of Classic Soul*, 173.

84. Tom Popson, "Vocal Variety Makes Isley Spinoff Distinctive," *Chicago Tribune*, March 28, 1986, 6.

85. "Rhythm and Blues Singer O'Kelly Isley Dead at Age 48," AP News, April 2, 1986, https://apnews.com/article/e748fce38ca8654fc04cd276b5a8c35b.

86. "O'Kelly Isley, 48, of The Isley Bros., Dies in N.J.," *Jet*, April 21, 1986, 52.

87. Gulla, *Icons of R&B and Soul*, 204.

Chapter 7. The Next Phase

1. Dennis Hunt, "Isley Brothers' Sailin' Back on the Charts," *Los Angeles Times*, July 3, 1987, 21.

2. "Angela Winbush Biography," Musician Guide, https://musicianguide.com/biographies/1608000066/Angela-Winbush.html.

3. "Happy 30th: Isley Brothers, Smooth Sailin'," Rhino, March 14, 2017, https://www.rhino.com/article/happy-30th-isley-brothers-smooth-sailin.

4. "Smooth Sailin' Tonight," performed by The Isley Brothers, track no. 5, *Smooth Sailin'*, Warner Brothers, 1987.

5. "The Isley Brothers," *Billboard*, "Smooth Sailin' Tonight," https://www.billboard.com/artist/the-isley-brothers/chart-history/tlp/.

6. The Isley Brothers, *Smooth Sailin'* Warners Brothers, 1987.

7. Patrick Goldstein, "Moonlighting on the Trail of an LP," *Los Angeles Times*, May 31, 1987, 86.

8. Hunt, "Isley Brothers' Sailin'," 21.

9. "Come My Way," performed by The Isley Brothers, track no. 7, *Smooth Sailin'*, Warner Brothers, 1987.

10. "The Isley Brothers," *Billboard*, "Come My Way," https://www.billboard.com/artist/the-isley-brothers/chart-history/tlp/.

11. "I Wish," performed by The Isley Brothers, track no. 8, *Smooth Sailin,'* Warner Brothers, 1987.

12. "The Isley Brothers," *Billboard*, "I Wish," https://www.billboard.com/artist/the-isley-brothers/chart-history/tlp/.

13. "Smooth Sailin'," The Isley Brothers, AllMusic, https://www.allmusic.com/album/smooth-sailin-mw0000194268.

14. "Way Back Wednesday Album Review: The Isley Brothers, Smooth Sailin'," Reviews and Dunn, https://reviewsanddunn.net/the-isley-brothers-smooth-sailin/.

15. "The Isley Brothers," *Billboard*, "Smooth Sailin'," https://www.billboard.com/artist/the-isley-brothers/chart-history/tlp/.

16. Isley-Jasper-Isley, *Different Drummer*, CBS, 1987.

17. Marc Taylor, *A Touch of Classic Soul: Soul Singers of the Early 1970s* (Ann Arbor: University of Michigan Press, 1996), 173.

18. "Isley-Jasper-Isley," AllMusic, "Different Drummer," https://www.allmusic.com/artist/isley-jasper-isley-mn0001202374.

19. Chris Jasper, *Superbad*, Gold City, 1988.

20. "Superbad," performed by Chris Jasper, track no. 1, *Superbad*, CBS, 1988.

21. Chris Jasper, "Superbad," Sony Music Entertainment, https://www.youtube.com/watch?v=pXOTvkLyaZM.

22. Gold City Records, "Chris Jasper," https://goldcityrecords.com/chris-jasper/.

23. Lou Downings, "Kizzy Supporter Joins WVON-AM," *Chicago Defender*, February 2, 1989, 2.

24. "Spend the Night," performed by The Isley Brothers, track no. 1, *Spend the Night*, Warner Brothers, 1989.

25. The Isley Brothers, "Spend the Night," Warner Urban Music, https://www.youtube.com/watch?v=VZWEDoYkWOc.

26. "The Isley Brothers," *Billboard*, "Spend the Night," https://www.billboard.com/artist/the-isley-brothers/chart-history/tlp/.

27. The Isley Brothers, *Spend the Night*, Warner Brothers, 1989.

28. Leo Sacks, "Their Own Words," *It's Your Thing: The Story of the Isley Brothers* (CD box set), Sony Music Entertainment, 1999, 36.

29. Bob Gulla, *Icons of R&B and Soul: An Encyclopedia of the Artists Who Revolutionized Rhythm* Vol. 2 (Westport, CT: Greenwood, 2007), 205.

30. "You'll Never Walk Alone," performed by The Isley Brothers, track no. 2, *Spend the Night*, Warner Brothers, 1989.

31. The Isley Brothers, "You'll Never Walk Alone," Warner Urban Music, https://www.youtube.com/watch?v=Z2SfKQ4Of8c.
32. "The Isley Brothers," *Billboard*, "You'll Never Walk Alone," https://www.billboard.com/artist/the-isley-brothers/chart-history/tlp/.
33. "One of a Kind," performed by The Isley Brothers, track no. 3, *Spend the Night*, Warner Brothers, 1989.
34. "The Isley Brothers," *Billboard*, "One of a Kind," https://www.billboard.com/artist/the-isley-brothers/chart-history/bsi/.
35. "Spend the Night (LP)," The Isley Brothers, AllMusic, https://www.allmusic.com/album/spend-the-night-mw0000201526.
36. Wilson and Alroy's Record Reviews, "The Isley Brothers, Spend the Night (LP)," http://www.warr.org/isleys.html.
37. Ernie Isley, *High Wire*, Elektra, 1990.
38. Wayne Robbins, "The Youngest Isley's Post-Hendrix Groove," *Newsday*, February 18, 1990, 21.
39. Greg Sandow and David Browne, "1990's Best (and Worst) Music," *Entertainment Weekly*, December 28, 1990, https://ew.com/article/1990/12/28/1990s-best-and-worst-music/.
40. Peter Watrous, "Sounds Around Town," *New York Times*, March 9, 1990, https://www.nytimes.com/1990/03/09/arts/sounds-around-town-019290.html.
41. Paul Freeman, "Isley Brothers Back on a Soulful Circuit/First Tour in Four Years," *San Francisco Chronicle*, April 8, 1990, 39.
42. Mike Boehm, "Pop Music Review: 'Shouts' Were Out, Ballads Were In at Isley Brothers Show," *Los Angeles Times*, April 23, 1990, 2.
43. "Lay Your Troubles Down," performed by Angela Winbush with Ronald Isley, track no. 4, *The Real Thing*, Polygram, 1989.
44. Emily Fagan, "Top 10 Angela Winbush Songs," Classic Rock History, 2021, https://www.classicrockhistory.com/top-10-angela-winbush-songs/.
45. Angela Winbush and Ronald Isley, "Lay Your Troubles Down," https://www.youtube.com/watch?v=Ug9RBtmSgQE.
46. "Isley Brothers, Angela Winbush, Marcia Griffith Show Relocated to the International Amphitheatre," *Weekend Chicago Defender*, December 29, 1990, 32.
47. The Isley Brothers, *The Isley Brothers Story, Vol. 1: The T-Neck Years (1969–85)*, Rhino, 1991.
48. The Isley Brothers, *The Isley Brothers Story, Vol. 2: The T-Neck Years (1969–85)*, Rhino, 1991.
49. "The Isley Brothers: 3 Decades of Hits," *New Pittsburgh Courier*, July 15, 1992, B-1.
50. "Rock Stars Join Hall of Fame," *Orlando Sentinel*, November 5, 1991, A2.
51. "Rock and Roll Hall of Fame Class of 1992," Cleveland.com, January 1, 2012, https://www.cleveland.com/rockhall/2012/01/rock_and_roll_hall_of_fame_cla_7.html.
52. "Three Boys Music v. Michael Bolton," *Law Blogs*, George Washington University, https://blogs.law.gwu.edu/mcir/case/three-boys-music-v-michael-bolton/.
53. Thom Duffy, Janine McAdams, and Jeffrey Jolson-Colburn, "Isley Sues Bolton over Song Right," *Billboard*, June 27, 1992, 13.
54. "Sensitive Lover," performed by The Isley Brothers, track no. 4, *Tracks of Life*, Warner Brothers, 1992.
55. The Isley Brothers, "Sensitive Lover," Sony Music Entertainment, https://www.youtube.com/watch?v=D3C93gSQIRA.

56. "The Isley Brothers," *Billboard*, "Sensitive Lover," https://www.billboard.com/artist/the-isley-brothers/chart-history/bsi/.

57. The Isley Brothers, *Tracks of Life*, Warner Brothers, 1992.

58. "The Isley Brothers," *Billboard*, "Tracks of Life," https://www.billboard.com/artist/the-isley-brothers/chart-history/bsi/.

59. "Whatever Turns You On," performed by The Isley Brothers, track no. 7, *Tracks of Life*, Warner Brothers, 1992.

60. "The Isley Brothers," *Billboard*, "Whatever Turns You On," https://www.billboard.com/artist/the-isley-brothers/chart-history/bsi/.

61. "Isley Brothers: Tracks of Life," Funknstuff, September, 18, 2022, https://funknstuff.net/isley-brothers-tracks-of-life-1992/.

62. "Tracks of Life," The Isley Brothers, AllMusic, https://www.allmusic.com/album/tracks-of-life-mw0000611909.

63. Wilson and Alroy's Record Reviews, "The Isley Brothers, Tracks of Life," http://www.warr.org/isleys.html.

64. Barry Jackson, "An Evening with the Isley Brothers," *Los Angeles Sentinel*, December 17, 1992, B2.

65. "Photo Standalone 13—No Title," *Chicago Defender*, February 18, 1993, 24.

66. "Angela Winbush, Ron Isley Wed in L.A. Ceremony," *Jet*, July 19, 1993, 38.

67. "July 1993 Black Film Festival," *New York Amsterdam News*, July 17, 1993, 31.

68. The Isley Brothers, *Live!* Elektra, 1993.

69. "Live," The Isley Brothers, AllMusic, https://www.allmusic.com/album/live%21-mw0000919608.

70. "The Isley Brothers," *Billboard*, "Live!," https://www.billboard.com/artist/the-isley-brothers/chart-history/bsi/.

71. Sonia Murray, "These Brothers Can Sing: Isley Brothers Being Rediscovered as Performers, Writers," *Austin American Statesman*, January 6, 1994, 14.

72. Earl Calloway, "Warner Bros. Releases Curtis Mayfield Tribute," *Weekend Chicago Defender*, March 5, 1994, 24.

73. "I'm So Proud," performed by The Isley Brothers, *A Tribute to Curtis Mayfield*, track no. 8, Warner Brothers, 1994.

74. "The Isley Brothers," *Billboard*, "I'm So Proud," https://www.billboard.com/artist/the-isley-brothers/chart-history/bsi/.

75. "Bolton Hit Essentially Is 1966 Isley Song, Jury Finds," *Los Angeles Times*, April 26, 1994, 2.

76. "Three Boys Music v. Michael Bolton."

77. The Isley Brothers, *Beautiful Ballads*, Epic/Legacy, 1994.

78. "The Isley Brothers," *Billboard*, "Beautiful Ballads," https://www.billboard.com/artist/the-isley-brothers/chart-history/bsi/.

79. RIAA, "Gold and Platinum," "Beautiful Ballads."

80. Rita Elizabeth Henderson, "Isley Brothers Serenade Trump Plaza Crowd," *New York Amsterdam News*, November 5, 1994, 32.

81. "Bits 'N Pieces," *Call and Post*, December 29, 1994, 7.

82. "Tradition," *Weekend Chicago Defender*, December 31, 1994, 22.

83. Arlene Vigoda, "War, Peace and Hemlines: [First Edition]," *USA Today*, February 1, 1995, 1D.

84. Various Artists, *Smooth Grooves: A Sensual Collection*, Rhino, 1995.

85. Arlene Vigoda, "Box Office: [Final Edition]," *USA Today*, January 23, 1995, 1D.
86. Various Artists, *Movin' On Up, Vol. 2*, The Right Stuff, 1995.
87. "Tryin' to See Another Day," performed by The Isley Brothers, *Friday (Original Motion Picture Soundtrack)*, track no. 7, Priority, 1995.
88. Various Artists, *Friday (Original Motion Picture Soundtrack)*, Priority, 1995.
89. John Fleming et al., "Audio Files Series: Audio Files: [City Edition], *St. Petersburg Times*, May 5, 1995, 12.
90. "Brownstone: New Group Makes Debut on Michael Jackson's Record Label," *Jet*, June 19, 1995, 59–61.
91. "Pop Eye: [Home Edition]," *Los Angeles Times*, May 14, 1995, 70.
92. J. D. Considine, "A Band to Shout About/The Isley Brothers Adapt to Stay Current," *Newsday*, August 13, 1996, B3.
93. Richard Harrington, "Longevity: It's the Isleys' Thing," *Los Angeles Times*, November 23, 2001, F22.
94. "Heaven's Girl," performed by Quincy Jones, featuring R. Kelly, Ron Isley, Aaron Hall, and Charlie Wilson, track no. 11, *Q's Jook Joint*, Quest/Warner Brothers, 1995.
95. "Down Low (Nobody Has to Know)," performed by R. Kelly featuring The Isley Brothers, track no. 8, *R. Kelly*, Jive, 1995.
96. R. Kelly featuring The Isley Brothers, "Down Low (Nobody Has to Know) (Full Version)," https://www.youtube.com/watch?v=VlIXR-O_AKY.
97. "R. Kelly," *Billboard*, "Down Low (Nobody Has to Know)," https://www.billboard.com/artist/r.-kelly/chart-history/hsi/.
98. "Best Selling Records of 1996," *Billboard*, January 18, 1997, 61.

Chapter 8. Brother, Brother

1. Various Artists, *Don't Be a Menace to South Central While Drinking Your Juice in the Hood: The Soundtrack*, Island, 1996.
2. Steve Hochman, "Pop Music Review: R&B Foundation Honorees Let Music Do the Boasting," *Los Angeles Times*, March 2, 1996, 2.
3. "Let's Lay Together," performed by The Isley Brothers, track no. 3, *Mission to Please*, T-Neck/Island, 1996.
4. "The Isley Brothers," *Billboard*, "Let's Lay Together," https://www.billboard.com/artist/the-isley-brothers/chart-history/bsi/.
5. The Isley Brothers, *Mission to Please*, T-Neck/Island, 1996.
6. "The Isley Brothers: Celebrating 4 Decades," *Los Angeles Sentinel*, September 12, 1996, B4.
7. "The Isley Brothers," *Billboard*, "Mission to Please," https://www.billboard.com/artist/the-isley-brothers/chart-history/bst/.
8. "Clinton Notes Black Music Month," *Philadelphia Tribune*, June 25, 1996, 8D.
9. Jack Lloyd, "An Isley's First Taste of Fame," *Philadelphia Inquirer*, January 17, 1997, 25.
10. "Black Music Organization Plans Gala," *Philadelphia Tribune*, June 14, 1996, 2E.
11. Eric Deggans, "Isley Brothers Do Their Thing and So Do Others," *St. Petersburg Times*, June 22, 1996, 2B.
12. "Twenty-Ninth Hampton Jazz Festival Continues Its Legendary Tradition," *New Journal and Guide*, May 1, 1996, 14.
13. RIAA, "Gold and Platinum," "Mission to Please."

14. Mark Sherman et al., "Atlanta Games Day 7 City Late Break," *Atlanta Journal-Constitution*, July 25, 1996, S28.

15. ChessNotCheckers, "Kelly Price Keeps It Real On Mariah Carey, Diddy and the Music Industry," https://www.youtube.com/watch?v=8_c-5T-MQeM.

16. Patricia Smith, "Isleys Satisfy Fans with Sanctified Soul," *Boston Globe*, July 27, 1996, C3.

17. ChessNotCheckers, "Kelly Price Keeps It Real."

18. "Isley Brothers Bring Soaring Vocals to Holiday Star Plaza," *Weekend Chicago Defender*, August 3, 1996, 16.

19. "Floatin' On Your Love," performed by The Isley Brothers, featuring Angela Winbush, track no. 1, *Mission to Please*, T-Neck/Island, 1996.

20. The Isley Brothers, *Floatin' On Your Love ft. Ronald Isley, Angela Winbush*, The Island Def Jam Music Group, https://www.youtube.com/watch?v=2Ogu2nptuGo.

21. "Floatin' On Your Love," The Isley Brothers, *Billboard*, https://www.billboard.com/artist/the-isley-brothers/.

22. Esther Iverem, "The Isleys, '90s Style; Mr. Biggs Upstaged at Constitution Hall," *The Washington Post*, September 23, 1996, D7.

23. "Tears," performed by The Isley Brothers, track no. 4, *Mission to Please*, T-Neck/Island, 1996.

24. The Isley Brothers, "Tears (Official Video) ft. Ronald Isley," The Island Def Jam Music Group, https://www.youtube.com/watch?v=K_Y-7iOX7Bo.

25. "The Isley Brothers," *Billboard*, "Tears," https://www.billboard.com/artist/the-isley-brothers/chart-history/bst/.

26. "Mission to Please," The Isley Brothers, AllMusic, https://www.allmusic.com/album/mission-to-please-mw0000647674.

27. "Mission to Please," The Isley Brothers, Lemon Wire, https://lemonwire.com/2018/03/29/isley-brothers-mission-to-please/.

28. Cherry Banez, "Entertainment: Tis the Season for Great Music," *Philadelphia Tribune*, November 29, 1996, A8.

29. "Three Boys Music v. Michael Bolton," *Law Blogs*, George Washington University, https://blogs.law.gwu.edu/mcir/case/three-boys-music-v-michael-bolton/.

30. "Photo Standalone 5—No Title," *Atlanta Daily World*, December 26, 1996, 7.

31. RIAA, "Gold and Platinum," "Mission to Please."

32. "Soul Train Hopefuls," *USA Today*, March 7, 1997, 6D.

33. Frances Hull, "Tradewinds of Funk Resonate the Beautiful Island of Aruba," *Atlanta Daily World*, June 12, 1997, 5.

34. John Serba, "Sound Waves of Summer: Muskegon's Summer Celebration Rides a Crest of Top Musical Acts," *The Grand Rapids Press*, June 22, 1997, G1.

35. Steve Jones, "Summer Festivals, Tours Get R&B Acts Together: Essence Spirit Imbues 'Party with a Purpose,'" *USA Today*, June 26, 1997, D8.1.

36. Ronald N. Bryant and Al Knight, "1997 Coors Light Festival Is July 18, 19, 20," *Call and Post*, July 17, 1997, 10.

37. Steve Jones, "A Big 'Ol Box of R&B Nostalgia Also on CD: Miles Davis Live, Classics by The Isley Brothers," *USA Today*, August 4, 1997, D3:1.

38. The Isley Brothers, *Greatest Hits*, Epic, 1997.

39. Wilson and Alroy's Record Reviews, "Rudolph Isley, Shouting for Jesus," http://www.warr.org/isleys.html.

40. "Marvin Isley, Isley Brothers Bassist, Dies of Diabetes at 56," *The Daily Beast*, June 10, 2010, https://www.thedailybeast.com/cheats/2010/06/10/marvin-isley-isley-brothers-bassists-dies-of-diabetes-at-56.

41. Ras Turner, "Annual Air Jamaica Jazz and Blues Festival," *Philadelphia Tribune*, November 7, 1997, 9E.

42. Chris Dickinson and Paul Hampel, "Hallelujah! The Annual Crop of Holiday Music Runs the Gamut for Christ," *St. Louis Post-Dispatch*, December 18, 1997, 20.

43. "The Isley Brothers," *Billboard*, "Special Gift," https://www.billboard.com/artist/the-isley-brothers/chart-history/bsi/.

44. Kimberly Roberts, "Isley Brothers on a 'Mission to Please,'" *Philadelphia Tribune*, January 32, 1998, 6E.

45. Kimberly Roberts, "Ernie Isley Shares the Family Secret," *Philadelphia Tribune*, January 30, 1998, 7E.

46. "Isley Brothers Still Going Strong After Four Decades on the Charts," *Philadelphia Tribune*, January 20, 1998, 4C.

47. Yvette C. Doss, "'Soul Food' and 'Angel' Are Tops in Image Awards," *Los Angeles Times*, February 16, 1998, 2.

48. "Honey Nut Cheerios Announces Sweetest Concert Tour of the Summer," *Business Wire*, June 23, 1998, 1.

49. Earl Calloway, "Stars Expected to Turn Out at WGCI Awards," *Weekend Chicago Defender*, November 14, 1998, 31.

50. Cathy Gardner, "Isley Brothers Dish Out 'Old School,'" *Chicago Defender*, December 28, 1998, 16.

51. "Other 11—No Title," *Philadelphia Tribune*, March 26, 1999, 11E.

52. Paula Crouch Thrasher, "Getaway: Quick Tips and Good Deals Southern Happenings," *The Atlanta Constitution*, April 21, 1999, D6.

53. Jonathan Takiff, "Kickin' Off the Jams: Suddenly Philly Radio Has a Hot New Player," *Philadelphia Daily News*, June 24, 1999, 39.

54. Steve Morse, "Isley Brothers Still a Potent Blow," *Boston Globe*, August 7, 1999, C6.

55. Various Artists, *Muppets from Space: The Ultimate Muppet Trip*, Sony/Epic, 1999.

56. Chris Morris Billboard, "Boxed Set Salutes 40 Years of Evergreen Isley Brothers," *The Commercial Appeal*, August 6, 1999, G12.

57. Geoffrey Himes, "The Isley Brothers: 'It's Your Thing: The Story of The Isley Brothers'; Epic Associated/T-Neck/ Legacy," *The Washington Post*, July 30, 1999, N16.

58. The Isley Brothers, *It's Your Thing: The Story of the Isley Brothers* (CD box set), Sony Music Entertainment, 1999.

59. Himes, "The Isley Brothers."

Chapter 9. Winner Takes All

1. John R. Schmidt, "The Panic of New Year's Eve 1999," WBEZ Blogs, December 31, 2012. https://www.wbez.org/shows/wbez-blogs/the-panic-of-new-years-eve-1999/1bdbe88d-5562-446d-a833-ee765feb1880.

2. Schmidt, "The Panic of New Year's Eve 1999."

3. "World Briefs," *The Salt Lake Tribune*, January 12, 2000, A2.

4. "Isleys Can Keep Songs Rights," *Philadelphia Tribune*, January 25, 2000, 7C.

5. Paul Farhi, "No Isley Estate for Bolton," *The Spectator*, February 26, 2000, W14.

6. "Isley Brothers Win Court Battle," *Alaska Highway News*, May 11, 2000, B1.

7. "Isley Brothers 'Shout' as Pullman Bond Deal Successfully Closes; The Pullman Group Finalizes Isley Pullman Bond Music Royalty Securitization With Legendary Hitmaking Isley Brothers Family," *Business Wire*, June 22, 2000, 1.

8. The Isley Brothers, *The Ultimate Isley Brothers*, Epic/Legacy, 2000.

9. "Ultimate Isley Brothers," The Isley Brothers, AllMusic, https://www.allmusic.com/album/ultimate-isley-brothers-mw0000100807.

10. "'Ultimate Isleys' Captures The Isley Brothers' Hit-Making Years 1959–1983," *Call and Post*, December 21, 2000, 4.

11. Mark Stryker, "These Box Sets Are Worth Unwrapping," *Detroit Free Press*, December 3, 2000, G1.

12. Neil Spencer, "Review: Music: POP," *The Observer*, December 10, 2000, 14.

13. Dan Aquilante, "Oldies but Goodies Going Digital," *New York Post*, January 9, 2001, O48.

14. The Isley Brothers, *Love Songs*, Epic/Legacy, 2001.

15. "The Isley Brothers," *Billboard*, "Love Songs," https://www.billboard.com/artist/the-isley-brothers/chart-history/bst/.

16. Billboard Staff, "Isleys Feel Vindicated In Bolton Case," *Billboard*, February 20, 2001, https://www.billboard.com/music/music-news/isley-feels-vindicated-in-bolton-case-80552/.

17. Kimberly C. Roberts, "Music Icon Receives Prestigious Award: Ronald Isley Accepts the Quincy Jones Award at the Soul Train Awards," *Philadelphia Tribune*, March 2, 2001, 3E.

18. Patricia Guthrie, "Mr. Isley, You Have Diabetes: After Years of Denial, the Youngest of The Isley Brothers Is Taking a Stand Against the Disease That Nearly Killed Him," *The Atlanta Constitution*, May 7, 2001, C1.

19. James R. Oestreich, "Where Music's Mission Is to Help Heal," *New York Times*, June 3, 2001, 2.27.

20. "Contagious," The Isley Brothers, Songfacts, https://www.songfacts.com/facts/the-isley-brothers/contagious.

21. "The Isley Brothers," *Billboard*, "Contagious," https://www.billboard.com/artist/the-isley-brothers/chart-history/bst/.

22. "Contagious," Songfacts.

23. "The Isley Brothers," Grammy Awards, https://www.grammy.com/artists/isley-brothers/14619.

24. The Isley Brothers, *Eternal*, DreamWorks, 2001.

25. Renee Minus White, "The Isley Brothers' Style Is 'Contagious,'" *New York Amsterdam News*, July 26, 2001, 17.

26. RIAA, "Gold and Platinum," "Eternal."

27. "Aaliyah, Isley Brothers Discussed Collaboration," *Moose Jaw Times Herald*, November 4, 2001, 19.

28. Kevin McKenzie, "Southern Heritage Concert Tonight Has Been Canceled," *The Commercial Appeal*, September 13, 2001, A8.

29. Associated Press, "Lennon Tribute Concert Is Staying Put," *The Record*, September 30, 2001, E05.

30. Nekesa Mumbi Moody, "Isley Brothers Still Generating Heat on Charts," *Columbian*, October 16, 2001, D3.

31. Kevin C. Johnson, "Isley Brothers Shine on R&B Classics and New Tunes," *St. Louis Post*, October 28, 2001, C7.
32. "Secret Lover," performed by The Isley Brothers, track no. 6, *Eternal*, DreamWorks, 2001.
33. "The Isley Brothers," *Billboard*, "Secret Lover," https://www.billboard.com/artist/the-isley-brothers/chart-history/bsi/.
34. The Isley Brothers, "Secret Lover (Official Video)," https://www.youtube.com/watch?v=cR8366Bvelc.
35. "JS," Biography, AllMusic. https://www.allmusic.com/artist/js-mn0000119887/biography.
36. "JS."
37. Richard Harrington, "Longevity: It's the Isleys' Thing," *Los Angeles Times*, November 23, 2001, F22.
38. "The Isley Brothers," *Billboard*, "Eternal," https://www.billboard.com/artist/the-isley-brothers/chart-history/bsi/.
39. "Keys, Isley Brothers Each Win Three Soul Train Awards," *North Bay Nugget*, March 22, 2002, C15.
40. "Eternal," The Isley Brothers, AllMusic, https://www.allmusic.com/album/eternal-mw0000010385.
41. Mark Anthony Neal, "The Isley Brothers Featuring Ronald Isley AKA Mr. Biggs: Eternal," PopMatters, August 6, 2001, https://www.popmatters.com/isleybrothers-eternal-2495943074.html.
42. Patty Jackson, "What's Up," *Philadelphia Tribune*, March 3, 2002, SM16.
43. "Angela Winbush Has Very Surprising New Career," I Love Old School Music, September 29, 2017, https://www.iloveoldschoolmusic.com/angela-winbush-has-very-surprising-career-thats-totally-different-from-her-singing-days/.
44. "Magic Mountain Unveils 'X,'" *Los Angeles Sentinel*, January 17, 2002, B6.
45. "Keys, Isley Brothers Each Win Three Soul Train Awards."
46. "City to Give Away Trees to Residents," *South Florida Sun*, May 29, 2002, 1.
47. "NAACP Upholds Freedom at 93rd Annual Convention in Houston; 'Freedom Under Fire' Theme Dominated Mobilization Efforts," US Newswire, July 11, 2002.
48. Billboard Staff, "Keys Tops 2002 Billboard R&B/Hip-Hop Awards," *Billboard*, August 10, 2002, https://www.billboard.com/music/music-news/keys-tops-2002-billboard-rbhip-hop-awards-74611/.
49. "A Star Is Born," *New Pittsburgh Courier*, March 29, 2003, B8.
50. "What Would You Do (featuring The Pied Piper)," performed by The Isley Brothers, track no. 3, *Body Kiss*, Dreamworks, 2003.
51. "Isley Brothers Are Booked for the Arie Crown Revue," *Weekend Chicago Defender*, April 5, 2003, 33.
52. "The Isley Brothers," *Billboard*, "What Would You Do?" https://www.billboard.com/artist/the-isley-brothers/chart-history/bsi/.
53. The Isley Brothers, *Body Kiss*, DreamWorks, 2003.
54. "Isley Brothers Are Booked for the Arie Crown Revue."
55. "The Isley Brothers," *Billboard*, "Body Kiss," https://www.billboard.com/artist/the-isley-brothers/chart-history/bsi/.
56. RIAA, "Gold and Platinum," "Body Kiss."
57. "The Isley Brothers," Grammy Awards, https://www.grammy.com/artists/isley-brothers/14619.

58. "Busted," performed by The Isley Brothers, track no. 5, *Body Kiss*, DreamWorks, 2003.
59. The Isley Brothers, "Busted ft. JS (Official Video)," https://www.youtube.com/watch?v=PDKGDPSq03A.
60. "The Isley Brothers," *Billboard*, "Busted," https://www.billboard.com/artist/the-isley-brothers/chart-history/bsi/.
61. "Prize Possession," performed by The Isley Brothers, track no. 8, *Body Kiss*, DreamWorks, 2003.
62. "The Isley Brothers," *Billboard*, "Prize Possession," https://www.billboard.com/artist/the-isley-brothers/chart-history/rba/.
63. "Body Kiss," The Isley Brothers, AllMusic, https://www.allmusic.com/album/body-kiss-mw0000028502.
64. Jim Fusilli, "Music Review: 'Body Kiss' from The Isley Brothers," NPR Music, June 13, 2003, https://www.npr.org/templates/story/story.php?storyId=1297987.
65. Mark Anthony Neal, "The Isley Brothers Featuring Ronald Isley AKA Mr. Biggs: Body Kiss," PopMatters, May 22, 2003, https://www.popmatters.com/isleybrothers-body-2495939937.html.
66. Luanne J. Hunt, "No Matter What the Times, Isley Brothers Do Just Fine," *Daily News*, August 30, 2003, U7.
67. Ronald Isley, *Here I Am: Isley Meets Bacharach*, DreamWorks, 2003.
68. Jim Farber, "'Smooth to the Taste,' Ron Isley Singing Burt Bacharach Makes for a Great Vintage," *New York Daily News*, November 9, 2003, 15.
69. "After 40 Years, We Don't Make Records Based On Luck and . . . ," *Pittsburgh Post-Gazette*, November 17, 2003, 27.
70. Farber, "'Smooth to the Taste.'"
71. "Ronald Isley," *Billboard*, "Here I Am: Isley Meets Bacharach," https://www.billboard.com/artist/ronald-isley/chart-history/tlp/.
72. Marquita Brown, "Isley Brothers Show Canceled; Fans Irked," *The Clarion Ledger*, August 7, 2004, B1.
73. Patty Jackson, "What's the 411?" *Philadelphia Tribune*, September 2, 2005, 39E.
74. The Isley Brothers, *The Essential Isley Brothers*, Epic, 2004.
75. "The Essential Isley Brothers," The Isley Brothers, AllMusic, https://www.allmusic.com/album/the-essential-isley-brothers-mw0000213535.
76. The Isley Brothers, *Taken to the Next Phase*, Epic, 2004.
77. "The Isley Brothers," *Billboard*, "Taken to the Next Phase," https://www.billboard.com/artist/the-isley-brothers/chart-history/bsi/.
78. "Taken to the Next Phase," The Isley Brothers, AllMusic, https://www.allmusic.com/album/taken-to-the-next-phase-mw0000167465.
79. "Tax Man Chasing Ronald Isley Again," *Chatham Daily News*, October 16, 2004, 9.

Chapter 10. The Heat Is On

1. "Ronald Isley Pleads Innocent to Tax Evasion," *Los Angeles Sentinel*, January 13, 2005, A33.
2. Patty Jackson, "What's the 411?," *Philadelphia Tribune*, May 27, 2005, 39E.
3. David Lindquist, "Good Times: Quality Entertainment Keeps Black Expo an Annual Favorite Destination," *Indianapolis Star*, July 3, 2005, I.1.

4. The Isley Brothers, *Summer Breeze: Greatest Hits*, Epic, 2005.

5. "Summer Breeze: Greatest Hits, The Isley Brothers, Official Charts, https://www.officialcharts.com/search/albums/summer-breeze/.

6. Patty Jackson, "What's the 411?," *Philadelphia Tribune*, September 2, 2005, 39E.

7. "Soul Legend Ronald Isley Weds Singer Kandy Johnson," *Jet*, September 5, 2005, 55–64.

8. "You Help Me Write This Song," performed by The Isley Brothers, track no. 11, *Baby Making Music*, Def Jam, 2006.

9. Patty Jackson, "What's the 411?," *Philadelphia Tribune*, September 2, 2005, 39E.

10. Billboard Staff, "Ronald Isley on Trial for Tax Evasion," *Billboard*, October 13, 2005, https://www.billboard.com/music/music-news/ronald-isley-on-trial-for-tax-evasion-61092/.

11. "Isley Brothers Singer Convicted on Federal Tax Evasion Charges," Press Release, Department of Justice, October 31, 2005, https://www.justice.gov/archive/tax/usaopress/2005/txdv05147.html.

12. "Nov. 6 Concert Postponed," *Los Angeles Sentinel*, November 3, 2005, B5.

13. "Just Came Here to Chill," performed by The Isley Brothers, track no. 3, *Baby Makin' Music*, Def Jam, 2006.

14. Ronald Isley, "Just Came Here to Chill," https://www.youtube.com/watch?v=3SOCNqLeydQ.

15. "The Isley Brothers," *Billboard*, "Just Came Here to Chill," https://www.billboard.com/artist/the-isley-brothers/chart-history/bsi/.

16. The Isley Brothers, *Baby Makin' Music*, Def Jam, 2005.

17. "Isley Brothers release 'Baby Makin' Music' featuring Mr. Biggs," *Call and Post*, March 16, 2006, 11.

18. "The Isley Brothers," *Billboard*, "Baby Makin' Music," https://www.billboard.com/artist/the-isley-brothers/chart-history/bsi/.

19. "Baby Makin' Music," The Isley Brothers, AllMusic, https://www.allmusic.com/album/release/baby-makin-music-mr0003693972.

20. David Weigel, "The Isley Brothers: Baby Makin' Music," PopMatters, May 24, 2006, https://www.popmatters.com/the-isley-brothers-baby-makin-music-2495679309.html.

21. Wilson and Alroy's Record Reviews, "The Isley Brothers, Baby Makin' Music," http://www.warr.org/isleys.html.

22. Patty Jackson, "What's Up?," *Philadelphia Tribune*, June 4, 2006, 14.

23. "Ronald Isley Gets 3 Years in Tax Evasion," *Chicago Defender*, September 4, 2006, 11.

24. Alonzo Weston, "Review: 'Beautiful Ballads' Series Offers Music for Romance," *St. Joseph News*, January 5, 2007.

25. The Isley Brothers, *Beautiful Ballads, Vol. 2*, Epic/Legacy, 2006.

26. "Beautiful Ballads, Vol. 2," The Isley Brothers, AllMusic, https://www.allmusic.com/album/beautiful-ballads-vol-2-mw0000447278.

27. Kimberly C. Roberts, "Isley Optimistic About Appeal, Ready for Tour," *Philadelphia Tribune*, February 16, 2007, 5E.

28. Kevin C. Johnson, "Isley Brothers Spice Up Their Legends with New Hits," *St. Louis Post-Dispatch*, April 22, 2007, F2.

29. Gary Graff, "Isley Brothers Writing New Tunes on Tour," *Billboard*, April 12, 2007, https://www.billboard.com/music/music-news/isley-brothers-writing-new-tunes-on-tour-1052862/.

30. Kimberly Roberts, "Isley Brothers Bid Farewell to Philly Fans," *Philadelphia Tribune*, May 1, 2007, 3C.

31. "The 2007 Essence Music Festival Presented by Coca-Cola Brings Together the Country's Largest Annual Gathering of African Americans to Celebrate Black Music and Culture," *PR Newswire*, July 5, 2007.

32. "ARTSCAPE 2007 to Feature Isley Brothers, Lupe Fiasco, Others," *Afro-American*, June 9, 2007, C5, C9.

33. Clarence Waldron, "Ronald Isley in Jail on Tax Evasion Charges," *Jet*, September 24, 2007, 39.

34. Kimberly Roberts, "Isley Due to Begin Jail Term," *Philadelphia Tribune*, August 7, 2007, 3D.

35. Steve Jones and Donna Freydkin, "Patti LaBelle, Isley Brothers to Spread a Little Holiday Soul," *USA Today*, September 28, 2007, E1.

36. The Isley Brothers, *I'll Be Home for Christmas*, Def Jam, 2007.

37. Jones and Freydkin, "Patti LaBelle, Isley Brothers," E1.

38. "The Isley Brothers," *Billboard*, "I'll Be Home for Christmas," https://www.billboard.com/artist/the-isley-brothers/chart-history/blp/.

39. Wilson and Alroy's Record Reviews, "The Isley Brothers, I'll Be Home for Christmas," http://www.warr.org/isleys.html.

40. "I'll Be Home for Christmas," The Isley Brothers, AllMusic, https://www.allmusic.com/album/ill-be-home-for-christmas-mw0000485398.

41. "Tune In Tuesday; Kid Rock Aims to Be Top Dog," *Courier-Journal* (Louisville, KY), October 9, 2007, E1.

42. The Isley Brothers, *The Definitive Collection*, Hip-O, 2007.

43. "The Isley Brothers," *Billboard*, "The Definitive Collection," https://www.billboard.com/artist/the-isley-brothers/chart-history/blp/.

44. "Isley Sentence Upheld," *Los Angeles Sentinel*, February 14, 2008, A15.

45. The Isley Brothers, *Original Album Classics*, Epic/Legacy, 2008.

46. "Original Album Classics," The Isley Brothers, AllMusic, https://www.allmusic.com/album/original-album-classics-2008--mw0000809706.

47. The Isley Brothers, *The Motown Anthology*, Motown/Universal UMC, 2009.

48. Alex Cohen, "Grammy Hall of Fame Adds 25 New Recordings to Collection," KPCC, November 25, 2009, https://www.kpcc.org/2009-11-25/grammy-hall-of-fame.

49. Bo Emerson, "Hendrix Lives On with Tour; Four Decades After His Death, Guitarists Gather to Celebrate His Genius," *The Atlanta Journal-Constitution*, March 21, 2010, E1.

50. "Entertainment Briefs," *Los Angeles Sentinel*, April 29, 2010, B5.

51. James Johnson, "Music: Our Critics Sound Off About This Week's Shows Hip-Hop," *Philadelphia Daily News*, May 7, 2010, 44.

52. Dennis Hevesi, "Marvin Isley, 56, Bassist in Isley Brothers: [Obituary; Biography]," *New York Times*, June 8, 2010, B15.

53. "No More," performed by Ronald Isley, track no. 2, *Mr. I*, Def Jam, 2010.

54. Ronald Isley, "No More," https://www.youtube.com/watch?v=_Zg8UjYb9c4.

55. The Isley Brothers, *Playlist: The Very Best of The Isley Brothers*, Epic, 2010.

56. "Experience Hendrix Tour to Make Second 2010 Run," *Independent*, August 31, 2010, https://www.independent.co.uk/arts-entertainment/music/experience-hendrix-tour-to-make-second-2010-run-2066307.html.

57. Ronald Isley, *Mr. I*, Def Jam Classics, 2010.

58. Jerry Shriver, "Inspiration Hit Singer in Prison," *The Windsor Star*, December 18, 2010, D2.

59. "What I Miss the Most," performed by Ronald Isley, track no. 7, *Mr. I*, Def Jam, 2010.

60. Ronald Isley, *Billboard*, "What I Miss the Most," https://www.billboard.com/artist/ronald-isley/chart-history/tlp/.
61. Steve Jones, "Ronald Isley: Mr I," *USA Today*, December 6, 2010, D8.
62. Rhonda Swan, "50 Years Later, Isley Still Going Strong Writing, Performing," *Palm Beach Post*, March 18, 2011, T24.
63. "Complete Grammy Nominations List," *Daily Breeze*, December 2, 2010.
64. Swan, "50 Years Later."
65. B. J. Hammerstein, "'Bachelor' Duo Might Be Done," *Detroit Free Press*, March 16, 2011, D2.
66. "Country Club Hills Kicks Off Summer Concert Season with Isley Brothers," *Chicago Defender*, June 8, 2011, S7.
67. Melissa Ruggieri, "Isley Brothers Hold 'Reunion': They Play Favorites in 90-minute Show," *The Atlanta Journal-Constitution*, September 2, 2011, D1.
68. Kevin C. Johnson, "Isley Brothers Not Ready to say Farewell," *McClatchy-Tribune Business News*, September 18, 2011.
69. Ruggieri, "Isley Brothers Hold 'Reunion.'"
70. "Concerts," *Telegraph-Herald*, January 29, 2012, E2.
71. "Tickets for 2012 Smooth Groves Music Fest in Fresno on Sale on Feb. 10," *Visalia Times-Delta*, February 6, 2012.
72. "Concerts: Statewide Listings This Week," *The Clarion Ledger*, May 24, 2012.
73. "Chene Park," *Detroit Free Press*, May 13, 2012, E4.
74. "The Long Beach Jazz Fest Celebrates 25 Years," *Los Angeles Sentinel*, August 9, 2012, B5.
75. "Holiday Happenings 12-20-12," *Times-News*, December 20, 2012.

Chapter 11. Forever Gold

1. Randy Cordova, "Smooth Survivor," *Arizona Republic*, April 7, 2013, AE1.
2. Michael Buckley, "Fantastic Indoor Concerts Coming Your Way This Spring and Summer," *Capital*, April 25, 2013, A11.
3. "Clark Atlanta University Hosts 2013 Spirit of Greatness Gala May 18," *Targeted News Service*, April 26, 2013.
4. "Dinner and a Movie," performed by Ronald Isley, track no. 2, *This Song Is for You*, eOne/Notifi, 2013.
5. Ronald Isley, "Dinner and a Movie," https://www.youtube.com/watch?v=7kWIsTqwRtQ.
6. "Ronald Isley," *Billboard*, "Dinner and a Movie," https://www.billboard.com/artist/ronald-isley/chart-history/tlp/.
7. Kevin C. Johnson, "Ronald Isley's New Album Shows 'Where Music Is Supposed to Be,'" *McClatchy-Tribune*, July 19, 2013.
8. Ronald Isley, *This Song Is for You*, eOne/Notifi, 2013.
9. Johnson, "Ronald Isley's New Album."
10. "Ronald Isley," *Billboard*, "This Song Is for You," https://www.billboard.com/artist/ronald-isley/chart-history/tlp/.
11. Marc Myers, "Soul Survivor," *Wall Street Journal*, July 15, 2013.
12. Johnson, "Ronald Isley's New Album."
13. "My Favorite Thing," performed by Ronald Isley featuring Kem, track no. 3, *This Song Is for You*, eOne/Notifi, 2013.

14. Ronald Isley ft. Kem, "My Favorite Thing," https://www.youtube.com/watch?v=zvnkt QDa3Fk.
15. "Ronald Isley," *Billboard*, "My Favorite Thing," https://www.billboard.com/artist/ronald-isley/chart-history/tlp/.
16. Teri Greene, "Isley Brothers to Headline ASU Show," *Montgomery Advertiser*, November 26, 2013, 1.
17. Bob Goldsborough, "R. Kelly's Mansion Sells to Isley Brothers for $587,000," *Chicago Tribune*, December 5, 2013, 2.
18. Kevin C. Johnson, "After Several Snubs, Grammys Honor Isley Brothers," *McClatchy-Tribune Business News*, January 25, 2014.
19. "Anthony Anderson Returns as Host, Grammy Winning Artists Jill Scott, The Isley Brothers and Tye Tribbett, Join Alice Smith, Sevyn Streeter, August Alsina and Spoken Reasons to Perform on UNCF Evening of Stars," Targeted News Service, March 20, 2014.
20. "About UNCF an Evening with Stars," Jesse Collins Entertainment, https://jessecollinsent.com/portfolio/uncf-evening-stars/.
21. Kirby Adams, "Kentucky Derby Festival; Electrifying," *Courier-Journal*, April 28, 2014, D1.
22. "Concerts & Events: Hot Tickets," *Atlanta Journal-Constitution*, April 18, 2014, D9.
23. Marshall Heyman, "'The Apollo Is 80 Years Young; A Benefit Concert for Harlem's Storied Theater," *Wall Street Journal*, June 11, 2014.
24. David Goodson, "Nightlife," *New York Amsterdam News*, August 28, 2014, 9.
25. A. J. Williams, "Chene Park Celebrates 30 Years with The Isley Brothers, En Vogue and Loose Ends for the Last Concert of the Year," *Michigan Chronicle*, August 28, 2014.
26. "Featuring: Macy's Great Tree Lighting," *The Atlanta Journal-Constitution*, November 23, 2014, NOS1.
27. "Music," *Orlando Sentinel*, December 26, 2014, M23.
28. "Go Guide Sunday," *The Atlanta Journal-Constitution*, December 28, 2014, E2.
29. Jennifer Brett, "Trumpet Awards Founder Aims to Inspire," *TCA Regional News*, January 14, 2015.
30. Alison Fensterstock, "Fantasia, Juvenile Join Isley Brothers on Zulu Coronation Ball Lineup: Tickets on Sale Now," Nola.com, November 18, 2014, https://www.nola.com/entertainment_life/music/fantasia-juvenile-join-isley-brothers-on-zulu-coronation-ball-lineup-tickets-on-sale-now/article_67f6c6bb-ccfb-5ac2-a085-194cdc8990cc.html.
31. "Mardi Gras 2023," History.com, February 17, 2023, https://www.history.com/topics/holidays/mardi-gras.
32. Fensterstock, "Fantasia, Juvenile Join Isley Brothers."
33. Carlton Fletcher, "Isley Brothers Hall of Fame Career Six Decades and Counting," *TCA Regional News*, March 11, 2015.
34. "Kendrick Lamar," Grammy Awards, https://www.grammy.com/artists/kendrick-lamar/17949.
35. "Let's Go! Weekly Entertainment Calendar 4-2-15," *Times-News*, April 2, 2015.
36. "The Timeless Isley Brothers, Ranked," *Courier-Journal*, June 11, 2015, 8.
37. "Road Trip: Around Louisiana," *The Daily Advertiser*, June 18, 2015, 25.
38. David Lindquist, "Summer Celebration Lineup Is Music to Fans' Ears," *Indianapolis Star*, July 14, 2015, A2.
39. The Isley Brothers, *The RCA Victor & T-Neck Album Masters (1959–1983)*, T-Neck/Epic/Legacy, 2015.

40. "Isley Brothers 1959–1983," *New Pittsburgh Courier*, August 5, 2015, B5.

41. Brian Mansfield, "Isley Brothers Take a Look Back," *USA Today*, August 18, 2015, D4.

42. Christina Maza, "Summer Jams: Barack Obama Edition," *The Christian Science Monitor*, August 14, 2015.

43. Donald James, "Aretha Franklin Comes Home to Chene Part," *Michigan Chronicle*, August 19, 2015, D2.

44. "'Legends: OWN at the Apollo' to Air as a Four-Part Primetime Special," Oprah.com, https://www.oprah.com/entertainment/legends-own-at-the-apollo-to-air-as-a-four-part-primetime-special.

45. "Legacy Recordings Announces Limited Edition Vinyl Exclusives for Record Store Day's Annual Black Friday Event (Friday, November 27, 2015)," PR Newswire, October 22, 2015.

46. The Isley Brothers, *Groove With You . . . Live*, T-Neck/Epic/Legacy, 2015.

47. Mesfin Fekadu, "Harrison Leads List of Hall of Fame Nominees," *Prince George Citizen*, October 6, 2015, A21.

48. Trevor Fraser, "Zora Neale Hurston Festival of the Humanities," *Orlando Sentinel*, January 22, 2016, M25.

49. "Santana IV Reunites Legendary Band Lineup: First Single 'Anywhere You Want To Go' to Be Released February 5, 2016," PR Newswire, January 21, 2016.

50. Allen Bush, "Rita Moreno, The Isley Brothers, Ludian Grainge, Milton Nascimento Honored at Commencement," Berklee College of Music, May 7, 2016, https://college.berklee.edu/news/rita-morno-isley-brothers-lucian-grainge-milton-nascimento-honored-berklee-commencement.

51. "16th Annual Soul Beach Music Festival Hosted by Aruba," *M2 Presswire*, May 27, 2016.

52. "Taste of Chicago: Full 2016 Music, Food Lineup," NBC Chicago, May 17, 2016, https://www.nbcchicago.com/news/local/taste-of-chicago-full-2016-music-food-lineup/115966/.

53. "Weekend Top 10," *Daily Press*, July 29, 2016, C3.

54. "Legendary Isley Brothers, Freddie Jackson, Chante Moore, and Ruben Studdard Ripped It at Wolf Creek Amphitheatre," *Atlanta Daily World*, August 25, 2016.

55. Ron Scott, "Hendrix Apollo Tribute, Chambers at Smoke, WeBop HAS," *New York Amsterdam News*, November 24, 2016, 23.

56. "Regional Highlights," *Telegram and Gazette*, January 8, 2017, G3.

57. Imhotep Gary Byrd, "Imhotep's Guide to Black Events," *New York Amsterdam News*, January 12, 2017, 29.

58. Jim Harrington, "Stone Soul Delivers a Strong Double Dose of R&B," *The Mercury News*, May 4, 2017, T14.

59. "The Isley Brothers and Santana 'Power of Peace' Set For 7/28 Release," *Glide Magazine*, https://glidemagazine.com/186785/isley-brothers-santana-power-peace-set-728-release/.

60. The Isley Brothers/Santana, *Power of Peace*, Legacy, 2017.

61. "Carlos Santana and Cindy Blackman Santana Join Forces with The Isley Brothers (Ronald and Ernie) on Power of Peace, a New Album Celebrating the Timeless Sounds of Funk, Soul, Blues, Rock, Jazz, and Pop: Available Friday, August 4 from Legacy Recordings," PR Newswire, June 5, 2017.

62. "The Isley Brothers," *Billboard*, "Power of Peace," https://www.billboard.com/artist/the-isley-brothers/chart-history/tlp/.

63. "Power of Peace," The Isley Brothers/Santana, AllMusic, https://www.allmusic.com/album/power-of-peace-mw0003062166.

64. Tristan Kneschke, "The Isley Brothers and Santana: Power of Peace," PopMatters, July 27, 2017, https://www.popmatters.com/the-isley-brothers-santana-power-of-peace-2495385051.html.

65. Doug Heselgrave, "Santana and The Isley Brothers: *Power of Peace*," Paste Magazine, July 28, 2017, https://www.pastemagazine.com/music/santana/santana-the-isley-brothers-power-of-peace-review/.

66. Stephanie Schulte, "Twist, Shout and Groove with the Commodores and The Isley Brothers at Fantasy Springs Resort Casino," *Redlands Daily Facts*, August 23, 2017.

67. "The Isley Brothers to Receive 2017 AutoZone Liberty Bowl's Outstanding Achievement Award," Targeted News Service, October 17, 2017.

68. Michael King, "The Isley Brothers Honored with Proclamation at Mable House Concert," 11 Alive News, July 15, 2018, https://www.11alive.com/article/entertainment/television/programs/the-a-scene/the-isley-brothers-honored-with-proclamation-at-mable-house-concert/85-573987496.

Chapter 12. Eternal

1. "'Legends Live Atlanta' R&B Concert Kicking Off Super Bowl Weekend," *Atlanta Daily World*, January 14, 2019.

2. "Dave Mustaine, Joe Satriani to Pay Tribute to Jimi Hendrix as Part of 2019 'Experience Hendrix' Tour," Blabbermouth.net, October 15, 2018, https://blabbermouth.net/news/dave-mustaine-joe-satriani-to-pay-tribute-to-jimi-hendrix-as-part-of-2019-experience-hendrix-tour.

3. Kevin C. Johnson, "Isley Brothers Are Latest Edition to St. Louis Walk of Fame in the Loop," *St. Louis Post-Dispatch*. April 19, 2019, G8.

4. Rashad Grove, "R&B Legends The Isley Brothers Announce Their 60th Anniversary Tour," *The Source*, May 17, 2019, https://thesource.com/2019/05/17/rb-legends-the-isleys-brothers-announce-their-60th-anniversary-tour/.

5. Kiki Camille, "Isley Brothers Seemingly Mute R. Kelly During 60th Anniversary Pitchfork Performance," *Chicago Defender*, July 23, 2019.

6. Dale Edwards, "Councilman Blaine Griffin Celebrates the Legendary Isley Brothers," *Call and Post*, October 30, 2019, 3C.

7. The Isley Brothers Announce 60th Anniversary UK Tour—Here's How to Get Tickets," Gold Radio UK, December 11, 2019, https://www.goldradiouk.com/news/music/the-isley-brothers-tour-tickets/.

8. "A Look into the Songwriters Hall of Fame," *University Wire* (Carlsbad), January 28, 2020.

9. Mark Kennedy, "Songwriters Hall of Fame 2022 Class includes Mariah Carey, Eurythmics, the Isley Brothers," *USA Today*, June 16, 2022.

10. "Songwriters Hall of Fame Reschedules 51st Annual Induction and Awards Dinner," Songwriters Hall of Fame, March 31, 2020, https://www.songhall.org/news/view/songwriters_hall_of_fame_reschedules_51st_annual_induction_and_awards_dinner.

11. Kevin C. Johnson, "Kandy Isley, Kim Johnson Spread Peace and Healing on New Single 'Free,'" *St. Louis Post-Dispatch*, June 12, 2020, G6.

12. Kevin C. Johnson, "Kandy Isley, Kim Johnson Dive Into Christmas with New EP," *St. Louis Post-Dispatch*, December 25, 2020, G7.

13. Andrew Unterberger, "The Isley Brothers vs. Earth, Wind & Fire in Funk Legends 'Verzuz' Battle: See Billboard's Score Card for the Event," *Billboard*, April 5, 2021, https://www.billboard.com/music/rb-hip-hop/isley-brothers-earth-wind-fire-verzuz-battle-scorecard-9551107/.

14. "Friends and Family," The Isley Brothers Featuring Ronald Isley and Snoop Dogg, track no. 13, *Make Me Say It Again, Girl*, RI Top Ten, 2022.

15. The Isley Brothers, "Friends and Family (Official Video) ft. Ronald Isley & Snoop Dogg," https://www.youtube.com/watch?v=Pq51JmcyBzY.

16. "The Isley Brothers," *Billboard*, "Friends & Family," https://www.billboard.com/artist/the-isley-brothers/chart-history/tlp/.

17. Shaylah Brown, "For the Love of Them: Englewood, Teaneck Rename Streets for The Isley Brothers," *North Jersey Herald News*, June 25, 2021, L1.

18. "Prep-Entertainment-Report," *The Canadian Press*, February 11. 2021.

19. Wendy Fox Weber, "Five Things to Do in the Southland and Nearby July 23–29," *Chicago Tribune*, July 19, 2021.

20. Emily DeLetter, "Isley Brothers to Headline Cincy Soul Fest in July," *Cincinnati Enquirer*, July 7, 2021, A7.

21. Briana Rice, "Black Music Walk of Fame to Open Next Year: First Four Inductees Honored at Ceremony on Saturday," *Cincinnati Enquirer*, July 25, 2021, A1.

22. "Louisville Shows This Week: Charlie Wilson, 'Gloria: A Life' and More; Saturday, Sept. 25," *Courier-Journal*, September 25, 2021, C2.

23. Kevin C. Johnson, "The Isley Brothers, Charlie Wilson Heading to Chaifetz Arena," *TCA Regional News*, August 23, 2021.

24. "Alex Isley," AllMusic, https://www.allmusic.com/artist/alex-isley-mn0003418239/biography.

25. Anjali Huynh, "One MusicFest Brings Thousands to Downtown Atlanta for H.E.R., Ari Lennox and More," *Atlanta Journal-Constitution*, October 10. 2021.

26. "Do You Have Your List Ready for Santa?" *Daily Journal* (Vineland, NJ), November 4, 2021, A5.

27. "Rapper Dead After Stabbing at Exposition Park Concert," *Los Angeles Sentinel*, December 23, 2021, A11.

28. "Miami Gardens' Musical Lineup on Tap This Weekend at 2022 JITG Festival," *Michigan Chronicle*, March 11, 2022.

29. Rae Johnson, "Kentucky Derby Week Brings Big Stars to Louisville," *Courier-Journal*, April 29, 2022, A6.

30. Chris Jordan, "Happy Mother's Day from The Isley Brothers," *The Record*, May 6, 2022, W4.

31. Mark Kennedy, "Songwriters Hall of Fame 2022 Class Includes Mariah Carey, Eurythmics, the Isley Brothers," *USA Today*, June 16, 2022.

32. DeArbea Walker, "In Texas, a Park Founded by Formerly Enslaved People Prepares to Celebrated Its 150th Juneteenth," *Insider*, June 18, 2022.

33. "Essence Festival of Culture's Roster Is Heating Up with Wizkid, City Girls, Beenie Man, Tems, Method Man, Raekwon, Ghostface, Kes, Mickey Guyton and More Still to Come," *Business Wire*, April 28, 2022.

34. "Go Guide: The Big A List," *The Atlanta Journal-Constitution*, July 3, 2022, E2.

35. "Make Me Say It Again, Girl," performed by Ronald Isley and The Isley Brothers featuring Beyoncé," track no. 1, *Make Me Say It Again, Girl*, RI Top Ten, 2022.

36. "Make Me Say It Again, Girl," The Isley Brothers, Songfacts, https://www.songfacts.com/facts/the-isley-brothers/make-me-say-it-again-girl-part-1-2.

37. Keithan Samuels, "The Isley Brothers Share New Album 'Make Me Say It Again, Girl,'" Rated R&B, September 30, 2022, https://ratedrnb.com/2022/09/the-isley-brothers-share-new-album-make-me-say-it-again-girl/.

38. "The Isley Brothers," *Billboard*, "Make Me Say It Again, Girl," https://www.billboard.com/artist/the-isley-brothers/chart-history/tlp/.

39. "Beyonce Wins Three Prizes at 2022 Soul Train Awards," *University Wire*, November 28, 2022.

40. The Isley Brothers, *Make Me Say It Again, Girl*, RI Top Ten, 2022.

41. Samuels, "The Isley Brothers Share New Album."

42. "The Plug," performed by The Isley Brothers featuring 2 Chainz, track no. 3, *Make Me Say It Again, Girl*, RI Top Ten, 2022.

43. "The Isley Brothers ft 2 Chainz—R&B Music Video Production," Zane Productions, https://www.zane-productions.com/isley-2chainz-plug-music-video.

44. "The Isley Brothers," *Billboard*, "The Plug," https://www.billboard.com/artist/the-isley-brothers/chart-history/bsi/.

45. Samuels, "The Isley Brothers Share New Album."

46. Duante Beddingfield and Julie Hinds, "Holiday Entertainment: Scrooge, 'Les Miz' and the Return of Noel Night," *Detroit Free Press*, November 13, 2022, E5.

47. Deborah Sengupta Stith, Eric Webb, and Earl Hopkins, "Bruce, Janet, SZA: Your Guide to Austin Live Music in 2023," *Austin American Statesman*, January 5, 2023, T1.

48. Maggy Donaldson, "Motown's Smokey Robinson, Berry Gordy Celebrated at Pre-Grammy Gala," *AFP International*, February 4, 2023.

49. Christi Carras, "Isley vs. Isley Over Trademark: Siblings Embroiled in Lawsuit for Rights to Isley Brothers Name," *Los Angeles Times*, March 22, 2023, E2.

50. Wes Woods, II, "Anderson .Paak Brings Smokey Robinson, Isley Brothers to Ventura Festival," *Ventura County Star*, May 13, 2023.

51. Adele Chapin, "10 D.C. Music Festivals You Can't Miss in June," *The Washington Post*, June 2, 2003.

52. Julia Conley, "Roots Picnic 2023 Honors Legendary Black Artists," *University Wire*, June 9, 2023.

53. Keithan Samuels, "AFRAM Festival 2023 Lineup Announced: The Isley Brothers and Ty Dolla $ign to Headline," Rated R&B, April 13, 2023. https://ratedrnb.com/2023/04/afram-festival-2023-lineup-the-isley-brothers-ty-dolla-sign-tamar-braxton/.

54. "The Isley Brothers Announce New Single 'Last Time.'" The Grateful Web, July 6, 2023, https://www.gratefulweb.com/articles/isley-brothers-announce-new-single-last-time.

55. "Last Time," performed by The Isley Brothers, track no. 7, *Make Me Say It Again, Girl*, RI Top Ten, 2022.

56. "The Isley Brothers," *Billboard*, "Last Time," https://www.billboard.com/artist/the-isley-brothers/chart-history/rbm/.

57. Jim Farber, "Rudolph Isley, Original Member of Brothers Group, Dies at 84," *Philadelphia Tribune*, October 15, 2023, 10B.

58. "Urban League's Gala Raises Almost $2.4 Million, Honors Community Leaders," *Chicago Defender*, November 7, 2023.

59. Paul Grein, "SZA, Usher & Victoria Monet Are Top Winners at 2023 Soul Train Awards: Full List," *Billboard*, November 26, 2023, https://www.billboard.com/music/awards/2023-soul-train-awards-winners-list-sza-usher-1235509200/.

60. Mary Caldwell, "15 Things to Do This Weekend in Metro Atlanta: MLK Events, Atlanta Boat Show and More," *TCA Regional News*, January 11, 2024.

61. Melissa Ruggieri, "Inside Clive Davis' Celeb-Packed Pre-Grammy Party: Green Day, Mariah Carey, More," *USA Today*, February 4, 2024.

62. "Tom Sandoval, Ween and Phoenix's Best Concerts This Week," *Phoenix New Times*, February 15, 2024.

63. "Ernie Isley," Songwriters Hall of Fame, May 26, 2024, https://www.songhall.org/profile/ernie_isley.

64. "The Guitar Center Music Foundation Hosts a Who's Who of L.A.'s Music Industry at Third-Annual Benefit Concert," *The Billings Gazette*, April 17, 2024.

65. Chris Rizik, "Happy Birthday to the Legendary Ronald Isley," Soul Tracks, May 26, 2024, https://www.soultracks.com/birthday-ronald-isley-2024.

66. "Music Legends Reunite: The Isley Brothers and Angela Winbush Live in Concert," Keciastourlife.com, June 16, 2024, https://keciastourlife.com/music-legends-reunite-the-isley-brothers-and-angela-winbush-live-in-concert/.

67. "Hollywood Walk of Fame Class of 2025 Announced by Walk of Famers Niecy Nash, Jimmy Jam and Joe Mantegna," Hollywood Walk of Fame, https://walkoffame.com/press_releases/hollywood-walk-of-fame-class-of-2025/.

68. "The Isley Brothers Bring Over 7 Decades to the Dell in Philadelphia," *New Pittsburgh Courier*, August 7, 2024.

Afterword

1. Chris Rizik, "Isley Brothers," SoulTracks, https://soultracks.com/artist/isley_brothers/.
2. RIAA, "Gold and Platinum."
3. RIAA, "Gold and Platinum."
4. Mark Elbert, "The Isley Brothers Talk About Extending Their Reign as 'Kings of Love Songs,'" *Billboard*, October 11, 2022, https://www.billboard.com/music/rb-hip-hop/isley-brothers-make-me-say-it-again-girl-interview-1235154320/.

Bibliography

"Aaliyah, Isley Brothers Discussed Collaboration." *Moose Jaw Times Herald*, November 4, 2001.
Adams, Kirby. "Kentucky Derby Festival; Electrifying." *Courier-Journal*, April 28, 2014.
"After 40 Years, We Don't Make Records Based On Luck and. . . ." *Pittsburgh Post-Gazette*, November 17, 2003.
"Ali, Bond, Gregory Asked to Adam Bash." *New York Amsterdam News*. February 18, 1967.
"All in My Lover's Eyes." Performed by The Isley Brothers. *The Real Deal*. T-Neck. 1982.
Allan, Blaine. "Musical Cinema, Music Video, Music Television." *Film Quarterly* 43, no. 3 (Spring 1990): 4.
AllMusic. "Alex Isley." https://www.allmusic.com/artist/alex-isley-mn0003418239.
AllMusic. "The Isley Brothers." https://www.allmusic.com/artist/the-isley-brothers-mn0000766893.
AllMusic. "Isley-Jasper-Isley." https://www.allmusic.com/artist/isley-jasper-isley-mn0001202374.
"All-Star Stage Bill Rules Regal Stage: Isley Brothers, Bill Doggett and Will Gains Star." *The Chicago Defender*, January 16, 1960.
"Angela Winbush, Ron Isley Wed in L. A. Ceremony." *Jet*, July 19, 1993.
"Anthony Anderson Returns as Host, Grammy Winning Artists Jill Scott, The Isley Brothers and Tye Tribbett, Join Alice Smith, Sevyn Streeter, August Alsina and Spoken Reasons to Perform on UNCF Evening of Stars." Targeted News Service, March 20, 2014.
"Apollo Re-Opens Friday with Top Holiday Fare." *New Pittsburgh Courier*, December 26, 1964.
Aquilante, Dan. "Oldies but Goodies Going Digital." *New York Post*, January 9, 2001.
"ARTSCAPE 2007 to Feature Isley Brothers, Lupe Fiasco, Others." *Afro-American*, June 9, 2007.
Associated Press. "Lennon Tribute Concert Is Staying Put." *The Record*, September 30, 2001.
"Ballad for the Fallen Soldier." Performed by The Isley Brothers. *Between the Sheets*. T-Neck. 1983.
Banez, Cherry. "Entertainment: Tis the Season for Great Music." *Philadelphia Tribune*, November 29, 1996.
Barkley, Elizabeth Isley. *One Isley Brother's Daughter*. Bloomington, IN: Xlibris, 2011.
BBC Review. Review of The Isley Brothers *Harvest for the World*. https://www.bbc.co.uk/music/reviews/fdfd/.

Beddingfield, Duante, and Julie Hinds. "Holiday Entertainment: Scrooge, 'Les Miz' and the Return of Noel Night." *Detroit Free Press*, November 13, 2022.
"Best Selling Records of 1996." *Billboard*, January 18, 1997.
Betts, Graham. *Motown Encyclopedia*. Scotts Valley, CA: CreateSpace, 2014.
"Between the Sheets." Performed by The Isley Brothers. *Between the Sheets*. T-Neck. 1983.
"Beyonce Wins Three Prizes at 2022 Soul Train Awards." *University Wire*, November 28, 2022.
Billboard. "The Isley Brothers." https://www.billboard.com/artist/the-isley-brothers/chart-history/bsi/.
Billboard. "R. Kelly." https://www.billboard.com/artist/r.-kelly/chart-history/hsi/.
Billboard. "Ronald Isley." https://www.billboard.com/artist/ronald-isley/chart-history/tlp/.
Billboard and Chris Morris. "Boxed Set Salutes 40 Years of Evergreen Isley Brothers." *The Commercial Appeal*, August 6, 1999.
Billboard Staff. "Isleys Feel Vindicated in Bolton Case." *Billboard*, February 20, 2001. https://www.billboard.com/music/music-news/isley-feels-vindicated-in-bolton-case- 80552/.
Billboard Staff. "Keys Tops 2002 Billboard R&B/Hip-Hop Awards," *Billboard*, August 10, 2002, https://www.billboard.com/music/music-news/keys-tops-2002-billboard-rbhip-hop-awards-74611/.
"Bits 'n Pieces." *Call and Post*, December 29, 1994.
Blabbermouth.net. "Dave Mustaine, Joe Satriani to Pay Tribute to Jimi Hendrix as Part of 2019 'Experience Hendrix' Tour." October 15, 2018. https://blabbermouth.net/news/dave-mustaine-joe-satriani-to-pay-tribute-to-jimi-hendrix-as-part-of-2019-experience-hendrix-tour.
"Black Berries (AKA The Blacker the Berrie)." Performed by The Isley Brothers. *The Brothers: Isley*. T-Neck. 1969.
"Black Music Organization Plans Gala." *Philadelphia Tribune*, June 14, 1996.
"Bless Your Heart." Performed by The Isley Brothers, *Get Into Something*. T-Neck. 1969.
Boehm, Mike. "Pop Music Review: 'Shouts' Were Out, Ballads Were In at Isley Brothers Show." *Los Angeles Times*, April 23, 1990.
Boissoneault, Lorraine. "Martin Luther King, Jr.'s Assassination Sparked Uprisings in Cities Across America." *Smithsonian Magazine*, April 4, 1968. https://www.smithsonianmag.com/history/martin-luther-king-jrs-assassination-sparked-uprisings-cities-across-america-180968665/.
"Bolton Hit Essentially Is 1966 Isley Song, Jury Finds." *Los Angeles Times*, April 26, 1994.
"Boy Singer Killed on Bike." *The Cincinnati Enquirer*, September 25, 1954. https://www.newspapers.com/article/the-cincinnati-enquirer/148304318/.
Boyd, Todd. *The Notorious Ph.D.'s Guide to the Super Fly '70s: A Connoisseur's Journey Through the Fabulous Flix, Hip Sounds, and Cool Vibes That Defined a Decade*. New York: Crown, 2007.
Branch, Kip. "The Isley Brothers: They're Really Brothers!" *Afro-American*, August 19, 1978.
Brett, Jennifer. "Trumpet Awards Founder Aims to Inspire." *TCA Regional News*, January 14, 2015.
Britannica. "Disco." https://www.britannica.com/art/disco.
Brown, Marquita. "Isley Brothers Show Canceled; Fans Irked," *The Clarion Ledger*, August 7, 2004.
Brown, Shaylah. "For the Love of Them: Englewood, Teaneck Rename Streets for The Isley Brothers." *North Jersey Herald News*, June 25, 2021.
"Brownstone: New Group Makes Debut on Michael Jackson's Record Label." *Jet*, June 19, 1995.

Bryant, Ronald N., and Al Knight. "1997 Coors Light Festival Is July 18, 19, 20." *Call and Post*, July 17, 1997.
Buckley, Michael. "Fantastic Indoor Concerts Coming Your Way This Spring and Summer." *Capital*, April 25, 2013, A11.
Bush, Allen. "Rita Moreno, The Isley Brothers, Ludian Grainge, Milton Nascimento Honored at Commencement." Berklee College of Music. May 7, 2016. https://college.berklee.edu/news/rita-morno-isley-brothers-lucian-grainge-milton-nascimento-honored-berklee-commencement.
"Busted." Performed by The Isley Brothers. *Body Kiss*. DreamWorks. 2003.
Byrd, Imhotep Gary. "Imhotep's Guide to Black Events." *New York Amsterdam News*, January 12, 2017.
Byrd, William. "Isley Brothers 25th Anniversary Tour Comes to the Fox." *Atlanta Daily World*, October 6, 1983.
Caldwell, Mary. "15 Things to Do This Weekend in Metro Atlanta: MLK Events, Atlanta Boat Show and More." *TCA Regional News*, January 11, 2024.
Calloway, Earl. "Bar-Kays Join Isley Brothers at Amphitheatre Saturday." *Chicago Defender*, August 25, 1976.
Calloway, Earl. "Black Stars Kept America Singing Jingling and Dancing in '76." *Chicago Defender (Big Weekend Edition)*, January 1, 1977.
Calloway, Earl. "Marvin Gaye Making Big Plans at CBS." *Chicago Defender*, December 28, 1981.
Calloway, Earl. "Stars Expected to Turn Out at WGCI Awards." *Weekend Chicago Defender*, November 14, 1998.
Calloway, Earl. "Warner Bros. Releases Curtis Mayfield Tribute." *Weekend Chicago Defender*, March 5, 1994.
Camille, Kiki. "Isley Brothers Seemingly Mute R. Kelly During 60th Anniversary Pitchfork Performance." *Chicago Defender*, July 23, 2019.
"Caravan of Love." Performed by Isley-Jasper-Isley. *Caravan of Love*. CBS. 1985.
"Carlos Santana and Cindy Blackman Santana Join Forces with The Isley Brothers (Ronald and Ernie) on Power of Peace, a New Album Celebrating the Timeless Sounds of Funk, Soul, Blues, Rock, Jazz, and Pop: Available Friday, August 4 from Legacy Recordings." PR Newswire, June 5, 2017.
Carras, Christi. "Isley vs. Isley over Trademark: Siblings Embroiled in Lawsuit for Rights to Isley Brothers Name." *Los Angeles Times*, March 22, 2023.
Carter, Ulish. "1970's: Golden Era Musically but Not Lyrically." *New Pittsburgh Courier*, January 12, 1980.
Carter, Ulish. "The Record Rack: Curtis' Latest Is a Downer." *New Pittsburgh Courier*, June 4, 1977.
Carter, Ulish. "The Record Rack: Isley Brothers Continue Class Young at Heart." *New Pittsburgh Courier*, June 25, 1976.
"CBS Stars Cut Tapes for Census Radio Spots." *Chicago Defender*, April 1, 1980.
Chapin, Adele. "10 D.C. Music Festivals You Can't Miss in June." *The Washington Post*, June 2, 2003.
"Charlie Cherokee." *Chicago Defender*, April 2, 1979.
"Chene Park." *Detroit Free Press*, May 13, 2012, E4.
ChessNotCheckers. "Kelly Price Keeps It Real on Mariah Carey, Diddy and the Music Industry." Accessed March 15, 2023. https://www.youtube.com/watch?v=8_c-5T-MQeM.

"Choosey Lover." Performed by The Isley Brothers. *Between the Sheets.* T-Neck. 1983.
Christgau, Robert. "The Isley Brothers." https://www.robertchristgau.com/get_artist.php?name=The+Isley+Brothers.
Christgau, Robert. "The Isley Brothers and Jimi Hendrix: *In the Beginning*...." Consumer Guide Album. https://robertchristgau.com/get_album.php?id=7056.
"City to Give Away Trees to Residents." *South Florida Sun,* May 29, 2002.
"Clark Atlanta University Hosts 2013 Spirit of Greatness Gala May 18." Targeted News Service, April 26, 2013.
Classic Motown. "The Isley Brothers." https://classic.motown.com/artist/the-isley-brothers/.
"Clinton Notes Black Music Month." *Philadelphia Tribune,* June 25, 1996.
Cohen, Alex. "Grammy Hall of Fame Adds 25 New Recordings to Collection." KPCC, November 25, 2009. https://www.kpcc.org/2009-11-25/grammy-hall-of-fame.
"Colder Are My Nights." Performed by The Isley Brothers. *Masterpiece.* Warner Brothers. 1985.
Coleman, Mark. "The Isley Brothers." *Rolling Stone* no. 769, September 18, 1997.
Collins, Carlton Robert. "Lincoln Heights: The Forgotten Black Wall Street." Medium, June 5, 2021. https://educ8drebel.medium.com/lincoln-heights-lessons-from-the-forgotten-black-wall-street-f670b2177c07.
"Come My Way." Performed by The Isley Brothers. *Smooth Sailin'.* Warner Brothers. 1987.
"Complete Grammy Nominations List." *Daily Breeze,* December 2, 2010.
"Concerts." *Telegraph-Herald,* January 29, 2012.
"Concerts and Events: Hot Tickets." *Atlanta Journal-Constitution,* April 18, 2014.
"Concerts: Statewide Listings This Week." *The Clarion Ledger,* May 24, 2012.
Conley, Julia. "Roots Picnic 2023 Honors Legendary Black Artists." *University Wire,* June 9, 2023.
Considine, J. D. "A Band to Shout About/The Isley Brothers Adapt to Stay Current." *Newsday,* August 13, 1996.
Corcoran, Patrick. "The Isley Brothers' 'The Heat Is On' Turns 45 | Anniversary Retrospective." Albumism, June 6, 2020. https://albumism.com/features/the-isley-brothers-the-heat-is-on-turns-45-anniversary-retrospective.
Cordova, Randy. "Smooth Survivor." *Arizona Republic,* April 7, 2013.
"Country Club Hills Kicks Off Summer Concert Season with Isley Brothers." *Chicago Defender,* June 8, 2011.
Defendorf, Richard. "The Isley Brothers (3 Star Edition)." *Orlando Sentinel,* December 1, 1985.
Deggans, Eric. "Isley Brothers Do Their Thing and So Do Others." *St. Petersburg Times,* June 22, 1996.
Deggans, Eric. "'Summer of Soul' Celebrates a 1969 Black Cultural Festival Eclipsed by Woodstock." NPR, July 1, 2021. https://www.npr.org/2021/07/01/1010306918/summer-of-soul-questlove-movie-review-harlem-cultural-festival.
DeLetter, Emily. "Isley Brothers to Headline Cincy Soul Fest in July." *Cincinnati Enquirer,* July 7, 2021.
Dickinson, Chris, and Paul Hampel. "Hallelujah! The Annual Crop of Holiday Music Runs the Gamut for Christ." *St. Louis Post-Dispatch,* December 18, 1997.
"Dinner and a Movie." Performed by Ronald Isley. *This Song Is for You.* eOne/Notifi. 2013.
"Disc Jockey Jamboree at Apollo." *New Pittsburgh Courier,* June 27, 1964.
Discogs. "The Isley Brothers." https://www.discogs.com/artist/47512-The-Isley-Brothers.
"Display Ad 38." *New York Amsterdam News,* August 13, 1966.

DJ Rob. "The Non-Isley Brother Who Made the Isleys Blow Up." *DJ Rob Blog*. September 19, 2016, https://djrobblog.com/archives/3515.

"Do You Have Your List Ready for Santa?" *Daily Journal* (Vineland, NJ), November 4, 2021.

Donaldson, Maggy. "Motown's Smokey Robinson, Berry Gordy Celebrated at Pre-Grammy Gala." AFP International, February 4, 2023.

"Don't Say Goodnight (It's Time for Love)." Performed by The Isley Brothers. *Go All the Way*. T-Neck. 1980.

Doss, Yevette C. "'Soul Food' and 'Angel' Are Tops in Image Awards." *Los Angeles Times*, February 16, 1998.

Douglass, Frederick I. "Black Experience: Isley Brothers." *Afro-American*, January 12, 1974.

Douglass, Frederick I. "Isley Brothers Burn!" *Afro-American*, July 10, 1976.

Downings, Lou. "Kizzy Supporter Joins WVON-AM." *Chicago Defender*, February 2, 1989.

"Down Low (Nobody Has to Know)." Performed by R. Kelly featuring The Isley Brothers. *R. Kelly*. Jive, 1995.

Duffy, Thom, Janine McAdams, and Jeffrey Jolson-Colburn. "Isley Sues Bolton over Song Right." *Billboard*, June 27, 1992.

Dunderbeck1980. "Go for Your Guns: 40 Years of a Funky Voyage to Atlantis with The Isley Brothers." *Andresmusictalk*. https://andresmusictalk.wordpress.com/2017/05/16/go-for-your-guns-40-years-of-a-funky-voyage-to-atlantis-with-the-isley-brothers/.

Dustygroove. "The Isley Brothers." https://www.dustygroove.com/item/75774/Isley-Brothers:Go-For-Your-Guns.

Edwards, Dale. "Councilman Blaine Griffin Celebrates the Legendary Isley Brothers." *Call and Post*, October 30, 2019.

Elbert, Mark. "The Isley Brothers Talk About Extending Their Reign as 'Kings of Love Songs.'" *Billboard*, October 11, 2022. https://www.billboard.com/music/rb-hip-hop/isley-brothers-make-me-say-it-again-girl-interview-1235154320/.

Emerson, Bo. "Hendrix Lives on with Tour: Four Decades After His Death, Guitarists Gather to Celebrate His Genius." *The Atlanta Journal-Constitution*, March 21, 2010.

En-Academic. "Ernie Isley." https://en-academic.com/dic.nsf/enwiki/958208.

"Entertainment Briefs." *Los Angeles Sentinel*, April 29, 2010.

"Entertainment Events." *New York Times*, November 15, 1969.

"Entertainment News." *Oakland Post*, July 30, 1978.

"Essence Festival of Culture's Roster Is Heating Up with Wizkid, City Girls, Beenie Man, Tems, Method Man, Raekwon, Ghostface, Kes, Mickey Guyton and More Still to Come." *Business Wire*, April 28, 2022.

"Etta James, Isley Brothers, Miller Sisters Next at Apollo." *New Pittsburgh Courier*, February 9, 1963.

Evans, Farrell. "The 1967 Riots: When Outrage over Racial Injustice Boiled Over." *History*. June 21, 2021. https://www.history.com/news/1967-summer-riots-detroit-newark-kerner-commission.

"Experience Hendrix Tour to Make Second 2010 Run." *Independent*, August 31, 2010. https://www.independent.co.uk/arts-entertainment/music/experience-hendrix-tour-to-make-second-2010-run-2066307.html.

Fagan, Emily. "Top 10 Angela Winbush Songs." Classic Rock History. 2021. https://www.classicrockhistory.com/top-10-angela-winbush-songs/.

Farber, Jim. "Rudolph Isley, Original Member of Brothers Group, Dies at 84." *Philadelphia Tribune*, October 15, 2023.

Farber, Jim. "'Smooth to the Taste,' Ron Isley Singing Burt Bacharach Makes for a Great Vintage." *New York Daily News*, November 9, 2003.

Farhi, Paul. "No Isley Estate for Bolton." *The Spectator*, February 26, 2000.

"Featuring: Macy's Great Tree Lighting." *The Atlanta Journal-Constitution*, November 23, 2014.

Fekadu, Mesfin. "Harrison Leads List of Hall of Fame Nominees." *Prince George Citizen*, October 6, 2015.

Fensterstock, Alison. "Fantasia, Juvenile Join Isley Brothers on Zulu Coronation Ball Lineup: Tickets on Sale Now." Nola.com. November 18, 2014. https://www.nola.com/entertainment_life/music/fantasia-juvenile-join-isley-brothers-on-zulu-coronation-ball-lineup-tickets-on-sale-now/article_67f6c6bb-ccfb-5ac2-a085-194cdc8990cc.html.

Ferguson, James. "Life of a Song: This Old Heart of Mine (Is Weak for You)—How Motown Created the Perfect Pop Song." Financial Times, October 4, 2021. https://ig.ft.com/life-of-a-song/this-old-heart.html.

"5th Annual: Image Awards." *Sacramento Observer*, November 4, 1971.

"5th Dimension Dionne Sing 'Grammy' Hopefuls." *Afro-American*, May 9, 1970.

"Fight the Power." Performed by The Isley Brothers. *The Heat Is On*. T-Neck. 1975.

Find a Grave. "Vernon Isley." https://www.findagrave.com/memorial/106424018/vernon-isley.

"The 500 Greatest Albums of All Time." *Rolling Stone*, September 22, 2020. https://www.rollingstone.com/music/music-lists/best-albums-of-all-time-1062063/.

Fleming, John, et. al. "Audio Files Series: Audio Files: [City Edition]." *St. Petersburg Times*, May 5, 1995.

Flemming, Steven E., Jr. "Eagles and Doves: With 'Givin' It Back' The Isley Brothers Sang of Joy and Pain." Albumism, September 25, 2021. https://albumism.com/features/tribute-celebrating-50-years-of-isley-brothers-givin-it-back.

Fletcher, Carlton. Isley Brothers Hall of Fame Career Six Decades and Counting." *TCA Regional News*, March 11, 2015.

"Floatin' on Your Love." Performed by The Isley Brothers, featuring Angela Winbush. *Mission to Please*. T-Neck/Island. 1996.

"For the Love of You." Performed by The Isley Brothers. *The Heat Is On*. T-Neck. 1975.

45cat. "Record Details: The Isley Brothers." http://www.45cat.com/record/131us2.

Fraser, Trevor. "Zora Neale Hurston Festival of the Humanities." *Orlando Sentinel*, January 22, 2016.

Freedberg, Mike. "Soul Dog." *Bay State Banner*, August 23, 1979.

"Freedom." Performed by The Isley Brothers. *Get Into Something*. T-Neck. 1969.

Freeman, Paul. "Isley Brothers Back on a Soulful Circuit/First Tour in Four Years." *San Francisco Chronicle*, April 8, 1990.

"Friends and Family." The Isley Brothers Featuring Ronald Isley and Snoop Dogg. *Make Me Say It Again, Girl*. RI Top Ten. 2022.

Fusilli, Jim. "Music Review: 'Body Kiss' from The Isley Brothers." NPR Music, June 13, 2003. https://www.npr.org/templates/story/story.php?storyId=1297987.

Gardner, Cathy. "Isley Brothers Dish Out 'Old School.'" *Chicago Defender*, December 28, 1998.

George Washington University. "Three Boys Music v. Michael Bolton." *Law Blogs*. https://blogs.law.gwu.edu/mcir/case/three-boys-music-v-michael-bolton/.

"George Wein Presents: On Tour . . . Kool Jazz Festivals." *Jet*, June 5, 1975.

"Get Into Something." Performed by The Isley Brothers. *Get Into Something*. T-Neck. 1969.

Gibbs, Kay. "In the Cut." *Bay State Banner*, December 30, 1971.
Giovanni, Nikki. "You See, Brother, Brother, Brother." *It's Your Thing: The Story of the Isley Brothers* (CD box set). Sony Music Entertainment. 1999.
Gipson, Gertrude. "Candid Comments: Nate Holden Party Sunday." *Los Angeles Sentinel*, May 18, 1978.
"Girls Will Be Girls, Boys Will Be Boys." Performed by The Isley Brothers. *Get Into Something*. T-Neck. 1969.
Glide Magazine. "The Isley Brothers and Santana 'Power of Peace' Set For 7/28 Release." https://glidemagazine.com/186785/isley-brothers-santana-power-peace-set-728-release/.
"Go Guide: The Big A List." *The Atlanta Journal-Constitution*, July 3, 2022.
"Go Guide Sunday." *The Atlanta Journal-Constitution*, December 28, 2014.
"Going All the Way Is a Way of Life." *Los Angeles Sentinel*, August 21, 1980.
Gold City Records. "Chris Jasper." http://goldcityrecords.com/chris-jasper/.
"Gold in Them Discs," *The Baltimore Afro-American*, November 17, 1962.
Gold Radio UK. The Isley Brothers Announce 60th Anniversary UK Tour—Here's How to Get Tickets." December 11, 2019. https://www.goldradiouk.com/news/music/the-isley-brothers-tour-tickets/.
Goldfine, Scott. "Isley Brothers: Tracks of Life." Funknstuff. September, 18, 2022. https://funknstuff.net/isley-brothers-tracks-of-life-1992/.
Goldsborough, Bob. "R. Kelly's Mansion Sells to Isley Brothers for $587,000." *Chicago Tribune*, December 5, 2013.
Goldstein, Patrick. "Moonlighting on the Trail of an LP." *Los Angeles Times*, May 31, 1987.
Golsen, Tyler. "James Brown Explains the Origins of Funk." *Far Out*, November 24, 2021. https://faroutmagazine.co.uk/james-brown-origins-of-funk/.
Goodson, David. "Nightlife." *New York Amsterdam News*, August 28, 2014.
"Got to Have You Back." Performed by The Isley Brothers. *Soul on the Rocks*. Motown. 1967.
Gould, Harry, Jr. "The Power and the Juice." *Philadelphia Inquirer*, August 14, 1983.
Graff, Gary. "Isley Brothers Writing New Tunes on Tour." *Billboard*, April 12, 2007. https://www.billboard.com/music/music-news/isley-brothers-writing-new-tunes-on-tour-1052862/.
Grammy Awards. "Isley Brothers." https://www.grammy.com/artists/isley-brothers/14619.
Grammy Awards. "Kendrick Lamar." https://www.grammy.com/artists/kendrick-lamar/17949.
The Grateful Web. "The Isley Brothers Announce New Single 'Last Time.'" July 6, 2023. https://www.gratefulweb.com/articles/isley-brothers-announce-new-single-last-time.
Green, Susan, Donothea Bickell, and Shirley Smith. "Our Readers Write: Modern Day Pied Piper." *Call and Post*, July 14, 1983.
Greene, Teri. "Isley Brothers to Headline ASU Show." *Montgomery Advertiser*, November 26, 2013.
Greenfield, Jeff. "1959: The Year That Changed Everything." CBS News, January 3, 2010. https://www.cbsnews.com/news/1959-the-year-that-changed-everything/.
Grein, Paul. "SZA, Usher and Victoria Monet Are Top Winners at 2023 Soul Train Awards: Full List." *Billboard*, November 26, 2023. https://www.billboard.com/music/awards/2023-soul-train-awards-winners-list-sza-usher-1235509200/.
"Groove with You." Performed by The Isley Brothers. *Showdown*. T-Neck. 1978.
Grove, Rashad. "R&B Legends The Isley Brothers Announce Their 60th Anniversary Tour." *The Source*, May 17, 2019. https://thesource.com/2019/05/17/rb-legends-the-isleys-brothers-announce-their-60th-anniversary-tour/.

"The Guitar Center Music Foundation Hosts a Who's Who of L.A.'s Music Industry at Third-Annual Benefit Concert." *The Billings Gazette*, April 17, 2024.

Gulla, Bob. *Icons of R&B and Soul: An Encyclopedia of the Artists Who Revolutionized Rhythm*. Vol. 2. Westport, CT: Greenwood, 2007.

Guma, Numa La. "The Most Creative Album of the Year." *Sun Reporter*, November 27, 1971.

Guthrie, Patricia. "Mr. Isley, You Have Diabetes: After Years of Denial, the Youngest of The Isley Brothers Is Taking a Stand Against the Disease That Nearly Killed Him." *The Atlanta Constitution*, May 7, 2001.

Hammerstein, B. J. "'Bachelor' Duo Might Be Done." *Detroit Free Press*, March 16, 2011.

Harrigan, Philip. "Funkadelic Leave Clinton, Lose Identity." *New Pittsburgh Courier*, April 4, 1981.

Harrington, Jim. "Stone Soul Delivers a Strong Double Dose of R&B." *The Mercury News*, May 4, 2017.

Harrington, Richard. "Longevity: It's the Isleys' Thing." *Los Angeles Times*, November 23, 2001.

"Harvest for the World." Performed by The Isley Brothers. *Harvest for the World*. T-Neck. 1976.

"Hear the Isley Brothers Do All Their Hits from Their Multi-Million-Dollar LP." *Jet*, September 11, 1975.

"Heaven's Girl." Performed by Quincy Jones, featuring R. Kelly, Ron Isley, Aaron Hall, and Charlie Wilson. *Q's Jook Joint*. Quest/Warner Brothers. 1995.

Henderson, Rita Elizabeth. "Isley Brothers Serenade Trump Plaza Crowd." *New York Amsterdam News*, November 5, 1994.

Heselgrave, Doug. "Santana and The Isley Brothers: *Power of Peace*." *Paste Magazine*, July 28, 2017. https://www.pastemagazine.com/music/santana/santana-the-isley-brothers-power-of-peace-review/.

Hevesi, Dennis. "Marvin Isley, 56, Bassist in Isley Brothers: [Obituary; Biography]." *New York Times*, June 8, 2010.

Heyman, Marshall. "The Apollo Is 80 Years Young; A Benefit Concert for Harlem's Storied Theater." *Wall Street Journal*, June 11, 2014.

Himes, Geoffrey. "The Isley Brothers: 'It's Your Thing: The Story of The Isley Brothers'; Epic Associated/T-Neck/Legacy." *The Washington Post*, July 30, 1999.

History.com Editors. "Mardi Gras 2023." History. https://www.history.com/topics/holidays/mardi-gras.

Hochman, Steve. "Pop Music Review: R&B Foundation Honorees Let Music Do the Boasting." *Los Angeles Times*, March 2, 1996.

Holden, Stephen. "Music Noted in Brief; Durable Isley Brothers Play Date at the Savoy." *New York Times*, November 16, 1981.

"Holiday Happenings 12-20-12." *Times-News*, December 20, 2012.

Hollywood Walk of Fame. "Hollywood Walk of Fame Class of 2025 Announced by Walk of Famers Niecy Nash, Jimmy Jam and Joe Mantegna." https://walkoffame.com/press_releases/hollywood-walk-of-fame-class-of-2025/.

"Honey Nut Cheerios Announces Sweetest Concert Tour of the Summer." *Business Wire*, June 23, 1998.

"Honorary Brother Jimi: Memories of James Marshall Hendrix." *It's Your Thing: The Story of The Isley Brothers* (CD box set). Sony Music Entertainment. 1999.

Hull, Frances. "Tradewinds of Funk Resonate the Beautiful Island of Aruba." *Atlanta Daily World*, June 12, 1997.

Hunt, Dennis. "Isley Brothers' Sailin' Back on the Charts." *Los Angeles Times*, July 3, 1987.
Hunt, Luanne J. "No Matter What the Times, Isley Brothers Do Just Fine." *Daily News*, August 30, 2003.
"Hurry Up and Wait." Performed by The Isley Brothers. *Grand Slam*. T-Neck. 1981.
Huynh, Anjali. "One MusicFest Brings Thousands to Downtown Atlanta for H.E.R., Ari Lennox and More." *Atlanta Journal-Constitution*, October 10, 2021.
"If He Can, You Can." Performed by The Isley Brothers. *Get Into Something*. T-Neck. 1969.
I Love Old School Music. "Angela Winbush Has Very Surprising New Career That's Totally Different from Her Singing Days," September 29, 2017. https://www.iloveoldschoolmusic.com/angela-winbush-has-very-surprising-career-thats-totally-different-from-her-singing-days/.
"I'm So Proud." Performed by The Isley Brothers. *A Tribute to Curtis Mayfield*. Warner Brothers. 1994.
"Insatiable Woman." Performed by Isley-Jasper-Isley. *Caravan of Love*. CBS. 1985.
"Inside You." Performed by The Isley Brothers. *Inside You*. T-Neck. 1982.
"I Once Had Your Love (And I Can't Let Go)." Performed by The Isley Brothers. *Grand Slam*. T-Neck. 1981.
"Isley Bros. at Apollo." *New York Amsterdam News*, July 3, 1971.
"Isley Bros. to Stage a Big Revue." *Chicago Defender*, January 27, 1976.
"Isley Brothers 1959–1983." *New Pittsburgh Courier*, August 5, 2015.
The Isley Brothers. *3+3*. T-Neck/Legacy. 1973/2003.
"The Isley Brothers: 3 Decades of Hits." *New Pittsburgh Courier*. July 15, 1992.
"Isley Brothers, Angela Winbush, Marcia Griffith Show Relocated to the International Amphitheatre." *Weekend Chicago Defender*, December 29, 1990.
"Isley Brothers Are Booked at Mill Run Theatre." *Weekend Chicago Defender*, June 20, 1981.
"Isley Brothers Are Booked for the Arie Crown Revue." *Weekend Chicago Defender*, April 5, 2003.
"Isley Brothers at Apollo." *New York Amsterdam News*, July 2, 1966.
The Isley Brothers. *Baby Makin' Music*. Def Jam. 2005.
The Isley Brothers. *Beautiful Ballads*. Epic/Legacy. 1994.
The Isley Brothers. *Beautiful Ballads, Vol. 2*. Epic/Legacy. 2006.
The Isley Brothers. *The Best . . . Isley Brothers*. Buddah. 1976.
The Isley Brothers. *Between the Sheets*. T-Neck/Big Break. 1983/2011.
The Isley Brothers. *Body Kiss*. T-Neck/Dreamworks. 2003.
"Isley Brothers Booked for Stadium." *Chicago Defender*, June 9, 1980.
"The Isley Brothers Bring Over 7 Decades of Music to the Dell in Philadelphia." *New Pittsburgh Courier*, August 7, 2024.
"Isley Brothers Bring Soaring Vocals to Holiday Star Plaza." *Weekend Chicago Defender*, August 3, 1996.
The Isley Brothers. *Brother, Brother, Brother*. T-Neck. 1972.
The Isley Brothers. *The Brothers: Isley*. T-Neck. 1969.
"The Isley Brothers: Celebrating 4 Decades." *Los Angeles Sentinel*, September 12, 1996.
"Isley Brothers Claim Faith Is Responsible." *New York Amsterdam News*, November 15, 1969.
"Isley Brothers Concert Is Set for Richfield Coliseum." *Call and Post*, July 26, 1980.
"Isley Brothers Control Recording Company." *Chicago Daily Defender*, April 1, 1969.
The Isley Brothers. *The Definitive Collection*. Hip-O. 2007.
The Isley Brothers. *Doin' Their Thing: Best of the Isley Brothers*. Tamla/Motown. 1969.

The Isley Brothers. *The Essential Isley Brothers*. Epic. 2004.
The Isley Brothers. *Eternal*. DreamWorks. 2001.
"The Isley Brothers: Floatin' On Your Love ft. Ronald Isley, Angela Winbush." The Island Def Jam Music Group. YouTube video. https://www.youtube.com/watch?v=2Ogu2nptuGo.
The Isley Brothers. *Forever Gold*. T-Neck. 1977.
The Isley Brothers. "The Isley Brothers: Friends and Family (Official Video) ft. Ronald Isley and Snoop Dogg." YouTube video. https://www.youtube.com/watch?v=Pq51JmcyBzY.
The Isley Brothers. *Get Into Something*. T-Neck. 1970.
The Isley Brothers. *Givin' It Back*. T-Neck. 1971.
The Isley Brothers. *Go All the Way*. T-Neck. 1979.
The Isley Brothers. *Go for Your Guns*. T-Neck/Big Break. 1977/2011.
The Isley Brothers. *Grand Slam*. T-Neck/CBS. 1981.
The Isley Brothers. *Greatest Hits*. Epic. 1997.
The Isley Brothers. *Greatest Hits, Vol. 1*. T-Neck. 1984.
The Isley Brothers. *Groove With You . . . Live*. T-Neck/Epic/Legacy. 2015.
The Isley Brothers. *Harvest for the World*. T-Neck/Legacy. 1975/2001.
The Isley Brothers. *The Heat Is On*. T-Neck/Legacy. 1975/2001.
The Isley Brothers. *I'll Be Home for Christmas*. Def Jam. 2007.
The Isley Brothers. *Inside You*. T-Neck. 1981.
The Isley Brothers. "The Isley Brothers: Ballad for the Fallen Soldier." Sony Music Entertainment. YouTube video. https://www.youtube.com/watch?v=H7oeayNHeh4.
The Isley Brothers. "The Isley Brothers: Busted ft. JS (Official Video)." YouTube video. https://www.youtube.com/watch?v=PDKGDPSq03A.
The Isley Brothers. *The Isley Brothers Do Their Thing*. Sunset. 1969.
The Isley Brothers. *The Isley Brothers Story, Vol. 1: The T-Neck Years (1969–85)*. Rhino. 1991.
The Isley Brothers. *The Isley Brothers Story, Vol. 2: The T-Neck Years (1969–85)*. Rhino. 1991.
The Isley Brothers. "The Isley Brothers: Tears (Official Video) ft. Ronald Isley." The Island Def Jam Music Group. YouTube video. https://www.youtube.com/watch?v=K_Y-7iOX7B0.
The Isley Brothers. *The Isleys Live*. T-Neck/Rhino. 1973/1996.
The Isley Brothers. *It's Our Thing*. T-Neck. 1969.
The Isley Brothers. *It's Your Thing: The Story of the Isley Brothers* (CD box set). Sony Music Entertainment. 1999.
The Isley Brothers and Jimi Hendrix. *In the Beginning. . . .* T-Neck. 1971.
The Isley Brothers. *Live!* Elektra. 1993.
The Isley Brothers. *Live at Yankee Stadium*. T-Neck. 1969.
The Isley Brothers. *Live It Up*. T-Neck/Legacy. 1974/2004.
The Isley Brothers. *Love Songs*. Epic/Legacy. 2001.
The Isley Brothers. *Make Me Say It Again, Girl*. RI Top Ten. 2022.
The Isley Brothers. *Masterpiece*. Warner Brothers. 1985.
The Isley Brothers. *Mission to Please*. T-Neck/Island. 1996.
The Isley Brothers. *The Motown Anthology*. Motown/Universal UMC. 2009.
"The Isley Brothers." *Oakland Post*, June 19, 1977.
"The Isley Brothers on TV's Soul Train." *Tri-State Defender*, December 14, 1974.
The Isley Brothers. *Original Album Classics*. Epic/Legacy. 2008.
The Isley Brothers. *Playlist: The Very Best of The Isley Brothers*. Epic. 2010.
The Isley Brothers. *The RCA Victor and T-Neck Album Masters*. T-Neck/Epic/Legacy. 2015.
The Isley Brothers. *The Real Deal*. T-Neck. 1982.

"Isley Brothers Release 'Baby Makin' Music' featuring Mr. Biggs." *Call and Post*, March 16, 2006.
"Isley Brothers Rock the Garden." *New York Amsterdam News*, October 19, 1974.
The Isley Brothers/Santana. *Power of Peace*. Legacy. 2017.
"The Isley Brothers: Sensitive Lover." Sony Music Entertainment. YouTube video. https://www.youtube.com/watch?v=D3C93gSQIRA.
The Isley Brothers. *Shout!* RCA Victor. 1959.
"Isley Brothers 'Shout' as Pullman Bond Deal Successfully Closes; The Pullman Group Finalizes Isley Pullman Bond Music Royalty Securitization with Legendary Hitmaking Isley Brothers Family." *Business Wire*, June 22, 2000.
The Isley Brothers. *Showdown*. T-Neck. 1978.
"Isley Brothers Singer Convicted on Federal Tax Evasion Charges." Press Release. Department of Justice, October 31, 2005. https://www.justice.gov/archive/tax/usaopress/2005/txdv05147.html.
The Isley Brothers. *Smooth Sailin'*. Warner Brothers. 1987.
The Isley Brothers. *Soul on the Rocks*. Motown. 1967.
The Isley Brothers. *Spend the Night*. Warner Brothers. 1989.
"The Isley Brothers: Spend the Night." Warner Urban Music. YouTube video. https://www.youtube.com/watch?v=VZWED0YkWOc.
"Isley Brothers Split to Form New Group, Record New Album and Hit Single." *Jet*, November 12, 1984.
"Isley Brothers Still Going Strong After Four Decades on the Charts." *Philadelphia Tribune*, January 20, 1998.
The Isley Brothers. *Summer Breeze: Greatest Hits*. Epic. 2005.
The Isley Brothers. *Taken to the Next Phase*. Epic. 2004.
The Isley Brothers. *Take Some Time Out for The Isley Brothers*. Scepter. 1966.
The Isley Brothers. *This Old Heart of Mine*. Tamla (Motown). 1966.
The Isley Brothers. *Timeless*. T-Neck. 1978.
"Isley Brothers to 'Go for Their Guns' Oct. 8 at Public Hall." *Call and Post*, October 1, 1977.
"The Isley Brothers to Receive 2017 AutoZone Liberty Bowl's Outstanding Achievement Award." Targeted News Service, October 17, 2017.
The Isley Brothers. *Tracks of Life*. Warner Brothers. 1992.
The Isley Brothers. *Twist and Shout*. Wand. 1962.
The Isley Brothers. *Twisting and Shouting*. United Artists. 1963.
The Isley Brothers. *The Ultimate Isley Brothers*. Epic/Legacy. 2000.
"Isley Brothers Win Court Battle." *Alaska Highway News*, May 11, 2000.
The Isley Brothers. *Winner Takes All*. T-Neck/Big Break. 1979/2013.
"The Isley Brothers: You'll Never Walk Alone." Warner Urban Music. YouTube video. https://www.youtube.com/watch?v=Z2SfKQ4Of8c.
Isley, Ernie. *High Wire*. Elektra, 1990.
Isley-Jasper-Isley. *Broadway's Closer to Sunset Blvd*. CBS. 1984.
Isley-Jasper-Isley. *Caravan of Love*. CBS. 1985.
Isley-Jasper-Isley. "Caravan of Love." Sony BMG Music Entertainment. YouTube video. https://www.youtube.com/watch?v=foFK6q7kF9Y.
Isley-Jasper-Isley. *Different Drummer*. CBS. 1987.
Isley-Jasper-Isley. "Insatiable Woman." Sony BMG Music Entertainment. YouTube video. https://www.youtube.com/watch?v=aTTYalYGXvY.

Isley-Jasper-Isley. "Kiss and Tell." Sony BMG Music Entertainment. YouTube video. https://www.youtube.com/watch?v=VeIqQ9bg2L8.
Isley-Jasper-Isley. "Look the Other Way." Sony BMG Music Entertainment. YouTube video. https://www.youtube.com/watch?v=AyFvhd_242I.
"Isleys, Austin to Appear at Football Game." *Bay State Banner*, September 20, 1973.
"Isleys Can Keep Songs Rights." *Philadelphia Tribune*, January 25, 2000.
"Isleys Head Bill at Oakland Arena." *Oakland Post*, April 14, 1974.
"It's Alright with Me." Performed by The Isley Brothers. *The Real Deal*. T-Neck. 1982.
"It's a Disco Night (Rock Don't Stop)." Performed by The Isley Brothers. *Winner Takes All*. T-Neck. 1979.
"It's Too Late." Performed by The Isley Brothers. *Brother, Brother, Brother*. T-Neck. 1972.
"It's Your Thing." Performed by The Isley Brothers. *It's Our Thing*. T-Neck. 1969.
"I Turned You On." Performed by The Isley Brothers. *The Brothers Isley*. T-Neck. 1969.
Iverem, Esther. "The Isleys, '90s Style; Mr. Biggs Upstaged at Constitution Hall." *The Washington Post*, September 23, 1996.
"I Wanna Be with You." Performed by The Isley Brothers. *Winner Takes All*. T-Neck. 1979.
"I Wish." Performed by The Isley Brothers. *Smooth Sailin'*. Warner Brothers, 1987.
Jackson, Barry. "An Evening with the Isley Brothers." *Los Angeles Sentinel*, December 17, 1992.
Jackson, Patty. "What's the 411?" *Philadelphia Tribune*, May 27, 2005.
Jackson, Patty. "What's the 411?" *Philadelphia Tribune*, September 2, 2005.
Jackson, Patty. "What's Up?" *Philadelphia Tribune*, March 3, 2002.
Jackson, Patty. "What's Up?" *Philadelphia Tribune*, June 4, 2006.
James, Donald. "Aretha Franklin Comes Home to Chene Part." *Michigan Chronicle*, August 19, 2015.
Jasper, Chris. Interview with the author. Atlanta, GA. July 27, 2022.
Jasper, Chris. *Superbad*. Gold City. 1988.
Jasper, Chris. "Superbad." Sony Music Entertainment. YouTube video. https://www.youtube.com/watch?v=pXOTvkLyaZM.
Jesse Collins Entertainment. "About UNCF an Evening with Stars." https://jessecollinsent.com/portfolio/uncf-evening-stars/.
John, Derek. "July 12, 1979: 'The Night Disco Died'—Or Didn't." NPR, July 16, 2016. https://www.npr.org/2016/07/16/485873750/july-12-1979-the-night-disco-died-or-didnt.
Johnson, James. "Music: Our Critics Sound Off About This Week's Shows Hip-Hop." *Philadelphia Daily News*, May 7, 2010.
Johnson, Kevin C. "After Several Snubs, Grammys Honor Isley Brothers." *McClatchy-Tribune Business News*, January 25, 2014.
Johnson, Kevin C. "Isley Brothers Are Latest Edition to St. Louis Walk of Fame in the Loop." *St. Louis Post-Dispatch*. April 19, 2019.
Johnson, Kevin C. "The Isley Brothers, Charlie Wilson Heading to Chaifetz Arena." *TCA Regional News*, August 23, 2021.
Johnson, Kevin C. "Isley Brothers Not Ready to say Farewell." *McClatchy-Tribune Business News*, September 18, 2011.
Johnson, Kevin C. "Isley Brothers Shine on R&B Classics and New Tunes." *St. Louis Post*, October 28, 2001.
Johnson, Kevin C. "Isley Brothers Spice Up Their Legends with New Hits." *St. Louis Post-Dispatch*, April 22, 2007.

Johnson, Kevin C. "Kandy Isley, Kim Johnson Dive into Christmas with New EP." *St. Louis Post-Dispatch*, December 25, 2020.
Johnson, Kevin C. "Kandy Isley, Kim Johnson Spread Peace and Healing on New Single 'Free.'" *St. Louis Post-Dispatch*, June 12, 2020.
Johnson, Kevin C. "Ronald Isley's New Album Shows 'Where Music Is Supposed to Be.'" *McClatchy-Tribune* News Service, July 19, 2013.
Johnson, Rae. "Kentucky Derby Week Brings Big Stars to Louisville." *Courier-Journal*, April 29, 2022.
Jones, Steve. "A Big 'Ol Box of R&B Nostalgia Also on CD: Miles Davis Live, Classics by The Isley Brothers." *USA Today*, August 4, 1997.
Jones, Steve. "Summer Festivals, Tours Get R&B Acts Together: Essence Spirit Imbues 'Party with a Purpose.'" *USA Today*, June 26, 1997.
Jones, Steve, and Donna Freydkin. "Patti LaBelle, Isley Brothers to Spread a Little Holiday Soul." *USA Today*, September 28, 2007.
Jordan, Chris. "Happy Mother's Day from The Isley Brothers." *The Record*, May 6, 2022.
"July 1993 Black Film Festival." *New York Amsterdam News*, July 17, 1993.
"Just Came Here to Chill." Performed by The Isley Brothers. *Baby Makin' Music*. Def Jam. 2006.
"Keep On Doin'." Performed by The Isley Brothers. *Get Into Something*. T-Neck. 1969.
Kennedy, Mark. "Songwriters Hall of Fame 2022 Class Includes Mariah Carey, Eurythmics, The Isley Brothers." *USA Today*, June 16, 2022.
"Keys, Isley Brothers Each Win Three Soul Train Awards." *North Bay Nugget*, March 22, 2002.
King, Michael. "The Isley Brothers Honored with Proclamation at Mable House Concert." 11 Alive News, July 15, 2018. https://www.11alive.com/article/entertainment/television/programs/the-a-scene/the-isley-brothers-honored-with-proclamation-at-mable-house-concert/85-573987496.
"Kiss and Tell." Performed by Isley-Jasper-Isley. *Broadway's Closer to Sunset Blvd*. CBS. 1984.
Kneschke, Tristan. "The Isley Brothers and Santana: Power of Peace." PopMatters, July 27, 2017. https://www.popmatters.com/the-isley-brothers-santana-power-of-peace-2495385051.html.
"Kool Jazz Festivals: The Events of the Year," *Jet*, April 26, 1979.
"Kool Jazz Festivals: The Only Way to Play It." *Jet*, April 30, 1981.
Laing, Dave. "Marvin Isley Obituary." *The Guardian*, June 9, 2010. https://www.theguardian.com/music/2010/jun/09/marvin-isley-obituary.
Lane, George. "Shades of Blue." *Bay State Banner*, June 14, 1979.
"Last Time." Performed by The Isley Brothers. *Make Me Say It Again, Girl*. RI Top Ten. 2022.
"Lay Lady Lay." Performed by The Isley Brothers. *Givin' It Back*. T-Neck. 1971.
"Lay Your Troubles Down." Performed by Angela Winbush with Ronald Isley. *The Real Thing*. Polygram. 1989.
"Legendary Isley Brothers, Freddie Jackson, Chante Moore, and Ruben Studdard Ripped It at Wolf Creek Amphitheatre." *Atlanta Daily World*, August 25, 2016.
"'Legends Live Atlanta' R&B Concert Kicking Off Super Bowl Weekend." *Atlanta Daily World*, January 14, 2019.
"Let's Go! Weekly Entertainment Calendar 4-2-15." *Times-News*, April 2, 2015.
"Let's Lay Together." Performed by The Isley Brothers. *Mission to Please*. T-Neck/Island, 1996.

Lewis, Femi. "Black History Timeline: 1960–1964." ThoughtCo. https://www.thoughtco.com/african-american-history-timeline-1960-1964-45443.
Lemon Wire. "Mission to Please." The Isley Brothers. March 29, 2018. https://lemonwire.com/2018/03/29/isley-brothers-mission-to-please/.
Lindquist, David. "Good Times: Quality Entertainment Keeps Black Expo an Annual Favorite Destination." *Indianapolis Star*, July 3, 2005.
Lindquist, David. "Summer Celebration Lineup Is Music to Fans' Ears." *Indianapolis Star*, July 14, 2015.
"Live It Up." Performed by The Isley Brothers. *Live It Up*. T-Neck. 1974.
"Livin' in the Life." Performed by The Isley Brothers. *Go for Your Guns*. T-Neck. 1977.
Lloyd, Jack. "An Isley's First Taste of Fame." *Philadelphia Inquirer*, January 17, 1997.
"The Long Beach Jazz Fest Celebrates 25 Years." *Los Angeles Sentinel*, August 9, 2012.
"Look the Other Way." Performed by Isley-Jasper-Isley. *Broadway's Closer to Sunset Blvd.* CBS. 1984.
"Lou Rawls 'Parade of Stars' Airs on WGN-TV." *Chicago Defender*, December 29, 1983.
"Louisville Shows This Week: Charlie Wilson, 'Gloria: A Life' and More; Saturday, Sept. 25." *Courier-Journal*, September 25, 2021.
"Love Is a Wonderful Thing." Performed by The Isley Brothers. United Artists. 1966.
"Love the One You're With." Performed by The Isley Brothers. *Givin' It Back*. T-Neck. 1971.
"Magic Mountain Unveils 'X.'" *Los Angeles Sentinel*, January 17, 2002.
"Make Me Say It Again, Girl." Performed by The Isley Brothers. *The Heat Is On*. T-Neck. 1975.
"Make Me Say It Again, Girl." Performed by Ronald Isley and The Isley Brothers featuring Beyoncé. *Make Me Say It Again, Girl*. RI Top Ten. 2022.
Mansfield, Brian. "Isley Brothers Take a Look Back." *USA Today*, August 18, 2015.
"Marvin Isley, Isley Brothers Bassist, Dies of Diabetes at 56." *The Daily Beast*, June 10, 2010, https://www.thedailybeast.com/cheats/2010/06/10/marvin-isley-isley-brothers-bassists-dies-of-diabetes-at-56.
"May I?" Performed by The Isley Brothers. *Masterpiece*. Warner Brothers. 1985.
Maza, Christina. "Summer Jams: Barack Obama Edition." *The Christian Science Monitor*, August 14, 2015.
McKeithan, Larry. "The Showdown." *New York Amsterdam News*, August 12, 1978.
McKenzie, Kevin. "Southern Heritage Concert Tonight Has Been Canceled." *The Commercial Appeal*, September 13, 2001.
McMillian, Stephen. "Funk My Soul—1975—The Heat Is On." FunkMySoul. https://www.funkmysoul.gr/the-isley-brothers-1975-the-heat-is-on/.
"Miami Gardens' Musical Lineup On Tap This Weekend at 2022 JITG Festival." *Michigan Chronicle*, March 11, 2022.
"Midnight Sky." Performed by The Isley Brothers. *Live It Up*. T-Neck. 1974.
Mitchell, Richard. "Isley Brothers: Music, Family and Funk." *Chicago Defender*, June 11, 1980.
Moddy, Walter. "All That Jazz." *Sun Reporter*, January 23, 1971.
Moody, Nekesa Mumbi Moody. "Isley Brothers Still Generating Heat on Charts." *Columbian*, October 16, 2001.
Moore, Marie. "Fiery Concerts: Black and White Smoke." *New York Amsterdam News*, October 9, 1976.
Moore, Marie. "Gil Scott Bringing Words of Wisdom." *New York Amsterdam News*, July 18, 1981.

Moore, Marie. "The Institution Called The Isley Brothers: Mama Isley." *New York Amsterdam News*, August 27, 1977.
Moore, Marie. "Musical Potpourri." *New York Amsterdam News*, September 3, 1977.
Morris, Al. "Theater Briefs." *New York Amsterdam News*, May 3, 1980.
Morse, Steve. "Isley Brothers Still a Potent Blow." *Boston Globe*, August 7, 1999.
Murray, Sonia. "These Brothers Can Sing: Isley Brothers Being Rediscovered as Performers, Writers." *Austin American Statesman*, January 6, 1994.
"Music." *Orlando Sentinel*, December 26, 2014.
Musician Guide. "Angela Winbush Biography." https://musicianguide.com/biographies/1608000066/Angela-Winbush.html.
Musician Guide. "The Isley Brothers Biography." https://musicianguide.com/biographies/1608004017/The-Isley-Brothers.html.
Myers, Marc. "Soul Survivor." *Wall Street Journal*, July 15, 2013.
"My Favorite Thing." Performed by Ronald Isley featuring Kem. *This Song Is for You*. eOne/Notifi. 2013.
Nard, Craig Allen, Michael J. Madison, and Mark P. McKenna. *The Law of Intellectual Property*. New York: Aspen, 2017.
Neal, Mark Anthony. "The Isley Brothers Featuring Ronald Isley AKA Mr. Biggs: Body Kiss." PopMatters, May 22, 2003. https://www.popmatters.com/isleybrothers-body-2495939937.html.
Neal, Mark Anthony. "The Isley Brothers Featuring Ronald Isley AKA Mr. Biggs: Eternal." PopMatters, August 6, 2001. https://www.popmatters.com/isleybrothers-eternal-2495943074.html.
"No More." Performed by Ronald Isley. *Mr. I*. Def Jam. 2010.
"Nov. 6 Concert Postponed." *Los Angeles Sentinel*, November 3, 2005.
Oestreich, James R. "Where Music's Mission Is to Help Heal." *New York Times*, June 3, 2001.
Official Charts. "Isley Brothers." https://www.officialcharts.com/artist/10762/isley-brothers/.
"O'Kelly Isley, 48, of The Isley Bros., Dies in N.J." *Jet*, April 21, 1986.
"One of a Kind." Performed by The Isley Brothers. *Spend the Night*. Warner Brothers. 1989.
Oprah.com. "'Legends: OWN at the Apollo' to Air as a Four-Part Primetime Special." https://www.oprah.com/entertainment/legends-own-at-the-apollo-to-air-as-a-four-part-primetime-special.
"Other 11—No Title." *Philadelphia Tribune*, March 26, 1999.
Ousley, Brandon. "Revisiting the Black Pop Liberation of Stevie Wonder and Earth, Wind &Fire, 40 Years Later." *Albumism*, September 26, 2016. https://www.albumism.com/features/revisiting-the-black-pop-liberation-of-stevie-wonder-and-earth-wind-and-fire.
Partipilo, Vic. "On Location." *Oakland Post*, February 23, 1979.
"Photo Standalone 5—No Title." *Atlanta Daily World*, December 26, 1996.
"Photo Standalone 13—No Title." *Chicago Defender*, February 18, 1993.
Plain Dealer Staff. "Rock and Roll Hall of Fame Class of 1992." January 1, 2012. https://www.cleveland.com/rockhall/2012/01/rock_and_roll_hall_of_fame_cla_7.html.
"The Plug." Performed by The Isley Brothers featuring 2 Chainz. *Make Me Say It Again, Girl*. RI Top Ten. 2022.
"Pop Eye: [Home Edition]." *Los Angeles Times*, May 14, 1995.
"Pop That Thang." Performed by The Isley Brothers. *Brother, Brother, Brother*. T-Neck. 1969.
Popson, Tom. "Vocal Variety Makes Isley Spinoff Distinctive." *Chicago Tribune*, March 28, 1986.

"Prep-Entertainment-Report." *The Canadian Press*, February 11. 2021.
Prescott, Virginia. "Stylin': Forty Years of Isley Fashion." *It's Your Thing: The Story of the Isley Brothers* (CD box set). Sony Music Entertainment. 1999.
"Prize Possession." Performed by The Isley Brothers. *Body Kiss*. DreamWorks. 2003.
R. Kelly featuring The Isley Brothers. "Down Low (Nobody Has to Know) (Full Version)." YouTube video. https://www.youtube.com/watch?v=VlIXR-O_AKY.
"Rapper Dead After Stabbing at Exposition Park Concert." *Los Angeles Sentinel*, December 23, 2021.
RateYourMusic. "Doin' Their Thing: Best of The Isley Brothers." https://rateyourmusic.com/release/comp/the-isley-brothers/doin-their-thing-best-of-the-isley-brothers/.
RateYourMusic. "Shout!" https://rateyourmusic.com/release/album/the-isley-brothers/shout/.
"The Real Deal." Performed by The Isley Brothers. *The Real Deal*. T-Neck. 1982.
Reed, Teresa. *The Holy Profane: Religion in Black Popular Music*. Lexington: University of Kentucky Press, 2003.
Reelblack One. "The Isley Brothers Live at Yankee Stadium (1969): It's Your Thing Movie Soundtrack." YouTube video, April 24, 2022. https://www.youtube.com/watch?v=JSMrMoSyxRU.
"Regional Highlights." *Telegram and Gazette*, January 8, 2017.
Reviews and Dunn. "Way Back Wednesday Album Review: The Isley Brothers, Smooth Sailin.'" https://reviewsanddunn.net/the-isley-brothers-smooth-sailin/.
Rhino. "Happy 30th: Isley Brothers, Smooth Sailin.'" March 14, 2017. https://www.rhino.com/article/happy-30th-isley-brothers-smooth-sailin.
Rhoden, William C. "Pride, Power and Politics: The Isleys Harvest the World." *It's Your Thing: The Story of the Isley Brothers* (CD box set). Sony Music Entertainment. 1999.
"Rhythm and Blues Singer O'Kelly Isley Dead at Age 48." AP News, April 2, 1986. https://apnews.com/article/e748fce38ca8654fc04cd276b5a8c35b.
RIAA. "Gold and Platinum: The Isley Brothers." https://www.riaa.com/gold-platinum/?tab_active=default-award&se=isley+brothers#search_section.
Rice, Briana. "Black Music Walk of Fame to Open Next Year: First Four Inductees Honored at Ceremony on Saturday." *Cincinnati Enquirer*, July 25, 2021.
Rizik, Chris. "Happy Birthday to the Legendary Ronald Isley." Soul Tracks. May 26, 2024. https://www.soultracks.com/birthday-ronald-isley-2024.
Rizik, Chris. "Isley Brothers." SoulTracks. https://soultracks.com/artist/isley_brothers/.
"Road Trip: Around Louisiana." *The Daily Advertiser*, June 18, 2015.
Robbins, Wayne. "The Youngest Isley's Post-Hendrix Groove." *Newsday*, February 18, 1990.
Roberts, Kimberly. "Ernie Isley Shares the Family Secret." *Philadelphia Tribune*, January 30, 1998.
Roberts, Kimberly. "Isley Brothers Bid Farewell to Philly Fans." *Philadelphia Tribune*, May 1, 2007.
Roberts, Kimberly. "Isley Brothers on a 'Mission to Please.'" *Philadelphia Tribune*, January 32, 1998.
Roberts, Kimberly. "Isley Due to Begin Jail Term." *Philadelphia Tribune*, August 7, 2007.
Roberts, Kimberly. "Isley Optimistic About Appeal, Ready for Tour." *Philadelphia Tribune*, February 16, 2007.
Roberts, Kimberly. "Music Icon Receives Prestigious Award: Ronald Isley Accepts the Quincy Jones Award at the Soul Train Awards." *Philadelphia Tribune*, March 2, 2001.

Roberts, Minor. "Jamaica Inn, Isley Bros. in $$$ Trouble." *New York Amsterdam News*, August 18, 1979.
Roby, Steven, and Brad Schreiber. *Becoming Jimi Hendrix: The Untold Story of a Musical Genius*. Cambridge, MA: Da Capo Press, 2010.
"Rock Stars Join Hall of Fame." *Orlando Sentinel*, November 5, 1991.
Rockwell, John. "Big Black Pop Bands Have Lost Excitement and Adventure." *New York Times*, December 6, 1981.
Rogers, Prentis. "Isley Bros: Good Live but Better on Record." *Atlanta Daily World*, October 27, 1977.
Rogers, Prentis. "Objectivity Key to Success of The Isley Brothers." *Atlanta Daily World*, July 2, 1978.
Ronald Isley. *Here I Am: Isley Meets Bacharach*. DreamWorks. 2003.
Ronald Isley. "Just Came Here to Chill." YouTube video. https://www.youtube.com/watch?v=3SOCNqLeydQ.
Ronald Isley. *Mr. I*. Def Jam Classics. 2010.
Ronald Isley. "No More." YouTube video. https://www.youtube.com/watch?v=_Zg8UjYb9c4.
Ronald Isley. *This Song Is for You*. eOne/Notifi. 2013.
"Ronald Isley Gets 3 Years in Tax Evasion." *Chicago Defender*, September 4, 2006.
"Ronald Isley Pleads Innocent to Tax Evasion." *Los Angeles Sentinel*, January 13, 2005.
Rowe, Billy. "Uncle Sam's Lien on Isley Bros." *New York Amsterdam News*, September 8, 1979.
Ruggieri, Melissa. "Inside Clive Davis' Celeb-Packed Pre-Grammy Party: Green Day, Mariah Carey, More." *USA Today*, February 4, 2024.
Ruggieri, Melissa. "Isley Brothers Hold 'Reunion': They Play Favorites in 90-Minute Show." *The Atlanta Journal-Constitution*, September 2, 2011.
Saalman, Austin. "The Isley Brothers—Reflecting on the 50th Anniversary of 'Brother, Brother, Brother.'" *Under the Radar*, May 2, 2022. https://www.undertheradarmag.com/news/the_isley_brothers_reflecting_on_the_50th_anniversary_of_brother_brother_br.
Sacks, Leo. "Their Own Words." *It's Your Thing: The Story of the Isley Brothers* (CD box set). Sony Music Entertainment. 1999.
Samuels, Keithan. "AFRAM Festival 2023 Lineup Announced: The Isley Brothers and Ty Dolla $ign to Headline." *Rated R&B*, April 13, 2023. https://ratedrnb.com/2023/04/afram-festival-2023-lineup-the-isley-brothers-ty-dolla-sign-tamar-braxton/.
Samuels, Keithan. "The Isley Brothers Share New Album 'Make Me Say It Again, Girl.'" *Rated R&B*, September 30, 2022. https://ratedrnb.com/2022/09/the-isley-brothers-share-new-album-make-me-say-it-again-girl/.
Sandow, Greg, and David Browne. "1990's Best (and Worst) Music." *Entertainment Weekly*, December 28, 1990. https://ew.com/article/1990/12/28/1990s-best-and-worst-music/.
"Santana IV Reunites Legendary Band Lineup: First Single 'Anywhere You Want To Go' to Be Released February 5, 2016." *PR Newswire*, January 21, 2016.
Schulte, Stephanie. "Twist, Shout and Groove with the Commodores and The Isley Brothers at Fantasy Springs Resort Casino." *Redlands Daily Facts*, August 23, 2017.
"SCLC Announces First New York Black Expo." *New York Amsterdam News*, October 23, 1971.
Scott, Ron. "Hendrix Apollo Tribute, Chambers at Smoke, WeBop HAS." *New York Amsterdam News*, November 24, 2016.
"Secret Lover." performed by The Isley Brothers. *Eternal*. DreamWorks. 2001.
"Sensitive Lover." Performed by The Isley Brothers. *Tracks of Life*. Warner Brothers. 1992.

Serba, John. "Sound Waves of Summer: Muskegon's Summer Celebration Rides a Crest of Top Musical Acts." *The Grand Rapids Press*, June 22, 1997.
Sherman, Mark, et. al. "Atlanta Games Day 7 City Late Break." *Atlanta Journal-Constitution*, July 25, 1996.
"Shout." Performed by The Isley Brothers. *Shout*. RCA Victor. 1959.
Shriver, Jerry. "Inspiration Hit Singer in Prison." *The Windsor Star*, December 18, 2010.
Simpson, Dave. "How The Isley Brothers Made Harvest for the World." *The Guardian*, July 6, 2020. https://www.theguardian.com/music/2020/jul/06/ernie-and-ron-isley-how-we-made-harvest-for-the-world-isley-brothers.
"16th Annual Soul Beach Music Festival Hosted by Aruba." *M2 Presswire*, May 27, 2016.
Smallwood, Bill. "Bill Smallwood." *Oakland Post*, September 2, 1971.
Smith, Patricia. "Isleys Satisfy Fans with Sanctified Soul." *Boston Globe*, July 27, 1996.
"Smooth Sailin' Tonight." Performed by The Isley Brothers. *Smooth Sailin'*. Warner Brothers. 1987.
"Solar Galaxy Stars to Sparkle at Holiday." *Weekend Chicago Defender*, July 25, 1981.
Songfacts. "Caravan of Love by Isley-Jasper-Isley." https://www.songfacts.com/facts/isley-jasper-isley/caravan-of-love.
Songfacts. "The Isley Brothers." https://www.songfacts.com/songs/the-isley-brothers.
Songfacts. "Music History Events: Legal Issues." https://calendar.songfacts.com/category/legal-issues/page-13.
Songwriters Hall of Fame. "Ernie Isley." May 26, 2024. https://www.songhall.org/profile/ernie_isley.
Songwriters Hall of Fame. "Songwriters Hall of Fame Reschedules 51st Annual Induction and Awards Dinner." March 31, 2020. https://www.songhall.org/news/view/songwriters_hall_of_fame_reschedules_51st_annual_induction_and_awards_dinner.
"Soul Explosion at the Oakland Coliseum." *Oakland Post*, September 4, 1977.
"Soul Legend Ronald Isley Weds Singer Kandy Johnson." *Jet*, September 5, 2005.
"Soul '70 at Cow Palace." *Sacramento Observer*, February 5, 1970.
"Soul Train Begins Second Season." *Bay State Banner*, September 14, 1972.
"Soul Train Hopefuls." *USA Today*, March 7, 1997.
Soul Train. "The Isley Brothers—Who's That Lady." YouTube video, May 20, 2022. https://www.youtube.com/watch?v=BW8-BRnbV-Q.
Spencer, Neil. "Review: Music: POP." *The Observer*, December 10, 2000.
"Spend the Night." Performed by The Isley Brothers. *Spend the Night*. Warner Brothers. 1989.
"Spill the Wine." Performed by The Isley Brothers. *Givin' It Back*. T-Neck, 1971.
"A Star Is Born." *New Pittsburgh Courier*, March 29, 2003.
"Stars Will Entertain Montague at Rockland." *New Pittsburgh Courier*, June 13, 1964.
Stith, Deborah Sengupta, Eric Webb, and Earl Hopkins. "Bruce, Janet, SZA: Your Guide to Austin Live Music in 2023." *Austin American Statesman*, January 5, 2023.
Stremes, Brecht. "The Origin and Influence of Doo-Wop Music." *Bertolt Press*, April 24, 2020. https://bertoltpress.com/2020/04/24/doo-wop-music-history/.
Stryker, Mark. "These Box Sets Are Worth Unwrapping." *Detroit Free Press*, December 3, 2000.
"Superbad." Performed by Chris Jasper. *Superbad*. CBS. 1987.
Swan, Rhonda. "50 Years Later, Isley Still Going Strong Writing, Performing." *Palm Beach Post*, March 18, 2011.

"Take Me in Your Arms (Rock Me a Little While)." Performed by The Isley Brothers. Motown. 1968.

"Take Me to the Next Phase." Performed by The Isley Brothers. *Showdown*. T-Neck. 1978.

"Take Some Time Out for Love." Performed by The Isley Brothers. *This Old Heart of Mine*. Tamla (Motown). 1966.

Takiff, Jonathan. "Kickin' Off the Jams: Suddenly Philly Radio Has a Hot New Player." *Philadelphia Daily News*, June 24, 1999.

Tapley, Mel. "About the Arts." *New York Amsterdam News*, June 7, 1980.

"Taste of Chicago: Full 2016 Music, Food Lineup." NBC Chicago. May 17, 2016. https://www.nbcchicago.com/news/local/taste-of-chicago-full-2016-music-food-lineup/115966/.

"Tax Man Chasing Ronald Isley Again." *Chatham Daily News*, October 16, 2004.

Taylor, Marc. *A Touch of Classic Soul: Soul Singers of the Early 1970s*. Ann Arbor: University of Michigan Press, 1996.

"Tears." Performed by The Isley Brothers. *Mission to Please*. T-Neck/Island. 1996.

"Testify." Performed by The Isley Brothers. T-Neck. 1964.

"That Lady." Performed by The Isley Brothers. *3 + 3*. T-Neck. 1973.

"Theatrical Spotlight." *New York Amsterdam News*, August 26, 1972.

"This Old Heart of Mine (Is Weak for You). Performed by This Isley Brothers. *This Old Heart of Mine*. Tamla (Motown). 1966.

Thrasher, Paula Crouch. "Getaway: Quick Tips and Good Deals Southern Happenings." *The Atlanta Constitution*, April 21, 1999.

"3 Record Stars in Regal Show." *Chicago Daily Defender*, December 31, 1962.

"Tickets for 2012 Smooth Groves Music Fest in Fresno on Sale on Feb. 10." *Visalia Times-Delta*, February 6, 2012.

"The Timeless Isley Brothers, Ranked." *Courier-Journal*, June 11, 2015.

"Tom Sandoval, Ween and Phoenix's Best Concerts This Week." *Phoenix New Times*, February 15, 2024.

Torres, Richard. "Sony Makes a Reissue Out of Isley Brothers." *Newsday*, September 14, 1997.

"Tradition." *Weekend Chicago Defender*, December 31, 1994.

"Tryin' to See Another Day." Performed by The Isley Brothers. *Friday (Original Motion Picture Soundtrack)*. Priority. 1995.

"Tune In Tuesday; Kid Rock Aims to Be Top Dog." *Courier-Journal* (Louisville, KY), October 9, 2007.

Turner, Ras. "Annual Air Jamaica Jazz and Blues Festival." *Philadelphia Tribune*, November 7, 1997.

"Twenty-Ninth Hampton Jazz Festival Continues Its Legendary Tradition." *New Journal and Guide*, May 1, 1996.

"Twist and Shout." Performed by The Isley Brothers. *Twist and Shout*. Wand. 1962.

"Twistin' with Linda." Performed by The Isley Brothers. *Twist and Shout*. Wand. 1962.

"The 2007 Essence Music Festival Presented by Coca-Cola Brings Together the Country's Largest Annual Gathering of African Americans to Celebrate Black Music and Culture." *PR Newswire*, July 5, 2007.

"'Ultimate Isleys' Captures The Isley Brothers' Hit-Making Years 1959–1983." *Call and Post*, December 21, 2000.

Unterberger, Andrew. "The Isley Brothers vs. Earth, Wind & Fire in Funk Legends 'Verzuz' Battle: See Billboard's Score Card for the Event." *Billboard*, April 5, 2021. https://www

.billboard.com/music/rb-hip-hop/isley-brothers-earth-wind-fire-verzuz-battle-scorecard-9551107/.

"Urban League's Gala Raises Almost $2.4 Million, Honors Community Leaders." *Chicago Defender*, November 7, 2023.

Various Artists. *Don't Be a Menace to South Central While Drinking Your Juice in the Hood: The Soundtrack.* Island. 1996.

Various Artists. *Friday (Original Motion Picture Soundtrack).* Priority. 1995.

Various Artists. *Movin' On Up, Vol. 2.* The Right Stuff. 1995.

Various Artists. *Muppets from Space: The Ultimate Muppet Trip.* Sony/Epic. 1999.

Various Artists. *Smooth Grooves: A Sensual Collection.* Rhino. 1995.

Vigoda, Arlene. "Box Office: [Final Edition]." *USA Today*, January 23, 1995.

Vigoda, Arlene. "War, Peace and Hemlines: [First Edition]." *USA Today*, February 1. 1995.

Vincent, Rickey. *Funk: The Music, the People, and the Rhythm of the One.* New York: St. Martins Griffin, 1996.

"Voyage to Atlantis." Performed by The Isley Brothers. *Go for Your Guns.* T-Neck. 1977.

Waldron, Clarence. "Ronald Isley in Jail on Tax Evasion Charges." *Jet*, September 24, 2007.

Walker, DeArbea. "In Texas, a Park Founded by Formerly Enslaved People Prepares to Celebrate Its 150th Juneteenth." *Insider*, June 18, 2022.

"Warpath." Performed by The Isley Brothers. T-Neck. 1971.

"Was It Good to You?" Performed by The Isley Brothers. *The Brothers Isley.* T-Neck. 1969.

Watrous, Peter. "Sounds Around Town." *New York Times*, March 9, 1990. https://www.nytimes.com/1990/03/09/arts/sounds-around-town-019290.html.

Weber, Wendy Fox. "Five Things to Do in the Southland and Nearby July 23–29." *Chicago Tribune*, July 19, 2021.

"Weekend Top 10. *Daily Press*, July 29, 2016.

Weigel, David. "The Isley Brothers: Baby Makin' Music." PopMatters, May 24, 2006. https://www.popmatters.com/the-isley-brothers-baby-makin-music-2495679309.html.

"Welcome Home Fete for Isley Bros. to Highlight Ohio Kool Jazz Festival." *Call and Post*, June 28, 1980.

"Welcome to My Heart." Performed by The Isley Brothers. *Inside You.* T-Neck. 1981.

Weston, Alonzo. "Review: 'Beautiful Ballads' Series Offers Music for Romance." *St. Joseph News*, January 5, 2007.

"Whatever Turns You On." Performed by The Isley Brothers. *Tracks of Life.* Warner Brothers.1992.

"What I Miss the Most." Performed by Ronald Isley. *Mr. I.* Def Jam, 2010.

"What It Comes Down To." Performed by The Isley Brothers. *3 + 3.* T-Neck, 1973.

"What Would You Do (featuring The Pied Piper)." Performed by The Isley Brothers. *Body Kiss.* Dreamworks. 2003.

White, Renee Minus. "The Isley Brothers' Style Is 'Contagious.'" *New York Amsterdam News*, July 26, 2001.

"Who Said?" Performed by The Isley Brothers. *Grand Slam.* T-Neck. 1981.

Wieben. "In the Beginning . . . The Isley Brothers and Jimi Hendrix." Rate Your Music. https://rateyourmusic.com/release/comp/the-isley-brothers-jimi-hendrix/in-the-beginning-the-isley-brothers-and-jimi-hendrix/.

Williams, A. J. "Chene Park Celebrates 30 Years with The Isley Brothers, En Vogue and Loose Ends for the Last Concert of the Year." *Michigan Chronicle*, August 28, 2014.

Wilner, Paul. "Isley Brothers: A Family Affair." *The New York Times*, March 13, 1977.

Wilson and Alroy's Record Reviews. "Isley Brothers." http://www.warr.org/isleys.html.
Winbush, Angela, and Ronald Isley. "Lay Your Troubles Down." YouTube video. https://www.youtube.com/watch?v=Ug9RBtmSgQE.
Winistorfer, Andrew. "The Isley Brothers Are the Most Important Band of All Time," Vinyl Me Please, https://www.vinylmeplease.com/blogs/magazine/isley-brothers-liner-notes.
"Winner Takes All." Performed by The Isley Brothers. *Winner Takes All*. T-Neck, 1979.
Woods, Wes II. "Anderson .Paak Brings Smokey Robinson, Isley Brothers to Ventura Festival." *Ventura County Star*, May 13, 2023.
"Work to Do." Performed by The Isley Brothers. *Brother, Brother, Brother*. T-Neck, 1972.
"World Briefs." *The Salt Lake Tribune*, January 12, 2000.
"You Help Me Write This Song." Performed by The Isley Brothers. *Baby Making Music*. Def Jam. 2006.
Zane Productiion. "The Isley Brothers ft 2 Chainz—R&B Music Video Production." https://www.zane-productions.com/isley-2chainz-plug-music-video.

Index

Aaliyah, 78, 107, 157, 158, 192, 224
"Aint Givin' Up No Love," 85, 87
"All in My Lover's Eyes," 103, 104, 132, 152–53
"Angels Cried," 12
Apollo Theater, 12, 19, 24–26, 30–32, 49, 190, 195, 198
"(At Your Best) You Are Love," 74, 78, 79, 84, 153, 157, 158, 160
Avant, 156

Babyface, 5, 137, 141, 170
"Baby Hold On," 101, 102
Baby Makin' Music, 172, 173
Bacharach, Burt, 164, 185, 189
Bailey, Philip, 158, 171
"Ballad for the Fallen Soldier," 106–8
Baraka, Amiri (LeRoi Jones), 26
Barkley, Elizabeth Isley, 11, 12, 218
Barrett, Richard, 12
Beatles, The, 3, 18, 22, 77, 189, 193, 203, 221, 224
Beautiful Ballads, 132
Beautiful Ballads, Vol. 2, 174
"Behind a Painted Smile," 31, 33, 39–40, 171
"Belly Dancer, The," 95, 97
Berns, Bert, 17
Best . . . Isley Brothers, The, 73, 74
Between the Sheets, 105–8, 111
"Between the Sheets," 5, 105, 106, 110, 111, 114, 131–33, 139, 140, 143, 152, 153, 158, 165, 170, 174, 175, 182, 188, 189, 190, 193, 205, 212, 218, 219, 224
Beyoncé, 72, 213, 214, 224

Billy Ward and the Dominoes, 9
Black Arts Movement, 26
"Black Berries," 41, 42
"Blacker the Berrie, The," 41, 73
Black Panther Party, 31, 47
Black Power Movement, 26, 30, 31
Black rock (music style), 5
"Blast Off," 172
"Bless Your Heart," 44
Bloom, Howard, 13
Blue Ash, Ohio, 8, 10
Body Kiss, 6, 160, 161, 162
Bolton, Michael, 127, 128, 131, 142, 150, 151, 153
Bone Thugs-N-Harmony, 5, 72, 107
Broadway's Closer to Sunset Blvd, 111, 112, 116
"Brother, Brother," 52, 62, 73, 88
Brother, Brother, Brother, 52–56, 143, 179
Brothers, The: Isley, 40–42, 143, 179
Brown, James, 4, 13, 24, 27, 100, 144, 147, 152, 159
"Brown Eyed Girl," 67, 132, 219
Brown Skin Models, 7
Brown v. Board of Education of Topeka, 9
Buddah Records, 34, 39, 40, 52, 63, 88
"Busted," 161–62, 163, 178

Calloway, Cab, 7
Cameo, 96, 170, 198
Caravan of Love, 114–16
"Caravan of Love," 115, 132, 143, 147, 152, 170, 224
Chaka Khan, 122, 132, 170, 182, 208, 220
Chambers Brothers, The, 14, 40

285

Charles, Ray, 16, 22
"Choosey Lover," 106, 108, 131, 132, 176, 217
Christians, The, 78, 79
Christmas with Kim & Kandy, 208
Cincinnati Black Music Walk of Fame, 210
Clara Ward and the Ward Singers, 8, 40, 46
"Colder Are My Nights," 113, 114
Cole, Nat King, 9
Coleman, Ornette, 13
"Come My Way," 118, 120
Commodores, The, 5, 147, 201
"Contagious," 154, 155, 157, 165, 175, 178, 224
Cooke, Sam, 9, 16, 22
"Coolin' Me Out," 85, 87, 133
Cornelius, Don, 54, 66
"Cow Jumped Over the Moon, The," 13
Crests, The, 11

Davis, Miles, 13, 16
Davis, Sammy, Jr., 8
Definitive Collection, The, 178
Diablos, The, 11
Different Drummer, 120, 121
"Dinner and a Movie," 186, 187
Disco, 3, 89–94
Dixie Hummingbirds, 9
D-Nice, 208
Doin' Their Thing: Best of The Isley Brothers, 39
Don't Be a Menace to South Central . . ., 135, 136
"Don't Hold Back Your Love," 101, 102
"Don't Let Me Be Lonely Tonight," 64, 66, 132, 143, 170
"Don't Say Goodnight (It's Time for Love)," 5, 94–97, 131, 132, 152, 175, 176, 178, 182, 196
Doo-wop, 3, 11
Do the Right Thing, 68
"Down Low (Nobody Has to Know)," 134, 140, 178

Earth, Wind & Fire, 67, 73, 79, 89, 93, 103, 108, 138, 144, 145, 158, 159, 171, 174, 195, 208, 209
"8th Wonder of the World," 120, 121
Epic Records, 63

"Ernie's Jam," 156, 159
Essential Isley Brothers, The, 165–67
Eternal, 6, 155–60
"Eternal," 156, 160, 161

"Fight the Power," 5, 67, 68, 70–73, 78, 84, 108, 110, 131, 133, 139, 140, 146, 151, 152, 154, 165, 178, 182, 188, 190, 193, 196, 205, 219, 223–24
"Fire and Rain," 49, 88
"First Love," 101–3
"Floatin' on Your Love," 136, 140, 178
"Footsteps in the Dark," 81, 131, 133, 139, 146, 153, 154, 171, 174, 190, 196, 205, 218
Forever Gold, 84
"For the Love of You," 5, 70, 71, 72, 84, 110, 131, 139, 152–54, 165, 170, 174, 182, 196, 217–18
Frankie Lymon and The Teenagers, 12
Franklin, Aretha, 36, 49, 70, 79, 100, 139, 152, 182–85, 189, 191, 195, 202, 205, 217, 220
"Free," 207
"Freedom," 47, 48, 73, 88
"Friends and Family," 209, 214, 216
Funk (music), 3, 4, 39

Gap Band, The, 96, 103, 146
Garrison, VeRon, 209
Get Into Something, 44–47, 143, 179
"Get Into Something," 47, 73, 88, 143
"Girls Will Be Girls, Boys Will Be Boys," 46
Givin' It Back, 49–52, 143, 179
"Givin' You Back the Love," 121
Go All the Way, 94–97
"Go All the Way," 96
Go for Your Guns, 80–84
"Go for Your Guns," 81, 196
Golden Age, 5, 6, 55, 58, 59, 111, 165, 223, 224
Goldner, George, 12
Goodstone, Elaine Isley, 212
Gordy, Berry, 4, 27, 34, 216
"Got to Have You Back," 33
Grammy Awards, 3, 4, 37, 46, 127, 155, 161, 180, 184, 188, 189, 192, 219, 223, 224
Grandslam, 98, 99, 100
Greatest Hits (1997), 143

Greatest Hits, Vol. 1, 109, 110
Great Soul Revue (concert series), 78
Gregg, Bobby, 23
"Groove with You," 85–87, 110, 131, 134, 139, 152, 174–76, 190, 196
Groove with You . . . Live!, 195–96

Hamilton, Andrew, 30, 31
Harlem Cultural Festival, 35
Harris, Howard C., 27
Harris, Jimmy "Jam," 5, 156, 159, 177, 224
Harvest for the World, 73, 74, 75, 78, 79, 163
"Harvest for the World," 74–78, 108, 143, 146, 152, 170, 189, 209, 219
Harvey, Steve, 141–42, 145, 208
Hawkins, Erskine, 9
Hawkins Singers, The, 40, 43
Heat Is On, The, 69–73, 161, 163, 213
"Heaven's Girl," 134
"Hello It's Me," 66, 67, 84, 131, 132, 139, 140, 152, 176, 190, 196
Hendrix, Jimi, 4–6, 23–25, 46–48, 52, 57, 59, 64, 127, 180, 181, 198, 203, 223
Here I Am: Isley Meets Bacharach, 6, 163–64, 189
"Here We Go Again," 95–97, 131, 174, 182, 195–96
"Highways of My Life, The," 59, 84, 143, 170
High Wire (Ernie Isley), 124
"High Wire," 124
Holland-Dozier-Holland, 27, 29–30, 34, 39
Hollywood Rockwalk, 160, 224
Hollywood Walk of Fame, 220–21
"Hope You Feel Better Love," 70, 84, 143
Houston, Whitney, 71, 106, 192, 224
"How Lucky I Am," 90, 153
"Hurry Up and Wait," 5, 99

I. B. Specials, The, 22
Ice Cube, 5, 139, 158, 203, 224
"If He Can, You Can," 45, 46, 88
"I Guess I'll Always Love You," 30, 171, 178
"I Know Who You Been Socking It To," 43, 88
I'll Be Home for Christmas, 6, 177–78
"I'm So Proud," 131, 147

"I Need You So," 44, 88
Ink Spots, The, 7
"Insatiable Woman," 114, 116, 174
Inside You, 101, 102
"Inside You," 101
In the Beginning . . ., 48
"I Once Had Your Love (And I Can't Let Go)," 98–99, 100, 132, 153
Isley, Alex, 210–11, 220
Isley, Corey, 182
Isley, Elaine (Rudolph's daughter), 218
Isley, Elaine Elizabeth Jasper, 11, 143, 188, 218
Isley, Ernie, 4–6, 8, 14, 23, 25, 36, 37, 57–59, 61, 64–67, 71, 72, 74, 76, 78, 82, 84, 85, 93, 96, 97, 104, 106, 108, 109, 111, 122, 124, 127, 130, 133–34, 137–40, 143–46, 148, 153, 154, 158–61, 163–65, 169, 171, 173, 174, 178, 180, 181, 183–85, 189–94, 197–200, 203–5, 209, 210, 212, 214, 217–21, 223, 224
Isley, Jalen, 182
Isley, Kandy Johnson, 146, 158, 160, 171, 175, 187, 188, 200, 204, 205, 207–9, 213, 214
Isley, Marvin, 4, 5, 8, 23, 34, 37, 47, 57, 58, 64, 68, 70, 76, 82, 83, 85, 87, 96, 109, 111, 122, 127, 143–44, 150, 154, 182, 193, 224
Isley, O'Kelly, Jr., 3, 5, 7, 13, 24, 25, 36, 37, 44, 54, 64, 76, 109, 112, 116, 117, 120, 122, 150, 151, 168, 193, 217, 224
Isley, O'Kelly, Sr., 7, 8, 11, 113, 116
Isley, Ronald, 3, 5, 6, 7, 9, 11, 13, 15, 23, 28, 36, 37, 47, 58, 64, 67, 68, 71, 72, 74, 76–78, 84, 93, 97, 106, 109, 112, 116–20, 122–25, 127, 128–35, 137–42, 144–46, 148–51, 153–61, 163–65, 167–69, 171, 173–78, 181–84, 186–93, 197–202, 204, 205, 208–10, 212–14, 216–18, 220–25
Isley, Ronald, Jr., 175, 176, 204
Isley, Rudolph, 3, 5, 7–14, 17, 25, 36, 47, 58, 109, 110, 112, 116–18, 122, 127, 135, 143, 150, 151, 165, 171, 188, 193, 209, 216–18, 224
Isley, Rudolph, Jr., 218
Isley, Sallye Bell, 7, 8, 14, 113, 116
Isley, Sheila Felton, 154
Isley, Sidney, 182
Isley, Tracy, 200, 204, 209
Isley, Valerie, 218

Isley, Vernon, 3, 8, 10, 11, 113
Isley Brothers, The: The Complete UA Sessions, 127
Isley Brothers, The: Summer Breeze Greatest Hits Live (DVD), 36
Isley Brothers Story, Vol. 1, The, 126
Isley Brothers Story, Vol. 2, The, 126
Isley-Jasper-Isley, 5, 111, 112, 114, 120, 147
Isleys' Greatest Hits, 62, 63
Isleys Live, The, 56, 57
"It's Alright with Me," 103
"It's a Disco Night (Rock Don't Stop)," 5, 90, 92, 93, 96, 143, 170, 196
"It's Too Late," 4, 56, 57, 73, 88, 174
It's Our Thing, 4, 36, 38, 39
"It's Your Thing," 4, 36, 37, 39–41, 44, 46, 49, 51, 53, 56, 62, 73, 88, 110, 131, 139, 143, 146, 152, 158, 159, 165, 171, 176, 182, 188, 190, 193, 205, 209, 212, 219, 223, 224
It's Your Thing (film), 41, 46
It's Your Thing: The Story of The Isley Brothers, 147, 148
"I Turned You On," 40, 41, 62, 73, 88, 193
"I Wanna Be with You," 89, 90, 93
"I Wish," 118, 120

Jackson, Mahalia, 9
Jamie Foxx Show, The, 144
Jasper, Chris, 4, 37, 57, 58, 61, 63, 65, 67, 71, 77, 83, 85, 86, 92, 94, 96, 97, 103, 109–11, 115, 121, 122, 150, 193, 194
Jasper, Elaine, 58
Jasper, Margie, 116
Jasper, Michael, 122
Johnson, Kim, 146, 158, 159, 161, 171, 175, 207, 208
Johnson, Krystal, 146, 158, 159, 171
JS (Johnson Sisters), 158, 159, 160
Juneteenth, 212–13
"Just Came Here to Chill," 172, 175, 178

Kaplan, Fred, 13
"Keep On Doin'," 44, 88
Kellman, Andy, 47
Kelly, R., 5, 6, 133, 134, 137, 138, 141, 155, 156, 158, 161, 163, 165, 172, 175, 185, 188, 192, 203, 224
Kem, 187, 188

Keys, Alicia, 158, 160, 170, 172, 185, 208
King, Martin Luther, Jr., 17, 33, 34, 77
"Kiss and Tell," 111
Knight, Gladys, 9, 19, 24, 131, 138, 139, 174, 184, 190, 195
Kool & The Gang, 64, 73, 94, 96, 100, 146

Lamar, Kendrick, 192, 211, 225
"Last Time," 214, 218
Lawrence, Trevor, 36
Lawrence, Vince, 92
Laws, Ronnie, 79
"Lay-Away," 52, 56, 62, 73
"Lay Lady Lay," 4, 51, 56, 73, 88, 132, 143
"Lay Your Troubles Down," 125
Lee, Spike, 68
"Let Me Down Easy," 74, 77–79, 174
"Let's Fall in Love," 90, 132, 182
"Let's Lay Together," 135, 136, 178
"Let's Twist Again," 18
Lewis, Terry, 6, 156, 159, 177, 224
"Life in the City," 90, 92
Lincoln Heights, Ohio, 7, 10
Live!, 131
Live It Up, 64–67
"Live It Up," 66, 84, 93, 110, 195, 224
Live at Yankee Stadium, 42, 43
"Livin' in the Life," 83, 196, 224
"Lonely Teardrops," 13
"Look the Other Way," 111
"Lost in Love," 128, 130
"Love Forever," 85, 87
"Love Is a Wonderful Thing," 30, 127, 131–32
Love Songs, 152, 153
"Love the One You're With," 4, 49, 56, 62, 73, 88, 143, 152, 170, 182
Lucas, Al, 23

Mack, Ted, 9
Make Me Say It Again, Girl, 6, 213–16, 218
"Make Me Say It Again, Girl," 70–72, 131, 132, 153, 160, 213, 214
Masterpiece, 112–14
Mayfield, Curtis, 22
"May I?," 113, 114
Maze Featuring Frankie Beverly, 83, 176, 187, 203, 211, 213, 216

McPhatter, Clyde, 9, 12
Medley, Phil, 17
"Midnight Sky," 66, 67
Mills Brothers, The, 7, 189
Mission to Please, 134, 136, 137, 139, 141, 142, 173
"Mission to Please You," 137, 140
Moore, Chante, 155, 198
"Most Beautiful Girl, The," 113, 114
Motown Anthology, The, 179–81
Motown Records, 3, 4, 6, 24, 26–28, 30, 33, 34, 39, 40, 80, 193, 216, 223
"Move On Over and Let Me Dance," 25
"Move Your Body," 155, 159
Mr. Biggs, 5, 6, 134, 140, 141, 145, 155, 158, 159, 161, 163, 172, 174, 176, 184, 198, 205, 217, 224
Mr. I, 6, 183, 184, 187
"My Favorite Thing," 187, 188

NAACP Image Awards, 145, 155
Naughty by Nature, 72
"Nobody but Me," 19
"No More," 182
"Nothing to Do but Today," 49, 88
Notorious B.I.G., 5, 106, 158, 189, 205, 224

"Ohio/Machine Gun," 49, 52, 56, 73, 88
"One of a Kind," 122, 124
Original Album Classics, 179
Original Amateur Hour, The, 9

"Papa's Got a Brand New Bag," 27
Parliament-Funkadelic, 73, 82, 94, 152
"Pass It On," 95, 97
Patterson, George, 3
"People of Today," 74, 78
Pitts, Charles, Jr., 36
Playlist: The Very Best of The Isley Brothers, 182
"Plug, The," 214–16
"Pop That Thang," 53, 54, 56, 62, 73, 88
Power of Peace, 6, 199–201
Price, Kelly, 138, 139, 192
"Pride, The," 5, 80, 81–82, 98, 143, 152
"Prize Possession," 161, 162
Public Enemy, 68

Pullman Group, 150, 151
"Put a Little Love in Your Heart," 52, 88

Questlove, 167, 217

RCA Records, 4, 13, 14
RCA Victor & T-Neck Album Masters (1959–1983), 193–94
Real Deal, The, 103, 104
"Real Deal, The," 103, 104
Red Caps, The, 7
"Release Your Love," 113, 114
"Respectable," 16, 23
Rice, Tony, 22, 23
Rock & Roll Hall of Fame, 3, 127, 191, 224
"Rockin' with Fire," 85, 87
Rock 'n' roll, 3, 4, 27
"Rubberleg Twist," 18

Saadiq, Raphael, 5, 156
Salt-N-Pepa, 18
Santana, 6, 197, 199, 224
Santana, Carlos, 199, 200, 220
"Say You Will," 95, 97, 196
Scepter Records, 4
"Secret Lover," 155, 158
"Sensitive Lover," 128
"Sensuality," 70, 71, 72, 132, 174
"Settle Down," 156, 159
Shout, 15, 16, 66
"Shout," 3, 4, 13–16, 23, 40, 56, 62, 109, 131, 139, 140, 146, 152, 155, 159, 165, 178, 188, 190, 193, 200, 203–5, 209, 212, 217, 219, 220, 223, 224
Shouting for Jesus (Rudolph Isley), 143
Showdown, 85–87, 89
"Showdown, Vol. 1," 161, 163
Sly & The Family Stone, 61, 223
Smooth Sailin', 5, 117, 119, 120, 122, 178
"Smooth Sailin' Tonight," 118, 131
Songwriters Hall of Fame, 196, 206, 210, 212, 216
Sonny Til and The Orioles, 9
Soul '70 (concert series), 44
Soul Brothers Summer Music Festival, 40, 42
Soul on the Rocks, 31, 32, 39
Soul Train, 54, 61, 62, 66

Soul Train Music Awards, 142, 153, 155, 159, 160, 162, 172, 182–83, 214, 218, 224
"So You Wanna Stay Down," 74, 78
Spaniels, The, 11
"Special Gift," 144
Spend the Night, 5, 122–24
"Spend the Night," 122, 131, 178
"Spill the Wine," 50, 62, 73, 88, 143, 152, 182
"Stay Gold," 113, 114
Stephens, Herman, 14
Steve Harvey Show, The, 141–42
Stewart, Rod, 28, 123, 131, 224
St. Louis Walk of Fame, 204
Stone, Angie, 94, 191
"Stone Cold Lover," 103, 105
Student Nonviolent Coordinating Committee (SNCC), 16
"Summer Breeze," 5, 63, 64, 66, 74, 139, 143, 146, 152, 153, 182, 189, 190, 196, 198, 205
Summer Breeze: Greatest Hits, 170–71
Superbad, 121
"Superbad," 121, 122
Superbowl LIII, 203
Supremes, The, 22, 27–29
Sweat, Keith, 137, 141, 165, 185, 212

"Take Me in Your Arms (Rock Me a Little While)," 34, 39, 178
"Take Me to the Next Phase," 85, 87, 176, 196
Taken to the Next Phase, 167, 168
"Take Some Time Out for Love," 29
Take Some Time Out for The Isley Brothers, 18
"Tears," 136, 141, 142
"Testify," 24
"That Lady," 5, 39, 58, 59, 61, 64, 66, 84, 110, 130, 131, 138, 143, 152, 154, 175, 176, 182, 189, 192–95, 198, 205, 212, 214, 219–20, 223
This Old Heart of Mine, 28, 30, 31, 39, 40
"This Old Heart of Mine (Is Weak for You)," 4, 27, 28, 29, 118, 123, 142, 170–71, 178, 188, 190, 223
This Song Is for You, 6, 187, 189
Three Boys Music Group, 151
3 + 3, 4, 59–61, 63, 64, 87, 179, 193, 194, 223
Timeless, 88

T-Neck Records, 4, 6, 22, 24, 26, 34, 40, 63, 64, 81, 84, 193, 209, 223
Top Notes, The, 17
Tracks of Life, 128, 129, 130
Triple Three Music, 151
Troop Beverly Hills, 14
Trumpet Awards, 191, 196
Twist and Shout, 18, 19
"Twist and Shout," 4, 17, 18, 23, 24, 26, 30, 39, 146, 152, 153, 158, 159, 164, 178, 180, 188–90, 200, 223
Twisting and Shouting, 19–21
"Twistin' with Linda," 18

Ultimate Isley Brothers, The, 152
"Under the Influence," 103, 105
United Artists record label, 22, 30, 127
Unterberger, Rich, 19

Valley Homes, 7, 8
Vance, Elmer, 10
Verzuz, 208
Vincent, Rickey, 27, 72
Vocal Group Hall of Fame, 3, 224
"Voyage to Atlantis," 5, 81, 82, 84, 131–33, 139, 153, 160, 182, 191, 196, 198, 209, 219

"Warm Summer Night," 156
"Warpath," 48, 49
Warwick, Dionne, 24, 31, 163, 164, 199
Waters, Ethel, 7
"Was It Good to You?," 41, 42
"Welcome to My Heart," 101
"Whatever Turns You On," 128, 129
"What I Miss the Most," 183
"What It Comes Down To," 61–62
"What Would You Do?," 160, 161, 175, 178
"When the Saints Go Marching In," 15
"Who Loves You Better," 73, 74, 78, 143, 182
"Who Said," 98, 99
"Who's That Lady," 22, 58
"Why Do Fools Fall in Love," 12
Wild in Woodstock: The Isley Brothers Live at Bearsville Sound Studio 1980, 193
Williams, Vanessa, 55, 79, 224
Wilson, Jackie, 9, 12, 13, 16, 24

Winbush, Angela, 5, 6, 117, 118, 122–25, 128, 129, 130, 132, 133, 137, 138, 140–42, 153, 156, 160, 165, 175, 204, 220
Winner Takes All, 89–93
"Winner Takes All," 5, 90–91, 93, 182
Wonder, Stevie, 24, 26, 34, 51, 54, 61, 72–73, 76, 77, 79, 117, 125, 144, 208, 216
"Work to Do," 54, 55, 62, 88, 139, 143, 152

"You Belong to Me," 9
"You Help Me Write This Song," 171, 172
"You Know When You're Gonna Fall in Love," 113, 114
"You'll Never Walk Alone," 122–24
You Make Me Wanna Shout—60th Anniversary Tour, 204, 205
"You're All I Need," 156, 159
"You're Beside Me," 90
"You're the Key to My Heart," 90, 132
"You Still Feel the Need," 74–75, 78
"You've Got a Friend," 183, 184, 189

About the Author

Photo by Russell J. Scott III

Trenton Bailey is a historian from Memphis, Tennessee, who currently resides in Atlanta, Georgia. An honors graduate of Morehouse College, he earned his PhD in humanities with a concentration in African American studies from Clark Atlanta University. Dr. Bailey has taught courses in African history, African American history, world history, and funk music, specifically. He was the coordinator for the Morehouse Oral History Project and has done extensive research on the history of Morehouse College. Dr. Bailey is a member of Alpha Phi Alpha Fraternity, Inc. and various organizations related to Black American life and culture. He is author of *Do You Remember? Celebrating Fifty Years of Earth, Wind & Fire*, published by University Press of Mississippi.

www.ingramcontent.com/pod-product-compliance
Lightning Source LLC
Chambersburg PA
CBHW030103170426
43198CB00009B/473